Borges and His Fiction

A REVISED EDITION   By Gene H. Bell-Villada

BORGES
and His Fiction

A GUIDE TO HIS MIND AND ART

 UNIVERSITY OF TEXAS PRESS, *Austin*

Texas Pan American Series

Acknowledgments:

Munro S. Edmonson, editor. From the translation of *The Book of Counsel: The Popol Vuh of the Quiche Maya of Guatemala* (pp. 24, 25, 27–28, 29). Copyright © 1971. Reprinted by permission of the Middle American Research Institute, Tulane University.

José Hernández. *The Gaucho Martín Fierro*
    From Part II, "The Return of Martín Fierro," transl. by C. E. Ward, annotated and revised by Frank Carrino and Alberto Carlos (pp. 479, 481, 495). Copyright © 1967. Reprinted by permission of the State University of New York Press.
    From the translation by Frank Carrino, Alberto Carlos, and Norman Mangouni (pp. 54, 62, 63, 64, 65, 67). Copyright © 1974. Reprinted by permission of the State University of New York Press.

Juan Mascaró, transl. From chapter 11 of *The Bhagavad Gita* (pp. 89–93 in the 1962 Penguin Classics edition). Copyright © Juan Mascaró 1962. Reprinted by permission of Penguin Books Ltd.

Gene H. Bell-Villada. A shorter version of chapter 11 was previously published as "Borges—Literature and Politics North and South" in *The Nation*, 21 February 1976 (pp. 213–217). Reprinted by permission of *The Nation*.
    Chapter 12 was first read as a paper at a conference on "Borges's Beginnings" at the University of Chicago in 1982. It was published as an essay in *Salmagundi*, spring-summer 1989. Reprinted by permission of Skidmore College.

Requests for permission to reproduce material from this work should be sent to Permissions, University of Texas Press, P.O. Box 7819, Austin, TX 78713-7819.

⊗ The paper used in this book meets the minimum requirements of ANSI/NISO Z39.48-1992 (R1997) (Permanence of Paper).

Library of Congress Cataloging-in-Publication Data

Bell-Villada, Gene H., 1941–
    Borges and his fiction : a guide to his mind and art / by Gene H. Bell-Villada. — Rev. ed.
    p.   cm. — (Texas Pan American series)
    Includes bibliographical references and index.
        ISBN 0-292-70877-7 (alk. paper) — ISBN 0-292-70878-5 (pbk.: alk. paper)
        1. Borges, Jorge Luis, 1899– —Criticism and interpretation.   I. Title.
    II. Series.
PQ7797.B635Z6342   2000
868—dc21   99-20938

For Audrey

For Estevan

For Kanani

For Valerie

and all that they have signified . . .

Contents

Part III   Borges's Place in Literature

Preface to the Revised Edition

Shortly after the first edition of this book came out in 1981, I experienced the enormous pleasure of receiving mail from complete strangers, broadly cultured nonspecialists who simply wanted to convey to me their appreciation as readers. A lawyer in Albuquerque, a painter in Chicago, a freelance writer in Connecticut, a schoolteacher in North Carolina—they and a number of others were to let me know, sometimes eloquently and at great lengths, just how much they liked and enjoyed the way that I had helped them understand Borges.

In the intervening years I also received letters and telephone calls from bright high-school students requesting further guidance and advice on the Argentine author. More recently, while the original edition was out of print, I heard from a good many individuals who, finding themselves overly dependent on borrowed copies, wrote or approached me to ask how they could secure a copy of their own.

Such moments meant a lot to me because, from the very start, I had conceived *Borges and His Fiction* as an object that could be picked up and consulted by anyone who wished to inform themselves and learn some useful things about my stated subject matter.

Eventually, I began hearing from college and secondary-school instructors who warmly and freely expressed to me their gratitude for having provided them a handy pedagogical tool. Every so often, someone at a conference or a social gathering would casually tell me that, the night before teaching a Borges text, they would reread my own analyses and reflections on the story and then make use of them in the classroom.

What has been particularly moving to me is the large number of schoolteachers, participants in the College Board's Advanced Placement program, who, time and again, with overwhelming enthusiasm and spontaneity, have indicated to me the crucial role my book has played in leading them and their students through the labyrinthine intricacies of Borges's mind and art. It is to those teachers, in great degree, that I owe this second edition; I've often thought of them, with a great deal of affection, in the process of correcting, updating, expanding, and revising my original text.

Borges and His Fiction, written in the 1970s, was first published in 1981. The original printing sold out in 1992. In the interim, in 1986, Borges died. A great deal of new material on the author, particularly new material regarding his life, has since come out. I have made every effort to bring in and integrate the essential aspects of that information within these pages, notably in chapter 2 (which focuses on Borges the man). In addition, I have tried to furnish a more complete look at Peronism and to sum up the peculiarities of that movement, both in chapter 11 and in my additional, new chapter 12.

When composing the text back in the 1970s, before Borges's death, I naturally described him in the present tense. Reflecting Borges's passing away, I have now changed many of the verbs to past tense. Moreover, the original—being my first published book—contained certain crudities of expression that, to the best of my ability, I have tried to polish and refine. Portions of the initial version also suffered from the stylistic tic of "reviewese"—understandably, inasmuch as most of my critical writing until then had appeared in general-interest magazines such as *Commonweal, New Republic, Boston Review,* and *The Nation.* Some of the less felicitous of these passages also have been recrafted.

I have also come around in my opinion of Borges's story "The South." In one of those little mysteries of the human heart, that evocative work did nothing for me two decades ago. Rereading it in the 1980s, I was struck by its spare and dreamlike beauty, and suddenly felt quite embarrassed at my earlier insensitivity to its incantatory prose and hypnotic power.

Finally, having since learned something about Borges's personal experience of mysticism, I have excised the erroneous and harsh judgments with which I had opened my chapter 9 and substituted for them passages that reflect the knowledge I have since gleaned of his early mystical encounters.

I can only hope that the final result delivered herein is a better, more palatable, and more mature work of letters.

Several individuals have aided and encouraged me in this project, but I should like to single out the late Thomas Smiley and also my colleagues in *Borgeología,* Professors Ronald Christ and Mary Lusky Friedman. My wife, Audrey, helped with the manuscript preparation, and Theresa J. May at the University of Texas Press has been a supportive voice. As I mention above, countless Advanced Placement participants have been urging me—for years now!—to find some way of reissuing *Borges and His Fiction,* but I especially must convey my heartfelt thanks to Dale Carter, Sylvia Coates, Robert DiAntonio, Marcela Holland, Bonnie Tucker Bowen, Silvana Millslagle, Aleyda González Mc-Kiernan, and Delia Montesinos, all of whom early informed me of their personal appreciation and esteem for the volume and, later, insisted that I seek to reprint it. Without their friendly, even obsessive, reminders, this book would not have had the privilege of a second life. I apologize for any undue omissions, and send my warmest and enduring gratitude to all—acknowledged or not—who have helped make this "revival" a physical reality, a shared artifact that readers can take home and, while sitting in the comfort of their armchairs, can hold in their hands, learn from, and savor.

G. B.-V.
CAMBRIDGE, MASSACHUSETTS
AUGUST 1998

Preface to the 1981 Edition

Writings on Borges now run in four figures. Despite this abundance, most commentators tend to give fragmentary views of Borges and his work. With a couple of exceptions, what has been lacking on the Borges studies scene is a broad and sensible look at the man and the artist, a book that would examine Borges's relationship to his stories and his times, and that would discuss his significance for literature both in the Hispanic and the larger Western worlds. Similarly, because practical criticism is out of favor in certain circles, there has been no complete story-by-story guide to Borges available as yet. This book, then, aims to fill the gap. In so doing, it is meant to be readable, informative, and directly useful for all concerned—for beginning and advanced students, full-time scholars, general readers, and lay people. Its underlying assumptions—that literature has to do with such things as cultural values and human emotions, that works of fiction and poetry have some connection, however oblique, with social life and the sense of history—go expressly against the grain of much fashionable critical theory. Although a discerning reader will find enough echoes of current literary thought in these pages, the language here employed is standard English and the critical-academic proper names are held to an absolute minimum. If occasionally I bring up the obvious, one might recall George Orwell's dictum that there are times when saying the obvious is our only antidote to prevailing sophistry and confusion. Among the elementary truths I insist upon here is the archaic and naive notion that readers read literature because they expect it to address their experience, because they wish to be moved or delighted or unsettled or amused. The rest, as the saying goes, is criticism.

Borges's high standing in academe has given rise to exaggerated and unfair claims for him and his work. Conventional wisdom has its well-worn clichés to the effect that Borges is a total "skeptic" who also has "read everything," whereas it would be far more helpful to define the limits of Borges's legendary skepticism and erudition, to seek out just what he believes, how much he knows, and in what ways he knows it. Moreover, in a curious mixture of proprietary condescension and servile awe, academic criticism treats Borges's art as a special world removed from the drift of human events. Borges himself is effectively cut off from history, stripped of his nonliterary opinions and experience, and transformed into a kind of pure aesthete. (I was once solemnly informed that mention of Borges's anticommunism is "unfitting.") Commentators of every political stripe mostly disregard such essential issues as Borges's deep roots in Argentine history, the vivid Buenos Aires setting of much of his best fiction and poetry, and the degree to which his cosmopolitanism and Europhilia are part of a definable tradition in Latin American intellectual life. There is the hagiographic strain: Borges is looked upon by his exegetes as a master who can do no wrong. His poetry and prose are indiscriminately judged of equal importance for world literature, when the truth of the matter is that Borges's verse shows few major innovations in specifically poetic realms such as diction, imagery, rhythm, and metrics. Though unmistakable in its voice and its moods, and oftentimes moving and quite beautiful, Borges's poetry is mostly of local and therefore secondary interest; he is a very good poet, if not a great one. By the same token, few academic critics attempt to distinguish between Borges's most highly inspired and his somewhat less successful fictions, let alone explain why certain Borges works have the power to move readers and why others do not. The ultimate in wrongheadedness is the all-too-frequent effort to make Borges into an original epistemologist and thinker.

Flattering though they may be, these misguided assessments only obscure Borges's genuine contributions to the literary and artistic realms, namely, his perfecting of a superb prose style; his raising of the detective and suspense genres to the level of a high art; his reintroduction of humor into Hispanic fiction; his restoring of the fantastical to a central and reputable place in imaginative literature; his synthesizing of new narrative forms in which realism and fantasy, fiction and essay are skillfully combined; and, of course, his having written some great and lasting short stories. These are impressive achievements, far more deserving of our respect than is the questionable role of metaphysical speculator too often assigned him by his critics. (Borges's art and temperament are metaphysical; that fact alone does not certify him as a metaphysician.) It is my hope that, in recognizing Borges's true accomplishments as an Argentine, Hispanic, and Western author, he can be reclaimed for the real world, and, as it were, brought down to earth.

Finally, it might be mentioned that the triumphal entry of European semiotic, structuralist, poststructuralist, and "deconstructionist" theory into art studies this side of the Atlantic, though helping to widen the technical vocabulary, methodological repertoire, and rhetorical strategies available to many an American critic, has also had the less positive effect of allowing the literary mandarinate to distance itself still further from its audiences—in some cases, from literature itself. A good deal of current literary criticism—with its name- and jargon-dropping, its leaden prose, its joyless professionalism, and its technocratic presumptions to being "value-free"—seems written for the purpose of impressing other critics rather than enlightening readers. Art for Art's Sake thus leaps into the doubly rarefied realm of Criticism for Criticism's Sake; the English language and good common sense endure much suffering as a result. To all who wish to share the experience of Borges's fiction, who want him rescued from all sectarian-critical cant, and who treasure his works as such, this book is warmly dedicated.

Acknowledgments

Numerous individuals have directly aided in the making of this book. To each and every one I wish to express my sincerest thanks. Different portions of the manuscript, in varying stages of its evolution, have been read by John Blegen of the State University of New York at Binghamton; by John Gliedman and Margery Resnick of Yale University; by Enrique Anderson-Imbert of Harvard University; by Morris Dickstein of Queens College and *Partisan Review;* and by Emile Capouya of *The Nation* and Baruch College, City University of New York. Last but not least, I must mention Malcolm L. Call, formerly of the University of North Carolina Press, who, by heeding my arguments during a critical moment, made this book possible. I also wish to thank Professor Michael Wood of Columbia University, who provided countless and indispensable editorial suggestions.

Equally indispensable information, from every conceivable field of knowledge, was furnished by the indefatigable polymath, John Gliedman; by James Irby of Princeton University, who kindly gave me access to his Ph.D. thesis (and also provided fine company and much appreciated hospitality); by Noreen Stack, Richard Nuccio, Brooke Larson, Sarah Roche-Gerstein, Glenn Yocum, John Stambaugh, and Marcella Mazzarelli, all of Williams College, and also by many students in my winter 1977 course on Borges; by Monique Tranchevent in Paris; by Professor Jean Franco of Stanford University; by Ronald Christ of Rutgers University and *Review;* by my mother, Carmen Villada Romero, of Albuquerque; by Sylvia Corona and Eduardo Barraza, of Mexico City; and in particular by Katherine Singer Kovács of the University of Southern California and Steven Kovács of New World Cinema, whose joint efforts made my trip to Argentina fruitful beyond all expectations.

In Mexico City, Jorge Aguilar Mora, Antonio Alatorre, Federico

Campbell, and Noé Jitrik furnished letters of introduction and much-needed encouragement.

I owe to the warmth and hospitality of countless *porteños* the access I was given to numerous papers and to many people. Through all of them I was able to acquire some feeling for the nuances of literary and cultural life in Buenos Aires, without which this book would have been sadly incomplete. In this regard, I wish to thank Enrique Pezzoni of Editorial Sudamericana; Pablo Urbanyi of *La Opinión;* Señor Vecino of *La Nación;* María Esther Vázquez; Ana María Barrenechea; Martha Beisim; Raúl Santana; Renato Rita; Gloria Autino; Willy and María Inés Bouillon; Manuel Pantín (of Reuters) and his wife Emily; Mirta Robilotte and her lovely relatives; Eduardo Gudiño Kieffer; Liliana Zukierman; Charles Driskell; Kenneth Kemble; Armando and Inés Parodi; Alicia Parodi and her literature students at the University of Buenos Aires; Alberto Vanasco; Fernando Lida; Jorge Lafforgue; Eduardo Irazábal (of Calicanto Editorial); the helpful employees of the Fulbright Commission; many casual strangers in cafés, restaurants, and taxis; and Señor Borges himself.

I wish also to thank Williams College for providing research funds and airfare to Argentina; Lee Dalzell and Sarah McFarland of the College Library, for securing many necessary items through the interlibrary loan service; and Professor George Pistorius, chairman of the Department of Romance Languages, for his encouragement and advice.

Finally I must express my deepest gratitude to two very special people: to the late Professor Raimundo Lida of Harvard University, whose lucid intellect, exigent standards, uncompromising rigor as scholar and teacher, and steady advice all helped me see beyond my then-youthful flaws, influencing my own development in the long process; and to my wife, Audrey, who aided in the shaping of this project in numerous places and countless ways, reading much material, furnishing discussion, and offering all manner of suggestions throughout many an afternoon and evening.

To all these individuals I owe whatever strengths are to be found in this book. All the weaknesses are my own.

G. B.-V.
CAMBRIDGE, MASSACHUSETTS
AUGUST 1979

Note on Page References

With minor exceptions, all references to books by Borges appear, parenthetically and abbreviated, within the body of the text. English volume and page number are cited first, followed by the Spanish ones. For example (L, 22; F, 101) signifies that the quotation under scrutiny appears on page 22 of *Labyrinths* and on page 101 of the Spanish *Ficciones*.

Although there exists an *Obras completas* (1974) in a single volume, as well as a later such compilation (1989) in four volumes, I have chosen to list page numbers from his individual collections. This I do for reasons of convenience, partly because many readers, though owning several books by Borges, may not possess those bulky tomes and partly because the *Obras completas*, the title notwithstanding, omit some of Borges's lesser or later writings.

Here follows a list of editions used, with their abbreviations.

English Translations

The Aleph and Other Stories, 1933–1969 (TA). Translated by Norman Thomas di Giovanni in collaboration with the author. New York: E. P. Dutton, 1978.

The Book of Sand (BS). Translated by Norman Thomas di Giovanni. New York: E. P. Dutton, 1978.

Chronicles of Bustos Domecq (CBD). Translated by Norman Thomas di Giovanni. New York: E. P. Dutton, 1976.

Doctor Brodie's Report (DBR). Translated by Norman Thomas di Giovanni in collaboration with the author. New York: E. P. Dutton, 1972.

Dreamtigers (D). Translated by Mildred Boyer and Harold Moreland. Austin: University of Texas Press, 1964.

Ficciones (F). Edited by Anthony Kerrigan. New York: Grove Press, 1962.

Labyrinths (L). Edited by James Irby and Donald Yates. New York: New Directions, 1962.

Other Inquisitions (OI). Translated by Ruth L. C. Simms. New York: Washington Square Press, 1966.

A Universal History of Infamy (UHI). Translated by Norman Thomas di Giovanni in collaboration with the author. New York: E. P. Dutton, 1972.

Spanish Editions

(All from Emecé in Buenos Aires, unless noted otherwise.)

El Aleph (EA). 1968.

Crónicas de Bustos Domecq (CBD). Adolfo Bioy Casares, coauthor. Buenos Aires: Losada, 1967.

Ficciones (F). 1966.

El hacedor (H). 1971.

Historia universal de la infamia (HUI). 1971.

El idioma de los argentinos (IA). Buenos Aires: M. Gleizer, 1928.

El informe de Brodie (IB). 1971.

El libro de arena (LA). 1975.

Otras inquisiciones (OI). 1966.

Any uncredited translations of foreign-language text, whether by Borges or other authors, are my own.

G. B.-V.

Chronology

second prize in annual Buenos Aires municipal literary contest.

Borges buys an eleventh edition *Encyclopaedia Britannica*.

1930   A right-wing army coup deposes the Radical government of Hipólito Yrigoyen.

Evaristo Carriego, essays.

1932   Civilian government is restored, with Conservatives retaining *de facto* power through the decade.

Discusión (Argument/Debate), essays.

1933   Borges is appointed literary editor for weekly arts supplement of *Crítica*, a tabloid.

1935   Borges's grandmother, Frances Haslam de Borges, a longtime resident of the family household, dies.

Historia universal de la infamia (A Universal History of Infamy), his first collection of stories.

1936   *Historia de la eternidad (A History of Eternity)*, essays.

1937   Borges's father dies. Borges begins work as an assistant cataloguer in a small branch library.

1938   Suffers a head wound, develops blood poisoning, barely escapes death.

1939   Spends several weeks in hospital. Begins writing his most important stories.

1941   *El jardín de los senderos que se bifurcan (The Garden of Forking Paths)*, eight stories.

Government of President Ramón Castillo openly favors Axis powers.

1942   *The Garden of Forking Paths* is nominated for the National Literary Prize, but a lesser author is awarded. *Sur* puts out the "Desagravio a Borges" ("Vindication of Borges"), a special issue in which twenty-one literary friends and acquaintances write in his defense.

1943   Anti-British military officers seize governmental power.

1944   *Ficciones*, stories.

1946   General Juan Domingo Perón is elected to the presidency by majority vote.

Borges is removed from his library post and is offered a position as poultry inspector, which he declines.

Accepts a number of teaching and lecturing jobs.

1949   *El Aleph (The Aleph)*, stories.

1951   *Fictions* is published in Paris, the first foreign translation of a
        Borges book.
1952   *Otras inquisiciones (Other Inquisitions)*, essays.
        Eva Perón dies.
1955   Perón government falls to a revolt by centrist army officers.
        Perón flees to Spain.
        Borges is appointed director of the National Library. The
        author becomes almost completely blind.
1956   New edition of *Ficciones*, with three additional stories.
1957   The University of Buenos Aires names Borges Professor of
        English Literature.
        With Margarita Guerrero: *Manual de zoología fantástica (A
        Handbook of Fantastic Zoology)*, vignettes.
1960   *El hacedor* (English version *Dreamtigers*), poems and short
        fictions.
1961   Shares with Samuel Beckett the first Formentor Prize, an
        international award granted by a group of European and
        American publishers.
        Teaches a semester at the University of Texas.
1962   *Labyrinths* and *Ficciones*, the first English collections of
        Borges's work, are published in New York.
1963   Visits and lectures in Europe.
1965   Travels in other Latin American countries.
1967   Marries Elsa Astete Millán.
1967–   Holds the Charles Eliot Norton Chair of Poetry at Harvard
1968   University.
        Delivers lectures throughout the United States.
1968   *El libro de los seres imaginarios (The Book of Imaginary
        Beings)*, expanded edition of the earlier *Manual de zoología
        fantástica.*
        Travels in Europe. Receives an honorary doctorate from
        Oxford University and numerous official honors on the
        Continent.
1969   *El informe de Brodie (Doctor Brodie's Report)*, stories.
        Elogio de la sombra (In Praise of Darkness), poetry.
        Visits and lectures in Israel.
1970   Borges is separated from his wife.
1971   Honorary doctorate from Columbia University.
        Jerusalem Prize.

1972   *El oro de los tigres (Gold of the Tigers),* poetry and prose.

1973   Perón is reelected to the presidency.
Borges resigns his post at the National Library.
Receives major prizes in Spain and Mexico.

1974   *Obras completas (Complete Works),* in a single volume.

1975   *El libro de arena (The Book of Sand),* stories.
La rosa profunda (The Deep Rose), poetry.
Prólogos (Prologues), collected prefaces.
Borges's mother dies at age 99.
Perón dies, is succeeded by his widow, Isabel.

1976   *La moneda de hierro (The Iron Coin),* poetry.
With Adolfo Bioy Casares: *Crónicas de Bustos Domecq
(Chronicles of Bustos Domecq),* satirical sketches.
Lectures at Michigan State University and attends conference
dedicated to his work at the University of Maine.
Right-wing army coup overthrows government of Isabel
Perón.

1977   Borges lectures in Buenos Aires and throughout Argentina.

1978   Travels to Paris for special homage at the Sorbonne.

1979   Celebrates his eightieth birthday.
Gold medal from the Académie Française, Order of Merit
from the Federal Republic of Germany, Cross of the Falcon
from government of Iceland.
Travels in Japan.

1980   Travels to Spain, is awarded the Cervantes Prize.
In Argentina, makes statements and signs protests against the
political repression and the "disappeared."
Siete noches (Seven Nights), lectures.

1981   Travels to Rome, is awarded the Balzan Prize.
Travels to Mexico City, is awarded the Ollín Yoliztli Prize.
Honorary doctorate from Harvard University.

1982   Attends conference on his work at the University of Chicago.
Military government invades the Falkland-Malvinas Islands
and is defeated by British naval forces. Borges condemns the
war.

1983   Awarded the insignia of the French Légion d'Honneur.

1984   Travels in Italy, Japan, and Greece. Honorary doctorates from
three Italian universities.
Atlas, poems, prose sketches, and photographs.

1985   Moves permanently to Geneva, Switzerland.
       Los conjurados (The Conspirers), poems and parables.
1986   Marries his personal assistant, María Kodama, on 22 April.
       Dies on 14 June of cancer of the liver. Is buried at the old
       Pleinpalais Cemetery in Geneva.

Part I

BORGES'S WORLDS

1 Buenos Aires and Beyond

bove all a superb author of fiction, but also a fine poet and a hauntingly original essayist, the elder Borges loomed infinitely larger as public figure than as flesh-and-blood individual—the personally shy, multilingually bookish, all but blind octogenarian who spent his final two decades living more or less alone in his native Buenos Aires. For, beginning in the 1960s, Jorge Luis Borges evolved as an international phenomenon, a name commonly invoked by literati from Stockholm to San Francisco, from Poland to Peru, a sculptor of words whose three- or four-dozen short stories and as many brief essays came to be mentioned in the same breath with the big tomes of Joyce or Proust or Faulkner, a man of letters whose mode of writing and turn of mind were so distinctively his, yet so much a revealed part of our world, that "Borgesian" eventually became as common a neologism as the adjectives "Orwellian" or "Kafkaesque."

Knowledge of Borges's work is now simply taken for granted by the myriad artists, scholars, and critics who choose to make casual mention of him. Alain Robbe-Grillet alludes to a well-known Borges conceit in his fiction manifesto, *For a New Novel;* high theorist Michel Foucault takes a bit of Borges whimsy (from the essay "The Analytical Language of John Wilkins" in *Other Inquisitions*) as a starting point on page 1 of *The Order of Things;* the exquisitely irreverent Jean-Luc Godard cites Borges in at least two of his movies, at the beginning of *Les Carabiniers* and toward the end of *Alphaville;* Italian filmmaker Bernardo Bertolucci makes the plot of Borges's story "Theme of the Traitor and the Hero" the basis for his drama of fascism, *The Spider's Stratagem;* American metanovelist John Barth hails Borges as *the* literary model for our time; and sociologist Daniel Bell quotes six full paragraphs from "The Library at Babel" to illustrate the modern epistemological dilemma in *The Coming of Post-*

Industrial Society. Perhaps the greatest artistic homage to the Argentine author is Umberto Eco's *The Name of the Rose,* a dazzlingly erudite detective novel set in a medieval monastery with an enormous manuscripts collection ("Borgesian" traits, all) presided over by a blind librarian named Jorge de Burgos (an obvious play on Borges himself).

On another level of discourse, *Time* magazine once likened the National Security Agency in Washington, D.C., to Borges's infinite Babel of books, and film critics routinely spice up their reviews with passing comparisons to Borges fantasies. The author's slim volumes have been displayed on American drugstore racks, are read by French students in the trains of the Paris Métro, were being studied by a hotelkeeper I once met in Warsaw, and are still varyingly imitated by a number of contemporary novelists in the United States. This is a renown truly remarkable for an author so learned, so difficult, and at times so precious as is Borges (approximate English pronunciation: BOR-hess).

His achievements as an artist aside, this global fame owes something to the fact that Borges's prose fiction translates and travels abroad quite gracefully, whereas the works of the great Chilean poet Pablo Neruda, the only Hispanic-American author to have gained a world following prior to Borges, appear almost exclusively in a medium not known for moving with ease across frontiers and oceans. On the other hand, Neruda justly received the Nobel Prize in 1971, an award that never was to be Borges's lot, presumably because of the Swedish Academy's original mandate to honor only those authors positively marked by moral idealism. (The idea that Borges's latter-day conservatism cost him the Nobel is not necessarily the case; after all, Octavio Paz was so honored in 1991, by which time he had become a figure of orthodoxy and a defender of the brutal *contra* wars in Nicaragua.)

Still, virtually every other international accolade managed to come Borges's way. His first leap into the world arena occurred in 1961 when he shared a major European publishers' award (the Prix Formentor) with another multilingual writer, the Franco-Irishman Samuel Beckett, after which the plaudits and publicity accumulated at a dizzying rate. Starting in the decade of the 1960s through the year of his death in 1986, Borges embarked on countless lecture tours across the Americas, Western Europe, and Asia, delivering hundreds of talks in four languages. In 1967–1968, for instance, he held the Charles Eliot Norton chair of poetry at Harvard University, a post previously held by, among others, T. S. Eliot, e. e. cummings, Ben Shahn, Aaron Copland, and Igor Stravinsky. In 1971

Borges received from the hand of Mayor Teddy Kollek the biennial Jerusalem Prize, whose recipients have included Bertrand Russell, Ignazio Silone, Eugène Ionesco, and Simone de Beauvoir. On different occasions, Oxford, Columbia, and Harvard Universities have granted honorary doctorates to Borges. One year General de Gaulle bestowed on the Argentine author, at André Malraux's request, the title Commander of the Order of Letters and Arts; another year he received the Order of Merit of Italy; yet another time he was appointed Knight of the British Empire by Queen Elizabeth; and in 1976 he addressed the United States Congress on the subject of Shakespeare. Whatever the ultimate worth of all this public adulation, these official honors reflected the degree to which Borges's writing had entered the mainstream of world literary culture.

It had not always been this way, and least of all in Borges's native Argentina. What was astonishing about this flood of recognition is that it came all at once, and late, when the author was well into his sixties. Before 1961 Borges had been writing in relative obscurity in Buenos Aires, his fiction and poetry read by a few hundred readers at most, praised by a handful of individuals (many of them personal friends and acquaintances), and ignored by his compatriots, who were slow in perceiving his worth or even knowing about him. The Argentine middle-class reading public, notorious for preferring translations from the French, gave Borges's own major works scant notice. On the other hand, during the nationalist 1940s and 1950s, when liberal, Europeanizing culture came under Peronist siege, Borges was more or less blacklisted by the official press, his name appearing only in *Sur* magazine and in the book supplement of *La Nación;* meanwhile, the local literary prizes regularly went to lesser talents who enjoyed political favor with the juries.

It was the French, in fact, who first gave Borges serious attention, boosting his reputation abroad and even at home. In 1925, Valéry Larbaud in *La Revue Européenne* praised Borges's youthful volume *Inquisitions,* singling out its great erudition and broad sense of culture. In 1933, Pierre Drieu La Rochelle traveled in Argentina and, upon returning to Paris, remarked, "Borges vaut le voyage" (Borges is worth the trip). Later, during the Nazi occupation, a number of French intellectuals— men of letters Roger Caillois and Paul Bénichou, photographer Gisèle Freund—were exiled in Argentina, where they met and read Borges. Back in liberated France they brought word of his tales and began placing them in magazines such as Sartre's *Les temps modernes.* The first foreign edition of Borges's stories, a volume entitled *Fictions,* appeared in France in 1951. The 1961 Prix Formentor (whose jury included the prestigious Gallimard publishing house) was the take-off point in Borges's recognition in Europe. Since then, structuralist theorists and critics such as Gérard Génette have found in Borges not just another exotic genius on whom to lavish high Gallic praise, but a wise master from whose doctrine of literary space they can learn a great deal and whose general theory of writing and reading brings forth major questions for study.[1] In a very real sense, it was the French who, as Borges himself once put it in an interview, made him visible.[2]

The Prix Formentor first caused Borges's name and face to be printed and publicized throughout his homeland. Fifteen years afterward, Borges remembered how, shortly after news of the award had appeared with his picture in the Argentine press, he was riding in a taxi, and at the end of the trip, the awed cabbie declined payment and asked to shake the author's hand—an episode suggestive of that impending avalanche of national acclaim.[3] As is often remarked, too many Argentines will accept a homegrown cultural product only if it has been applauded overseas. A standard instance in this regard is the tango, a musical form that, owing to its humble origins, was deemed beneath contempt by educated Argentines at the turn of the century. Suddenly, in the 1910s, the tango became a European rage: it was sung at the Moulin Rouge, praised occasionally by French intellectuals, and danced by fashionably dressed demoiselles at "tea-and-tango parties"—at which point Argentine tastemakers put aside class prejudice and claimed this music as their own. In much the same way, the larger Argentine readership began seriously to recognize Borges only when his books came back with the official seal of French fame.

Borges's onetime neglect at home now seems strangely remote, almost idyllic. If anything, the Borges of the 1970s and 1980s appeared in the Argentine mass media with dizzying frequency. His public lectures were attended by people of all educational levels, class backgrounds, and ages—needy students as well as ladies in furs—who often contended for standing-room space in crowded auditoriums, in what seemed less a cultural event than a religious service. The literati, even those who deplored and despised the conservatism of the elder Borges, admiringly quoted his lyrics in private gatherings and cafes, while pop-music composers set tango tunes to lines by Borges. When the author would go for his afternoon stroll in downtown Buenos Aires, casual strangers used to walk up and chat with him, requesting his autograph, while young girls would ask if they could kiss him. As a culminating irony, his one-thousand-page, single-volume *Obras completas* (*Complete Works,* 1974), bound in green leatherette, was on display for sale in newsstands throughout the capital city. The book was reportedly a big seller during holidays.[4]

Outside Argentina, across the southern continent, Borges's literary contribution stands as accepted fact. Throughout the Spanish-speaking world, even leftist intellectuals (Cuban ones included) cite him, if at times grudgingly. The only sectors staunchly resisting Borges's art, both in Argentina and elsewhere, have been the more hard-line nationalist elements. Whether it was the right-wing Hispanophiles of the 1930s and 1940s (who would have their art steeped in old Iberian ways) or the left-leaning regionalists of earlier and later date (who, by contrast, agitate for native Argentine lore), readers and critics from all nationalist factions have tended to dismiss Borges's writings as too European, too British, too remote from Spanish American concerns.

It was these spiritual adversaries whom Borges had in mind when preparing his well-known talk "The Argentine Writer and Tradition" (1951), a key document in Borges's aesthetic, a defense of literary cosmopolitanism in reply to Iberophiles and nativists both. On his left, to the local-color advocates, Borges aims the argument that a literature confined to immediate national subjects needlessly narrows its material range, and that (in a striking observation) Racine is no less French a poet and playwright for having concentrated on ancient Greek myths and characters. On his right, to those who would stand strictly on their Iberian cultural roots, Borges responds with a radical premise, namely that "Argentine history can unmistakably be defined as a desire to become separated from Spain" (L, 182; D, 158); here Borges goes so far as to pronounce that the appreciation of Spain's authors is a taste that is learned and acquired, whereas French or English books come naturally to Argentine readers.

Borges's premise about cultural roots grows out of and reflects certain peculiarities of the history, society, and culture of the Republic of Argentina, especially Buenos Aires. In the nineteenth century, of course, many South American countries, following political independence from Spain, also repudiated in varying extents their Hispanic heritages, looking to England and France for their models. In Argentina, though, this dynamic was taken considerably further—some Argentine leaders even toyed idly with the idea of adopting French as the national language, for instance. Obviously an unrealistic proposition, though they did manage to ban bullfighting in Argentina—and not out of pro-taurine sympathies, either.[5] Even the original colony had been exploited less for precious metals than for agriculture and livestock, historical circumstances that were to generate a national style very much its own. Whereas in other parts of the empire, both under Spain and after independence, the indigenous peoples were absorbed as slave labor for the mines and haciendas (as often as not remaining culturally unassimilated), in Argentina the Indians were swept off the land and mostly liquidated, in conscious imitation of the U.S. model.

Argentina, moreover, is the only Latin country into which Britain's Empire, under the encouragement of liberal, Anglophile politicians like Sarmiento, managed to penetrate politically and culturally (unlike, say, Cuba and Mexico, countries that have waged successful battles against foreign invaders, a fact that inevitably reinforces antiforeign modes of feeling). Finally, massive immigrations from Italy, Eastern Europe, and (to a lesser degree) the British Isles would inevitably transform the Argentine demography, particularly that of the capital, which became, like New York, a cosmopolitan city, differing markedly from the Argentine provinces, which have far more in common, socially and culturally, with the rest of Hispanic America.[6] A full 40 percent of the Buenos Aires population, for instance, is of Italian origin[7]; another half a million (most of them now assimilated) are of Jewish descent. Spoken Spanish in Buenos Aires has an unmistakable Italian lilt, and styles of dress are strongly European and British. (There is even a large Harrod's in the middle of the city.) One revealing symptom of the non-Hispanic character of Argentina is a relatively low incidence of that distinctive Spanish trait: double family names.

In the visual realm, much of Buenos Aires's architecture, storefronts and street signs, and even its arboreal arrangements are virtual facsimiles of those of France. This "look" is the result of a conscious political decision made in the early twentieth century, when Argentina's elites set out to make their city into the Paris of Latin America. The great mansions of the high oligarchs were modeled after French villas and châteaux. When master architects were not brought in directly from France and Germany to do the job, they were simply commissioned to draft their designs in the comfort of their European offices. Meanwhile, Argentine architects either trained at the Ecole des Beaux Arts in Paris or followed the lead of the French school's hegemonic ideas. And then there are the famous boulevards of Buenos Aires, which were laid out in unabashed imitation of the renowned urban-renewal programs carried out in Paris by Baron Haussmann under Napoleon III. In sum, though Argentina may belong, politically and economically, to the Third World, the cultural resources, appearances, and flavor of its capital city are strongly—some would say deceptively—European.

Borges's life is closely linked with Buenos Aires and all that it represents. Born in what is known as the *microcentro,* he was to spend most of his existence in various parts of the city, frequently alluding in his work to its buildings and streets, and in old age residing in an apartment just five minutes' walk from the street where he was born. A dyed-in-the-wool *porteño,*[8] he always professed the cosmopolis dweller's snobbish indifference to much of the rest of Argentina—the Andean cordillera, or the far south for instance. Even the famed Iguazú falls, which he never visited, aroused no interest in him. It is the non-Hispanic, cosmopolitan, European drift in Argentina's national history, then, with its vivid incarnation in the urban metropolis, that underlies and sustains Borges's bold proposal that the Argentine writer make use of "all of Western culture" (L, 184; D, 160)—which is to say, the entirety of European *and* local phenomena. To Borges it is not a matter so stark as choosing between rural gaucho legends and German philosophy but of reaping the riches to be found in both. To illustrate his point, Borges takes from American sociologist and economist Thorstein Veblen a well-known analogy: the Jews in Europe who, long associated with Western culture without being part of it, have felt less tied to its past, less bound to its traditions, and thus have tended to be discoverers of new forms, originators of new ideas rather than curators of the old. Another analogy favored by Borges is Ireland, an area on Britain's periphery that has given the world more than its share of English-language authors. In the twentieth century, as is well known, the chief "British" poet, novelist, and dramatist—Yeats, Joyce, and Shaw, respectively—were Irish.

Of course, as is the case with all such programmatic statements, Borges's general theory grows out of his concrete practice as an Argentine writer of the cosmopolitan type. Poised on the periphery in a remote Western outpost, Borges takes on whole chunks of European experience—the Greek myths, the Roman Empire, early Christian doctrine, medieval Islamic thought, Jewish mysticism, academic theology, philosophical idealism, French symbolism, Victorian orientalism, Irish republicanism, English sleuth yarns and spy thrillers—and then remakes these variegated disciplines, subcultures, and genres (playfully, ironically, irreverently, fancifully, sometimes magically) into fresh forms and new structures. On the other hand, conspicuously absent in Borges's later writings, save for many allusions to Cervantes, are Spain and its literature. At the same time, it is unfair to say, as do many of his detractors, that Borges turns his back on local materials, for his works include numerous stories dealing with Argentine subjects such as gauchos, rural toughs, urban gangsters, the Martín Fierro legend, and the nineteenth-century civil wars. For that matter, as we have seen, even the cosmopolitanism of Borges's celebrated fantasies reflects a specific and identifiable quality in the Buenos Aires way of life, a set of values that has played a key role in Argentine history.

Borges's universalism has its Latin American side as well. The intimate history of that continent presents numerous individual figures who, by dint of reading all the books, manage to absorb more of European culture than most Europeans could ever imagine. From the seventeenth-century nun Sor Juana Inés de la Cruz (who studied vast amounts of philosophy and theology on her own, wrote some first-rate specimens of Baroque poetry, and also displayed an uncanny sense of scientific method, all of whose talents were eventually stifled by colonial Catholicism and male prejudice) to the twentieth-century poet and novelist José Lezama Lima (who gave the impression of carrying all of world literature within his square head and gigantic body, and yet scarcely ever set foot outside his native Cuba), Spanish America has produced these freak intellects who live a kind of vicarious cultural ecumenism while remaining as local as the next fellow in their daily lives. A familiar fictional instance of this is Aureliano Babilonia in García Márquez's *One Hundred Years of Solitude,* the last scion of the Buendía household, a bookworm who seldom leaves his study and somehow learns everything, including the street names of Brussels and Rome and even some practical Sanskrit too.

Borges's defense, indeed advocacy, of the cosmopolitan position dates from the 1940s. In its wake, in the novels of the so-called Latin American boom, his formulation has been keenly borne out and vindicated. Authors like Cortázar, García Márquez, Carpentier, Cabrera Infante, and Puig in their very best books have judiciously shunned the pitfalls of excess localism. Though the Cuban novelist Alejo Carpentier was actively involved in Fidel Castro's revolution, his greatest book, *Explosion in a Cathedral,* is set in Haiti, France, Guadeloupe, Spain, and various ships on the ocean, as well as his native Cuba. Similarly, the action of Cortázar's *Hopscotch* moves to Buenos Aires from the Latin Quarter in Paris, with much discussion on subjects ranging from Zen Buddhism, American jazz, and Argentine tangos along the way. Even when a work by these novelists depicts a small provincial town, the larger outside world is shown to enter and affect the locality, be it in the direct form of travelers or through the cultural medium of foreign movies and books (as Puig does in his novels). García Márquez's *One Hundred Years of Solitude* portrays a remote village in Colombia, yet Colombia and its geography are seldom mentioned, though convincingly evoked; at the same time, there are tales of journeys across the globe, with numerous place-names given. García Márquez's cast of characters includes a learned gypsy, an Italian dance teacher, a Catalan bookseller, a Belgian entomologist, various North American banana-company types, and even the Wandering Jew. The range of cultural references in these authors' work is also quite vast, with artifacts, names, and assorted "isms" from Europe entering freely into the texts—if only to be held up for subtle criticism.

In reality, the issue of local versus cosmopolitan, national versus universal, is a deceptive, probably false, opposition, for neither portion of the dichotomy has greater intrinsic value than the other and each one in its pure form can be harmful. A cosmopolitanism without some local roots easily becomes lifeless and academic, sterile, snobbish, and abstract, while a localism unmitigated by broader outside influences leads to small-minded gossip or self-congratulatory xenophobia. Any art worthy of esteem finds an adequate blend of both, or, as the critical commonplace says, great works of art are somehow both concrete and universal.

Though Borges's stories are the works most immediately associated with his name, they form but a fraction of his total output—some forty books and probably thousands of magazine articles. Moreover, as we saw earlier, not a few of those stories make use of Argentine subjects; in the same way, roughly half of Borges's lyric verse (some three or four hundred pages) has a nativist touch and deals with Buenos Aires landmarks or Argentine historical figures. Borges's literary journalism—written for local consumption and published in small journals, news dailies, and middlebrow magazines such as *Hogar* (Home), where in the 1930s Borges reviewed foreign books[9]—far outweighs, in terms of bulk, the fine-grained stories on which his global fame rests. Hence, throughout his life as a man of letters, Borges has written not for foreigners but for interested Argentine readers and friends. And though his universalism is obviously essential to his work, it is something picked up on native ground, through family ties and from wide reading at home. Borges never went the route of self-exile, which has been the lot of many an author of peripheral origins since the Yankee James and the Irishman Joyce. Except for his seven years as a late adolescent and young adult in Europe, and his globetrotting dating from the 1960s, Borges's life and work are experientially rooted in the world of Buenos Aires.

Borges's personal identity, moreover, originates in the historical reality of Argentina. Names of his ancestors figure prominently in the nation's books, archives, and street signs. They are men who founded and governed colonial settlements, who fought in the wars of liberation from Spain, who took part in the politics of early independence, and who spearheaded the frontier warfare that shaped the Republic. Among Borges's ancestors are Juan de Garay, founder of Buenos Aires; Jerónimo Luis de Cabrera, who founded Córdoba (Argentina's second largest city); a distant great-uncle, Francisco Narciso de Laprida, who, at the 1816 Congress of Tucumán, declared the independence of "the United Provinces of South America" from Spanish control; great-grandfather Colonel Isidoro Suárez, who led a decisive battle against the Spaniards in the early nineteenth century; and his grandfather, Colonel Francisco Borges, who fought against Indians and gaucho insurgents. The Borges line is one rich in martial antecedents, a fact of which the author was always proud. As a boy, he grew up with swords, knives, and other such battle gear decking the walls of the family home. As a poet, he often wrote movingly of them, both the men and the instruments.

Needless to say, bookish Borges stands far removed from this world of fast action, blood, and gore—except through the vicarious medium of those poems dealing with military battles and his stories depicting gauchos. Thomas Mann in his novel *Buddenbrooks* gave striking shape to this historical phenomenon in the character of young Hanno, a delicately artistic boy, who emerges and flourishes only at the point when the grand old Buddenbrooks family is in decline, is indeed nearing the end of its existence. The real-life artist Borges vividly incarnates Mann's notion, for he is the very last of the immediate Borges line, there being no brothers or sons to perpetuate the name. Beyond the family, Borges himself once remarked to some reporters that his career as author closely coincides with the secular decline of the Argentine nation.[10]

The paradox, then, is that Borges's greatest writing—universalist and cosmopolite but also *porteño* in outlook—issues from a man whose roots lie deep in his country's past. As a minor indication of this, Borges's Argentine interviews differ substantially in content from his hundreds of published conversations with foreign interlocutors; for in the company of compatriots his allusions, hints, and echoes are of an extremely local kind, recognizable only by other Argentines.[11] In a quite literal sense, Borges's family past and personal handiwork are part of the national history; he is as much an Argentine author as, say, Robert Lowell (whose Boston-Brahmin origins are analogous to Borges's own background) is an American one.

The strong British and even Anglophile streak in Borges also comes, to some extent, out of family ties. His grandmother, Frances Haslam, was a Victorian lady who, on a chance visit to her sister in Argentina in 1870, happened to meet Colonel Francisco Borges and there married him within a year; tragically widowed in 1874, she stayed on with the family in Buenos Aires until her own death, six decades later, in 1935. Among the offspring of the union was Borges's father, Jorge Guillermo, bilingually raised; Jorge Guillermo in turn nurtured his son Jorge Luis—"Georgie," as he was affectionately called—on both Spanish and English, while Grandmother Haslam used to recite to him from the King James Bible, much of which she knew from memory. (Borges once recalled how, as a child learning to talk, he found himself addressing his Argentine grandma one way, his English one another; it was only some time later that he realized he had been employing different languages.) [12]

In sum, the author-to-be grew up in what was a happy blend, a richly harmonious world of two languages and their cultures: military-historical Argentina and nineteenth-century England, with the intellectual and political attitudes of each. It is thus understandable that Borges should see no conflict between European and Argentine cultural values, inasmuch as he stems from and is a beneficiary of both. These nativist-cum-foreign strands in Borges's genealogy are also the basic constituents of his artistic makeup, persisting throughout his life as a man of letters.

2 A Sort of Life, a Special Mind

Much of the shape of Borges's artistry and intellect can be traced to his home life as a growing boy.[1] Born at the final stages of the nineteenth century, in 1899, he received no public schooling until his tenth year, owing to the Spencerian-libertarian beliefs of his father, who distrusted all activities of the State. Instead, he and his sister Norah received their first lessons from a resident tutor called Miss Tink, the daughter of a British couple who had settled in Argentina. Similarly, Borges's adult literary acculturation was to come to him not so much via formal schooling as from personal contacts, private study, and idiosyncratic reading of slightly unorthodox works.

Alongside those military artifacts and memories mentioned earlier, the Borges household boasted a substantial English-language library, which the bookish and Anglophile author later would describe as "the chief event in my life" (TA, 209). There he devoured the fanciful works of Stevenson, Wells, Kipling, and Poe (authors who were to remain prime influences on Borges's mature writing), as well as adventure yarns and gaucho novels (seeds of what would eventually become the higher art of his knife-and-action tales).

The family could claim literary credentials. Borges's great-uncle, Juan Crisóstomo Lafinur, was among the first poets in the newly formed Argentine republic. Jorge Guillermo Borges, a lawyer and professor who taught psychology from the William James textbook and liked reciting Keats to his two children, Jorge Luis and Norah, was himself something of a writer. Over his sixty-four-year life span, the father would produce unpublished sonnets, short fiction, the first translation into Spanish of Fitzgerald's *Rubaiyat,* and a novel entitled *El caudillo.* A handsome man, with British movie-star good looks, papa Borges also had his eccentric side, practicing vegetarianism in a beef-eating country and briefly founding an anarchist colony in Paraguay.

As childhood amusement, young Borges and his sister Norah used to act out dramatizations of stories from Wells, Poe, and the *Arabian Nights*. With his father, Jorge Luis began discussing philosophical problems at age ten. A boy wonder, he was already producing the literary equivalent to Mozart's childhood minuets. He penned his first story, "La visera fatal" ("The Fatal Vizor"), when he was seven years old; at age nine, he did a translation of Oscar Wilde's fairy tale "The Happy Prince," which, after being printed in the Uruguayan newspaper *El País*, was mistakenly read by a family friend as the handiwork of Borges's father; and in his thirteenth year, he published his first original piece, a story entitled "El rey de la selva" ("King of the Jungle"), narrated from the point of view of a proud tiger who is being preyed upon by a distant and shadowy huntsman (the form of the action thus clearly anticipating "The House of Asterion" in *El Aleph*).

The home environment, then, strongly reinforced the child prodigy's talents. Indeed Borges's father actively encouraged him to write even as he imposed highly stringent standards. During the author's adolescence, the elder Borges was to exhort him, "Leé mucho, escribí mucho, rompé mucho, y no te apures en publicar" ("Read a lot, write a lot, tear up a lot, and don't rush into print").[2] When Borges finally had the manuscript of *Fervor de Buenos Aires* ready for publication—his fourth attempt, previous efforts having been found wanting and, as per instructions, torn up—his father footed the printing bill of 300 pesos. Hence, as we can see, the entire household set the stage for Borges's development, groomed him for the role, molded his sense of himself as a writer. In contrast to the varieties of home opposition encountered by many young artists, Borges's family would recognize his gifts, nurture them, and even finance them.

In 1908 Borges finally began attending public school, which came as something of a shock after his sheltered existence. Male classmates taunted him and roughed him up on account of his formal, Eton-style coat and tie, as well as his spectacles (calling him "four-eyes" and occasionally breaking them), and their working-class *lunfardo* slang had him totally bewildered. Schooling aside, the young boy grew up mostly in Palermo, then a suburb at the very edge of Buenos Aires, but today simply another chic section of the sprawling megalopolis. (The name comes not from the capital of Sicily but from Juan Domínguez de Palermo, a Spaniard who owned an *hacienda* there during the early colonial period.) The Palermo of Borges's childhood included a slum area inhabited by knife-toting gangsters and street toughs, who later would crop up as protagonists in his stories.

Then, in 1914, the family set sail for Europe to do something about the fast-deteriorating eyesight of papa Borges, who at age forty could no longer read the legal documents he was supposed to sign and had had to resign from both his jobs. For the next few years the family would live off some modest rents. (It should be noted that, their patrician origins notwithstanding, the Borges family was not rich.) The outbreak of the Great War caught Borges's parents on German soil, where aliens suddenly were not allowed to leave. The Borgeses managed to get out only with a bribe to a compliant official, the Argentine peso at the time being a highly valued currency.

The family's original plans for settling in Paris now shattered, they moved instead to the neutral security of Geneva, living at 17 Rue Malagnou (today Ferdinand Holder). There young Jorge Luis attended the Collège de Genève on Rue de la Vallée, one of various secondary schools founded in the sixteenth century by none other than John Calvin. An austere-looking building with a red roof, it housed an academically serious environment, and Borges was greatly esteemed by his classmates, two of whom remained lifelong friends and even make occasional cameo appearances in his fiction. Under his *genevois* professors (who pronounced his last name to rhyme with "forge"), the teenaged boy soon became fluent in French and also picked up Latin. Later, during the war, taking advantage of the nightly blackouts and curfews, Borges hid away in his bedroom and taught himself German. In a matter of months, he could read Heine and Stefan George fluently, and he first savored *Leaves of Grass* in a Teutonic version. He also studied contemporary German Expressionist poets, whom he much admired and whose work he was the first to translate into Spanish. Borges eventually published articles on German literature in Swiss newspapers. Among the readers impressed with these pieces was Martin Buber, who requested a meeting with their author—and was astonished to find him so young.[3]

After receiving his Swiss *baccalauréat*—his highest earned academic degree—Borges spent the 1919–1921 years in Spain. The family initially settled for ten months at Palma, in Majorca, out of economic motives—the Balearic Islands had not yet become a tourist center and were hence inexpensive. There Borges's father finished writing his novel *El caudillo;* a twenty-year-old Borges for his part studied more Latin with a local priest and penned (in French) his first book review ever, of two volumes by Azorín and Pío Baroja, for a Swiss journal called *La Feuille*. From there Borges moved on to Seville, where he met local adepts of the *ultraísta* movement—a toned-down Iberian answer to Dadaism, Futurism, and other vanguard vogues of the time—and thence to Madrid, where he quickly made friends with the core group.

Based in the Café Colonial, the *ultraístas* were essentially held together by the charismatic Rafael Cansinos-Assens, a minor poet but brilliant intellect who in time learned eleven foreign languages, and who—in a courageous position for that era—insisted on his alleged Jewish ethnic-cultural ancestry. (In one of those odd little corners of history, Cansinos also happens to have been an uncle of Rita Hayworth, originally baptized Margarita Cansinos.)

Cansinos-Assens was much taken with the brilliant late adolescent from Argentina, whom he warmly encouraged. Borges in turn was dazzled by the man's erudition, effervescence, and free-ranging spirit. Seeing in Cansinos-Assens his first literary master, he remained loyal to the man for the rest of his life, and paid him a disciple's visit in Madrid in 1963. (He always liked noting how Cansinos was too poor to afford bookshelves and therefore kept his countless volumes stacked up in columns that reached the ceiling.) Borges would later describe Cansinos-Assens as an ironic sort of leader, an informal teacher who above all wanted young writers to study the avant-garde canon (Mallarmé, Apollinaire, et al.) in order to bring a tired and provincial Spanish culture up to date with the Modernistic arts of Europe. Appropriately, *ultraísmo* displayed those very same garish features—youthful irreverence toward the old and established, a heady taste for grand assertions and manifestos, a love of Bohemian impudence in various forms—that brought regular notoriety to its internationally visible opposite numbers across the Pyrenees. As part of his youthful rebellion, Borges around this time published some immature poems in praise of the Russian Revolution. Years later, as a result, in one of those little ironies of history, during the McCarthy period Borges's name appeared on the U.S. immigration blacklist and he was denied a visa as a "Communist."[4]

Borges then took *ultraísmo* to Argentina, where he more or less single-handedly reestablished the movement, enlisting devotees among a few young literati and pulling off modest capers such as pasting copies of *Prisma* (*Prism*), a mural magazine that resembled Marinetti's Futurist posters,[5] all over Buenos Aires walls and fences. In these broadsides, Borges and his cohorts breezily rejected in their overstated prose the "garrulous anecdotalism" and "bluish tattoos" of the *modernista* poet Rubén

Darío, while counterproposing the use of metaphor for its own sake, calling for an end to all connectives, adjectives, and adornments in verse, and extolling the "unseen visions," the "undiscovered aspects" of this world. Borges later came to feel embarrassed about this boyish episode, finding the public gestures silly, the poetry negligible, the theory simply wrong. His mild exercises in revolt did help him get launched as a literary person, though, when the editor of *Nosotros,* the most prestigious Argentine literary magazine of the time, invited Borges and his friends to contribute to the journal. Among Borges's cohorts was Guillermo de Torre, today known for his panoramic survey of the European avant-garde,[6] but at that time a roving young Spanish journalist whose contacts in publishing also helped Borges's poems see print in anthologies and books. In the process, the poet gained a relative, for de Torre eventually courted and married Borges's sister Norah. The union did cause some dissension, not least because of anti-Spanish prejudices within the family ranks.

The prime intellectual influence on Borges back home was a slight, graying man with a huge forehead, a perpetual bowler hat, and a Mark Twain moustache. Bearing the unlikely name of Macedonio Fernández, he had attended law school with Borges *père* and joined him in the brief Paraguayan anarchist-colony adventure. After a stint as a law clerk, Macedonio (as everybody still calls him) chose to dedicate himself to pure thought, playing with philosophical ideas both alone and in public. Borges met the man upon returning from Europe and immediately fell under his spell, meeting him every Saturday at the Café Perla. Though Macedonio knew many of Buenos Aires's leading intellects, he preferred meeting with younger minds, drinking *maté* tea with them and channeling their philosophical discussions with his celebrated silences, which he would interrupt only with the occasional, "Well, I suppose you must've noted" this or that or the other.

A drifter, Macedonio lived in boarding houses, often leaving manuscripts behind when he shifted living quarters (which was often). Whenever his admirers expressed dismay at these losses, he would answer, "Do you guys think I'm capable of thinking up anything new?"[7] Some of his more fanciful notions suggest a *porteño* Oscar Wilde, as in his suggestion that the city authorities install better street lighting, so that the thieves would not have to ply their trade by day. Legendary for his absentmindedness, he sometimes neglected to put addresses on envelopes. In what became an oft-cited letter, Macedonio once wrote to Borges, "You must excuse me for not having shown up last night. So forgetful am I that while on my way I forgot that I'd stayed at home instead. These distractions are shameful, and I even forget about feeling ashamed." [8] Borges's mother, on the other hand, was not pleased with her son's disreputable friend, and many were the times when the aspiring writer had to go see Macedonio on the sly.

Macedonio died in 1953. Over the years Borges would recall him as the most extraordinary individual he'd ever met. A complete original, he left his unmistakable imprint on the developing writer's ways of thought and feeling. He was the comic Socrates to a young disciple's playful Plato, "the embryo of the humorist there is in Borges, the humorist concealed within the metaphysician," [9] as one of his biographers so neatly puts it.

T he Argentina to which Borges returned in the 1920s was a land awash in postwar prosperity and was at a social and political peak as well. The recent celebrations of the Centennial of Independence had generated a climate of nationalism, helping further accentuate officialdom's bright prospects for the nation's future. [10] And Argentina was rich, with a strong currency. One of the world's big granaries, it seemed destined to become, at the very least, another Canada or Australia. Similarly, revenues from beef—a product that was at times blithely discarded into the swamps and rivers—appeared inexhaustible. [11] The political situation also held high promise. Due to a recent law granting universal manhood suffrage, the immigrant-based Unión Cívica Radical, a mildly reformist party known simply as "los Radicales," had swept the polls in 1916 and was to remain in power for a full fifteen years. The result was what historian Félix Luna has described as "a quiet egalitarian revolution." Even though the wealth and privileges of the landowning class remained untouched, during that period the benefits of public education were to be shared liberally with the immigrant masses, and political posts ceased being the exclusive property of the old oligarchy. [12] To most every well-meaning citizen, it looked as if the Argentine republic— thanks to unending food exports, modest industrial growth, and wise government patronage—was destined to live on in conditions of permanent well-being. Both for immigrants and for the more progressive elements of the enlightened middle class, it was a situation in which a young Argentine writer of the time could honestly believe.

Into this vigorous and confident country—then compared to the United States but today a shambles—the formerly expatriated Borges now sought reentry as a writer and as an Argentine. Reflecting a harmony between his loyalties and the dominant political tenor of the times, Borges mixed with intellectuals who were Radical-connected and even affiliated himself with the Radical party, joining a committee to re-elect President Yrigoyen in 1928. In addition, in something of a reaction to his parents' aristocratic Europhilia, Borges began cultivating an interest in the fashionable folklore of street toughs and gauchos, and secretly read the nineteenth-century gaucho epic *Martín Fierro*—a book which, for political reasons, was res non grata in the Borges household. Sharing in the national emotions of the moment, and clearly compensating for his years abroad, Borges in these years wrote poetry that was passionately localist and nationalist in flavor, utilizing a free-verse medium frankly modeled after that of Walt Whitman. Some of the titles of his books of poetry and prose speak for themselves: *Fervor de Buenos Aires* (1923), *El idioma de los argentinos* (1928), and *Cuaderno San Martín* (1928; the title refers to a schoolboy notebook bearing the name of the Argentine national hero).

Borges's poetry from the 1920s is, in retrospect, surprisingly direct, romantic in feeling, and, though obviously highly crafted and polished, nonetheless quite unallusive and unliterary, its apparent spontaneity a far cry from the self-consciousness of his later prose. These poems, as the book titles might suggest, express an intimate personal identification with Buenos Aires. The very first lines of Borges's first book reads, "Las calles de Buenos Aires / ya son la entraña de mi alma" (OP, 17; "The streets of Buenos Aires / are now part of my inner soul"). Throughout these collections he wistfully evokes the sights and sounds of the old city—its side streets, cemeteries, patios, parks—as symbols of a gracious and old-fashioned way of life being eclipsed by industrialism and social change. This nostalgic mood remained present throughout Borges's writing career and later became a key theme in some of his more famous stories. Curiously, there are almost no contemporary people—whether Argentine or immigrant—in the Buenos Aires of his early verse. The emphasis is on the sites and places, especially those associated with older, Hispanic creole ways.[13]

The youthful essays of this period, noted today for their many bald statements and frontal attacks (all of which the mature Borges repudiated), are often openly programmatic in their literary nationalism. One piece contains the overt declaration, "I want to speak to the natives: to the men who experience life and death in this land, not to those who believe that the sun and moon are in Europe."[14] (The gentle, twenty-something Borges, it bears noting, was indifferent if not precisely hostile to the immigrant wave from Europe. Later, in "The Waiting" and "Emma Zunz," two of his most powerful tales of crime, he would create characters who are the offspring of immigrant Italians and Jews, respectively.)

One of Borges's early prose works is entitled *El tamaño de mi esperanza* (*The Extent of My Hope*), that "hope" being no less than to find a poetry and musicality that might express the grandeur of Buenos Aires.[15] His personal parti pris is eloquently summarized in the poem "Arrabal" ("Outlying Slum"),[16] which ends with the words "Los años que he vivido en Europa son ilusorios / yo he estado siempre (y estaré) en Buenos Aires" (OP, 39; "The years I have lived in Europe are illusory / I have always been, and will be, in Buenos Aires"). Although these lines speak for a Borges now buried in the distant past, worlds apart from the Europhile antinationalist of the 1940s and 1950s, they in one sense proved prophetic, for Borges was to live almost uninterruptedly in his native city for nearly forty years.

O n the morning of 6 September 1930, the inhabitants of Buenos Aires found themselves awakened by overflying planes and tanks in the city streets. The show of force signaled a conservative military coup by General José Félix Uriburu, an anti-Radical move ordered and financed by right-wing, nationalist, xenophobic elements in the old oligarchy. Though Uriburu's dictatorship lasted only eighteen months, it was the opening shot in what was to become a new, chaotic, completely unresolved Argentina—the one we know today. The prime cause was the global slump, which had adversely affected world food markets, thereby shattering the Argentine economic prosperity and social consensus of the 1920s. As a result, in reaction to the Radical years, a now-polarized Argentina was to witness the rise of nationalist movements on the Mussolini-Franco model, eventually leading to widespread Axis sympathies during the early 1940s. The ideological basis of these nationalisms was a narrow, quasi-racist notion of *Hispanidad,* i.e., a fervid glorification of the culture of old Spain, complemented by anti-British, anti-Semitic, and anti-immigrant attitudes.[17]

In the eyes of Argentina's liberals, cosmopolites, and even leftists, national kinds of emotion were now discredited. Borges, accordingly, abandoned his earlier nativist aesthetic, defined himself as a non-nationalist, and took his stand within the more enlightened space of the Europhile intelligentsia, which as of 1930 suddenly found itself in the opposition. In "Nuestras imposibilidades" ("Our Impossibilities"), a dense, brooding essay first written in 1931 and included shortly thereafter in the first edition of *Discusión,* Borges broadly laments the street-level chauvinism and xenophobia he notes rampant among ordinary Argentine folk, and toward the end of the piece he deplores most of all the "incomparable spectacle of a conservative government that is forcing the entire republic to turn to socialism, only to ruin and sadden a party of the center."[18]

European culture had thus finally succeeded in claiming the thirty-two-year-old poet as its standard-bearer, a connection that was to stay with Borges through five more decades, his own pro-Europeanism sometimes reaching absurd heights during old age. In its origins, though, this Europhilia was a stance of explicit opposition to those pro-Hispanic nationalists who, having virtually declared war on liberalism and antifascism, inevitably drove Borges and other such figures into the cosmopolitan camp. In a minor incident, a nationalist publication entitled *Crisol* (*Crucible*) leveled at Borges the supposed charge of being Jewish. Retorting with irony, Borges humbly described having gone into the archives to research and confirm his Jewish ancestry but, he was sad to reply, had no such kin. Borges also belonged briefly to a committee to protest Argentine anti-Semitism.

Politics aside, Borges spent the 1920s and 1930s living the life of an extremely busy literary man-about-town, reading many books (among them much of the celebrated eleventh edition of the *Encyclopaedia Britannica*), getting himself associated with newspapers and ephemeral magazine projects, and writing essays and verse. Throughout these years Borges regarded himself as a poet; fiction he did not take up in any serious way until 1933, with little of major intrinsic significance issuing from his pen until some years later. The immediate set of circumstances that goaded Borges into seriously writing fiction was to become legendary: his accident on a dark stairway at home on Christmas Eve in 1938, his serious head injury, his near-death from blood poisoning followed by three weeks of delirium. As he lay convalescing, Borges once again felt his writer's itch but, fearing that a temporary block or minor lapse would appear to him as a permanent loss of control over his prime medium, he dared not touch poetry. Borges thereupon decided to try his hand at fiction. The result was his now-classic "Pierre Menard, Author of the *Quixote.*"

The story was later gathered in *El jardín de los senderos que se bifurcan*

(*The Garden of Forking Paths*), a slim book containing eight of those three-dozen narratives that eventually brought Borges world acclaim. At the time (1941), however, it drew public attention only from personal friends and learned critics. Though the volume was submitted to the jury of the National Literary Prize for consideration, the top awards that year went to a few minor authors, an event prompting the memorable "Desagravio a Borges" ("In Defense of Borges," 1942) that filled half an issue of *Sur,* the prestigious literary monthly, in which the leading Argentine intellects eloquently spoke up for Borges and his little collection of tales.[19] In the eyes of his personal friends and admirers, Borges was vindicated, but he remained a marginal figure until the 1950s, when the honors and attention started trickling in from overseas.

Borges's long and sedentary existence was one defined almost exclusively in literary terms. Reflecting on this fact, Borges in 1932 wrote in the preface to *Discusión,* "Life and death have been lacking in my life" (10). These words were particularly true at the time. He was thirty-three, an age at which many men have held regular jobs, been married, fathered children, and suffered bereavement, all of which Borges had not. But even now Borges's personal history seems staid and uneventful; few nonliterary happenings loom very large in his eighty-six years. Among the best-known of these is the fact of his blindness, which became nearly total in his sixties. The ailment was a hereditary one from the English branch of the family; a great-grandfather of Borges suffered from so unusual an eye condition that, in the early nineteenth century, an article about his case appeared in the British medical journal *Lancet.* Father Borges, as we have seen, was similarly afflicted. Borges the son, always severely nearsighted, felt the worst to be imminent in the 1920s. Fortunately he underwent eye surgery in 1929 at the hands of an Argentine doctor—a move considered dangerous by every European surgeon the family had consulted but which virtually restored Borges's eyesight for some three decades.

The late 1930s and 1940s were the most difficult years in Borges's long life. Whatever he had never before experienced seemed to swoop down on him simultaneously: the death of his father, Borges's own nearly fatal accident, and his first full-time drudge job as library clerk.[20] World politics compounded his woes, with local enthusiasm for early Fascist victories adding to his isolation. In 1946 Borges himself became a minor victim to local politics when a minor functionary in the newly elected Perón régime took away his library position and assigned to him the fabled slot of chicken inspector, an offer he declined. Luckily a job came through at a British school, the Instituto Anglo-Argentino. With the counsel of a local psychotherapist named Miguel Cohen-Miller (or Kohan-Miller), who suggested that Borges thoroughly memorize all his lectures and practice them constantly, the once painfully shy author overcame his fear of public speaking and began teaching courses on English and American literature. Meanwhile, Borges found himself shadowed by the security police, his erudite lectures studiously attended by plainclothesmen.

When Perón fell in 1955, Borges's record was cleared and he was appointed director of the National Library. This prestigious sinecure (he actually did very little at the job)[21] Borges held until 1973, when he quietly took retirement—nominally for reasons of age, but to all an obvious resignation in protest against Perón's return to power. In addition to his high-level library post, at around the same time Borges received an appointment as a professor of literature at the University of Buenos Aires, where his classes acquired a reputation for being eccentric, undemanding, and fun—the perfect choice for lazy students. Borges's assignments and examinations required less in the area of facts, dates, and ideas than in a simple love of literature. He failed practically no one during his twelve-year academic career.

With the beginnings of Borges's global fame in the 1960s, his life and fortunes inevitably changed. No longer the struggling, underpaid, somewhat obscure and embattled writer, he metamorphosed into a public presence, *the* grand old man, perhaps, of international letters. Moreover, as María Esther Vázquez observes, he was one of those rare individuals whom old age actually helps, "imparting to them a charm and a distinction they lacked in their youth . . . His figure took on style, his facial features sharpened, and his head of hair, which he retained to the very end of his life, went through all shades of gray until achieving the silvered clarity of silk."[22] Finally, world book sales and countless speaker's fees brought him considerable wealth. Money and luxurious possessions, however, were of scant interest to Borges; now he took on the study of Old English and Old Norse—perfect subject matters for a blind man— via informal weekly meetings with some of his more dedicated students. And he continued to live modestly at his apartment on Calle Maipú, with his aging mother (when he was single) until her death at the age of ninety-nine in 1975, and thereafter with his dedicated housekeeper Fani Úveda de Robledo (and her albino cat Beppo). A brass plaque on his front door bore the simple inscription "Borges"; and casual visitors were often welcome.

Borges's love life is a delicate and complex matter, an unhappy history further complicated by some nasty yet unfounded rumors, among them the claim that the man was physically incapable of sexual relations, or that he was a compulsive masturbator. Certain biographical works published in the years since Borges's death, however, have helped clarify the mystery and shed much-needed light on this obscure topic.

From his early twenties through old age, Borges fell serially (and seriously) in love with anywhere between a dozen and two dozen women, courting them with compulsive if polite passion. Almost all of them ended up amiably spurning the man's marriage proposals. Borges's lonely bachelorhood inevitably aggravated his combined political isolation and personal unhappiness from the 1930s through the early 1950s. Then, with the increased recognition and respect he was gaining as a writer, he began yearning for a normal domestic life, away from the daily presence of his widowed mom, and with home, hearth, and children of his own to sustain him in his growing public life.[23]

Among the many objects of his affections was Estela Canto, an intelligent, highly cultured, unusually experienced and emancipated, and very sexy twenty-eight-year-old Uruguayan whom Borges met in late 1944. For a year or so the two conducted an intense though essentially chaste relationship, meeting almost daily for long strolls and literary conversations. At the time deeply engrossed in writing his great story "The Aleph," Borges repeatedly told Estela that she was Beatrice to his Dante and could help steer him out of his hell. (The published story is dedicated to her.) Eventually developing as a novelist in her own right, Canto published in 1989 an unusually revealing memoir of their liaison, providing along the way a fascinating close-up of the intimate Borges.

Almost at the outset, Canto notes that Borges's attitude toward sex was one of "panic and terror."[24] Nevertheless, he did "get aroused as any normal man would," even if, ultimately, "sexual fulfillment was terrifying to him."[25] She vividly describes his bafflement and ineptitude with the entire universe of eroticism—his kisses, for example, which were "always ill-timed" and "awkward, brusque."[26] Though she genuinely appreciated and admired the author, she did not love him, and when he surprised her by blurting out one evening, "Estela, eh, would you marry me?" her somewhat perverse reply, in English, was, "I'd be glad to, Georgie. But don't forget, I'm a disciple of George Bernard Shaw. We can't get married unless we go to bed together first."[27] The suggestion, as Estela expected, was never acted upon, and the relationship eventually soured when she realized that Borges had a habit of regularly phoning his mother to report on his whereabouts, and that the elder lady (who tended to monologue about her illustrious ancestors and always chaperoned them whenever Estela visited) disapproved of Canto as a choice for her son's wife. Though the two drifted apart, Canto and Borges remained friends.

Borges's profound sexual anxieties seem to have originated in a curious incident from his Swiss days. At that time—among male Hispanics particularly—any erotic activity with one's female equals was out of the question, and young bloods customarily received their sexual initiation at a brothel. With this in mind, and concerned about his growing boy's late virginity, papa Borges gave him the name and address of a prostitute and sent him to Geneva's red-light district, the Place Dubourg de Four. Once at the assigned place, the teenager became obsessed with the notion that his dad was her "client," and so found himself incapable of bedding down with that woman—and, consequently, with any woman.[28]

So goes the story, as reported in recent biographies. If true, it does help explain Borges's lifelong difficulties with the opposite sex. For years afterward, his parents apparently interpreted the problem as simply physiological and provided him an array of tonics and medications (including a treatment for liver deficiency).[29] In 1946, however, Dr. Cohen-Miller, the same psychotherapist who was to help Borges overcome his fears of public speaking, concurrently diagnosed him as "far from impotent" yet a victim of "exaggerated sensitivity, fear of sex, and guilt feelings."[30] Dr. Cohen-Miller suggested, in fact, that Borges learn to address audiences as part of his sexual cure, and also that he get married. Later, in the 1950s, Borges mentioned to friends that he had achieved sexual relations with a dancer.

As regards marriage, the big challenge was in finding someone available, appropriately mature, and willing. This finally happened in 1967, when Borges renewed a relationship with Elsa Astete Millán, a woman he had first met, fallen in love with, and pursued in the late 1920s. For a few months in that earlier era, Borges had called on her every Saturday. She was pretty, frivolous, and just seventeen, and their courtship had come to a sudden stop when Elsa's mother received him one morning and told a rather bemused Borges that the young girl had married someone else only yesterday. The marriage to Ricardo Albarracín—a satisfactory union, with a son—had ended when Elsa's spouse died of lung cancer in 1964.

Through a series of chance social events, Borges now met up with Elsa once again, and their engagement and marriage happened fairly fast, with his mother's approval. The entire relationship, however, was a terrible mismatch, and Borges knew he had erred long before their 4 August 1967 wedding day rolled around. Elsa knew nothing about literature, spoke no foreign languages, and seems to have been interested mainly in shopping and small talk; among her chief conversational topics was discussing Buenos Aires bus routes.[31] During the author's U.S. lecture tours she reportedly would do such things as announce, on the very night of an event, an increase in Borges's speaker's fee (which led to an emergency passing of the hat among the audience),[32] or, at receptions, call attention to herself by singing and strumming her guitar when the purpose of the gathering was to listen to Borges's words.[33]

Trapped in domestic misery, Borges by 1970 wanted out, yet also feared the inevitably angry scene should he inform Elsa of his desires. Besides, divorce in Argentina was illegal. With the combined help of Norman Thomas di Giovanni (Borges's then-translator and amanuensis) and a lawyer friend, a secret plan was concocted. On 7 July, Borges left for the office as on any normal work day but made for the airport instead; he and di Giovanni took a flight to Córdoba, where the author had some speaking engagements. Meanwhile, back "home," Elsa heard the doorbell ring around noontime; thinking it was Borges returning for lunch, she opened the door and was confronted by five strangers: a lawyer and his son, both of them legally authorized to remove the writer's properties (books, mostly), and three hired movers, who proceeded with their assigned task. The estranged couple did not meet again; a legal separation was secured, and Elsa never recovered from her shock at the way in which her second husband's departure had been handled.[34]

There was, at long last, a happy ending to Borges's decades of sadness as a man. In 1975 he hired a new secretary, María Kodama, approximately thirty. Born and raised in Argentina of a Japanese father and a German-Jewish mother, she had first met the author in her twelfth year and had participated in his Old English study group as a university student. Having eventually earned her doctorate in English from the University of Buenos Aires, she was ideally qualified to work as Borges's professional assistant. For years they maintained a properly professional and correct relationship, even addressing each other with the formal "Usted" pronoun. One outsider describes Kodama as almost otherworldly and characterizes her attitude toward him as "reverential."[35] It is also worth remarking that, unlike numerous other individuals who became close to Borges, she never attempted to "cage" him or to exploit their ties for her own advantage.[36]

Over the years, a tenderness began to grow between older master and younger employee. Age in this case was not the major obstacle. Kodama herself came from a broken home and feared repeating in her life the trauma of spousal separation. In addition Borges, being too much the "Victorian gentleman," once again did not wish to embark on a non-marital affair. Finally, in 1985, events moved apace. Borges was diagnosed with cancer of the liver, a fact that the author, his doctor, and Kodama kept concealed.[37] Weary of Buenos Aires, Borges now decided to live out the remainder of his life in the Geneva of his adolescence. Once there, he and Kodama came to a mutual decision, freely and mutually arrived at, and, on 24 April 1986, took their marriage vows—though by proxy, in Paraguay, since, according to Argentine law, Borges was still married to Elsa.

Eight weeks later, on 14 June, the author breathed his last. (His agnosticism notwithstanding, Borges heard confession and was granted absolution on his deathbed.) The death was not completely foreseen; his mother's near-century of existence had generated hopes of comparable longevity for the son. He was buried in Geneva's Pleinpalais Cemetery, under a yew tree, a few yards from the tomb of John Calvin.[38] A rough-hewn gravestone bears inscriptions in both Old English and Old Norse.

Borges's belated, final romance freed him from many old ghosts and brought him a new serenity. He died, in certain ways, a happy man.[39] Still, the attendant circumstances scarcely added up to a pretty picture. Due to some family and financial squabbles, Borges had designated Kodama his all but exclusive heir, and even an originally generous legacy for his housekeeper Fani had been reduced to two thousand dollars. The marriage was publicly criticized by Borges's sister Norah and his nephews, who, following his death, launched a campaign against Kodama in the local and European press.[40]

In *The Book of Sand* (1975), Borges's last full volume of fiction, he included a sweet, romantic tale entitled "Ulrike." It is his only love story, and moreover the sole work of his that portrays sexual love in a positive, indeed joyous, light. Kodama has described the text as evocative of her own relationship with Borges,[41] but this seems unlikely, inasmuch as "Ulrike" was written a couple of years before she started working for him.

In a touching gesture, however, Kodama included on Borges's tombstone the dedication, "From Ulrike to Javier Otálora," referring to the pair of strangers who, within the story, chance to meet and enjoy their mutual pleasures during a single winter's night in the old city of York. Love, literature, and life thus fuse—in death—into a single myth, an encompassing fable. As of this writing, Kodama keeps alive the memory of her husband in her capacity as head of the Fundación Jorge Luis Borges, with offices next door to the house where the Borgeses resided in the 1930s.

H is personal ups and downs aside, the full picture of Borges's biography, temperament, and talents presents that unusual case of a man doing exactly what he likes to do, doing it in his own way, and being superbly gifted at doing it—abilities that were manifest from early childhood and adolescence. (Even relatively late in life Borges was treated like something of a child prodigy.) For anything connected with language and literature Borges evinced an uncanny personal intuition and a rare brilliance: the feat of teaching himself German in three months comes to mind. Later, in his forties, Borges took to reading in the original the novelist Eça de Queiroz, with no previous exposure to Portuguese; whenever a phrase stumped him, Borges would read it aloud and then could grasp the meaning of the phrase. To get to his library job, Borges faced a daily bus ride of an hour each way. During this trip he tackled Dante's *Divine Comedy* in an annotated English-Italian bilingual edition by John Aitken Carlyle; his method was to read a page in the English translation to absorb the sense, and then to experience the same lines in Italian; by the time he had reached the *Purgatorio,* Borges realized he could read Italian fluently.[42] Throughout his life Borges also showed a prodigious memory for poetry, with thousands of lines of verse (in English, Spanish, French, German, and Latin) stored somewhere in his head, a living literary record from which he freely called forth material, be it for conversation or for a written page.

Unlike his fellow Formentor prizewinner Samuel Beckett, who was noted for shunning all publicity, or his own Argentine compatriot Julio Cortázar, who simply preferred not to be set upon by solicitors, Borges, a friendly and loquacious man, always enjoyed being approached for conversation, even by strangers. When he was a visiting lecturer at Harvard University in 1967, he actually complained that too few students were dropping in on him at his Hilles Library office—a rare lament from writers-in-residence. His many private and public talks appeared in print, and during the 1960s practically every North American literary magazine was publishing interviews with Borges. Because of the many Boswells and their tape recorders, we know far more about Borges the man—his opinions, his strengths and gaps in knowledge, his personal style—than we usually do about an author. It is true that in these interviews (as commentators often remark) the talk centers chiefly around books, with scarce references to Borges's private life. Nonetheless, this is perfectly fitting for a man whose entire life has been consecrated to, organized around, and conceived in terms of imaginative literature. Even one of his closest confidantes, Alicia Jurado, could not help but remark that the numerous entries in her personal diary pertaining to her conversations with Borges seldom mention more than the literary topics discussed by them that day.[43]

Borges once remarked that, just as politics in the 1960s could be a passion among the young, in his own time the realm of literature, the relations between literature and life, and the theoretical and artistic possibilities of language could arouse similar enthusiasm.[44] The word "enthusiasm" is an essential factor in Borges's personal aesthetic; at age sixty-eight he could unabashedly state that "people should get a kick out of literature."[45] Books are a visceral, not a coolly professional, matter with him; of entering the National Library, he notes, "I feel, almost physically, the gravitation of the books" (D, 10; H, 7). In the same way, writing for Borges is akin to a religious vocation, a destiny, not an occupation or a job or a set of techniques. Because of his intensely personal, unacademic approach to books in general, Borges—in contrast to practitioners of much of the contemporary, campus-based higher criticism—looks upon poetry and fiction as a way of life, as something produced by living, inherently interesting human beings. Borges can thus shed new light on Coleridge, whom he considers an uneven poet but an engaging literary *person;* similarly, he will note the aesthetic limitations of Whitman's and Valéry's verse but bring the two individuals together with the striking observation that the contrasting kinds of poet, the types of men represented and contained in their poetry, are what we readers most esteem and value. This is the outlook that leads Borges in *Dreamtigers* to speculate imaginatively as to what Homer and Shakespeare may have been like as individual personalities.

The life (no word fits better) led by Borges with books is nicely summed up by his well-known self-characterization as "a hedonistic reader." Following only his tastes and temperament, blissfully ignoring established canons of worth, Borges read either what he liked or whatever happened to fit his writing needs. A vast amount of curious, out-of-the-way, bookish lore stayed with him in the process, the celebrated "erudition" so dazzling to Borges's admirers. That Borges "read everything" is a commonplace of criticism. And yet, the learning evinced by Borges stands out above all for its being slightly odd, marginal, archaic. To a great extent it is a knowledge that originates in "what nobody reads anymore," as André Maurois puts it in his foreword to *Labyrinths* (L, ix)—for example, obscure church heresies, somewhat faded works of metaphysics, nineteenth-century orientalist scholarship, non-Western mystical writings, and, above all, fanciful esoterica from a variety of periods and places.

Borges's literary culture, moreover, was something picked up mostly on his own. In great measure a self-taught man, his most advanced academic degree was a Swiss secondary school certificate (for which, incidentally, he never took the final, comprehensive examinations that were required for university admission).[46] Before he began teaching for a living, when he was well into his forties, Borges had had very little to do with universities or the higher-education system. If anything, his college "classrooms" were the literary cafés in Spain and Buenos Aires, his professors the nonacademic, anti-academic masters Cansinos-Assens and Macedonio Fernández. This "gap" in Borges's educational background is simply astounding when one remembers just how profoundly bookish a man he was. Moreover, as is usually the case with self-taught men, Borges's learning was as idiosyncratic and lopsided as it was aglow with enthusiasm.

Néstor Ibarra, Borges's translator into French, said of the author, "Il n'est que lacunes" ("He is all gaps"). Ibarra notes, for instance, that Borges is ignorant of French literature and has read only a tenth of what any man of letters has. Borges sees no harm, says Ibarra, in reading secondhand summaries of books as he in fact did for *Ulysses*. Metaphysical in temperament and exclusively literary in lifestyle, Borges, Ibarra asserts, reads no newspapers, cares little about science, and has never once set foot in a concert hall or museum.[47] Hence the virtual absence in all of Borges's oeuvre of any allusions to the fine arts, to the social and natural sciences, or to current affairs. Borges himself admitted more than once to being tone deaf and caring little about the visual arts. (The extent of his interest in music is uncomfortably displayed in his answer to a question posed to him by Richard Burgin: "Gustav Mahler. I never heard him.")[48] Similarly, when Borges equates dialectical materialism with Nazism and anti-Semitism in "Tlön, Uqbar, Orbis Tertius," he reveals his reading gap in Marxist thought and, for that matter, in much of the significant social philosophy of the preceding ninety years.

Borges's literary interests show a similarly curious imbalance. William H. Gass forcefully points out how the authors dear to Borges are essentially "cranky, wayward, even decadent . . . [and] marginal" figures, the purveyors of "works at once immature and exotic, thin though mannered, clever rather than profound, neat instead of daring, too often the products of learning, fancy and contrivance to make us comfortable."[49] The thinkers who most captivate Borges tend not to be the very best in their respective fields and indeed are often of second rank: Zeno instead of Plato, Bishop Berkeley instead of Hobbes or Locke or Hume, Schopenhauer instead of Kant or Hegel, Herbert Spencer instead of John Stuart Mill, Jung instead of Freud. The same applies to his literary favorites: Stevenson, Kipling, and H. G. Wells are recurrent Borgesian references, and G. K. Chesterton he once hailed as nothing less than "my master." At the same time, he pronounced *Ulysses* a failure, found Virginia Woolf boring, considered Frost a better poet than Eliot, and expressed serious reservations about Proust.

These eccentricities Borges was wont to carry over into his life as critic and teacher. Ronald Christ reports a Buenos Aires student complaining to him that Borges's lectures on English literature dealt mostly with the personal whims of Jorge Luis Borges, much undue attention being given, for example, to William Morris.[50] Even when discussing Shakespeare, Borges's written references revolve around pet topics: the play-within-a-play in *Hamlet* (to Borges a magical device), the idea gleaned from *Julius Caesar* that past events may repeat themselves, and fanciful speculation in *Dreamtigers* as to Shakespeare's multiple personality. He did write a piece on Flaubert—not, however, on *Madame Bovary* (which he deemed awkward) or *Sentimental Education* but on that bookish fantasia of the intellect, the almost Borgesian creature entitled *Bouvard and Pécuchet* (in D, 137). Though a major world literary figure, he cared little for his international contemporaries. Frequently likened to Beckett and Nabokov, he displayed no particular interest in them. Wallace Stevens, in many ways a North American counterpart, was little more than a name to Borges and—in one of his rarely stated opinions on recent European writers— he once dismissed Alain Robbe-Grillet and Michel Butor as "a couple of fools."[51]

How does one account for this strange drift in Borges's interests? Youthful passions for one are at work here. The writings of Wells and Stevenson were literally the first books handled by Borges at age five, while Chesterton and Schopenhauer came during his teens in Geneva. At the time when he was growing up, of course, these authors were highly regarded, even world famous, but when their public reputations gradually ebbed, Borges remained ever faithful to them. Borges was often likened to a little boy who never grew up, and certainly his cult of a long-vanished nineteenth-century frontier *machismo* as well as the nostalgic sentiments that predominate in his verse bespeak a mind strongly attached to things past.

Whatever the psychological reasons for Borges's offbeat literary preferences, these marginal men were nonetheless key sources in his development as an artist. Intrinsically their works are minor, but they contain techniques hitherto neglected, procedures that Borges was to appropriate and recast into something unmistakably his. Wells's *The Time Machine* and Stevenson's *The Strange Case of Dr. Jekyll and Mr. Hyde* are narratives that stand completely outside the literary mainstream of their time, that is, the realist novel of character analysis and individual psychology, a genre which Borges, for a number of reasons, actively and notoriously dislikes. For Borges the novel is formally hazy, the behavior of its characters irrational and false, and the attempt to "represent" reality a pernicious illusion that leads a Proust or a Tolstoy to overburden their works with irrelevant detail. The young Borges thought Dostoevski the greatest of all novelists but later found his books filled with exaggerated, unconvincing attitudes. He continued to esteem *Don Quixote* and *Huckleberry Finn* later in life, though thinking them both shapeless. Significantly, Borges's literary essays contain only scant references to such major nineteenth-century novelists as Balzac, Dickens, and George Eliot.

What Borges was to find in these minor authors was an alternative to realism and psychologism; from them he could glean other literary ways long ignored and forgotten. In Robert Louis Stevenson, a man generally unread today by serious students of literature, he rediscovered the narrative of action stripped of any psychological causation and subjective introspection; accordingly, quite a few Borges pieces—fast-moving vignettes in which men kill simply because they kill, with no reasons or subtle motives given—are in this same tradition of the adventure story but with an added magical or metaphysical twist.

More important, Borges found in Stevenson's *The Strange Case of Dr. Jekyll and Mr. Hyde* (and to a lesser degree in *Markheim*) the artistic possibilities inherent in the idea of double identity. Stevenson may ultimately have furnished Borges with his well-known and persistent, almost obsessive, notion about one man literally being two. Stevenson himself had his Dr. Jekyll postulate a theory about the twoness of man: "With every day, and from both sides of my intelligence, the moral and the intellectual, I thus drew steadily nearer to that truth by whose partial discovery I have been doomed to such a dreadful shipwreck: that man is not truly one, but truly two. . . . It was on the moral side, and in my own person, that I learned to recognize the primitive duality of man; I saw that, of the two natures that I could rightly be said to be either, it was only because I was radically both."[52] Stevenson, of course, is actually positing a late-nineteenth-century pseudobiological cliché about the hidden beast in man, a doctrine that really does not concern Borges, who is drawn more to the purely formal literary implications of Dr. Jekyll's conceit, the idea of being "radically both." Borges once remarked that the title of Stevenson's Jekyll-Hyde novella suggests two different persons, the reader then finding out to his surprise that the two names belong to one man. In like fashion, Borges's stories that sport such titles as "Theme of the Traitor and the Hero" and "The Theologians" end with the disquieting revelation that the differing characters in the title are really one person.[53]

H. G. Wells, once widely admired and respected as a novelist and social thinker, is today consumed mostly by science-fiction buffs, who regard him as an important and innovative pioneer. His original literary contribution is what we might call—in contrast to Poe's tales of absolute, unfathomable mystery—the fantastic but seemingly explainable. I say "seemingly" because, Wells's use of science notwithstanding, his applied physics and biology are rather fantastical and illusory; by all known experience so far, the situations depicted by him are simply not possible occurrences. This is why, when Jules Verne read Wells's *The First Men in the Moon*—an unlikely yarn about the forging of an artificial metal not subject to ordinary gravitation and the discovery of some antlike creatures made of glass who live *inside* the moon—he exclaimed, "Mais il invente!" ("He's dreamt it up!"). Wells's visionary art is a strange hybrid of objectively realist representation, pseudoscientific fact, and utterly unreal events; despite the pretensions to science in *The Time Machine*, the farfetchedness of its conception puts it much closer to such Borges tales of fantasy as "The Secret Miracle" or "The Immortal," both of which attempt to go beyond ordinary conceptions of time. *The Island of Dr. Moreau*, in which two men engineer the successful blurring of the boundaries separating man and animal, builds upon a notion even more extravagant than Borges's fancies about loss of personal identity. And the unreal situation of Wells's invisible man is not so remote from the utter unreality of the dreamer in "The Circular Ruins."

Wells was always one of Borges's favorites. In his eloquent appreciation of the author in *Other Inquisitions,* Borges touches lightly on one of the Englishman's narrative procedures—the fact that Wells normally starts out from an unlikely situation, then proceeds to develop the logical consequences of that situation. Hence, what counts about the invisible man is neither his personal history nor his psychological makeup but the far more radical circumstance of his invisibility, which forces him to behave in a predetermined way; all of his actions stem from the need to conceal his predicament. This approach closely resembles Borges's own methods. In "The Immortal," for example, the multiple activities and roles undertaken by the protagonist derive not from his background or inner personality (of which we know little) but from the broader horizons generated by his incapacity to die.

G. K. Chesterton's dogmatic Catholicism always bored the agnostic, free-thinking Borges. Nevertheless, the arch-conservative Briton opened Borges's eyes to what could be done with detective fiction. This genre has a special appeal to Borges because of its minimal psychology and peculiar narrative mechanics. The actions in a detective story are dictated not by personality traits but by a strict set of possibilities inherent in a situation. Any typical detective story tends to stress *how* things happen rather than *who* does them—the criminal who is eventually found being simply the final link in a logically deduced problem.

Chesterton's Father Brown stories are delightful, polished gems of wit and intelligence in which a bewildering series of facts and events are coldly demystified by a super-reasoner (who happens to be a Catholic priest). Significantly, the stories bring magical and exotic elements to bear on the action (characters from remote lands, occult spells), seemingly frightening and unmanageable facts that, in the end, reorder themselves into neatly rational patterns. As Borges describes Chesterton's art, "Each story in the Father Brown saga presents a mystery, proposes explanations of a demoniacal or magical sort, and then replaces them at the end with solutions of this world" (OI, 86; OI, 119). Borges proceeds in precisely this way in his own detective stories "Death and the Compass" and "Ibn-Hakkan al-Bokhari."

Chesterton is particularly fond of extended impersonations and identity tricks. In *The Man Who Was Thursday,* we read at first of a group of six anarchist agents, known only as "Monday," "Tuesday," and so on through "Saturday." As the book progresses, we find out that each and every one of the agents is a counterspy, a double agent working for the other side—a trick later exploited by Borges himself in "The Shape of the Sword," where the speaker turns out to be the very coward he has been vilifying throughout his narrative. Similarly, in Chesterton's story "The Dagger with Wings" a man impersonates his brother, whom he has just murdered; but Father Brown notes certain logical inconsistencies in the man's conduct and there and then denounces him. Likewise, Borges tells of an Arab prince who poses as his own dead cousin in "Ibn-Hakkan al-Bokhari"; years later, the mathematician Unwin solves the mystery by noting the loose ends and inconsistencies in the actions of the Arab prince.

In his middle years, Borges did a fair amount of translating, and the same patterns that characterized his literary preferences and his own approaches to storytelling can be discerned in the works he translated. These translations—which were done primarily for the extra money—include Virginia Woolf's *Orlando* (1937), a novel portraying the divers personal and even sexual transformations of an Elizabethan gentleman over a three-hundred-year period (a kind of preliminary exercise for "The Immortal," which stretches the time span to three thousand years and shows a character becoming Homer, a Roman military officer, the Wandering Jew, and many, perhaps all, men); Faulkner's *The Wild Palms* (1940), a rather curious narrative of two completely separate individuals who never once meet but have a thematic relationship that unites them in the mind of the reader (a precursor to Borges's "Story of the Warrior and the Captive," in which two stories centuries apart are also brought together by a striking insight in Borges's mind); and Melville's *Bartleby the Scrivener* (1944), a Kafka-like tale about an office clerk who refuses to obey orders, simply saying "I prefer not to" in reply to his boss (a harbinger of "The Life of Tadeo Isidoro Cruz" and "The Waiting," stories which similarly reduce whole lives to a single act or set of acts).

What is particularly noteworthy is that the period in which Borges worked on these translations, 1937 to 1944, closely coincides with the years when his major fictional works either were produced or were in gestation. The time pattern appears too close to be merely casual; Borges was probably well aware that he was dealing with writers whose literary methods were not unlike his, and hence he felt he could learn something from the extensive exposure to them. Borges remarks in a famous essay that Kafka *created* his precursors, that his mode of writing modifies our view of works from the past. In a very real sense, Borges has created his own precursors by recasting them in his native tongue.

Borges's attraction for minor philosophers can be analyzed in much the same way as his fondness for lesser authors. For example, as a systematic theorist of morals or knowledge, Zeno and his contributions are slight, but his clever sophistries helped nourish Borges's own fascination with paradox and mental conceits. The idea that a man will never leave this room because first he will walk one-half the distance to the door, then one-fourth, then one-eighth, and so on ad infinitum is an elegantly specious artifice, an elaborate structure of arguments built on unreal premises much like a well-written treatise on unicorns. Borges is so fond of this sort of thing that he wrote two different essays dealing with Zeno's argument to the effect that Achilles, for like mathematical reasons, never catches up with the tortoise. Entire stories by Borges can hinge on such a sophistry. "Pierre Menard" is a richly textured argument in defense of an author who writes another man's work verbatim, indeed, claiming with ironclad logic that Menard's effort is commendable precisely because he wrote someone else's writing.

Bishop Berkeley's absolute idealism, which holds that physical matter does not exist and that the universe is nothing more than a projection of our minds, is seldom taken seriously by philosophers today other than as a means of eliciting discussion. Berkeley's hypothesis and his defense thereof is a classic sophistry in that it accepts no arguments from outside its own thought-provoking parti pris. Because of its very outrageousness, however, absolute idealism can engender similarly extravagant, farfetched, and thought-provoking corollaries.

Already in his twenties, Borges—in *Inquisitions,* a book he later rejected, destroying any copy of it that came his way—brought out an article sympathetically summarizing Bishop Berkeley's position, with many of the materialist counterarguments ingeniously handled and purportedly demolished. Borges also frankly hails Berkeley as a prime stimulus to his own thought. In that same volume, moreover, Borges included an essay called "The Insignificance of Personality," which sets out to demonstrate that, quite simply, "No hay tal yo de conjunto" ("There is no such thing as an overall self"). Borges develops this audacious notion in a way that looks forward to his most famous stories, where personality plays a minimal role in the action and where in fact the self is shown to be double or even multiple. In a more familiar essay, "A New Refutation of Time" (gathered in *Other Inquisitions*), Borges takes the idea even further. He argues that if matter and space do not exist, then time too must be an illusion. And of course the fanciful concept of an insubstantial, idea-permeated universe, although it may be argued and extrapolated within the realm of the abstract, can be narratively depicted as well, visibly mapped out with all its logical ramifications, as Borges does in "Tlön, Uqbar, Orbis Tertius." A similar conceit serves as the philosophical basis for "The Circular Ruins," where men turn out to be merely incorporeal dreams generated by the minds of others—who may also be dreams themselves.

Borges never wrote any systematic exposition of Schopenhauer's thought, as he once did with that of Berkeley. This is understandable, given that the German metaphysician was a far more ambitious thinker than the Irish clergyman. Borges is fond of alluding to him, however, and often lists him when mentioning his other literary favorites. In his "Autobiographical Essay," Borges pays Schopenhauer the highest possible tribute: "Today, were I to choose a single philosopher, I would choose him. If the riddle of the universe can be stated in words, I think these words would be in his writings. I have read him many times over, both in German, and with my father and his close friend Macedonio Fernandez in translation" (TA, 216–217). Extremely popular with intellectuals some decades ago, Schopenhauer is rarely read today except by historians of ideas and students of German culture, who are well aware of the direct link between him and his far greater successor Nietzsche. With his rather cloying, self-indulgent pessimism, Schopenhauer now tends to appeal mostly to troubled adolescents. Yet Borges remained steadfastly loyal to Schopenhauer, and in the numerous rereadings one might expect the ideas of the German metaphysical speculator to rub off on the Argentine metaphysical fiction maker.

Among the key ideas shared by Schopenhauer and Borges is the concept of the universe as a vast, total oneness in which individuality is but an illusion. A prime target of Schopenhauer is what he contemptuously terms the "principle of individuation." For Schopenhauer, the ordinary man is beguiled by immediate accident and sees misleading distinctions rather than continuities. Hence, in Schopenhauer's view, pain and pleasure are not opposites but essentially the same thing, and even good and evil are "but different sides of the manifestation of the one will to live." This leads logically to the conceit, found here and there in the philosopher's work, that the executioner and his victim are one. A parable that figures among Schopenhauer's favorites comes from a passage in the *Upanishads,* where a student sees all the beings in the world parade successively before his eyes, and, as each one files past, he hears a voice announce to him, "Tat twam asi" ("This thou art"). A man is not his self, but essentially others.

It is no accident that the passages and conceptions quoted above read like statements for the themes of Borges stories. "Tat twam asi" ("This thou art") is precisely what Tadeo Isidoro Cruz suddenly realizes when he fights against Martín Fierro or what Señora de Borges feels in the "Story of the Warrior and the Captive" when confronted by the Indian-English girl, whose fate she partly shares. At the end of the latter piece, in fact, Borges ventures the speculation that the lives of two different persons may really be one single story. We can also see at work, in other Borges narratives, the Schopenhauerian notion that killer and killed are one. This concept appears in "The Waiting," where Villari and his victim are alluded to by the same name throughout the piece, or in "The Theologians," at the end of which a scholar denounced as a heretic and the personal rival who denounced him are shown to be the same man.

The various mystical writings of which Borges is fond similarly furnished him concrete methods of perceiving and organizing the universe in ways that transcend immediate physical reality, psychological perception, and realistic reporting; the mysticism, however, may be subjected to parody and humor, as in "The Aleph," and the mystical outlook may suggest insanity, as in "The Zahir." In his essay published in *Discusión,* "A Vindication of the Cabbalah," Borges defends not the doctrinal content of Hebraic mysticism but the literary potential to be mined from its numerical-alphabetical techniques; later he was to structure his story "Death and the Compass" around cabbalistic material. Likewise, Vedantaism, a Hindu school of philosophy that sees all men as one and considers individuality a mere illusion, had the same fruitful intellectual function for Borges, who produced numerous stories on similar lines. Of all the Hindu sects, Vedanta is the one that most completely denies the existence of the world and, even more explicitly, the individual personality; as Borges himself once put it in his essay on Bernard Shaw, "the Self . . . Vedanta condemns as a capital error" (OI, 175; OI, 221). Finally, it should be noted that all these idealisms and mysticisms have in common their conception of the universe as ultimately unreal; and unreality, as Ana María Barrenechea pointed out in her pioneering study, is the formal, intellectual, and artistic basis of all Borges's work as storyteller and poet.

Herbert Spencer, a target of ridicule even for Borges's great favorite Bernard Shaw, is a more curious case, bringing us to the question of what Borges himself believes. Unfortunately, many critics tend to take all of Borges's statements at face value or to accept certain of his self-characterizations and disregard others. One of these believed half-truths is Borges's fabled "skepticism," for example, his blunt assertion that "I disbelieve all interpretations, including my own." Borges's afterword to *Other Inquisitions* notes a tendency "to evaluate religious or philosophical ideas on the basis of their esthetic worth" rather than by what is true or false, valid or invalid in them. And it is undeniable that Borges manifests a mischievous pleasure in playing around with different doctrines purely for the imaginative possibilities they evoke and the degree of wonder they can arouse. Borges, like Samuel Beckett, is interested not in the content but in the shape of ideas.[54] We might say that Borges treats ideas as if they were compositional elements in a still-life painting; since he deems all systems of thought basically arbitrary, he tends to link them together in formal arrangements, in equally arbitrary but aesthetically intriguing contexts.

But there are limits even to Borges's skepticism. Montaigne, who has been compared to Borges and whom Borges admired, doubted everything except the existence of God. Similarly, Borges playfully ponders all ideas but, as with his idealist thinkers on planet Tlön, cannot countenance materialism, be it the empirical or the dialectical variety. Borges's attitude is partly understandable since, from an artistic point of view, materialism, in contrast to the occult sciences or the-world-as-idea, cannot possibly be mined for the fantastic. As Borges once remarked to an interviewer, "if you're a materialist, . . . you're tied down by reality."[55] This is why Borges is drawn to Jung (who shares Borges's fascination with universal myths and the uses of imagination for its own sake) but finds the materialist Freud "a kind of madman . . . laboring over a sexual obsession."[56] This is also why Borges evinces no interest in the natural or social sciences, inasmuch as these disciplines assume the material existence of their respective objects of study. And though Borges will not go so far as to believe, with Berkeley, that the physical world is one vast illusion, he does state frequently enough that Schopenhauer (whose best-known book begins with the assertion, "The world is my idea—this is a truth which holds good for everything that lives and knows") provides the definitive explanation for the riddle of the universe.

Borges's skepticism also has its limits in the political realm. Being a sensible man, he never went in for intellectual or aesthetic games with Nazism, a movement which (as was definitely *not* the case with T. S. Eliot, Ezra Pound, Henry Luce, William Randolph Hearst, and most Western conservatives in the 1930s) Borges absolutely loathed. Borges's skepticism never went so far as to doubt the rightness of the Allied cause. By the same token, however, he was rigidly anti-Communist, having on differing occasions supported the Bay of Pigs invaders and simplistically interpreted the war in Vietnam as a conflict between "Western culture and Soviet imperialism." When Borges denounced Nazism, moreover, he had in mind specifically Hitler's treatment of the Jews, the French, and the city of London, whereas the Eastern front and the wholesale destruction of Russia, with her twenty-five million dead, never elicited much public sympathy from him. Borges once designated himself a "mild liberal" in the nineteenth-century sense, one who believes above all in individual freedom and thinks good government governs little. Hence his admiration for Herbert Spencer, an extreme defender of laissez-faire capitalism whose social ideas Borges, on some metaphysical level, seems generally to share.

Borges, of course, is not a philosophical or political thinker—something he himself always conceded. This is not the same thing, however, as saying Borges is a total skeptic who believes in nothing at all. In the 1960s he joined the Conservative party, a move he justified on numerous occasions as proof of his skepticism—a rather specious explanation since, if anything, it revealed Borges's frank adherence to backward-looking social solutions, to an Argentina as it was before 1910. (As so often happens in political discourse, "skepticism" is a neutral word that Borges employed as a camouflage for his deeper meaning, "opposition to social change.") Borges's ideas outside of the world of poetry and metaphysics may have been old-fashioned and simplistic, even crude, but he nevertheless valued certain principles and banished others both from his life and his art. The mind of Borges could absorb a great deal, though not that which would logically negate its own workings. Like a modern Descartes, he doubted everything except his right, and above all his desire, to doubt everything. It is a mind very much of the nineteenth-century world and the old liberal family into which it was born.

3   What Borges Did for Prose Fiction

Borges is one of the foremost literary innovators of the twentieth century, a true originator and discoverer, a master artisan and meticulous maker, a man whose verbal inventions have effectively altered, in both the Americas and in Europe, the guidelines for writing, reading, and judging prose fiction.

Within the Hispanic American world, from Buenos Aires to Mexico City, Borges's thirty-odd stories stand as an event of immeasurable cultural importance. Quite simply, had Borges not existed or had he died before producing the *Ficciones,* the panorama of Latin American literary life in the later twentieth century—with its awesome standards of performance, its high level of discourse, its intellectual freshness and vigor, its seriousness of craft, its artistic originality—would have been noticeably different. Borges's work played a primal role in nurturing the writers of the celebrated Latin American "boom." Julio Cortázar's numerous collections of fantastic fiction stand in a direct line of succession from Borges's own tales of time travel and double identity in *El Aleph,* and such major novelists as García Márquez, Cabrera Infante, and Cortázar himself were to assimilate, expand upon, and transcend the lessons of Borges in such far-reaching books as *One Hundred Years of Solitude, Three Trapped Tigers,* and *Hopscotch.*

Although nearly every younger Hispanic author deplored the retrograde politics of the elder man, writers in Lima or Mexico City or Havana had to reckon with the author Borges, whether they accepted his writings whole, singled out certain aspects of his art, or ultimately rejected him outright. Attitudes toward Borges, even on the part of his admirers, have varied widely. Literary specialists tend to give equal time and assign equal value to the entire Borges oeuvre of poetry, essays, and fiction; general readers know him mostly by his fanciful tales and an occasional essay; and a small minority group (one that includes, among others, the Argentine novelist Ernesto Sábato) discounts Borges's prose narratives as ivory-tower escapism, yet considers him a major poet in Spanish. Cuban literary critics on the island, inevitably at odds with Borges's politics, are given to citing him frequently, if with some discomfort. Whether one likes the fact or not, Borges is there, politically a relic of the nineteenth century but artistically a recognized universal genius, one whose labyrinthine imaginings constitute a fruitful presence and a milestone in Spanish American cultural history.

Pablo Neruda—famed and beloved Chilean poet, Nobel Laureate for 1971, dedicated Marxist activist, and one of the first victims of General Augusto Pinochet's dictatorship—once characterized the Argentine author with words that fully sum up the ambiguous pride with which Latin American intellectuals look upon Borges:

> He's a great writer, and good heavens! All Spanish-speaking peoples are very proud that Borges exists. And Latin Americans in particular, because before Borges we had very few writers to compare with European authors. We have had great writers, but a universal one, such as Borges, is a rarity in our countries. He was one of the first. I can't say that he is the *greatest,* and I only hope there may be a hundred others to surpass him, but at all events he made the breakthrough, and attracted the attention and intellectual curiosity of Europe toward our countries. That's all I can say. But to quarrel with Borges, just because everyone wants to make me quarrel with Borges—that I'll never do. If he thinks like a dinosaur, that has nothing to do with my thinking. He doesn't understand a thing about what's happening in the modern world, and he thinks I don't either. Therefore, we are in agreement.[1]

Neruda forgives Borges his latter-day conservatism in recognition of the vast prestige rendered to the Hispanic world by his stories, those cosmopolitan artifacts that, for the first time, have forced Europeans to take Latin American culture seriously and to accept that an Argentine writer can be as worthy of consideration as a French or an English one. This in itself is a major breakthrough for the status of Hispanic letters, the first decisive step in the rise to world prominence of the Latin American novel in the second half of the twentieth century.

One issue on which there is almost unanimous agreement in Latin America is the matter of Borges's style, a painstakingly wrought instrument that is shorn of the airy bombast, the overblown grandiosity, and the oratorical assertiveness traditionally endemic to Hispanic prose. Borges's distinctive medium displays precisely the reverse features: crisp understatement, rigorous compression, disciplined attention to expressive nuance, and strict avoidance of facile bluster. Though Borges frequently repeats himself from one piece to another, within the boundaries of a single story he states his business briefly, succinctly, and seldom more than once. A prose style neither inaccessible nor obscure, it nonetheless has an intellectual density that makes no concessions to the lazy reader.

Numerous Latin American authors have frankly acknowledged Borges's importance in the area of language. When asked by an interviewer about the possible influence of Borges on his own fantastic stories, Julio Cortázar, oddly enough, denied any real link in subject matter and content between himself and his elder compatriot. What Cortázar does single out in Borges is his "implacable search for an expressive rigor that will encourage true creativity, rather than stifle it under the thickets of South American rhetoric." According to Cortázar, he and Borges coincide in their "search . . . for a style," one that will correct the literary vices of Argentina, where "people write so sloppily, you think you're reading a hastily produced translation, like the ones you see piled up in Buenos Aires bookstores." [2] The task of forging an authentic Argentine literary language is, for Cortázar, nothing less than "an ethical problem, a question of decency."

Similarly, the great novelist Gabriel García Márquez, when asked about his feelings concerning Borges, replied that "Borges is one of the authors whom I most read—and whom I probably like the least. I read Borges for his extraordinary ability at verbal artifice; he's a man who teaches you how to write, teaches you to sharpen your instrument for stating things." [3] Like many an Hispanic intellectual, the author of *One Hundred Years of Solitude* openly esteems Borges's linguistic contribution, while simultaneously expressing discomfort with his "escapist literature." Nevertheless, García Márquez admits to no special difficulty in admiring Borges, whose *Complete Works* were "all I bought when in Buenos Aires. And I'll read them every day. He is a writer I cannot stand. And yet I love the violin he makes use of for expressing himself, because we need him for exploring language—a serious problem." [4] The earnestness with which García Márquez evokes the serious problem of exploring language strongly parallels Cortázar's statement cited above about the ethical problem of prose style.

Probably the best-known and most eloquent appreciation of Borges's linguistic achievement comes from the pen of Mexican novelist Carlos Fuentes:

> Borges confronts the Spanish language with all its lacks. . . . This daz-
> zling prose of his, so cold it burns one's lips, is the first ever to relate us
> [Latin Americans] . . . pulling us out of our discrete compartments and
> hurling us out into the world, a language which, in relativizing us, does
> not lessen but rather *constitutes us.* The ultimate significance of Borges's
> prose—without which, quite simply, the modern Latin American
> novel would not exist—is that it attests basically to the fact that Latin
> America is in want of language, and that therefore it must be consti-
> tuted. To do so, Borges blurs all genres, rescues all traditions, kills all
> bad habits, creates a new order, rigorous and demanding, on which
> irony, humor, and play can be built . . . and . . . constitutes a new Latin
> American language which, by sheer dint of contrast, reveals the lie,
> the submission, and the falseness of what traditionally passed for "lan-
> guage" amongst us.[5]

Fuentes hails Borges's prose not only as an artistic fact, which deserves ultimate credit for the major novels of today, but also as a revolutionary cultural entity, a "Latin American language" serving as a means of disci-pline and an active instrument of solidarity. It is a fact well worth noting that, though these three novelists (respectively an Argentine, a Colom-bian, and a Mexican) are in varying degrees left-wing sympathizers who have praised and even (in the case of García Márquez) worked for socialist governments in Cuba and Central America, they can nonetheless ignore Borges's right-wing politics and welcome his prose, which, in their view, is an indispensable, positive force for Latin America.

Borges once described to an interviewer the exacting methods he em-ployed when producing his tales. His first lengthy effort would go into molding the opening sentence of the story then in question, ceasing work on it only after it had taken on precisely the shape he desired. He then slaved over the paragraph itself, redoing it many times over until it seemed absolutely satisfactory. Only at that point would he venture on to the following paragraph. The process then repeated itself again and again up to the final line of the story.[6]

Such painstaking craftsmanship bespeaks the profound commitment of Borges to the microtexture of prose, the importance allotted by him to the fullest possible realization of written language. Borges's role as a

model artisan of prose style in Latin America is thus historically analogous to that of Flaubert (who could spend a week on a single paragraph)
in European letters. Prose, Borges revealed, deserves as much love and
labor as is customarily assigned to verse. This view of craftsmanship is
shared by many of the Latin American writers who followed in his wake
(by García Márquez, for example, who, when working on his own short
stories, reportedly produces about three lines per day).

Borges's fictions are often thought of as cold and unfeeling; what is at
work here, however, is a verbal restraint uncommon in Hispanic writing.
Actually, most Borges narratives have their well-placed shows of emotion,
little *frissons* which, at certain strategic moments, break through the
tautly forbidding surface. For example, at the end of "Death and the
Compass," Lönnrot, having just discovered the unpleasant truth and
grimly awaiting his execution, "felt faintly cold. And he felt, too, an impersonal—almost anonymous—sadness. It was already night; from the
dusty gardens came the futile cry of a bird" (L, 86; F, 157). While there
is sadness here, it is characterized (as befits Borges's distaste for subjectivity) as "impersonal," "anonymous." Moreover, the pain and defeat
surely felt by Lönnrot, rather than being feebly described by abstract
words of emotion, is given external shape via subtle and objective images
of desolation, such as the dusty gardens, the nightfall, and the solitary bird.

In similar fashion, "The Circular Ruins," at the moment when the
Dreamer realizes he too is being dreamt, ends with a favorite stylistic
device of Borges—an intense emotional state, deftly summed up in a
haunting series of three: "With relief, with humiliation, with terror, he
understood that he too was a mere appearance . . ." (L, 50; F, 66). Borges
here directly lists a number of disparate emotions, but he subjects these
to tight organization by collocating them in ascending order of potency
("terror" is a more vivid sensation than "relief"), further tempering their
effect through repetition of the word "with."

Such overt displays of feeling ruffle only occasionally the austere ele-
gance of Borges's prose; in traditional Spanish writing, by contrast, they
would be far more extensive and numerous. Borges does not eliminate
affectivity; he retains human emotion but reserves it exclusively for the
high point of the narrative, polishing it, refining it, relativizing and shaping it to the context. Just as Flaubert succeeded in correcting the formal
and sentimental crudities of Hugo and Balzac by fiercely paring down his
expressive apparatus, Borges pursues the same path in order to furnish a

concrete alternative, a countermodel to the historic burden of rhetorical excess in Spanish America.

Another contribution of Borges to Spanish American writing is his lightness of touch, his subtle and sophisticated sense of humor. Until Borges, literature in South America had, as a virtual rule, taken itself very seriously. Whether it was Rubén Darío and his sweeping reforms in poetic language, José Hernández and his eloquent defense of the Argentine gaucho, or the early social novelists (Gallegos, Rivera) and their naive attempts at depicting broad continental conflicts, with few exceptions the Latin American writer had taken on his or her task with an awesome, almost Germanic solemnity. Of the complete works of the Cuban novelist Alejo Carpentier, one of Borges's outstanding contemporaries, only his later novels, *Reasons of State* and *Concierto barroco,* treat us to more than an occasional light moment. Even the mighty poet Pablo Neruda, for all the vastness of his imagination, seemed mostly unaware of the literary potential of humor until the publication in the 1950s of his delightful *Elementary Odes.*

Most Borges fictions, on the other hand, have at least some faintly whimsical side and several of them are openly tongue-in-cheek. Borges's first major narrative piece, the sprightly put-on "Pierre Menard," bristles throughout with paradox and wit. Another story, "Funes the Memorious," conjures up via the skewed thinking of its hero various comically far-fetched languages and draws humor out of the infinity of ways of looking at an ordinary dog in mid-afternoon. In "The Aleph" the narrator sees a great cosmic vision in the musty basement of a condemned house, with absurd comments by a grandiloquently bad poet, who actually asks Borges if the Aleph came to him in color. One humorous mode that Borges has found especially fruitful is parody; two of his detective stories are essentially lampoons of the genre, and one of his lesser volumes introduces a sleuth named "Isidro Parodi." Sometimes Borges's wit is purely learned and mental; for example, the recherché language described by the Babel librarian is "a Samoyedic-Lithuanian dialect of Guaraní, with classical Arabic inflexions" (L, 54; F, 89). On other occasions he is outrageous, as in his suggestion ("Three Versions of Judas") that God may really have come down to earth not as Christ—but as Judas. One well-known Borges joke is typographical, literary, mock-religious, and scatological at the same time—the reference in "The Lottery in Babylon" to "a sacred latrine called Qaphqa" (L, 33; F, 71). Borges has even contributed to an underground tradition of humor with his "Sect of the Phoenix," a story that from beginning to end alludes, solely by hints and circumlocutions, to the sex act.

Here too Borges's innovations set the tone for subsequent Latin American writing. However much Julio Cortázar, Gabriel García Márquez, and Guillermo Cabrera Infante differ in outlook and temperament, one common ground shared by them is their creation of some of the funniest books in Spanish. Of course, their respective senses of humor vary widely, from Cortázar's imaginative mixture of the Marx Brothers and surrealism, to Cabrera Infante's verbal tomfoolery with Cuban accents and European culture, through García Márquez's blend of Dickensian caricature, rural magic, and bawdy sex. Differences aside, the comic achievements of these authors build upon Borges, whose stories establish humor as a legitimate literary strain in Spanish America. Julio Cortázar even sees the forging of comic literary traditions as an essential cultural project, one that, by showing that humor need not be the "privilege of Anglo-Saxons," helps contribute to Argentine national maturity.[7] (Deploring the general absence and low esteem of humor in South American letters, Cortázar waggishly suggests a corrective: pictures of Buster Keaton in every Latin American schoolhouse.) Matthew Arnold once proposed "high seriousness" as the touchstone for great literature. In Latin America, though, the problem has long been an excess of supposed "high seriousness" or, as Cortázar puts it, too much equating of seriousness with solemnity. Borges, who venerates literature as much as Arnold did, is the first major Hispanic American author to lay aside this august principle; actually, he stands it on its head, for he brings to South American writing a new dimension and crystallizes a new element of high playfulness.

To the writing of fiction, both within Latin America and without, Borges's best stories contribute a new praxis and sensibility, a fruitful artistic mode that breaks away from psychology and realism, which for some two hundred years had been the fundamental materials of prose narrative. Rather than restrict themselves to recognizable people and places, with meticulous attention to character traits and physical detail, the fictions of Borges aim instead to tap the artistic potential of unreality, to put fantasy to work in literature, to allot to the imagination a role beyond its traditional job of reorganizing and refining everyday life; indeed, to restore to human thought its capacity for dreaming up infinite notions and for fashioning something new.

For Borges, who is temperamentally averse to nineteenth-century narrative, one of the chief errors of the traditional novel was its misconceived attempt to reproduce reality. Realism, in Borges's view, mistakenly attempts to make the reader "forget [the novel's] quality of verbal artifice" and tries to be a ready-made mirror instead of a written object. As a result, even the greatest novelists tend to overburden their works with what Borges feels is superfluous descriptive or psychological baggage. The very titles of Borges's books, by contrast, hint subtly at a contrasting set of principles. The volume translated into English as *Dreamtigers* originally bore the name *El hacedor,* "The Maker." A rare word in Spanish (thereby drawing attention to itself), it refers to Homer, portrayed by Borges as one driven to *make* epic poems. Borges's well-known title *Ficciones*—unlike the expected conventional rubrics, *cuentos* or *relatos* ("stories")— points specifically to the fact of untruth, to the unreality of the book's content. It is no accident, moreover, that "fiction" derives from the Latin *fingere* (whence also comes "feign"), meaning "to form, to mold, to devise," all synonyms of "to make." Similarly, the second half of *Ficciones* is labeled "Artificios" ("Artifices"), a word that suggests inventiveness, artful expertise, and an artificer.

This heightening of invention and imagination in literature is Borges's concrete reply to a question frequently posed by modern novelists and critics alike: namely, what is to be done, what *can* be done, after Joyce and Proust, after Woolf and Kafka? For the past fifty years it has become a commonplace that the novel of linear plot and in-the-round characterization, with its distinctive features of logical sequence, personal choice, and a prevailing normality in the natural and social worlds, belongs to another era, a distant nineteenth century of philosophical positivism, optimistic individualism, and comparative peace. It was a time when, to a far greater degree than at present, educated readers largely believed in and accepted the reality before them. Numerous literary people have since intuited, however vaguely, that the current century, which is characterized by global conflict, vast economic combines, mass movements, and assorted social pathologies, cannot be adequately dealt with through traditional realism.

Hence many serious writers, faced by a disquieting landscape and radically altered human circumstances, sense the need for new literary modes and forms, new ways of conveying experience. Samuel Beckett, to cite but one major instance, filters the objective world through the reduced myopic consciousness of an old and decrepit loner, whose contacts are pared down to his immediate world of scattered personal effects (a bicycle, a knapsack, a pocketful of stones), a run-down garret, and (when venturing out of doors) a great deal of mud. By so narrowing the scope of reality and by portraying the individual subject as floundering bleary-eyed in his environment, Beckett effectively crystallizes the solipsism, the opaque and fragmentary nature of late twentieth-century human existence. Vladimir Nabokov, on the other hand, though ordinarily linked with Beckett and Borges, clearly believes in the reality of his choice—his childhood idyll under the czars, the experience of Russian emigrés, and the folkways of American academe. Most of Nabokov's writing actually retains the essential nineteenth-century framework, with its remaining spaces taken up by hidden patterns, parodic games, and sheer verbal virtuosity.

In contrast to Beckett and Nabokov, who purposely select a few segments of reality and deal with them as such, Borges breaks further away from traditional fiction, for the realities he depicts (usually quite meticulously) are invariably tinged and at times permeated by some brand of unreality. Though in some stories its presence may be slight, unreality is nonetheless at the core of Borges's aesthetic ("one of art's prerequisites," he remarks in "The Secret Miracle"). "Borgesian" narrative and its theory deftly combine the physical and the mimetic with the inventive and imaginary; it intermingles the mundane with the miraculous and hallucinatory.

A few basic distinctions should first be made, however, between Borges's brand of fantasy and other seemingly analogous phenomena of the twentieth century such as science fiction, surrealism, or Tolkien-style escapism. Science fiction, for all its imaginative adventures and cosmic range, still operates mostly within the traditional framework of plot and character; moreover, its acceptance of, and fascination with, technology is fundamentally alien to the Borges of mental and metaphysical artifice. Nor is "Borgesian" fantasy akin to that of the surrealists, whose violent intensity and Freudian inquiry into the nature of dreams Borges openly dislikes; in fact, he once lumped them with Nazis. (Though Borges is interested in dreams for his own purposes, he has no desire to sound the dark recesses of the unconscious—perhaps out of his own psychological fears.) Least of all are his stories a soothing means of escape into pure fantasy for its own sake à la Tolkien. Borges's unrealities are, in the last analysis, disquietingly suggestive of this world; his characters may at times inhabit remote realms (Babylon, ancient Rome) or haunt imaginary ones (the Babel Library, the vaguely Eastern circular ruins), but the fictive situation still refers, however obliquely, to our own. Borges has stated on more than one occasion that his fantastic tales are essentially parables, veiled comments on real human problems. Thus, even when Borges depicts an unreality, he is alluding to reality indirectly by other means.

Conversely, when Borges's fictions have recognizable, real settings, unreality somehow intrudes, disrupting nature's laws or at least questioning them. To build on our earlier contrast: Beckett's Unnamable lives trapped in a jar, where he tries endlessly to make sense of the outside world, whose fleeting shadows he perceives. On the other hand, Borges's Tzinacán, held in prison by Spanish conquistadores in "The God's Script," attempts and gains no objectively scientific knowledge of the outside world; instead, by contemplating the spots on the tiger (jaguar) that occupies the adjoining cell, he achieves mystical understanding and magical powers (though of course the experience may be taking place solely in Tzinacán's head). Similarly, in "The Secret Miracle," a story set in Nazi-occupied Prague (with dates and city landmarks all accurately rendered), Hladík attempts not to cope with the German onslaught but pleads for, and seemingly obtains, divine intervention. The contrast between our two authors may yet be further generalized by noting that Beckett's personages, their desperate plight notwithstanding, seek their consolations in the real world (they form relationships, take trips, wait for help, rebel) whereas Borges's characters are inextricably caught up in the library, the lottery, the madness of Tlön, or whatever vast network of unreality happens to encompass their lives.

Of course, the unreality in Borges's three-dozen major stories varies widely in degree. The abstracted, dreamlike quality of "The Circular Ruins" is nearly absolute; on the other hand, the antiworlds of "The Library of Babel" and "The Lottery in Babylon," though similarly self-contained and imaginary, have the luminosity of parables or poetical meditations on specific human concerns. Some stories ("The God's Script," "The Zahir") depict intensely powerful visions or vivid subjective experiences that in all probability are not "really happening" other than mentally. "Funes the Memorious," a story about an ordinary peasant with the gift of total memory, is quite the opposite; it is an account of a rare phenomenon, a miracle even, but one that in our earthly reality does arise now and then. Many Borges stories actually have basic realistic formats and features that are modified by an accompanying conceit or a mental fancy through which events are refracted. This technique occurs in "The Waiting," where a hoodlum who is soon to be shot inexplicably adopts his executioner's name, and in "The Dead Man," where throughout the narrative the protagonist is actually not dead at all, except in the fanciful, extended sense of being doomed to die, as indeed we all are. At the farthest end of the unreality spectrum are stories like "The End" and "The Life of Tadeo Isidoro Cruz," unreal only insofar as they are fictions based on *Martín Fierro,* a preexistent fiction.

T he literature of unreality, needless to say, hardly originates with Borges. But it had, for the 150 years that precede *Ficciones,* been relegated by the hegemonic, realist aesthetic to the status of a minor art. The fiction writers we normally associate with the nineteenth century are all realists of some shade or other: Balzac, Flaubert, Dickens, George Eliot, Henry James, and Tolstoy. Some of these realist authors did dabble in fantasy, but their efforts in this mode, though sometimes impressive, are still in the minority. Balzac wrote *La peau de chagrin,* but it is certainly a lesser book when compared to *Lost Illusions* or *Cousin Bette.* Flaubert created "St. Julian the Hospitator" and *Bouvard and Pécuchet,* but there is no doubt that *Madame Bovary* and *Sentimental Education* are his greatest works. James wrote some very famous fantastical stories and was also at work on a fantastical novel, *The Sense of the Past,* when he died. On the whole, however, James scholars tend to regard these works as atypical.

Those Western authors who did habitually practice fantastic narrative occupy a peculiar position in the established literary canon. Poe, for instance, is regarded by English-language critics as a minor writer, at best a premature talent and at worst a crank. G. K. Chesterton is looked upon as an eccentric author of amusing spy stories and anachronistic Catholic beliefs. The fantastical narrations of H. G. Wells and Robert Louis Stevenson are still widely read by adolescents and avid connoisseurs of science fiction, but none of these works enjoys the highest esteem among those empowered to make critical opinion. We saw in our previous chapter how even such an up-to-date literary man as William Gass considers these authors to be "cranky, wayward, even decadent . . . marginal figures."

The marginal status of fantastic narrative in the nineteenth century is well illustrated in a theoretical statement by that classically realist Edwardian novelist, E. M. Forster. In his set of lectures entitled *Aspects of the Novel,* Forster actually gives an entire chapter over to the subject of "Fantasy"—and his attitude is uncomfortable and essentially negative. At one point he considers the case for fantasy: "why should any question arise about an angel, except whether it is suitable? Once in the realm of fiction, what difference is there between an apparition and a mortgage?"[8] Yet immediately thereafter, Forster personally rejects the idea: "I see the soundness of this argument, but my heart refuses to assent." In that same chapter, moreover, Forster compares fantasy to a sideshow not once but twice; for example, he makes the remark that fantastic narratives are "sideshows inside the main show."[9]

On the other hand, Latin America in the past one hundred years has seen some worthy practitioners of fantastic literature—for example, Ricardo Palma, Rubén Darío, Leopoldo Lugones, and Horacio Quiroga; indeed, these writers brought out (before the advent of Borges and the "boom") some of the better, more interesting, and certainly more original prose fiction in Spanish. Conversely, the realistic novel in South America presents a sad and indifferent history; it is, with a few notable exceptions, an arid panorama of lifeless imitation and uncritical adherence to Transatlantic models, in part because nineteenth-century Hispanic Americans were slavishly Europhile in their tastes, and in part because, unlike their French or English counterparts, Latin American realists lacked legitimate native, bourgeois realities within which they could work.

The apparent irrationalism of most South American history, by contrast, seems to accord more fruitfully and fit more adequately within the explicitly nonrational literature of fantasy. Before Borges, the fantastic was a vaguely defined and uncertain tradition. After him it becomes a mode that takes on clear shape and direction on a global scale. For one of Borges's lasting achievements is to have invested literary fantasy with unprecedented respectability. His precursor Poe was definitely a kindred spirit and even an originator, but he was a virtual loner with no local base or following; moreover, he was a writer whose foreign standing is a trifle disproportionate to the intrinsic merits of his work. In contrast, Borges is an author of undisputed genius, one whose world stature inevitably legitimizes and draws attention to his kind of writing.

In various essays, Borges himself singles out some of the material aspects distinguishing fantastical from traditional fiction—aspects that, of course, give the former its edge of superiority over the latter. As correctives to narrative psychologism, with its alleged structural and epistemological flabbiness, Borges at different points suggests two possibilities: the adventure story and the use of magical causality.

In his foreword to *The Invention of Morel,* a short novel by his friend and collaborator Adolfo Bioy Casares, Borges asserts his own preference for narratives of adventure over the "slow-paced" novel of character. As

Borges accurately notes, the tale of adventure, in order to avoid succumbing to episodic looseness, is obliged to set forth a series of incidents with
rigor and precision, and no more; it pursues its inexorable narrative path
minus any psychological nonsense (the latter the chief cause, for Borges,
of novelistic amorphousness). Subtleties of motivation, which are quite
out of place in a fast-moving thriller, are perforce eliminated; in their
stead we find pure physical action, unencumbered by any Dostoevskian
ponderings as to the dark reasons behind the act.

These same principles are visibly at work in Borges's own adventure
stories. His tentative first fiction "Streetcorner Man," as well as his gangster yarns in *El Aleph,* all deal with power struggles, brawls, and murders
that take place without much explanation. One particularly revealing
headline in the early *History of Infamy* volume—"MUERTES PORQUE
SÍ" (literally, "DEATHS JUST BECAUSE")—hints at the conception
of narrative to be developed in Borges's later small thrillers.[10] Hence, the
louts in "The South" taunt and challenge Dahlmann not from any notable feelings of hostility but because that happens to be their function in
the piece. Otálora in "The Dead Man" rises to power not out of personal
choice but because of the machinations of blind fate. Finally, in "The
Waiting," the hero simply awaits his killer without even considering fighting back or fleeing, and with no reason given by the narrator for such
inaction.

As yet another substitute for the novelistic machinery of motivational
analysis, Borges reconsiders the question of magic. In 1932 (years before
he had even attempted writing stories) Borges brought out an essay entitled "El arte narrativo y la magia" ("Narrative Art and the Magical"), a
kind of defense of, and tentative manifesto for, nonrealism in fiction.
There Borges acknowledges, just as Forster argues in his chapter on
"Plot" in *Aspects of the Novel,* that "the central problem of the novel is
causality" (D, 88), i.e., that there must be reasons, explicit or implied, for
the events. But, Borges observes, the "lethargic" novel of character presents "a succession of motives that purport not to differ from those of the
real world"—in Borges's view an ultimately unworkable assumption.
The realist novel, by definition, represents the presumed working of natural laws. And yet, Borges remarks, nature has "infinite and uncontrollable
operations" (D, 91), forces that are far too numerous to pin down in a
fiction and are therefore beyond formal control. The novel, to Borges, is
thus caught up in a contradiction between its suggested philosophy and
its intrinsic capabilities, its narrative aims and material means.

In contradistinction to this naturalistic and psychological mimeticism, Borges argues for the restoration of magic in fiction; to him magic is the "crowning height" of causality, not its contradiction. For, unlike the thinkers and practitioners of the Western rationalist tradition, Borges sees in magic not chaos or mystification but a fruitful artistic mode, a means of clarity and rigor. It has the evocative advantages of the atavistic, but it is also formally lucid and intellectually diverse; "it is governed by all natural laws, and by imaginary ones as well" (D, 89). Interestingly enough, these ideas of Borges, albeit somewhat diffuse in their original exposition, anticipate by thirty-five years the theories of Tzvetan Todorov, the Franco-Bulgarian structuralist who in 1967 devised the term "imaginary causality," a category denoting those events which, though seemingly attributable to blind chance, are actually impelled by a vaster, more generalized, more mysterious order of things.[11]

Magic is the very basis of all the action in several Borges stories. In "The Immortal," what induces the protagonist and his companions to passively indulge their contemplative natures is the simple, magical fact that they will never die. Similarly, the mysterious changes in the accepted facts about Pedro Damián's biography in "The Other Death" originate with his last-minute hallucinations, which, by becoming the dominant reality, alter the way in which others see him. Likewise, in "The Zahir," an ordinary Argentine coin, now endowed with mystic, magical powers, drives the narrator-protagonist insane.

In an unpublished lecture, delivered in Montevideo in 1949, Borges furnished a yet more thorough insight into his artistic procedures. (By the time of this lecture, of course, Borges had fully mastered his new fictional mode.) There Borges suggested that unreality in literature can be evoked by any of the following: (1) the work of art within another work of art, (2) the contamination of reality by dreams, (3) the journey through time, and (4) the Double.[12] The list is a trifle unprecise; one might add "and by the imagination" to category 2. When applied to specific narratives, moreover, the classifications may appear both too overlapping and too cramped. "The Secret Miracle," for instance, fits somewhat into each of the first three divisions. Nevertheless, this little catalogue reveals much about Borges's way of writing fiction. The Double, which can be construed as any blurring or any seeming multiplication of character identity, is found in, among others, "Ibn-Hakkan al-Bokhari," "The Waiting," "The Shape of the Sword," "Three Versions of Judas," "Theme of the Traitor and the Hero," and "Story of the Warrior and the Captive." Device number 3, the journey through time, is well exemplified in "The Immortal," while "The Circular Ruins" and "The Other Death" depict an external world modified by one man's dreamings.

Borges is especially renowned for his use of the first device, the work of art within another work of art. Some of his most celebrated tales ("Pierre Menard," "Tlön, Uqbar") deal with nonexistent books and authors. Borges even has a special essay, "Partial Magic in the *Quixote*," that deals with a kind of derivative phenomenon: those works in which a literary character finds himself depicted in a book or a play (the well-known experience of Claudius in *Hamlet* and of Don Quixote in part 2 of that novel). Borges conceives of this little artifice (commonly described as the "hall-of-mirrors" effect) as a means of unreality. This is something of a maverick viewpoint, however, inasmuch as the device is generally perceived as *heightening* the credibility and reality of the fictional characters involved. Borges's striking defense of his little conceit is that the magical aura of a fiction-within-a-fiction derives from the possibility that we, the readers of the outer fiction, may in turn be fictional characters—being read about, at the very same time, by someone else! (This, mutatis mutandi, is what the hero of "The Circular Ruins" finds out.)

More an imaginative leap of faith than a logical conclusion, Borges's argument recalls the sophistry noted by Chesterton in "The Blast of the Book" and developed by Borges himself in "Ibn-Hakkan"; the sophistry hinges on the fact that things occurring in a related series have a psychologically compelling quality, even though their logical or empirical bases may be questionable or indeed untrue. At the same time, Borges's fanciful notion links logically with his own characteristic speculations (derived from mystical readings) about the world being one (one book, one person, one divinity, etc.). After all, the long-run implication of Borges's supposition is that, in the end, we are all characters in a gigantic book of creation, being read about by an ultimate reader—a perfectly conceivable "Borgesian" plot for a fantastic fiction.

Whatever the merits of Borges's logic, he singles out a most useful and highly suggestive illusionistic device, one to be employed with great success by other Latin American authors. In "Continuity of Parks," for example, a short story by Borges's fellow Argentine Julio Cortázar, a man casually finds a book, a thriller that happens to deal with a situation much like his own; he goes home, relaxes in an armchair, and proceeds to read about his own impending murder in an armchair, which is about to occur as the story ends. In *Hopscotch,* by the same author, the novelist "Morelli" has built up reams of notes for a book resembling *Hopscotch;* he delineates possible deviant behavior for his characters, a pattern borne out by the protagonist of Cortázar's novel. Certainly one of the most stirring moments in all literature is the dizzying finale of García Márquez's *One Hundred Years of Solitude,* where Aureliano Babilonia, having just seized the hidden meaning (as the readers have) of Melquíades's prophetic history of Macondo, finally reaches the end of the manuscript, where he reads about Aureliano Babilonia reading Melquíades's history of Macondo (while we readers in turn read about Aureliano reading about Aureliano, etc.); then comes the famous windstorm, and death.

The spirit of unreality, well exemplified in Borges's theories and his art, is one that a mischievous Borges even brings to the world of real books. To take the best-known instance (there are hundreds of others), one of his favorite literary moments is episode 602 of the *Arabian Nights,* in which Scheherazade reportedly begins telling her very own story of the precarious relationship she has so far been sustaining with the Sultan. This intriguing occurrence is, alas, a fabrication of Borges's, who seems to have invented the whole thing, most probably in order to have at his disposal yet another authority from the past—and thereby literally creating a precursor for himself. It is often remarked that Borges's work has become the raw material for a literary industry, as happened earlier with Eliot and Joyce, whose erudite asides kept many an academic critic busily hunting down and explicating their more obscure sources. The duties of the scholar-detective, however, have been still further expanded, for Borges has furnished them the additional task of establishing which of his (Borges's) allusions are authentic and which ones fake.

I n addition to resurrecting the unreal as viable literary content, Borges has simultaneously fashioned, as a vehicle for his imaginings, a distinctly new literary form. Borges's *ficciones* have little in common with the short stories of Chekhov or Hemingway or Joyce. The portrayal of character, traditionally thought of as the essential business of prose narrative, is of minor importance in Borges. Readers remember Pierre Menard, Emma Zunz, or "Villari" because of the complex of logical relations in which they operate or because of their abstract situations, not because physically or psychologically they "are" a certain way. In many Borges stories (for example, "The Library of Babel," "The Lottery in Babylon"), the characters remain nameless and unidentified throughout, and one, "The Sect of the Phoenix," really contains no characters at all.

With the exception of his adventure yarns, plot is correspondingly meager in Borges. Some of the stories for which he is best known (again, "The Library of Babel," "The Lottery in Babylon") are virtually without action. What Borges's narratives present is either a fantastic situation (one characterized by mystical, magical, or otherwise imaginary elements) or a seemingly realistic situation that is mystified, made strange, or rendered unreal by magical forces, by means of one of the four devices discussed above. As Ronald Christ has remarked, the quintessence, the point of departure in a Borges story is not plot or character but an intriguing idea, even a clever sophistry.[13] A *ficción* starts from some eccentric notion, curious premise, or unlikely situation such as immortality, absolute memory, a completely idealist world, or a library with all possible letter combinations in all possible books. Borges then proceeds to spin the consequences logically generated by this subjective fancy. His method is the *als ob* ("as if") philosophy of the inhabitants of planet Tlön, applied in his case to literature.

Since Borges's stories deal more with general circumstances and logical arguments than with the movement of human-caused events or psychological individuality, it only follows that his fiction should have much in common with the essay form. In fact, Borges frankly admitted in an interview that he had consciously aimed at a fusion of essayistic and fictional modes.[14] Accordingly, the "Postscript" to "Tlön, Uqbar," refers to the latter item as an "article," and the piece does in fact look outwardly like a journalistic examination of a notorious literary curiosity. In similar vein, "The Approach to Al'Mu-tasim" is a spurious book review, and "Pierre Menard" and "Herbert Quain" are learned appreciations of nonexistent authors. "Funes the Memorious" could be a magazine profile (in *The New Yorker,* say) of a colorful rustic figure of unusual interest, while "The Sect of the Phoenix" has the flavor of a traveler's account of a distant civilization. The "Story of the Warrior and the Captive" does not even contain any material that is (by Borges's own admission) at all fictive; both the Lombard warrior and the British-Indian woman are actual personages out of history. In reality, the "story" of the warrior and captive is not a story at all but a personal inquiry into a thought-provoking phenomenon—the inexplicable shift in an individual's cultural or national allegiances; as such, it is formally indistinguishable from Borges's real essays in *Other Inquisitions.*

The actual essays of Borges are of special note. Despite his bookish nature, Borges's nonfictional prose is curiously offhand and informal. Very few of the essays in his collections go beyond four or five pages; they are mostly occasional pieces conceived as enjoyable and readable copy for little magazines, not for learned journals. Almost conversational in flavor, they are, as Ronald Christ observes, highly "personal expressions of insight, interest, and enthusiasm"[15] through which Borges casually shares his private notions with the magazine's readers (many of whom happened to be his close friends). His articles somewhat recall Montaigne; when reading essays either by the Frenchman or the Argentine, we directly experience a man's own thoughts on a chosen topic as, in an easy-going manner, they range freely over the subject, giving the impression of a civilized man of letters ruminating out loud before us. Their respective generic labels also suggest spiritual points of contact: Montaigne's literary neologism *essais* ("attempts") implies a tentative endeavor, giving an idea a "try." Borges's titles (*Discusión, Inquisitions*) suggest a comparable attitude of informal debate and inquiry.

A word is in order regarding what is best known in Borges's work—his "themes," the subjects and notions that permeate his writing. Some of the more outstanding of these are: the hallucinatory character of human existence; the illusory nature of the physical world; the inevitable arbitrariness of all rational thought; infinity, and infinite possibilities; the idea that the most minuscule event implies and contains the entire universe; the idea that everything we can imagine has either happened already or will happen eventually; the conceit that every man is also another man and even all men; a character who realizes he is better off as someone else; a character who believes he is winning when he is really losing; time as but another illusion; "circular time" and especially "eternal recurrence"—the idea that the number of personal experiences, though vast, is finite and that, consequently, events can occur again in the future; remote settings (Babylon, Prague, Araby); an attitude of amazement (Borges cannot understand authors like Fitzgerald or Sinclair Lewis who do not "marvel at the universe"); hatred of mirrors because they multiply reality; and the sudden moment of mystical insight and total understanding. Most significant, of course, is the famous and omnipresent labyrinth, Borges's most characteristic motif, just as sweetly whimsical machines and moons are immediately identifiable as Paul Klee's fancies, bowler hats and floating apples as those of Magritte. The labyrinth sums up Borges's delight with multitudinous possibilities and symbolizes the idea of a bewildering universe, the complexities fashioned by men.

Part II
BORGES'S FICTIONS

4   The Apprentice Fiction Maker

Borges's first attempts at fiction appeared in the oddly titled *Historia universal de la infamia* (1935; English translation, *A Universal History of Infamy,* published in 1972). It was a kind of entry through the back door, since this literary curiosity was initially conceived and produced not as a book but as journalism. The bulk of its contents first saw light in a weekly entertainment supplement, edited in part by Borges and included weekends in *Crítica,* a mass-circulation daily. *Crítica* was actually little more than a sensationalistic scandal sheet, but its owner had cultural pretensions and therefore gave his literarily inclined employees a certain amount of leeway. At the time a stranger to prose narrative, Borges had amused himself—as he later would describe the process—writing what he then thought of as ephemera, and he was later surprised when his publisher suggested gathering the pieces into a single volume.

In a preface added by the author to the 1954 edition, Borges characterizes the book's sonorous title as "excessive." Some years later, though, on a French radio interview, he admitted having wished to shock his readers by using "a bombastic word."[1] The title is actually parodical; countless Spanish-language history books (school texts especially) bear the name *Historia universal* (their equivalent to the English formula "World History"). Borges's reading public would thus immediately have responded to this familiar set phrase, which is then curiously and ironically juxtaposed with the rather theatrically, almost operatically charged *infamia.*

Borges's subject matter is of course neither infamy nor its universal history. The book is mainly a loose collection of thumbnail sketches— fast-moving biographies of hustlers, gangsters, poseurs, thieves, charlatans, street toughs, and otherwise colorful rogues. Among these figures are Lazarus Morell, who made a fortune freeing slaves and then reselling them elsewhere to other slaveholders in the American South; Arthur Orton-Tom Castro, who for years posed successfully as the long-lost son of a gullible English lady; a Chinese piratess, who engages in cunning relations with the imperial court; Billy the Kid, who at age twenty-one had bumped off as many persons—"not including Mexicans" (UHI, 61; HUI, 65)—and who died cursing in Spanish; and Monk Eastman, who is a New York gangland boss with a bloody history.

These figures are all taken from a few real books (listed in back of the *Universal History*) in which their true lives are told. Borges pilfered from these sources the basic materials for his vignettes. The titles include a history of piracy by Philip Gosse (London, 1932), a thick volume by Herbert Asbury dealing with the New York City gangs (New York, 1927), a 1915 history of Persia by one Sir Percy Sykes, Mark Twain's *Life on the Mississippi*, and the celebrated eleventh edition of the *Encyclopaedia Britannica*.

Borges's rogues roughly correspond, in essential background and biography, to their real-life originals. He often adds to or modifies reported facts, however, either for increased vividness or seeming exactitude. For example, Mark Twain's John Murrel is rechristened "Lazarus" by Borges, obviously for the mock-Biblical overtones that befit a professional redeemer. Tom Castro's birth date does not appear in the *Britannica* article on which the story is based, so Borges added a seemingly factual tidbit for the purposes of narrative precision.[2] Certain evocative set pieces, such as the Chinese emperor's antipiracy decree, the hundred gunmen in the Monk Eastman sketch, and Morell's method of disposing of his "liberated" slaves, are entirely invented by Borges.[3]

At times Borges builds on and remakes the given data with a view to tightening and strengthening the main lines of his narrative. His account of Billy the Kid fuses the well-known cowboy's adult life with the childhood of another Billy, a New York tough discussed by Asbury.[4] In the Castro story, Borges takes on Bogle (briefly mentioned in the *Britannica* as a Negro manservant who gave the real Orton a bit of coaching) and transforms him from the vague supernumerary which he originally was into Orton's co-protagonist and mastermind.[5]

Borges's two prefaces (respectively dated 1935 and 1954) to the *Universal History* point to the basic characteristic of these stories and of later ones as well. The 1934 preface indicates that these vignettes "stem . . . from my rereading of Stevenson and Chesterton" (UHI, 15; HUI, 7). Borges thereby claims for his book a dual tradition—in Stevenson's case, the narrative of events rather than of character; in Chesterton's, the mixture of the crime thriller with metaphysics and magic. Further along in the preface, Borges makes it clear that the stories "are not, they do not try to be, psychological" (UHI, 15; HUI, 7). At the very outset of his career as a fiction writer, then, Borges has adopted an alternative aesthetic, a set of assumptions and procedures contrary to those hitherto predominant in prose narrative. It goes without saying that Borges's description of these stories is an accurate one. We find out nothing about his rogues' inner lives, their finer points of personality, their hopes or fears or other such feelings. Motivation is absent or at best is implied in the kinds of action; the psychological forces presumably driving the characters (money, hunger, power, lust, simple vengefulness, or sheer sadism) are left unmentioned.

In that same preface, Borges apologizes for his bothersome peccadilloes, to wit: "random enumerations, sudden shifts of continuity, and the paring down of a man's life to two or three scenes" (UHI, 15; HUI, 7). Authorial modesty notwithstanding, these same devices would be fruitfully employed in later stories. The "random enumeration" of a myriad things in "The Aleph," for instance, is surely one of Borges's most dazzling pages. Within the *Infamy* volume, moreover, some of the enumerations are in themselves fascinating—the teeming catalog of sordid criminals at the beginning of the Monk Eastman piece, or the infinity of phenomena listed as emanating from Father Las Casas's overtures to the African slave trade (one of Borges's more famous passages, as a matter of fact):

> To this odd philanthropic twist we owe . . . endless things—W. C.
> Handy's blues; the Parisian success of the Uruguayan lawyer and
> painter of the Negro genre, don Figaro; . . . the mythological dimen-
> sions of Abraham Lincoln; the five hundred thousand dead of the Civil
> War; . . . King Vidor's film *Hallelujah*; . . . the Negro killed by Martín
> Fierro; the deplorable Cuban rumba "The Peanut Vendor"; . . . the
> *habanera*, mother of the tango; another old Negro dance, of Buenos
> Aires and Montevideo, the *landombe*.
> And further, the great and blameworthy life of the nefarious
> redeemer Lazarus Morell. (UHI, 19–20, HUI, 17–18)

The reader will instantly recognize a number of "Borgesian" preoccupations in this passage. A single fact—Las Casas's slavery proposal—implies and generates a host of others; or, to reverse the argument, had black slavery never been instituted in the Americas, none of the above would have come into existence, Lazarus Morell included. In addition, Borges's recurrent obsession about forces larger than the individual (developed in stories as diverse as "The Circular Ruins," "The Library of Babel," or "The Dead Man") is present here. Lazarus Morell functions in a world vaster than himself and owes his very existence to an enormous system brought into being three hundred years ago by another person. In the same way, Monk Eastman, first mentioned in his own story at the tail end of a long list of New York hoodlums, is thereby introduced as one criminal among countless others.

The other features for which Borges excuses himself in his preface (the "sudden shifts in continuity, and the paring down of a man's life to two or three scenes") also anticipate certain key characteristics of his major fiction. The distinctive mark of the *Infamy* pieces undoubtedly is their jagged, disjointed quality (deriving from the influence of gangster films), a brusqueness that is further enhanced by the "headlines" bobbing up every few paragraphs (a device attributable to the yellow-journalism origins of the stories). Borges later retained something of this kind of narrative pacing, though without the youthful, overstated breeziness of these sketches. The so-called life of Tadeo Isidoro Cruz (in *El Aleph*), for example, despite the much smoother presentation of the background facts, is deceptively free of rough transitions or abrupt shifts. Borges moves rapidly from one scene to another in the hero's past and summarizes Cruz's married years in a single sentence. As in these early tales, many of Borges's mature fictions end curtly with a terse report of the hero's death. The statement, "Ireneo Funes died in 1889, of pulmonary congestion" (L, 66; F, 127), is related thematically to the biography of Funes in a way that many of the analogous episodes in the *Infamy* pieces are not; but as information it is just a shade more elaborate than the final datum given about Tom Castro, "On April 2, 1898, he died." Borges's apology for having reduced men's lives to two or three scenes, moreover, appears somewhat ironic in retrospect. His superb portrait of Funes the Memorious is provided via no more than the three visits paid by an anonymous, mature narrator to the youthful protagonist.[6] Other comparable pieces deal with Pedro Damián ("The Other Death"), Droctulft ("Story of the Warrior and the Captive"), and "Villari" ("The Waiting") in terms of only one particular phase within their respective lives. In a well-known passage of the Cruz story, Borges goes so far as to assert doctrinally that a man's whole life can be narrowed down to *"a single moment"* (emphasis is Borges's), that moment when "someone finds out who he is" (TA, 56; EA, 55).

Borges repudiated the *Universal History* later in life—"utter rubbish" he once called it[7]; his 1954 preface dismisses its contents as "the irresponsible game of a shy young man who dared not write stories and so amused himself by falsifying and distorting . . . the tales of others" (UHI, 12; HUI, 10). Yet this procedure, so resoundingly condemned by the fifty-five-year-old author, is actually a cruder, less developed manifestation of Borges's profoundly bookish approach to art. That much of Borges's best work builds on other writings is common knowledge among the author's fans. In his mature stories, of course, Borges would never plunder materials from other books outright, let alone trot out a bibliography of books raided. But the essential method is still there: two Borges stories ("The End" and "Biography of Tadeo Isidoro Cruz") have the *Martín Fierro* narrative poem as their point of departure; "The House of Asterion" retells the Theseus legend from a new perspective; "The Immortal" builds on the legend of the Wandering Jew and identifies, at the end, the narrator's numerous allusions to books; and some of Borges's most celebrated pieces humorously distort an entire literary genre, the detective story.

One of Borges's most enduring personal doctrines, moreover, is the idea that no work of literature is truly original, that every book derives in some measure from books in the past. By extension, Borges often says as much about the actions of men, who in his stories tend to repeat, unbeknownst to them, another person's deeds—as in "The Plot" (in *Dreamtigers*), a parable in which some violent rural gauchos unknowingly reenact the murder of Julius Caesar. Finally, it is worth noting that, even at the height of his writing powers, Borges was scarcely innocent of falsifying other people's stories, the best-known instance of this being his spurious episode 602 of Scheherazade.

T he types of characters in the *Universal History,* their actions, and their manner of portrayal all look forward to the hoodlums and toughs that populate *Ficciones* and *El Aleph.* A major trait of the early rogues is their systematic use of fraud and deceit, their appearing to be what they are not, their posing as opposites and becoming their own doubles. Borges in later stories will have cowards feigning courage, traitors cited for heroism, victims posing as victimizers, and also vice versa. In this book, Lazarus Morell claims to liberate but actually recaptures slaves; Hakim of Merv hides his leprous face behind a mask and plays successfully at being God. Arthur Orton's pose is double, his identity triple: he first changes his name to Tom Castro and later casts himself as Roger Tichborne, even though Tichborne was delicately dark and trim and Orton boorish, freckled, and fat. One gangster, née Osterman, is first alluded to as "Edward Delaney, alias William Delaney, alias Joseph Marvin, alias Joseph Morris, alias Monk Eastman" (UHI, 51; HUI, 55)— a man of multiple selves, like the Immortal.

In addition to this play of personalities, the *Universal History* is studded with casual statements about the essential elusiveness of identity. Lazarus Morell's physical appearance is reportedly an utter mystery; Borges makes the fanciful point that all existent daguerreotypes of the ersatz liberator (as befits a professional poseur) are false. Orton's facial traits, in turn, "could hardly be made out," a bit of Borgesian exaggeration since there are in fact photographs of the real Orton.[8] Billy the Kid, his frontier fame notwithstanding, is here described as "the most anonymous figure" in the West. When Hakim of Merv is forced to remove his godlike mask, the features he reveals are so horrifying that, paradoxically, his real face is likened by Borges to a mask. Gangster Monk Eastman's aliases are as "distressing as a masquerade, in which one is not quite certain who is who"; Borges even puts Eastman's own name further in doubt by speculating "whether there is such a thing as a real name" (UHI, 53; HUI, 56).

Still more vivid harbingers of the mature Borges are the occasional conceits, the odd way in which events are at times refracted. When Monk Eastman is sentenced in court, Borges writes that the judge "*prophesied* for him, with complete accuracy, ten years of prison" (UHI, 59; HUI, 62; emphasis added)—a clever twist on the very idea of prophecy. A comparable play of fancy is the description of Billy the Kid watching melodramas, unaware that "they were signs and symbols of his destiny" (UHI, 62; HUI, 66); this story anticipates "The Waiting," in which the hoodlum protagonist watches gangster movies, never aware that they depict his own way of life. Borges similarly invests ordinary mechanical weapons with a wondrous quality: when Billy fires his gun, the "invisible bullets, . . . like *magic,* killed at a distance" (UHI, 61; HUI, 65; emphasis added).

Perhaps the most striking of these early conceits of Borges is the account of the death of Bogle as he strolls about London, in search of a new scheme: "We will never know whether he found it. Shortly before reaching Primrose Hill, there loomed out of the dark the dreaded vehicle that had been in pursuit of him through the years. Bogle saw it coming, he cried out, but salvation eluded him. Dashed violently against the stone pavement, his skull was split by dizzying hoofs" (UHI, 38; HUI, 39). It is a recognizable "Borgesian" turn of mind to see an apparent accident as ultimately predestined, as the end result of a long process of pursuit.

Nonetheless, although the *History of Infamy* displays most of the distinctive features of "Borgesian" narrative, these components are still present in their most rudimentary form; most crucially, the basic elements are not fully proportioned and fail to cohere. On the whole, there is something unsatisfying about the book's contents. Some Borges scholars have given the volume lavish (and unjustifiable) praise, but even the author himself—as pointed out—would just as soon have banished the book from existence. The aesthetic value of the *Universal History* lies somewhere between Borges's harsh estimation and the overstated claims of his exegetes. The narratives do exhibit obvious and familiar strengths: they are fanciful, provocative, clever, brilliant in their prose style (notably the catalogues), and filled with an almost untypical physical exuberance. At the same time, they suffer from formal awkwardness, a brittle and inorganic quality, and they lack (precisely because of their brusque, flashy episodism) a page-by-page smoothness. Underlying the often gratuitous fragmentary form is a yet more serious lack—the absence, in nearly every story, of a central governing image or idea; despite the occasional fancies and conceits, none manages to dominate the action in a unifying way, as is typically the case in Borges's later hoodlum pieces such as "The Waiting," "The Dead Man," and "The Life of Tadeo Isidoro Cruz."

Most ironic of all, the *Infamy* stories abound in precisely what Borges finds wrong with traditional narrative; that is, they contain an excess of geographical, historical, biographical, and physical reportage. For example, the Mississippi River's past and present are lengthily summarized and certain rogues are described in close detail. These early fictions, moreover, are surprisingly visual, and in ways that are seldom convincing. Borges's preface, of course, acknowledges influences from the cinema; within the stories there are overt allusions to film, and the Wild West landscapes and saloons seem in conscious emulation of Hollywood, though with no sense of irony or distance. The overall impression is of a young Borges straining for visual shock effect and of a man quite out of his element. Even when his eyesight was still fairly good, Borges's was not a visual imagination—unlike Neruda or Nabokov, whose verbally crafted optics invariably ring true. By contrast, in the Argentine author's best stories, adventure yarns included, the visual element is completely subordinate to mental patterns. Indeed, the very strength of Borges's mature fiction is its avoidance of strictly visual matters, whereas in these early tales the mental element is only embryonically and fragmentarily present.

Finally, despite the parody in the title and the nearly cartoonlike, rapid-fire depiction of events, these sketches lack the fine humor and urbane wit that are so much a part of Borges's best products. The *History of Infamy* is simply not very funny, nor does it have the blood-and-guts appeal of a good old-fashioned, swashbuckling thriller. Its stories are the skewed first attempts of an emerging talent, an apprentice still finding his way in a new field; they show a rare spark of originality and a high sensitivity to prose but no coherent vision or practice. It is certainly no accident that, whereas *Ficciones* and *El Aleph* command the admiration of many sophisticated readers worldwide, the readership for the *History of Infamy* scarcely extends beyond a cozy circle of full-time Borges aficionados.

The exception to the above statement, the one intrinsically valuable piece in the volume, is "El hombre de la esquina rosada" ("Streetcorner Man"). In many ways a most curious story, of the sketches gathered in the *History of Infamy,* it is the only completely original narrative, i.e., one based not on books but on something resembling real life. Moreover, the piece soon became an anthology favorite, enjoying a success unusual for Borges's work before the 1960s, and was even made into a movie in 1961—understandably, inasmuch as it is certainly an exciting, spine-chilling drama of (those reliable ingredients) power, violence, and sex.

All this is atypical enough, but "Streetcorner Man" especially stands out in that, of dozens of Borges stories, only it evokes a particular linguistic and regional atmosphere—in a word, employs local color. The piece is in fact written in a highly oral language, a stylized form of *lunfardo* (Buenos Aires underworld idiom). Borges even goes so far as to transcribe tough-guy talk phonetically—"pa" for "para," "acreditao" for "acreditado," and the like, the Hispanic equivalents of "fer," "comin'," or "gonna" in popular American dialect. And he includes three *lunfardo* vocabulary items: "quilombo," "lengue," and "biaba." [9]

Borges modeled the vivid oral style of this sketch on the distinctive way of speaking of an old hood he met with in 1927, a murderer named Nicolás Paredes (who is alluded to in the text). Later remembering his friendly meeting with the man at a bar in the Palermo district, Borges would note his soft-spokenness and good manners, a façade that nevertheless belied a sinewy toughness and sense of local power. Mustachioed, with a large and "insolent" head of hair, he had lived from gambling, and he taught Borges a thing or two about card games and left a lasting impression on the budding author.[10]

In the several months he took to compose the story, Borges strove to recreate Paredes's colorful speech patterns by reading each sentence out loud, deleting any word or phrase that rang too literary or sounded unlike the original, real-life street tough (TA, 238). Borges never again engaged in this sort of thing; even in his own translation of the piece thirty-five years later (done in collaboration with Norman Thomas di Giovanni), there was no attempt to anglicize the oral-linguistic peculiarities just cited, and many such turns of phrase were considerably ironed out.

As the story begins, an unnamed narrator casually recalls the events, prompted by a listener identified in the end as "Borges." The setting is a dance hall, where a roistering party is shaken up by the ominous arrival of Francisco ("the Butcher") Real, hulk of a hoodlum dressed in black (like the bad guy in a Western) and accompanied by seven henchmen. Real gives a long speech saying he's "looking for a man," and defies Rosendo Juárez, the local boss. Rosendo simply walks off, forever branded a coward. Real now takes over and goes off with Rosendo's woman, La Lujanera. The somewhat perturbed narrator steps out, presumably for air, speculating that the hoodlum and La Lujanera are "going at it in a ditch." He goes back inside; suddenly, La Lujanera returns in a daze, followed by Real, who, bleeding profusely from chest wounds, drops dead. La Lujanera blurts out that, while Real and she were out in a field, a stranger challenged Real and stabbed him. There are additional bits of suspense with Real's body and the police, after which the narrator heads home and "took out my knife again. . . . It was as good as new, innocent-looking, and there wasn't the slightest trace of blood on it" (UHI, 100; HUI, 107). So the culprit was the narrator.

Because of what he calls its "stagy unreality," Borges came to dislike this original vignette almost as much as he did the ones based on books (TA, 282). He even produced a revisionist sequel many years later (included in *Doctor Brodie's Report,* which is a quiet vindication of the disgraced Rosendo, the seeming coward who, we find out, in reality had seen himself in the "Butcher" and hated what he saw, thereupon stalking out and changing his ways). Still, despite its uncharacteristically feverish melodrama and the author's brief infatuation with oral dialect, "Streetcorner Man" vividly evokes that ambiance of street toughs, an ambiance familiar to Borges from his boyhood in Palermo and the subject of roughly half his later narratives. A conspicuous presence in the text is the observer "Borges," supposedly listening awestruck to this tale of crime, a role familiar to him from his youth and a function he was to assign himself in numerous future stories.

Accidents of tone and language aside, however, this story employs certain kinds of artifice recognizable from well-known Borges pieces. Partly because of the spectacle of an enormously powerful villain dressed all in black and largely because of the mystery and drama surrounding his death, there is something eerie about the tale. Of course, the mystery is only apparent; in the manner of a typical detective story (Borges's single favorite genre and the specific form of some of his best pieces), the narrator throughout his account drops casual hints as to his true role. His opening sentence—"Fancy your . . . asking me, of all people, about the late Francisco Real" (UHI, 89; HUI, 95)—suggests a special relationship ("me, of all people") between him and the late "Butcher." The narrator recalls laying eyes on Real only three times, which is one time too many: had the narrator not stabbed him, the correct number would have been two (Real's two entrances into the dance hall). Quick on the draw, the first person to jump the "Butcher" as he bullies his way in is the narrator, who soon feels a grim anger about the swaggering Real's takeover and thus has a motive for killing him. When the revelers later dispose of Real's corpse, the narrator stands aloof, looking the other way; meanwhile, an old man stares at him, probably out of suspicion.

The matter of La Lujanera furnishes a racy subplot and also more clues. The events occur the same night that "La Lujanera decided to come round to my place and bed down with me" (UHI, 89; HUI, 95). This seemingly casual remark is not followed up until the final paragraph (and in a sense only after that). At the height of public commotion over the murder, La Lujanera leaves the dance hall; when the narrator goes home, he notes in his window a burning candle that mysteriously goes out as he approaches; at that point, the reader knows (though the narrator as yet does not) that La Lujanera, always drawn to the current top dog, awaits him for a night of pleasure. There are other hints about the Lujanera-narrator connection. When she stutters out her incomplete version of the knife fight, the narrator wonders "whether anyone would believe her" (UHI, 98; HUI, 104), thereby implying falsehood on her part. Borges then throws out deceptive clues by having Real's henchmen accuse her of murdering their boss. The narrator promptly defends her, for reasons still unknown to us. Soon thereafter, La Lujanera slips away to her surprise trysting place.

In its own peculiar way, "Streetcorner Man" is a miniature master-piece. The language, the narrative continuity, the plot lines of the four characters, and the tone are all in sharp focus and control. Quite unlike the other stories in the volume, the emotions are clear, consistent, and low-key; though the narrator takes on Real out of combined anger, manly honor, and sheer hate, these motivating sentiments are scarcely stated. One minor stroke of genius is the way in which Borges completely omits the two central episodes—the knife fight and the narrator's sexual con-quest—and leaves these "offstage" for the reader to reconstruct. Hence the highest points of the drama remain secret, nearly as elusive to us as they are to the dance-hall types.

For reasons cited above, Borges later saw in "Streetcorner Man" not a starting point in his fiction-writing trajectory but a temporary byway, a dead end. Soon shedding his literary nationalism, he would also abandon such youthful attempts at reproducing Argentine speech and write in a distilled, "standard" Spanish instead. As he once remarked, the vignette "stands there as a kind of freak" (TA, 238). The paradox is that the other stories in the *History of Infamy,* though decidedly inferior to this one, nonetheless have the shape of Borges's works to come.

Borges's next fictional foray, "The Approach to Al'Mu-tasim," first appeared in a collection of essays, *Historia de la eternidad* (1936; the portentous title of the book alludes to nothing more than the subject of the major piece, a chronological survey of the idea of eternity since Plato). The story was later reincorporated into *Ficciones.* Borges labeled the story a *nota,* a book review ostensibly dealing with an East Indian detective novel entitled *The Approach to Al'Mu-tasim* (whose existence, it should be stated at the outset, is a complete invention of Borges). The "review" opens with an elaborate history of the supposed fortunes of this fictional volume: the runaway sellout in 1932 of four Bombay printings; the 1934 edition by the prestigious London publisher Victor Gollancz, now prefaced by Dorothy Sayers (the famed medievalist and detective novelist); the mixed press given it by actual critics. All of this, of course, is perfectly spurious. So convincing was this pseudofactual rendition, however, that one of Borges's readers, his friend Bioy Casares, actually put in an order with Victor Gollancz in London for the novel *The Approach to Al'Mu-tasim!*

Borges then provides a lengthy plot summary. A Bombay law student (a freethinker of Islamic background) gets involved in a religious riot, kills a Hindu, and hides in a tower, where he encounters a Parsee bum stealing gold teeth from corpses. From there the student hustles his way through the subcontinent (under which pretext Borges extensively catalogues the geographic settings of the hero's varied exploits). In the course of his odyssey the student falls in with the dregs of society—criminals, beggars, vagabonds. One day he sees a derelict radiating such tender spirituality that he concludes such riffraff can only be a reflection of someone else, a higher being, the culmination of a vast series of superior human links. The hero then spends nineteen chapters in search of that ultimate man, Al'Mu-tasim. Finally, he approaches a seedy hovel from whence resounds Al'Mu-tasim's "incredible voice." The novel at that point ends. As in any normal book review, Borges now offers "criticisms." He praises the book in part, censures its allegorical tendencies, and points out its essential derivativeness from the *Colloquy of the Birds* (a real work of Persian literature).

Strictly in terms of procedures and subjects, the Borges of the major stories now stands unmistakably before us. His analysis of a spurious literary work and the notion of a book originating from a former one are both eminently recognizable as the materials of "Pierre Menard." (In earlier editions of *Ficciones,* "Tlön, Uqbar," "The Approach," and "Pierre Menard" are all lined up in succession—a presumably calculated arrangement.) The idea of a man who is the mere shadow of someone else obviously suggests "The Circular Ruins," while the converse conceit of a man who is all others looks forward to "The Immortal," as do the student's wide travels. The search for an ultimate, higher level of knowledge Borges was later to evoke vividly in "The God's Script." Last but not least in this emergent "Borgesian" world is the remote, almost unreal setting. These exotic materials and the formal artifice of book-within-a-book help distance us from the mystical plot, thereby presenting the latter as twice fictional, a mere story. At the same time, they furnish an illusion of objectivity, lending substance to the element of mysticism and never putting its likelihood into doubt.

All this is clearly the "literary" Borges, the Borges of mental conceits, the artist of books and mind. The piece even toys with one of his most enduring doctrinal-aesthetic concerns, the apparent fusion of mystical allegory with detective materials in the alleged book from Bombay. The Indian novel thus exhibits the "Chestertonian" mixture that soon became one of Borges's distinctive trademarks. The detective-story label, however, seems somewhat inapplicable to the "book" under review; even though the Indian novel does depict a rationalist intellectual who, by fol-

lowing the lead of a single stray clue, solves a mystery, Borges's own detailed plot summary suggests a narrative of travel and adventure—yet another "Borgesian" interest—rather than the cool-headed analysis of a
sleuthing yarn. (One gathers that Borges simply wished to air an idea then
much on his mind, whether or not it was all that germane.)

From the point of view of Borges's artistic development, "The Approach to Al'Mu-tasim" is a decided advance over most of the stories in
the *Universal History of Infamy*. It unmistakably inaugurates virtually all
of Borges's key practices and ideas. Certain basic problems still remain,
though, notably some awkward holdovers from the *Infamy* phase. I refer
in particular to the abundance of adventures, of which there is simply too
much detail crowded onto three pages. This concatenation of incidents is
as emotionally flat, as monochrome, as lacking in specific tone and focus
as were the earlier stories; it is almost a list, with no episode standing out
or dominating over the others. In the same way, though the story exhibits
most all of Borges's distinctive themes and devices, the precise trouble,
again, is that there are too many of them. Later, at the height of his
powers, Borges would organize each one of his stories around only one
or two sets of conceits and would allude in passing to other fancies.

"The Approach," moreover, while launching the technical innovations of "Tlön, Uqbar" and "Pierre Menard," does so without notice-
able drive or radiance. In "Pierre," for instance, every last detail of the
Frenchman's past is made to connect, in a rigorously mock-logical way,
with his literary exploit; there Borges plays on the curious contradiction of a bookish aesthete who, via *Don Quixote*, glorifies war—a riddle
Borges humorously resolves by invoking Nietzsche's influence as well
as Menard's love of pure irony. By contrast, many elements in "The
Approach" appear gratuitous (the myriad adventures, the Indian place
names) or worked in for the sake of local color (Hindu-Islamic riots,
Parsee ghouls). Yet potential sources of rich philosophical conflict, such
as the paradox of a freethinking law student deeply involved in mystical
searches and religious intrigues, are not made much of.

For these reasons, the story by itself is rather flat and uncompelling. It
lacks the sinister historical forebodings of "Tlön, Uqbar," the bristling
ironies, comic anger, and contrived dialectics of "Pierre Menard," and
the far-fetched heterodoxy of "Three Versions of Judas." (Perhaps it is
because of these lacks that Borges excised the story from later editions
of *Ficciones,* as well as from his 1974 *Complete Works.*) One could reason-
ably speculate that, had Borges died soon after publishing "The Approach," this piece (and not "Streetcorner Man") would now be seen as

the freak, its long-range artistic implications and potential lost on even the most discerning reader. "Al'Mu-tasim" appeals to Borges scholars and critics less because of its inherent worth than because, projecting onto it the future major works of Borges, we see there the immediate precursor to the great fictions of the 1940s. In retrospect, "The Approach to Al'Mu-tasim," though not a key story in its own right, is the final link, the decisive transition from Borges's initial attempts to full maturity. It is the work of a highly advanced apprentice finding his own true way, or, rather, of a journeyman storyteller on the brink of finally achieving mastery.

5   *Ficciones* I

DOUBLES, DREAMERS,
AND DETECTIVES

Borges's genius as maker of fiction at long last became fully manifest in 1941, his forty-second year, when *El jardín de los senderos que se bifurcan (The Garden of Forking Paths),* a thin volume containing eight fantastic tales, appeared. (This was also the year of the local scandal in which Borges did *not* receive the National Literary Prize for a group of stories that would eventually earn Borges, and Argentine letters, worldwide fame.) These narratives were reissued in 1944, under the now-familiar collective title *Ficciones,* with a supplementary section, consisting of six stories, labeled "Artificios" ("Artifices"). To this last section Borges was to add yet another three pieces in the 1956 edition.

As we saw in chapter 2, the immediate reason commonly cited by Borges for his having taken up story writing was his almost fatal bout with septicemia. As Borges repeatedly would tell his interviewers, "Pierre Menard," produced during convalescence, was a useful means of steering himself away from poetry—his preferred medium—and thereby fending off writer's panic had the result been found wanting. The writing of prose fiction served as proof to Borges that he was still a writer.

It is a dramatic and even convincing anecdote. Nevertheless, artists are notoriously fond of launching and perpetuating humorous half-truths, of hiding behind faintly absurd smokescreens when interrogated about the touchier aspects of their own lives. In the same way, one could not expect Borges, a shy man, to enjoy reminiscing out loud with a casual interviewer on the subject of his very worst years, especially when that faithful old chestnut, "How did you first begin writing stories?" invariably comes up for discussion.

In any event, the larger facts of the time suggest a situation more complex than that of a Borges producing superb fictions merely by default.

Actually, Borges had written almost no verse since 1930; it is difficult to conceive of his feeling suddenly compelled to do so once again. On the other hand, as we noted in the preceding chapter, the author had been experimenting for some six years with prose fiction, seeking out a viable means of organizing narrative fantasy, theorizing some, writing some, and even achieving notable success in the case of "Streetcorner Man." It is evident to us now that Borges, in the *Infamy* pieces and in "The Approach to Al'Mu-tasim," was consciously feeling his way through new territory—was "onto something," without being yet sure of what that something was. What is far more likely, then, is that Borges's illness and recovery furnished him concrete incentives, an emotionally charged moment of leisure during which certain ideas, long on his mind but not yet fully worked out, could definitively crystallize and assume their most fitting shape.

The years intervening since "The Approach to Al'Mu-tasim," moreover, had been confronting Borges with certain crises and extraliterary tensions, had been putting him in touch with basic human problems rather than merely bookish and metaphysical ones—in short, had been exposing him to the world of everyday conflict and concrete reality, elements hitherto quite absent from his life and art. Until 1937 Borges's existence had been mostly unproblematic and carefree; in the period following, he inhabited for the very first time the darker passages of life. Borges's father died in 1938; some months later Borges's own illness nearly killed him. In addition to these dramatic personal shocks, there were Nazism in Europe and growing military dictatorship at home—larger social developments that were putting Borges, together with his relatives and friends, on the defensive. And of course there was his personal loneliness.

Moreover, because the family's finances had by now dwindled severely, the author had had to start earning his living full-time—and under highly unpleasant conditions as it turned out. In 1937, Borges accepted a poorly paid post as cataloguer in a drab suburban library. A seedy place, its employees cared only for—in Borges's own words—"horse races, soccer matches, and smutty stories" (TA, 241). Literature did not figure among their interests; a favorite recollection of Borges concerns a fellow clerk who, casually leafing on one occasion through an Argentine encyclopedia, happened upon the entry for "Jorge Luis Borges" and marveled at the coincidence that his fellow cataloguer and a nationally recognized author should somehow share the same name.

The job gave Borges a meager living and "nine years of solid unhappiness" (TA, 241). The cataloguing system at the library, however, was conveniently slow, so that Borges fulfilled his daily quota in the early hours, then spent the remainder of the day reading in the basement and writing the great stories that now constitute *Ficciones*. Fantastic narrative was thus Borges's defense, his sole means of coping with unresolved tensions in a hostile environment, and the temporal basis of this group of tales, their greater context, is one of overwhelming personal sadness. While convalescence may have provided the immediate impulse for the writing of one story (as Borges insists), still, those numerous other misfortunes constitute the ultimate cause, the fundamental determinants, for they spurred a Borges who was then almost fully formed as a fictionist. More important, they enriched Borges's artistry, endowed his emerging skills with a new anguish and intensity, and imparted to his stories a seriousness transcending the purely literary preoccupations and mental pleasures that had characterized his earlier work.

Considering the thinness of the volume *Ficciones* (there are fewer than two hundred pages of actual text), its variety of subgenres and subjects astounds all the more. In this book there are miniature political thrillers, knife-fight yarns, tales of nearly absolute fancy, a personal memoir of an unforgettable young man, and a couple of the most ingenious crime tales ever to have been written. In addition to this assortment (essentially highly refined distillations of certain popular and even pulp literary forms), *Ficciones* contains several instances of Borges's two best-known contributions to the art of narrative: the illusory book-within-another-book and the fantasy world that reflects earthly reality—fictional devices that, though employed previously by other authors, achieve a rare and classic perfection through Borges's mastery of language and form. Because these narrative modes hold a special place in his work, we reserve the discussion of Borges's most characteristic short stories for the following chapter.

As often obtains with story collections, the *Ficciones* also vary to some degree in artistic excellence. Of the two pieces set in the Irish Republican struggles, for instance, one is scarcely more than clever. Nevertheless, their subject matter—traitors—is one rich in fantastic possibilities. An enemy posing as friend automatically constitutes a Double, his behavior by itself presenting two opposed meanings. A traitor's actions provide constant interplay between apparent foreground and hidden background; a reader in turn observes the curious spectacle with a kind of double vision, as if she were closely observing an acquaintance and the distorted reflection at the same time.[1] The major drawback of this theme, on the other hand, is its very handiness, its ease; there is a temptation to rely too much on the intrinsic appeal of the subject and lapse thereby into the mechanical. Significantly, of Borges's stories dealing with betrayal, the one with the greatest impact—"Three Versions of Judas" (examined in chapter 6)—stretches the idea of treachery to its most absurd extremes and further props its outlandish arguments with an elaborate scaffold of erudition, wit, and even warmth.

Of all his mature tales, Borges likes "The Shape of the Sword" the least; he once dismissed it, somewhat justifiably, as a mere "trick story." [2] It deals with a mysterious Irishman, a settler in rural Argentina, whose outstanding trait is the crescent-shaped scar on his forehead. When "Borges" cautiously inquires about this odd feature, the foreigner agrees to explain: In the 1920s, when he fought in the Irish Republican ranks, the man's unit took in a Communist affiliate with the name of Vincent Moon. Moon is characterized via the traditional anti-Communist stereotype; in the narrator's words, he was a gloomy and dogmatic ideologue who "reduced the history of the universe to a sordid economic conflict" (L, 69; F, 131). Moon also perpetrated (to Borges) the other unpardonable sin: cowardice. When fear paralyzed Moon in battle, the Irishman had to save him; later Moon informed on his comrade, and the Irishman, in revenge, slashed at Moon's face with a cutlass. Moon then fled, probably to South America. The narrator pauses, listener "Borges" sits, still baffled; finally the Irishman blurts it out, "I am Vincent Moon. Now despise me" (L, 71; F, 135).

This able essay into double identity recalls certain crime tales by Chesterton, in which an elusive stranger, cryptically discussed, turns out to be someone quite obvious, say, the raconteur himself. In anticipation of Borges's own later volume *El Aleph,* with its numerous stories in which one man is many or two men really one, Moon's recollection is told as if he were someone else, the betrayed and not the betrayer. The narrative is thus literally ambiguous in that it has two meanings.

Moon's duplicity (the word applies here in its descriptive as well as pejorative sense), though unrevealed until the final line, is hinted at here and there. The protagonist's scar, mentioned at the outset and also given indirectly in the title, is described as crescent-shaped, that is, like a waxing moon, and thus serves as a hidden clue in Spanish (though of course less hidden in the English translation). Moreover, the speaker at one point lets out metaphysical doubts as to his own identity: "Whatever one man does, it is as if all men did it. Perhaps Schopenhauer was right: I am all other men, any man is all men, Shakespeare is in some manner the miserable John Vincent Moon" (L, 70; F, 133). If, as Moon says, any man is all men, the watchful reader might infer that the speaker is another man. Midway through his *récit,* in fact, the Irishman virtually gives away the ending: "This frightened man mortified me, as if I were the coward and not Vincent Moon" (L, 70; F, 133). The "as if" eventually emerges as the true reality.

The sure hand of Borges the artificer is as evident here as elsewhere. His two successive narrators provide differing points of view—first "Borges," who, on his casual visit to Moon, furnishes a first impression from outside; then Moon's account, with its initial objectivity (actually opposition) slowly shading over into personal guilt. Hence Borges in this short piece elaborates an architecture, sets up a series of receding depths; formal design and metaphysical reflection help give shape and continuity to what is basically a rather slight tale. Whether all these ultimately suffice in terms of substance is another matter. "The Shape of the Sword" is also marred by its peevish and heavy-handed political judgments, intrusions most unworthy for a Borges purportedly hostile to *littérature engagée.* To debunk Communists, after all, is every bit as much a social stance as to glorify them, and to portray them as cowards, moreover, is a distortion of the historical record, inasmuch as throughout the twentieth century Communist partisans have notably figured among the most daring of military troops.

"Theme of the Traitor and the Hero," another Irish tale, follows directly after Moon's story in *Ficciones,* thus indicating some affinity between the two. Set simultaneously in 1824 and some one hundred years later, its hero, one Fergus Kilpatrick, is a martyred nineteenth-century rebel leader. Ryan, his great-grandson and biographer-to-be, puzzles over Kilpatrick's murder, noting its odd resemblance to the deaths of Macbeth and Julius Caesar in Shakespeare's plays. Ryan at first dismisses the very idea of life imitating art, but upon finding out that one Nolan, a comrade-in-arms of Kilpatrick, had worked in theater, Ryan pieces together the entire riddle in the privacy of his room, as follows:

At a secret rebel meeting, during a time of popular unrest, Nolan unmasked a mysterious traitor—none other than Fergus Kilpatrick himself. The latter duly confessed, pleading for speedy execution. The timing was poor, however; a much-loved leader's public disgrace would have demoralized the Irish people, weakening their will to rebel. Nolan then conceived his ingenious scheme: rather than simply execute Kilpatrick, one would assassinate him at the theater, an event that would spark off an angry revolt. The assassination was to be modeled after scenes from

Shakespeare, but for purely practical reasons—as a means of using existent knowledge and to avoid having to plan from scratch. The ruse succeeded; the people rebelled; and a high-level conspiracy kept things absolutely secret, up to and including sleuth-biographer Ryan, who, though
in possession of the damaging facts, now writes a book celebrating great-
grandfather Kilpatrick's heroism.

"Theme" is an incomparably better story than "Shape of the Sword,"
richer formally and more suggestive intellectually. With political striden-
cies left out and with a certain empathy somehow present, the narrative
tone improves. And the central paradox—national hero and secret traitor
in one—has a scope that transcends the narrowly abstract and personal
theme of courage versus cowardice; rather than hinge exclusively on a
final jolt, the piece raises issues of greater substance. Kilpatrick's double
identity is revealed early in the story—on first appearance a disaster for
the conspirators. They nonetheless engineer his duplicity to get good results in two opposed spheres—a political undesirable is disposed of and a
nationalistic populace is roused to arms. Indeed, the end result owes its
very success to traitor Kilpatrick's elaborate pose as martyr. Borges thus
gives readers a suggestive taste of the grim ironies and the confusing dia-
lectic of history—the unforeseen gains that can derive at times from
losses (as well as vice-versa), the exploitation of unsavory facts for the
advantage of a political cause, and the creation of myths that bind people
socially but also deceive them.

The narrative structure of "Theme of the Traitor and the Hero" basically parallels Vincent Moon's story, the action being perceived through
two individuals—Borges first, then Ryan. Their relationship to the events
is more complex, however, owing to Ryan's latter-day stake in his ancestor's political reputation. Ryan's ensuing silence, moreover, implies a
long and even endless series of men who know of Kilpatrick's treachery
but will never tell. In addition to these perceivers, there are Nolan and
ultimately Shakespeare, both of whom literally stage the events later examined by Ryan.

Borges's own opening contains more elements of artifice; he labels the
piece "Theme" and not "Story," thus emphasizing the abstractness of
the situation. Borges develops the idea by announcing that he is only
considering writing this story; hence, what we read is only a tentative and
incomplete version, a draft being produced before our eyes. (Here in embryo is that preoccupation of American writing during the 1960s and
1970s: the work of art that deals primarily with itself.) In an apparently
offhand way, Borges chooses Ireland as his setting and christens his char-

acters with stereotypically Irish names (Ryan, Nolan, and the folksy-poetical Fergus Kilpatrick). By indicating that the action could unfold in any "oppressed and tenacious" country and also by employing the most common of family names, Borges calls attention to the universal and not the local features of his account. This applicability to any time or place was fruitfully recognized by Bernardo Bertolucci, whose made-for-TV film *The Spider's Stratagem,* closely based on the plot of "Theme of the Traitor and the Hero," has Mussolini's Italy as its setting.

Two pieces in *Ficciones*—"The End" and "The South"—deal with gaucho duels, raw violence stripped of any political or other significance. Borges of course began his career in fiction with a group of tough-guy vignettes; years later, during the Perón era, themes of this sort dominated many of his narratives, beginning with the collection *El Aleph* (1949). These two narratives of blood and gore may seem out of place in the rather bookish *Ficciones,* and indeed their presence here is fortuitous; both were composed in the 1950s, when Borges had knives and hoodlums on his mind. The products of a later phase, Borges added them to his earlier book in its 1956 reprinting.

"The End" takes as its point of departure the famed gaucho classic by José Hernández, *Martín Fierro.* Actually it is a kind of closing sequel to *The Return of Martín Fierro,* itself a sequel. The episodes on which Borges builds are the last three chapters of Hernández's long poem, in which Fierro and a Negro singer engage in a singing-and-riddles duel. The Negro, after responding quite well to the hero's trick questions, is stumped when Fierro throws him a riddle that involves spelling (the Negro is illiterate). The black man now renounces singing, suddenly turns hostile, and reveals himself as the brother of another Negro killed by Fierro in an earlier chapter. The two men are about to fight to the death when bystanders separate and calm them. Fierro then gives fatherly advice to his children, he departs, and Hernández's book ends.

Borges's narrative, presented as the aftermath to that episode seven years hence, is seen through the eyes of a passive outsider, an invalid bar-keeper named Recabarren. In the background a black man strums his guitar, referring casually to the incident between Fierro and himself—without any names as yet, however. A horseman in a poncho now shows up; he exchanges harsh words with the Negro, reminding him that he, the horseman, wished neither this fight nor the previous one. Before they draw their knives, the Negro alludes bitterly to his brother's murder. Only on the last page do we find out who the contenders are; there we also see, for the very first time, Martín Fierro losing a battle and dying. It is quite literally "the end" for him, something that does not appear in Hernández's celebrated book, which is simply rounded off with a nostalgic, conciliatory leave-taking by Fierro.

In his prologue to "Artifices," Borges modestly disclaims any originality for this story, assuring us that "everything in it is implied in a famous book." And indeed numerous elements from Hernández's narrative go into the making of this piece. For one, the germs of this last battle can be discerned in certain sentiments voiced by the original contenders. In Hernández's poem, the last words of the Negro are, "You'll all find out afterwards / what destiny has in store" (pt. II, lines 4467–4468)[3]—an open-ended statement that anticipates something, however vague, in the future. A few stanzas later Fierro adds his own musings; his remarks refer to his inevitable death and also furnish Borges the title of his story: "I can't tell what's going to happen . . . / but I'll follow my right road / steady on to *the end*—everyone is bound to carry through / the law of his own destiny" (pt. II, lines 4481–4486, emphasis added). Borges's Fierro, like Hernández's, invokes this force of destiny, which "has made me kill, and now, once more, it has put a knife in my hand" (F, 161; F, 179).

The story shows further points of contact with Hernández's narrative. Borges's Fierro recalls his children, whom he has not seen in seven years: "I saw them that day . . . I gave them some good advice . . . I told them, among other things, that one should not shed another man's blood" (F, 161; F, 179). The original Fierro's giving of fatherly counsels, in fact, was his last major act before the closing of Hernández's poem. One of the gaucho's major points of advice was to avoid killing men "just to satisfy a whim," for—and this is precisely what Borges's narrative brings out—"blood that is spilt will never be forgotten / till the day you die" (pt. II, lines 4434–4439). There are also hidden allusions to the poem in Borges's play of doubles. The first Negro scars Fierro's face, before being stabbed by the gaucho; here, on the other hand, it is the Negro who gets scarred, Fierro who dies. In the poem, after the knifing of the Negro, Fierro reports, "[I] cleaned my knife on the grass, / I untied my colt, / I mounted slowly, and went off / . . . towards the lowland" (pt. I, lines 1249–1252). Now that the Negro has taken his revenge on Fierro, he accordingly "wiped his bloodstained knife on the turf and walked back toward the knot of houses" (F, 162; F, 180).

At the same time, however, Borges incorporates into "The End" certain ingredients all his own, ideas by no means present in Hernández's poem. One major addition is that of Recabarren, the barkeeper, described as having been present at the first duel and being stricken with paralysis the day after.[4] He serves as a link with the past and is witness to a history that repeats and this time reverses itself. His inability to move suggests a static, timeless, changeless situation, and his very name—with its prefix *re,* in combination with the root of the verb *acabar* ("to finish")—suggests something that ends twice, perhaps definitively. One immediately recognizable, purely "Borgesian" conceit in the story is the passing observation that the Negro, by killing Fierro, "had become the stranger," presumably because he was taking over Fierro's role of hero, scars and all, though Borges's well-known obsession about the Double seems a trifle gratuitous here.

What is most "Borgesian" in this story, however, is the showing of the famous gaucho as defeated and dead—Borges thus inverts the Martín Fierro legend, much as he stands the detective myths on their heads in "Death and the Compass." There is, in this regard, virtually nothing in Hernández's account that presages Fierro's doom at the hands of his enemies. Borges's assertion that such an outcome is among the things implied in the poem perhaps was intended as a self-effacing apology for the sheer farfetchedness of the idea—to Argentine readers something as inconceivable as, say, a defeated Lone Ranger or a rich and aged Huckleberry Finn to Americans, or a destroyed Sherlock Holmes to Baker Street cultists. Dependent in some degree on its final surprise, "The End" qualifies as something of a trick story, though not so flagrant as "The Shape of the Sword." It is, however, a distinctly minor piece, one necessarily predicated on the reader's knowledge of, and systematic reference to, a single other literary work. It is worth noting that, in the panorama of Western literature, no writings of this type (including those poems of Tennyson and Eliot which recreate characters and scenes from Shakespeare) have managed to attain major stature.

A knife fight that we never witness is the real subject of "The South." From its first appearance in print, Borges—in prefaces, essays, and interviews—has repeatedly characterized this story as his best. It is certainly his personal favorite, for it exalts bravery, something that, Borges once told an interviewer, meant a great deal to him since he was not particularly courageous himself. Bravery is implicit in the very title: the word "South" has overtones of romantic violence in Argentina that are comparable to those of "the West" in the United States. And, in Borges's view, it is in the South—a world far from city softness, a place where personal courage still enjoys esteem and carries moral weight—that the protagonist Juan Dahlmann finds himself meeting a manly death.

A library worker of mixed German-ecclesiastical and Argentine-military background, Dahlmann is painfully aware of the discordant strains in his ancestry. He lives his heroic side vicariously—he owns a sword, likes popular music, reads *Martín Fierro,* buys himself a ranch out on the plains. Then, a crisis: in 1939 Dahlmann bumps his head on a door and ends up in a hospital, where he undergoes an ordeal of nausea and pain, very nearly dying of septicemia. In the autumn he is released, boards a train, and heads south for his ranch; as he sees the plains unfold, he looks exultantly forward to being in an older and tougher world, despite his own ignorance of rural ways. A train mix-up obliges him to get off at an earlier stop. At the local bar he is taunted by some young toughs. Dahlmann is not surprised when the bartender, telling him not to worry, addresses him by name. Eventually Dahlmann walks up to and confronts the hoodlums, and one of them challenges him to a fight. Unarmed, he suddenly finds himself furnished with a dagger by an old gaucho sitting in the corner. Dahlmann now finds himself bound to fight, even though he will certainly lose and be killed. But he realizes that, were he still in the hospital, he would have preferred this death. He sees the moment, then, not as a calamity but as "a liberation, a joy, a festive occasion" (F, 174; F, 195) and heads calmly out to the plain, ready for the end.

Aside from the obvious theme of courage in the face of defeat, of subjective triumph even when one is appearing ridiculous, "The South" also depicts the moment of complete personal fulfillment, of self-discovery followed soon thereafter by death—the outcome of works as different as George Eliot's *The Mill on the Floss* or Hermann Hesse's *Magister Ludi.* More importantly, the story is, as anyone acquainted with Borges's life will note, frankly autobiographical. The protagonist, a library employee, suffers the same accident and almost dies in the same way Borges nearly did, and in the same year. Moreover he is part German, Borges part English. "Dahlmann" is clearly an assonant echo of "Haslam," the family name of Borges's paternal grandmother; and Dahlmann's grandfather, "Francisco Flores," is a parallel in career and almost in name to Colonel Francisco Borges, Jorge Luis's grandfather who died in battle. Dahlmann's background is military-cum-clergy, Borges's military-cum-literary. Although their two fates are obviously dissimilar, both underwent, in a time of illness and possible death, the experience of self-discovery—physical courage in Dahlmann's case, the writing of fictions in Borges's. One can understand why this story should be so dear to Borges's heart.

"The South" is not, however all that it appears to be on the surface. Borges, in his foreword to "Artifices," states, somewhat elusively, that the story can be read as a straight narrative and also "in another way." When asked about this in an interview, Borges replied that the events following the protagonist's own convalescence can also be construed as a prolonged hallucination experienced by a Dahlmann who in reality simply dies in the sanitarium.[5] Thus interpreted, Dahlmann's rural adventure becomes in Freudian terms an illusion, a subjective wish-fulfillment of the death he would have preferred, i.e., in active combat, rather than passive and supine. This alternate reading explains the curious correspondences between the two halves of the story: the hackney-coach that takes Dahlmann both to and from the sanitarium, the copy of the *Arabian Nights* Dahlmann examines just before his accident and later on the southbound train, and the exact likeness between the hospital orderly and the rural bartender (who somehow knows Dahlmann's name). These are "residues," as Freud might have called them, carried over by Dahlmann's mind from his last days to his final dream.

Borges's second reading also renders comprehensible certain other incongruities in the story. The old gaucho in the bar, with his archaic clothing, exemplifies a rustic type no longer existent in 1939. Sitting aloof and silent in a corner, the gaucho scarcely acts, save to spur Dahlmann on to action; he is more of a presence, "a summary and cipher of the South" and its old macho ways. He is thus a nostalgic figure out of history, the incarnation of a life longed for by Dahlmann—not a real person but a myth, a stereotype, a legend made concrete by the power of delirium.

Certain references in the text also become secret clues and take on added meaning in the light of Borges's explanation. When Dahlmann caresses a black cat, he thinks of the contact as "an illusion"; on the train, he feels "as if he were two men at one time" (F, 170; F, 191). The train ride itself is described as giving the impression of a trip "into the past, and not merely south." The slow nightfall gives the events an eerie cast; and when the two men step outside to fight, Dahlmann's thoughts are oddly relayed to us via the conditional tense: a knife fight "*would have been* a liberation, . . . this *would have been* the death he would have chosen or *dreamt*" (F, 174; F, 191, emphases added). The verb forms utilized imply uncertainty or doubt, and the word "dreamt" adds to the unreal quality of the drama. Finally, from the hellish treatment that Dahlmann is subjected to at the hospital, on through the shifting colors of daylight, the declining sun, and the vastness of the plains that fascinate the protagonist on his trip south, Borges succeeds in creating an entire hallucinatory atmosphere, a reality that somehow feels more imagined than merely perceived.

The two contrasted readings of the story interlock with yet another fantastic theme—the Double. Dahlmann is hardly described, other than in terms of his two divergent selves, which are already in conflict before his mishap. (There is but a passing reference to current family and friends.) Illness only intensifies a chronic problem, to the point where Dahlmann comes to detest his very identity. Later, on the train, he ponders his duality: on the one hand, the restored man traveling through the "fatherland" ("la patria," a word with heroic overtones), on the other, the convalescent trapped in medical "servitude." Needless to say, Dahlmann's two equally possible fates correspond to his disparate origins and life-styles—the clergyman's son and sedentary librarian who perishes in the hospital, and the colonel's grandson and ranch owner who is to be killed in battle.

"The South" can be read and appreciated for either one of its outcomes or for both. Significantly, Borges's exegetical indications closely foreshadow what the Franco-Bulgarian structuralist Tzvetan Todorov was to single out in 1967 as the "hesitation effect." An indispensable trait, as Todorov sees it, of fantastic literature, this so-called hesitation stems from an essential ambiguity as to the precise nature of the given events in a fantastic narration—factual versus hallucinatory, realistic versus symbolical, objective versus subjective. This radical elusiveness unsettles the reader, who "hesitates" between the two possible readings and never succeeds in resolving them.[6] Years before Todorov's path-breaking study of the fantastic, in which this key theory was abstractly formulated, Borges had already noted the existence of the "hesitation effect" in one of his fictions.

The combination of doppelgänger fantasies with thuggish violence in this story is undoubtedly what inspired Nicholas Roeg to quote extensively from "The South" in his film *Performance.* The movie also makes much use of a copy of Borges's *Personal Anthology* and of Borges's dust-jacket photograph, images woven by the director into a bizarre yarn that culminates in an exchange of identities between Mick Jagger and a mobster on the lam—goings-on unmistakably "Borgesian." While personal considerations no doubt prompted Borges's oft-stated fondness for this work, its richly conceived fabric of dreams and doubles, time-travel and knife-fights—those familiar obsessions of his—also places this unusually accessible piece among his most striking and inspired creations.

Another excellent Borges story that is equally subject to two such readings is "The Secret Miracle," a piece deceptively artless in its simplicity and free of the strictly autobiographical dependencies of "The

South." This is one of the most directly compelling of Borges's fantastic works.

On 14 March 1939, Jaromir Hladík, a Jewish scholar-writer in Prague, dreams of a vast and infinite chess game—only to be shaken back into reality by the Nazi blitz. The Germans take him prisoner and sentence him to death by firing squad. Terrified of death as he sits in his dark cell, Hladík entreats God to grant him a year's respite, in order that he may complete his masterpiece, an unfinished three-act drama entitled *The Enemies.* On the eve of execution, Hladík has a magical dream: among the 400,000 volumes of the Clementine Library (an authentic building of the University of Prague), he singles out the one letter that contains God. This stroke of sheer luck causes Hladík's wish to be fulfilled. As he faces the guns the following morning, the physical universe suddenly stops. Faced for 365 days with the very same raindrop, the same bee and its shadow. and the same tobacco smoke, Hladík finishes and polishes his drama within the confines of his head—after which there inevitably comes the "quadruple blast" and death.

"The Secret Miracle" was composed at the height of World War II. Borges's choice of protagonist was no doubt made because of his sympathy for those who were (together with gypsies, socialists, and homosexuals) the prime victims of Nazism, and because the figure of the Jewish scholar-intellectual represents most aptly the ideal of an urbane and unaggressive culture, a civilized mode of life easily snuffed out by brute force, by a militarism against which the powers of creative intellect are pathetically slight. The one small consolation in a battle so unequal is the mythic relationship of the imagination with divine forces greater than oneself. And if an amoral Faust, bored by existence, can strike a deal with Satan, it is quite fitting that a bookish and unworldly savant, faced with death, should be able to work out an arrangement with God.

Hladík of course enjoys, in Borges's own words to an interviewer, a rather "unassuming miracle"[7]—indeed, a miracle so unassuming that its true nature, actual or fantastical, cannot be finally ascertained. As with the protagonist's final journey in "the South," Hladík's silent year can be interpreted as a real occurrence or as a vivid hallucination dominating his last moments, a case of the imagination heightened by the onset of death.

Numerous elements within the narrative point to the possibility of a last-minute illusion. Hladík himself is portrayed as something of a dreamer; the story opens with his dreaming vividly about an infinite chess game between two families. (As the protagonist awakens, Borges notes that "the terrible clocks ceased"—an anticipation of the long moment when the clocks also "cease" for Hladík.) In prison Hladík daydreams, actively and profusely, about the ways in which he might die; he conceives of the building outside his cell as a visually fascinating labyrinth, a fantasy later belied by the prosaic iron stairway that takes him to the firing squad. Hladík's unfinished play (its title, *The Enemies,* parallels his chess dream) depicts little more than a prolonged delirium, with time never passing (as ultimately happens to Hladík) and with the same events repeating themselves. The night before his execution, Hladík again dreams of the future miracle, obtained by a gamble in itself miraculous.

Hladík furthermore exhibits a marked propensity for mystical and occult readings: Boehme, Fludd, the *Sepher Yetsirah.* Given these literary tastes, his oneiric preoccupations, and his own tendency to dream, it would be an entirely logical inference to construe his year-long respite as only the very last in a series of personal fantasies. The events in the paragraph that immediately precedes the falling-in of the firing squad, moreover, could be interpreted other than at simple face value:

> Hladík, more insignificant than pitiable, sat down on a pile of wood. He noticed that the soldiers' eyes avoided his. To ease his wait, the sergeant handed him a cigarette. Hladík did not smoke; he accepted it out of politeness or humility. As he lighted it, he noticed that his hands were shaking. The day was clouding over; the soldiers spoke in a low voice as though he were already dead. Vainly he tried to recall the woman of whom Julia von Weidenau was the symbol. . . . (L, 90-91; F, 165; ellipsis in the Spanish original)

Though the squad reportedly takes up its position immediately thereafter, one could just as convincingly see the above episode as blurring with the actual death-wound to Hladík. The burning cigarette easily merges in the imagination of nonsmoker Hladík with gunfire; the day is said to cloud over, a minor incident that could be caused by more than clouds; the soldiers speak "as though he were already dead" (the kind of "as if" statement that is never of casual import in Borges); Hladík's odd inability to reflect on his own play may be caused by something other than the tension of waiting—by the shock of the bullets, for instance; and the three little dots hint at some dark, unspoken business. In the final line of the story, Hladík is reported as dying at 9:02; the execution was scheduled for 9:00. During the two minutes that elapse, there is much that Hladík's dreamy mind could have imagined.

Nevertheless, because the action is told exclusively from Hladík's point of view, this alternate interpretation cannot be established with any finality. One indeed could reason equally convincingly that the miracle simply happens, together with everything else, as indicated in the text. For in this story, all of reality (both the mental and the physical) is not only vivid but precise and exact. The date of the entry of the Nazis is accurate, their accusations typical. The Prague landmarks alluded to by Borges are all authentic (for example, the protagonist resides on a major thoroughfare, Zeltnergasse, the same street where the Kafka family lived). The behavior of the soldiers on the motorcycle and at other moments is entirely in character, as is Hladík's horror of death as he sits in prison. A reader could just as well conceive of Hladík's secret miracle as another awesome event, the logical culmination of a reality turned completely monstrous, inhumanly bizarre.

When writing this piece, Borges may have had in mind a remarkably similar story by Ambrose Bierce entitled "Occurrence at Owl Creek Bridge." It deals with Peyton Farquhar, a man being hanged by the Confederate Army for a crime almost as obscure as Hladík's. Suddenly the rope snaps and Farquhar falls in the river. Braving soldiers' bullets, he swims to the warmth and safety of his family—a hallucination, as it turns out: the last paragraph shows a lifeless Farquhar dangling desolately over the river.

Unlike Bierce's story, however, there is in Borges's a radical uncertainty as to the fantasy or unreality of Hladík's final experiences. In addition, there lingers in this parablelike narrative an added element of metaphysical complication—namely, whether something perceived only by Hladík does or does not constitute a fact or, conversely, whether a miracle lived through by only one man's mind is or is not a miracle. On the other hand, Hladík's capacity for writing a drama under utterly hopeless circumstances in itself amounts to something of a miracle; implicit in Borges's story is the idea of artistic creation quietly triumphant, spiritually victorious, in absolute adversity, however unknown the achievement remains outside of its creator.

"The Secret Miracle" is one of Borges's most effective stories. Though it does not evoke the wealth of issues touched upon in his greater works, within its range it suggests all that can be suggested. Its success derives in great degree from the perfect tone it strikes. Fantasy and reality are flawlessly blended, evenly balanced, with each element maintaining as intense and convincing a level as the other. Absent, moreover, are the political interpolations that, in "The Shape of the Sword," detract from and encumber the narrative pace; the events by themselves demonstrate the brutality of the Nazis, and there is no need to preach to the reader on that score.

Like "The South," "The Secret Miracle" contains autobiographical references—none of them obtrusive, however. Borges first characterizes his protagonist as follows: "Hladík had rounded forty. Aside from a few friendships and many habits, the problematic exercise of literature constituted his life" (L, 90; F, 161). This is an accurate summary of Borges's own age and activities at the time he wrote the story. Hladík's writings also recall Borges's; one study by the former combines a history of philosophic conceptions of eternity with a negation of time, the respective subjects of two well-known Borges essays. In the 1920s Hladík wrote some Expressionist verse, somewhat to his later regret; Borges in that decade likewise flirted with Expressionism and comparable vanguards, repudiating these interests years later. Hladík's elaborate drama (its plot an exaggerated play on the doubles motif) is meant to "cover up his defects and point up his abilities" (L, 91; F, 163); as we have seen in the earlier chapters, Borges's development as author was precisely one of weeding out narrative weaknesses and emphasizing his imaginative strengths. Finally, the story's plot corresponds to the basic pattern of Borges's existence in the 1940s: the creative spirit isolated under harsh political circumstances, besieged by military violence and barbarism. Borges's Czech setting, however, puts the autobiographical material literally at a suitably objective remove from his own past.

"The Circular Ruins" also hinges on a dream-related pact with a deity, though it differs from "The Secret Miracle" in being unequivocally about dreams. Borges considers this oft-anthologized piece among his less-successful products and feels that it suffers from an excess of "fine writing" of the Virginia Woolf variety (TA, 267). "The Circular Ruins" is no doubt highly poetical, its prose distilled to a Mallarmé-like refinement and density; the language offers virtually no respite in the way of dialogue or action, no names of places or of people, no fights or excitement, no events prior to those in the narrative (other than certain implied ones), no struggle other than that of the individual mind's determination to generate a man. "Everything is unreal" in this piece, as Borges notes in his 1941 preface. Not even books receive mention in "The Circular Ruins," which is perhaps Borges's least concrete story, the tale that is most removed from daily experience.

An old man gets off a boat, kisses the "sacred mud," and installs himself in the ruins of an ancient circular temple. His aim is nothing less than to dream a man and "insert him into reality" (L, 46; F, 60). In this "minimum of visible world" he goes through a number of fertility rites and false starts, chronically unable to dream a man who will stay alive when the Dreamer awakes. Eventually he makes a pact in a dream with the god of Fire (whose animal-like statue presides over the temple): if the Dreamer will solemnly hand over his offspring to the god, so that the boy can dedicate his entire existence to him, then the Dreamed Man will gain life. The Dreamer now succeeds in dreaming a man; he raises him and finally sends him off to his duties as servant of the god of Fire. Some undetermined time later, the Dreamer hears a rumor that, at the other temple downstream, a "charmed man" has been seen walking through fire unharmed—obviously the Dreamer's son, protected by his tutelary deity. The Dreamer is frightened lest his son should realize he is a mere shadow, a projection of someone else. Suddenly, fire begins to ravage the Dreamer's own temple. Resigned to his fate, he approaches the flames expecting death, but, as his own body passes through the holocaust undamaged, the Dreamer realizes he too is being dreamt by another.

Its austerity and absolute unreality notwithstanding, "The Circular Ruins" is one of Borges's better-wrought tales. Its materials, though limited, are perfectly consistent, with no notable unessentials. Unstinting in its exclusion of simple guideposts or transitions, the piece is consequently a bit difficult. The strange elusiveness of "The Circular Ruins" derives in part from its skilled combination, at the most basic level, of hermeticism and vagueness. In keeping with the misty, remote quality of the few events, characters remain shadowy (indeed, in the end are shown to be literally so). The Dreamer is a "gray man" (the vaguest of colors); his son and the workmen who bring the Dreamer rice and fruits are not described at all. The faces of the two oarsmen, who bring to the Dreamer the wondrous news about his son, cannot be perceived in the dark. The tutelary god atop the circular temple is both more vivid and more vague than the characters; in the opening paragraph he is either "a stone tiger or horse," who at times takes on "the color of fire," at other times "that of ashes." In the hero's dream, the deity is both tiger and horse and also "a bull, a rose, and a storm" (L, 48; F, 63).

At the same time, "The Circular Ruins" is held together by numerous clues that foreshadow the final outcome. The story opens during a "unanimous night" (that is, "one-souled"), thus calling attention to the oneness of the context, with a suggestion that the universe (as Vedantism maintains) may be but one vast soul. As the man climbs up the river bank, there is the speculation that he might not feel the blades lacerating his flesh, a hint of some lack of the ordinary sense of pain, anticipating the eventual disclosure of his invulnerability to fire. When raising his son, the Dreamer is actually "troubled by the impression that all this had happened before" (L, 49; F, 64). Before sending the boy off to the next temple, the Dreamer erases all of the boy's memories of his youth, "so that he would be thought a man like others" (L, 49; F, 64); in an obvious parallel, its significance brought out only at the end, the Dreamer too possesses no knowledge of his own years before his arrival at the temple.

The ruins themselves present similar structural connections. The Dreamer inhabits a burnt-out temple, "whose god no longer received the homage of men" (L, 45; F, 59); downstream, it is pointed out, there is another such temple in a comparable state of oblivion and decay. Months afterward, the god of Fire (still active, it turns out) demands that the Dreamer's son be directed precisely toward this other set of ruins—the place from which the eventual news of the boy's wizardry arrives. The god alludes dimly, moreover, to other such circular temples, once the settings for certain forgotten rites and sacrifices. The epigraph from Lewis Carroll also enters here in this regard. The quotation is from the scene in which Tweedledum and Tweedledee tell Alice about the Red King; they explain to her that the king is actually dreaming of her, and, were he to awake, Alice would simply vanish (*Through the Looking-Glass*, ch. 4). Borges's implication is not only that, were the Dreamer to awake, his son would vanish, but also that, if the mysterious man dreaming the Dreamer were to awake, he too would vanish—and so on and on. In all, "The Circular Ruins" suggests an endless series of burned-out ruins where dreamt men dream of other men. The very title of the story combines familiar "Borgesian" hints of recurrence and decay.

This story exhibits yet another instance of the "hesitation" pointed out by Todorov, though of a rather different sort from that in "The South" or "The Secret Miracle." The problem lies not in the nature of the events but in their significance. One of the prime impressions "The Circular Ruins" has on a reader is its elusive, uncertain meaning. The interpretive dilemma, the "hesitation," hinges on whether to accept the story as a simple little tale, vaguely oriental in atmosphere, about some full-time dreamers and their god or to construe Borges's narrative as a metaphysical parable, an allegory for something else. In the end both approaches are incomplete; the former, literal and modest, rather limits the piece artistically, but the latter has its intellectual perils—it offers too attractive a pretext for spinning the critical wheels and engaging in airy speculation.

Nevertheless, the story does seem to hint at more than its surface plot. At the most obvious level of indirect allusion, there is the idea of the problems of paternity: the efforts and tensions involved in reproducing and rearing, the eventual aftermath of the latter ("all fathers are interested in the children they have procreated"—L, 50; F, 65), the ever-growing consciousness of traits shared by child and parent, and the corollary that perceives these traits as a continuum extending from one's forefathers. All of this of course puts in doubt the notion of an autonomous individuality. Extrapolating from this point, however, one could just as convincingly see "The Circular Ruins" as a parable not just of procreation but of creation in general; one could conceive that our products and actions may reflect our own wills, but they stem ultimately from the desires of other beings. On a more abstract plane, there lies deeply imbedded in this story a denial of time, of history, and of human change; it is a vision in which a subject unwittingly repeats the past; one's ontogeny recapitulates phylogeny with no awareness of doing so, if only because vast "inhuman laws" (evoked by Borges at the end of "Tlön, Uqbar" and embodied here in the evasive god of Fire) control our lives in ways that no single dreamer-father-creator ever could grasp. Any exegesis of this type, however, must be undertaken with maximum care.

T o move from the hermeticism of "The Circular Ruins" to the wit and flippancy of "Death and the Compass" may at first seem inappropriate. Both stories, however, depict the same basic situation: a man who thinks his own intelligence and will are achieving something, only to discover that someone else is determining his acts. Of course, the means are quite different; "The Circular Ruins" has the solemn resonance of a metaphysical parable, but "Death and the Compass" is gory detective fiction, albeit of a peculiarly literary sort.

The story opens in a hotel room with the murder of Yarmolinsky, a bearded Russian rabbi. Inspector Treviranus believes it a simple case of murder-by-mistake, committed by a crook who was seeking the jewels down the hall. Detective Erik Lönnrot, however, does not find this interesting enough and asserts that what they have on their hands is a Jewish murder mystery. Lönnrot's imagination is triggered by a pile of mystical books in the rabbi's room and especially by a cryptic sentence—"The first letter of the Name has been uttered"—left on a piece of paper inside the rabbi's typewriter. Lönnrot now suspects Jewish intrigues. A month later to the day, a notorious bandit named Azevedo is found dead in an alley, with the words "The second letter . . ." scribbled on the wall. Exactly another month hence, one Ginsburg (or Ginzberg) phones Treviranus to explain the two sacrifices and is cut off by whistles and horns. The call is traced to a boardinghouse, where the owner tells a strange yarn about one Gryphius, recently seized by two Yiddish-speaking kidnappers dressed as harlequins. Inspecting Gryphius's room, Treviranus finds more Jewish books and a third message about "the last of the letters," and he suspects a hoax. Lönnrot, meanwhile, is enticed by Gryphius-Ginzberg's use of the word "sacrifices."

As it turns out, the sites of the three murders—all of which have occurred on the third of the month—form an equilateral triangle. Then, on 1 March, Lönnrot receives an anonymous note hinting at an approaching crime for 3 March, at an equidistant fourth point that completes a rhombus. When Lönnrot arrives at that final coordinate, he comes upon and wanders through an oddly symmetrical, mirror-decorated mansion. Suddenly two goons seize and handcuff him. Lönnrot is now confronted by his long-standing enemy, Red Scharlach, who explains all the events. A dour Scharlach informs Lönnrot that the rabbi's murder had been just as Treviranus said—a mistake; and the cryptic message about the Name was simply the opening line of a learned article begun by the rabbi shortly before his death. Through the press Scharlach found out that Lönnrot, suspecting Hassidic sacrifice, hoped to crack the mystery through Judaic mysticism. Scharlach engineered all the rest: he had the bandit Azevedo killed, later played "Gryphius" himself, using these elegant symmetries to trap his hated enemy in an obsessively symmetrical house. Lönnrot now requests that, in a future avatar, the labyrinth employed by his enemies be a less complicated one—a straight line. Scharlach assents to this and shoots.

Where "The Circular Ruins" is almost forbidding in its smoothness and intensity, "Death and the Compass" bristles with all manner of clever tricks. It is, for one, an ingenious spoof on the old detective-story formula. In Borges's topsy-turvy world of crime, the criminal nabs—indeed handcuffs!—the detective; Scharlach further preempts Lönnrot's normal role at the end by recalling all the facts and piecing them together for the captive reader. In the same vein, certain people who are usually wrong in ordinary crime fiction turn out to be right in this case. Lönnrot is— like Poe's Dupin or Chesterton's Father Brown, like Sherlock Holmes or even Perry Mason—the classic detective, the pure thinker who solves mysteries through erudition and intellect alone. On the other hand, Treviranus—the tough-talking, cigar-chomping inspector—is Lönnrot's rival in the police department, a typical "dumb cop" in the tradition of Poe's Monsieur G., Doyle's Inspector Lestrade, Chesterton's Inspector Greenfield, or Gardner's Lieutenant Tragg; he is the stodgy bureaucrat who always comes up with the most obvious, simple-minded—and therefore mistaken—solution to a crime. In this revisionist detective story, however, Treviranus is twice proven right; Yarmolinsky's murder was accidental, victim Gryphius-Ginzberg-Ginsburg a mere hoax. The thinker-detective here only complicates matters, destroying himself in the process.

The mystical-occult elements in "Death and the Compass" evoke an atmosphere of the supernatural; at the same time, in a Chestertonian way, they serve to distract both Lönnrot and reader from the more prosaic facts of the case. The mystical references are nonetheless authentic. Hovering over the incidents is the tetragrammaton, that is, the four consonants (JHVH) that form God's Hebrew name Yahweh, considered too sacred to be uttered or written in full by Jewish mystics. (Lönnrot gets the notion, from Yarmolinsky's learned books and from the unfinished sentence about the "Name," that Jewish extremists seek to incarnate the tetragrammaton by sacrificing four Jews at equidistant points.) The Baal Shem, accordingly, is a generic title for those who hold the secrets of the tetragrammaton; it is also employed, however, to allude specifically to the revered Israel Baal Shem Tov, founder of the Hassidim—a well-known mystical sect whose history figures in Yarmolinsky's library. The *Sepher Yetsirah* ("Book of Creation") is a legendary work of mysticism dating back at least 1500 years; it purports to relate the entire cosmos to the ten primary numbers and the twenty-two letters of the Hebrew alphabet. One of Yarmolinsky's books defends the Cabbalah, the long-lived mystical undercurrent in Jewish life, known for its inspired cryptographic approach to scripture. (The title *A Vindication of the Cabbalah* is a private joke: Borges has an essay by that very name in his collection *Discusión*.) Another volume in the rabbi's library examines the work of Robert Fludd, a seventeenth-century British occultist credited with founding the Rosicrucian sect.

Through most of these occultisms there runs a common cryptographic thread, a tendency to perceive the world not as mere physical matter but as a divine manifestation of certain letters, words, numbers, and names. As befits a narrative so steeped in doctrinal legerdemain, Borges's narrative engages in elaborately systematic play with the numbers 3 and (to a lesser degree) 4. The former is associated throughout with factual and concrete reality; the latter, by contrast, stands for the occult, the farfetched, the fabled sectarians of the tetragrammaton, and the mystic manias of Lönnrot.

The number 3 all but pervades "Death and the Compass." The commonsense inspector's family name is made up of the Latin words *tre* and *vir*—"three" and "man" respectively. Borges thereby furnishes a secret clue to the facts of the case: that only "three men" are to be disposed of. In the same vein, the crimes occur on the third of the month; the rabbi is attending the Third Talmudic Congress, after enduring "three years of war" and "three thousand years of oppression"; the telephone rings on the next day at 11:03; the hotel is prism-shaped, that is, three-sided; and the inspector's opening remark is "no need to look for a three-legged cat"—meaningless in English, but a common Spanish idiom more or less signifying "no sweat." In the Gryphius-Ginsburg-Ginzberg caper (note the three names), three men (two short, one tall) are involved—the very same trio who nab Lönnrot in the end (when Scharlach informs us about his brother's arrest three years ago). The Gryphius harlequins also note that "the last of the letters . . . has been uttered," making it clear that the sequence is finished: the right number is 3.

Tied up with the number 3 is a color sequence. The Hotel du Nord, where the first crime takes place, reportedly displays one color, white; at the scene of the second crime, the colors are two, "yellow and red rhombs"; the harlequins who capture Gryphius in the third episode wear rhombs in "yellow, red, and green," but at the mansion where Lönnrot is held, the diamond-shaped windows remain similarly three-colored, reminding us of the story's iron law of three. The climax to this play of triple numerology fittingly comes at the third crime, where an old book is found opened at its thirty-third dissertation; it is a scholarly tome by a real author, Johannnes Leusden, an eighteenth-century professor of languages who produced a set of three philologies, of which the *Hebraeo-Graecus* cited in the narrative is—need I say?—the third.

The crux of the action and of the two series of opposed numbers is the Latin quotation from *Philologus,* where Lönnrot reads that "the Hebrew day begins at sundown and lasts until the following sundown." This, Scharlach later elucidates, is what misleads Lönnrot into believing the crimes (all of which occur late at night) have transpired not on the third day of each month but on the fourth; Lönnrot thence infers an additional fourth crime standing for the fourth letter of the tetragrammaton. This fourfold set also is present throughout the story. The original target for the first murder was the Tetrarch of Galilee; tetra, of course, means "four" in Greek. This man, nominally one of four administrators, is also the ultimate if forgotten source of the four ensuing events. Azevedo, moreover, was originally assigned to burglarize the Tetrarch on 4 December; the heist was attempted a day earlier only because of Azevedo's drunkenness and irresponsibility. As things quite accidentally turn out, then, the true reality is three. Scharlach then plants false clues to deceive his adversary into thinking in terms of four—the rhombs at the paint shop where Azevedo is stabbed, the rhombs worn by the harlequins in the Gryphius-Ginzberg incident, the bit of information in the *Philologus*. Appropriately, the windows at Triste-le-Roy, where Lönnrot is caught, are also diamond-shaped. The narrative thus begins with an attempt, planned for the fourth, on a Tetrarch's jewels and ends with a murder amid four-sided windows on what in Jewish terms is the fourth of the month, but which, in the reality that has taken shape on the prevailing Christian calendar, is the third. For that matter, only three men (not four) are murdered, with Lönnrot conveniently serving as number three. (One minor quibble: for all of Lönnrot's intelligence, it never crosses his mind that, due to the completely different organization of the Jewish calendar, the days on which the murders have occurred would be not the fourth of the month but actually some other date.)

There is a comparable legerdemain in the character's names. As befits a story in which cop and criminal exchange roles, their names share various shades of a single color. Aside from his obvious first name, "Red," the murderer's surname "Scharlach" suggests "scarlet" (and in fact means "scarlet" in German), making the murderer not once but twice red. "Lönnrot," by a similar token, contains echoes of German *rot,* also meaning "red." In addition, the sleuth's first name brings to mind the most famous Erik of them all, Erik the Red. Yet another more literary pun lies concealed within the criminal's surname, which closely resembles nothing less than "Sherlock"—appropriately, since Red Scharlach usurps the functions of his sleuthing enemy. The Jewish names employed in "Death and the Compass" are genuine. Borges claims having chosen "Yarmolinsky" because the work struck him as "strange," [8] though perhaps he had in mind the fact that Russian *yarmo* means "yoke"—the rabbi is emphatically described in terms of enduring oppression. "Treviranus," as we saw above, is a play on "three men" but is also an authentic German surname.

The immense villa where Lönnrot dies is obsessive in its symmetry—every room, every stairway, every fountain, is correspondingly duplicated. This labyrinthine, mirrorlike edifice, languidly named Triste-le-Roy, heightens the atmosphere of mystery at the culminating point of the narrative. The mansion serves also as the vivid concretization of Lönnrot's mania for symmetry. Its diamond-shaped windows evoke and magnify the rhombs brought back from earlier episodes and feverishly multiply the single rhombus drawn by Scharlach to entrap Lönnrot. As for the fantastical city, its four corners ranged over by criminals and cops, it is no less than Borges's own Buenos Aires, artfully disguised by the French, German, Jewish, Irish, and Nordic toponyms and surnames. For those acquainted with his hometown, Borges has pinpointed each spot (see his "Commentary" to this story in *The Aleph and Other Stories*).

Death and the Compass"—rich in content, crisp in its emotions, almost perfect in form—is one of Borges's greatest performances. "The Garden of Forking Paths," the other detective story in *Ficciones,* also has its own scaffold of bookish artifice and exotica yet succeeds somewhat less as a total structure. And what "The Garden" gains in depth of sentiment and irony, it correspondingly loses in the way of humor and brisk wit—emotions that are basic to police fiction.

Set in England during World War I, the story opens with a reference to B. Liddell Hart's standard history of that conflict. The report of a postponed British attack on Serre-Montauban, however, is mostly "Borgesian" invention. Hart does allude to a battle in 1916 near Montauban, in which the same number of British divisions (thirteen) were involved, but there is no mention of a postponement; and the heavy rains took place in November, not July, as Borges indicates. The allusion to Liddell Hart's history serves above all to provide Yu Tsun's ensuing narrative with a larger field of action, as well as some supposedly explanatory value and importance.

The pages "missing" from Yu Tsun's statement help plunge us immediately into the intrigue (a common thriller device), with its furtive telephone call, Anglo-Irish spy, and assassinated fellow-agent. The Chinese protagonist, a German operative on the verge of capture, has found out the secret whereabouts of a British artillery park. Desperately in need of conveying this strategic information to his bosses in Berlin, Yu Tsun hatches an obscure plan (not to be revealed until his next-to-last sentence). He grabs a revolver and boards a train with the Anglo-Irish agent hot on his heels; at his destination some schoolboys address him and, anticipating his question, volunteer directions to Stephen Albert's house (a seemingly mysterious occurrence, eventually clarified by Albert's renown as a sinologist). The approach to Albert's place casually reminds Yu of his great-grandfather T'sui Pen, who, at the height of his career, abandoned politics in order to compose a vast novel and erect a hitherto-undiscovered labyrinth. On arriving at the gate, Yu is taken aback by the sounds of Chinese music and by Albert's greeting him in Chinese. He is further astonished when he learns that the Englishman holds in his possession nothing less than the original manuscript of T'sui Pen's vast novel.

That novel, Albert now tells Yu Tsun, was also T'sui Pen's cryptic labyrinth. On first inspection a hopelessly chaotic book, the title—*The Garden of Forking Paths*—hints at its secret structure, now decoded for the first time by Albert: to wit, each of its incidents leads to not just one but all possible outcomes. Hence, when T'sui Pen's novel depicts a stranger entering one Fang's house, we read of (1) Fang killing the intruder, (2) the intruder killing Fang, (3) both escaping, and finally, (4) both dying. Albert now recites from the manuscript, and Yu marvels at the strangeness of it all: on an imperial island halfway around the globe, in a sordid spy intrigue, an Englishman is reading to him in Chinese from a once-inscrutable literary monstrosity written in the hand of Yu's very own blood-ancestor—a perfectly luminous conjuncture of events, an almost magical moment, however fragile and brief. Despite the book's chaotic appearance, Albert then explains, it is not really a novel (in China a scorned genre) but rather a cosmic parable about T'sui Pen's conception of the simultaneity of time. Yu feels a heady vertigo in the face of these revelations but also senses the urgency of minutes ticking by. Just as he sees his Anglo-Irish pursuer outside, Yu Tsun shoots Albert from behind. In the end we read that Yu's fell purpose was to inform Berlin: newspapers the next day carried reports of a senseless murder of sinologist Stephen Albert by one Yu Tsun—the latter thus tipping off German intelligence about a British artillery park located at the French city named Albert.

"The Garden of Forking Paths" once won second prize in the annual *Ellery Queen's Mystery Magazine* story contest. One inevitably wonders what the first-prize winner was like—in all probability better as a thriller but also without the formal and metaphysical suggestiveness of Borges's story. Indeed, the very idea of a book that depicts every possible narrative sequence (with examples given to boot) excites the imagination, as do the artifices of a book-within-a-book and the themes linking the "book" with the rest of the piece.

The basic outline of the story is made up of a series of enclosed narratives (the so-called Russian dolls or Chinese boxes effect)—first Liddell Hart's history, then Yu Tsun's sworn confession, then Albert's presentation of T'sui Pen's novel, and, at the core, the gigantic draft of T'sui's book itself (interpreted via Albert). The inner narratives present a chain of cryptograms, each one carrying, via the decoder, its creator's vindication. At the center is the hundred-year-old puzzle, decoded by Albert, who translates it into a cosmic riddle about time. T'sui Pen thereby stands vindicated with his great-grandson, who until now had joined in the chorus of disdain for the politician-turned-novelist. Albert's name, in turn, is a cryptogram, sent out by T'sui Pen's own great-grandson to a German intelligence chief, described as "sitting in his arid office in Berlin, endlessly examining newspapers" (L, 20; F, 90—this latter allusion is probably the only clue to the ending in the entire piece). The German then decodes Albert's name in the newspapers and translates it into a single point in space. Yu Tsun is thereby vindicated with his German boss, who apparently is something of a sinophobe; the Chinese agent has proved that "a yellow man" could do meaningful field work, just as Albert has proved that a much-misunderstood yellow man could have written a meaningful text. Even as the personal honor of a despised Chinese ancestor is restored a hundred years later near London, the military prestige of another despised Chinese (a descendant of the former) is enhanced several hundreds of miles away in Berlin.

Closely interlaced with these various codes and vindications is a series of deaths. At the very outset we read of the elimination of Yu's fellow agent, Victor Runeberg, at the hands of Richard Madden, who then goes on to chase Yu in the hope of killing him. The real interlinking series, however, begins with Yu's recollection that T'sui Pen, after spending many years writing his book, was murdered by a stranger. Albert, in turn, after spending many years deciphering T'sui's book, is now murdered by a stranger who is—of all things—T'sui's great-grandson. Yu Tsun himself is soon to die at the hands of yet another stranger, a British hangman. And, finally, Yu's act of treason has brought about the military deaths of countless strangers at the battle of Albert, France. Hardly by coincidence, the two excerpts that Albert cites from T'sui's "novel" happen to deal with the same subjects of Borges's own story—one large and epical, the other immediate and inter-personal: a bloody confrontation between two great armies on the one hand, the murders that can result from the arrival of an intruder at someone's house on the other.

The subject of time (or rather its denial), in addition to pervading T'sui's book, figures prominently among Yu's inner thoughts—anticipating and paralleling Albert's exposition, but also suggesting inherited family attitudes and the transmission of philosophical concerns over the generations. For example, shortly after the opening, as Yu sits in his bedroom, pondering his past and wondering what to do, he reflects metaphysically that "everything happens to a man precisely, precisely now. Centuries of centuries, and only in the present do things happen" (L, 20; F, 98). Later, as Yu walks towards Albert's house, hounded by fear and dread, he offers a bit of advice founded on the same premises as those of the above observation—Yu thus applies this idea not to the past but to the future: *"The author of an atrocious undertaking ought to imagine that he has already accomplished it, ought to impose upon himself a future as irrevocable as the past."* (L, 22; F, 101; emphasis in the original). This strand of thought is picked up once again near the end when, just after Albert has completed his elucidation of T'sui's book, Yu remarks out loud, "The future already exists"—a sentence suggestive of T'sui's book—and shoots the Englishman. Yu's casual musings inadvertently present piecemeal and thematically reinforce the obsession once nourished full time by his great-grandfather: that is, the simultaneity and convergence of all past, present, and future experiences, regardless of passing time. And yet, even though Yu's own off-the-cuff speculations hint at an undeveloped personal metaphysic of converging and forking times, even though they reveal a fascination with the idea of an "eternal present" as exemplified in T'sui Pen's preposterous novel, as a man of action Yu ultimately recognizes that, in our earthly reality, we each of us have but one future and no more.

Finally, one might note that Yu's narrative is held together by an underlying unity of tone and sentiment—a combination of fear, sadness, and guilt. Yu Tsun is neither the hard-boiled nor the coldly rational operative. Indeed, for a spy he is oddly sensitive and conscience-ridden, a man obsessed by doubts and even by such abstract principles as family honor, personal loyalty, and morality. Dr. Yu's complex intellect (he is a professor, after all) ponders the metaphysics of time, the horrors of violence, the vicissitudes of fate, and the Goethian stature of Dr. Stephen Albert. All of this introspection necessarily establishes Yu Tsun as a man aware of life's subtler ironies, one who, given his personal depth, inevitably feels guilt about his actions but who, for the sake of his own self-respect, must nonetheless destroy a man that has renewed Yu's regard for his own great-grandfather. As Borges himself once observed, there is something disquieting and sad about this proverbially family-conscious member of the Chinese upper class, who, owing to circumstance, is compelled to murder the very individual responsible for redeeming a much-maligned ancestor.[9] Equally sad, we might observe, is the fact that, as befalls Hladík in "The Secret Miracle," a gentle man of learning such as Albert must be singled out for liquidation for the most sordid reasons of state.

F unes the Memorious" was Borges's other favorite story in this collection—and understandably so, since "Funes" stands among the author's freshest, most accessible, and warmest works. Part of the reason for its undeniable appeal must be its almost flesh-and-blood protagonist—a freak of nature, vividly portrayed through the eyes of an apologetic upper-class narrator who is himself something of a colorful eccentric. Moreover there is in this story a compassion that is unusual for Borges.[10]

Set in the nineteenth century, in a remote region of Uruguay (chosen by Borges because of its raw, primitive character), the story tells of Ireneo Funes, an ordinary rural roustabout who, when first seen, can tell the time of day without use of a watch. Later, after being thrown from a horse, he becomes physically paralyzed but in turn receives the gift of absolute memory. The narrator visits Funes in his dark bedroom and finds the nineteen-year-old declaiming in Latin from Pliny's *Natural History* (Book VII, ch. 24) on the more dramatic examples of memory (a typical hall-of-mirrors effect: someone with a perfect memory reciting from memory a passage on memory). Funes, however, finds the alleged wonders of the past quite inferior, for he can remember absolutely everything he perceives: the cloud shapes of a particular day, the foam on a river, the streaks on a book. In a raw, quantitative way, he has more memories than all mankind does.

Funes's faculty of perception in the present, moreover, has turned equally absolute: he can see and of course remember every leaf and fruit on a tree, every single hair on a horse. As a result, in Funes's world everything is always fresh, strikingly new; the grass appears different from one day to the next, having grown some; his own reflection in the mirror astounds him with its recent wrinkles and facial hair. On top of this, Funes's consciousness takes into account the differing perspectives of the viewer. For example, a dog seen sideways at 3:14 is to Funes a totally different phenomenon from the same dog seen frontwise at 3:15. Consequently, all languages, long-existent as well as recent man-made ones, strike Funes as "too general"; the word "dog," for instance, is overly inclusive of all breeds, all specimens, all perspectives on each dog, and all moments of a dog's existence. Hence, with a view to pigeonholing every single object and moment and thereby imparting some order to all that he sees, Funes devises purely arbitrary linguistic and numerical systems of classification. Sadly, what Funes has gained in memory, he loses in the realm of general concepts; he is all discrete memories and perception, with no capacity to organize these into categories. His mind is, as he puts it, a vast "garbage heap" of overly differentiated, ever-new facts from past and present. And because his mind is always vividly recollecting to the level of pathology (Bergson's *mémoire involontaire* elevated to the absurd), Funes can barely sleep. Two years after the narrator's visit, Funes dies of lung congestion.

The story is a tiny masterpiece, not only because of the very provocativeness of the central character, but especially because of Borges's skillful handling of context. The earlier introduction of Funes as a person who can give the exact time of day without a clock—a gift in itself uncanny—helps render acceptable to readers the following, far more curious step in Funes's parapsychological development. In addition, the unnamed narrator necessarily provides a conceptual framework, a perspective not unlike ours—though with irony. Florid and genteel, fatuous and condescending, given both to captious criticism and overstated wonder, he serves as intermediary between Funes and ourselves. He voices our own mixed feelings about this extraordinary creature but also, in his tendency to prissiness and exaggeration, gives them a special twist, even a touch of parody.

Every datum furnished by Borges about Funes himself is aimed at underlining the boy's problematic existence. Funes's bodily paralysis symbolizes his fundamental impotence, his incapacity to transform his vast range of perceptions into meaningful action. Chronically bedridden, immobile in his contemplation, he is in more ways than one the helpless prisoner of his gift. Hence, though the world he sees may be varied and rich, the life he leads is monotonous and poor. The darkness in his room—the means by which Funes keeps the endless onslaught of images at a minimum—also emphasizes the contradiction between Funes's immense factual knowledge and the eternal night in which he and his mind figuratively must live. Not accidentally is Funes associated throughout the piece with darkness. The narrator's first momentary encounter with Funes before the accident occurs at dusk, under a slate-gray, stormy sky; all that he can see of the boy are his peasant clothes and burning cigarette. The later interview with Funes the Memorious takes place at night; only toward the end does the sun peep out, revealing Funes's face for the very first time in the story. This dominant chiaroscuro imagery is further reinforced by Funes's name, a word strongly suggestive of certain Spanish words variously meaning "funereal," "ill-fated," and "dark."

In much the same vein, Funes's youthful nineteen years bring out the fact of his personal and intellectual immaturity. His illegitimate origins already make of him—even prior to his accident—legally a powerless person, a marginal and ineffectual figure in society. His fatal congestion of the lungs neatly parallels the mental congestion that has rendered his life useless. Finally, Funes's death before reaching the adult age of twenty-one drives home his basic incapacity for growth and development. It also accentuates the essential frailty of his gift; in a broader way, his early death suggests the ephemeral quality of all such wonders, reminds us of the delicate balance of forces that allows for the emergence, let alone the persistence, of any human prodigy.

A year before "Funes the Memorious" appeared, Borges published an article on James Joyce in which he also discussed a preliminary draft he had sketched for the story. The essay provides a fascinating documentary record of the artistic transformation of the character Funes in Borges's mind. Borges then wrote:

> the protagonist of that fiction . . . , around 1884, is a generally
> unhappy country boy from Fray Bentos or Junin. His mother works as
> an ironer; his father, rumor has it, has been a free-lance scout. The
> truth is that the boy has the blood and taciturnity of an Indian. Years
> ago he was expelled from grade school for slavishly reproducing a
> couple of chapters, with pictures, maps, vignettes, boldface letters and
> typos to boot. . . . He dies before turning twenty. He is incredibly lazy;
> most of his life he has spent lying on a cot, his eyes fixed on a fig tree
> or a cobweb. At his wake the neighbors recall the scattered, sad dates
> of his history; a visit to the stables, another to the brothel, another to
> so-and-so's ranch . . . "

From Borges's initial germ to the finished product there stretches an enormous gap, essentially the gap separating nineteenth-century from twentieth-century fiction. Almost the entire biographical material cited above was left out of the version now standing. The only details kept by Borges are the setting, the date, and the boy's ironer mother. The scouting profession of the father is retained, but only as one of several other possibilities; the man's identity is thus rendered uncertain—and Funes's status becomes not just low-class but illegitimate.

One important fact from Borges's first presentation does survive: the boy's passivity and chronically supine state. Here again, however, the change is indicative of Borges's originality as narrator. The Funes we know stays in bed not because he is, as was his prototype, "incredibly lazy"—a motive which, in its traditional psychologism, recalls the nineteenth-century Russian character Oblomov—but because of a combination of freak accident and miracle. In the same way, the plagiarism perpetrated by the boy in Borges's initial sketch comes as the result of a certain moral-psychological lassitude and not because of any unusual qualities of mind. Borges's final version does mention the boy's typical rustic features and dress, thereby placing Funes as a recognizable type, but nonetheless he is a figure without individual traits other than his monstrous memory. As with all of Borges's characters, what stands out about Funes is not a temperament or personality but his extraordinary circumstances.

Borges once said over French radio that "Funes the Memorious" is an autobiographical "metaphor of insomnia." He wrote it during a troubled period when "I'd close my eyes and find myself imagining the furniture, the mirrors, the house" and try in vain, as poor Funes does, to get to sleep. The piece was written, according to Borges, as a means of staving off insomnia (a therapeutic trick that Borges claims did its work).[12] As Borges sees it, then, the story is a fable about the need, and the concomitant difficulty, of being able to forget—a cleverly pointed inversion of Proust.

Far more important than Borges's own interpretation, however, are the story's obvious hints, both comical and suggestive, concerning the intricate relationships between objective reality, sense perception, and organized language and thought. "Funes the Memorious" is an informal inquiry into the nature of human understanding, an amusing philosophical divertissement that flirts with the question of what constitutes knowledge. Somewhat resembling the Babel librarians in Borges's other well-known epistemological fable, the boy Funes "knows," has at his personal disposal many (too many) of the discrete elements of the world, but fails to achieve a minimal synoptic comprehension thereof. The difference here, of course, is that, rather than succumb to the Babelites' metaphysical anxieties and doubts, Funes takes ceaseless pleasure in his growing store of data and has no desire to go beyond raw accumulation. He is perfectly content to add to the vivid, encyclopedic, and ultimately useless grasp he has on reality. As well befits this difference between the two stories, the tone that predominates in "Funes the Memorious" is not the Babel librarians' cosmic despair but a tender and sympathetic irony.

"Funes the Memorious" qualifies as fantasy in that it portrays a miracle, albeit one that—if we disregard Funes's more farfetched plans—is quite conceivable in the real world. Most everyone has at least heard of someone with powers and limits of mind resembling those of Funes. One noteworthy example of a real-life Funes appears in a full-length book called *The Mind of a Mnemonist* by the eminent Russian psychologist A. R. Luria. The subject of Luria's study is one S., a Soviet citizen who was gifted and accursed with a memory approaching the grandeur and the absurdity of Funes's. Apparently S. suffered from a deep-seated incapacity for thinking in terms of general ideas. Luria remarks of S. that "details which other people would overlook . . . took on independent value in his mind, giving rise to images that tended to scatter meaning."[13] The result of these "proliferating associations," writes D. W. Harding (in a review of Luria's book), was that S. had difficulty selecting "the relevant from the irrelevant." S., though not stricken with physical paralysis (which in the story is more of a literary device aimed at enhancing meaning), nonetheless had enormous difficulty leading a normal life; the only steady employment he could find was as a performing mnemonist in shows and circuses. It is of course doubtful that Borges ever knew of S. specifically. There would actually have been no need, though, for such a specific example, given that the consequences of being afflicted with total recall can be logically inferred; in addition, people with Funes's curious aptitudes tend to share certain problems. Still, the biographical congruences between the historical S. and the fictional Funes are as impressive as they are revealing.

6   *Ficciones* II

THE WORLD WITHIN A BOOK

With characteristic understatement, Borges points out in his preface to *Ficciones* that "The Lottery in Babylon" is a piece "not entirely free of symbolism." It is curious that Borges should so single out this one story, since all his narrative writings from this period have the symbolic aura ordinarily associated with his kind of fantasy. Indeed, close to one-half of the stories in *Ficciones* are symbolic parables that evoke human problems and situations. Some pieces do this by sketching before our eyes imaginary antiworlds, whose rituals, arts, and history are variously suggested; others hint at a larger reality by focusing upon the smaller but denser intellectual space of an invented book or the invented writings of a concocted author. The most impressive story of them all—"Tlön, Uqbar, Orbis Tertius"—fuses a fabricated book and a fancied antiworld into a single entity: an imaginary encyclopedia that deals with an imagined planet. These fictional devices, mined by Borges for all their suggestive potential, are at the basis of his reputation as narrative innovator.

The small gem entitled "The Sect of the Phoenix" provides a striking instance of an imagined world that obliquely represents our own. Borges himself termed the story an "allegory." It deals with a mysterious sect with a single bond that unifies its members: an unmentionable "Secret," a "simple ritual" that is "trivial, momentary, and does not require description" (L, 103; F, 183). The narrative opens with a formidable barrage of learning, an erudite mock controversy that considers purported allusions to the sect in sources as diverse as ancient Egyptian inscriptions, medieval chronicles, and nineteenth-century philology. Borges soon drifts into a more descriptive vein, with seeming recollections of talks about the "Secret" with Swiss artisans. This sect differs from the Jews or gypsies, we are told, in that its members do not stand out in any way; their looks and language resemble those of everyone else. Hence the sectarians are never singled out for attack; but, because the people of the Phoenix are found among all possible nationalities and groups, they share in whatever misfortune befalls their compatriots. At one time their "Secret" had religious significance; now it is only a received tradition, varyingly interpreted as punishment, pact, or privilege. The story ends with Borges observing that he has met followers of the Phoenix on three continents, sectarians who at first were shocked by the "Secret," but for whom it is now instinctive.

"The Sect of the Phoenix" can puzzle first-time readers; after one has guessed the rather banal identity of the "Secret," however, the story comes to life as one of Borges's most accessible, refreshing, and even amusing works. Borges here constructs a seemingly vast enigma, an exotic but lighthearted fable, a sophisticated literary puzzle about the sex act. (In case there are doubts, Borges once told Ronald Christ, "the act is what Whitman says 'the divine husband knows, from the work of fatherhood,'" adding that as a child he was shocked upon realizing that his own parents had done it.[1]) The sectarians, in turn, are no less than the entire human race, from artisans to lawyers, ancient Egyptians to Uruguayan settlers. They resemble all the men in the world for the obvious reason that they *are* all men in the world.

The first references to the so-called sect logically would appear in Egyptian inscriptions, the oldest extant literary writings known to man. Of course, in that remote era, the "Secret" was invested with religious significance (as it still is in certain societies), but to the modern, secular-minded, more shallow sectarians, it has become rather ordinary, something clinical or simply hedonistic. Temples are unnecessary for the ritual since "a ruin, a cellar or an entrance hall" (L, 103; F, 183) will suffice for privacy (Borges prudently shuns mention of a bedroom). For devout Christians, who think of the sex act as Adam and Eve's original sin, the "Secret" is God's "punishment"; on the other hand, for couples who agree to perform the ritual, in or out of wedlock, it is in some measure a "pact"; and for Don Juans, polygamous sheiks, and other comparably highly placed or able individuals, the "Secret" is an enjoyable "privilege," one of those perquisites of power. In the end, however, all sectarians who practice the rite can achieve "eternity" by the obvious avenue of procreation. Borges in this regard inserts a subtle pun: his allusion to the repeated performance of the rite, "generation after generation," plays etymologically on the root verb "to generate." In a broader way, the chosen words *secta* and *secreto,* repeated numerous times throughout the narrative, take on the character of punning substitutes, of quasi-soundalikes, of slightly distorted close duplicates for the unmentionable word *sexo*.

Such verbal play is appropriate here. Sexual puns are legion; the double entendre pervades every level of human discourse, from barroom banter and subliminal language in glossy advertisements to innocuous Freudian slips and a poet's evocation of the sea at nightfall. As the narrator of the story himself points out, all words allude to the rite—frequently to the discomfort of both speaker and listener—with the result that the hallowed "Secret" can often seem "ridiculous." At the same time, certain sectarians abstain from the rite and thereby gain prestige, for example, priests and nuns. Finally, many of the faithful became horrified when learning about the ritual, as happened to Borges and to many of us when that era of our innocence came to an end.

One set of references in this story inevitably baffles readers—the curious mention of "cork, wax, or gum arabic" as required materials. Here, however, Borges is alluding to commonplace objects, if in devious ways. The word *corcho* signifies not only "a cork" but, in Spain at least, "a mat or small mattress" as well. The "wax" may refer not solely to the substance exuded by bees but to the petroleum-derived waxes (Vaseline, for instance) that can serve as supplementary lubricants. "Gum arabic" does seem a complete mystery; at first one is hard put to see how this sticky substance, extracted from acacia trees for use in candies, has any connection whatsoever with the sex act. As it turns out, though, for the medieval alchemists, gum arabic was "a symbol for the seminal substance." [2] Equally cryptic on first reading is the statement that "In the liturgy, mud is mentioned" (L, 103; F, 183); the giveaway here, however, is that Borges mentions this "liturgy" a few lines after having established the complete absence of traditions or scriptures among the sect. Hence Borges actually has in mind the liturgy of Christianity, a religion that notoriously emphasizes the baseness of the body, sees it as a transient entity made from substances such as "earth," "mud," and "slime." Thus the *légamo,* which is "often used" in the secret ritual, happens to be nothing less than the human body.

Despite its brevity and concealed ribaldry, "The Sect of the Phoenix" boasts numerous erudite or mock-erudite references. A few of these— Herodotus, Tacitus, Martin Buber—are the common property of generally educated persons, but most of the names cited mean next to nothing to a reader uninitiated in antiquarian scholarship. For example, Heliopolis is the Greek name for the city of Ra—the center for Egyptian sun worship in the fourteenth century B.C., known for its vast temples and powerful priesthood. Flavius Josephus (A.D. 37–93) was a historian of Jewish origin who became court chronicler to the emperor Titus; his histories of Jewry were pro-Rome in their bias. The *Saturnalia* is a loose aggregate of travel lore and Virgil criticism by the fifth-century Latin author Macrobius. Hrabanus (or Rabanus) Maurus was a librarian, teacher, and scholar of the Carolingian period, whose quite unoriginal writings derived mostly from Isidore of Seville.

From the recent past Borges digs up Ferdinand von Gregorovius (1821–1891), a German scholar best known in the nineteenth century for his history of Rome. Cited further on is Franz von Miklosich (1813–1891), a professor at the University of Vienna who, in his hundreds of studies on the East European languages, laid the foundations for Slavonic philology; among his numerous publications are some works on gypsies, in which he speculates on the origin of that people's tongue (works which Borges may have in mind in his paragraph dealing with gypsies). Toward the end of the narrative Borges alludes to another philologist, Charles Fresne du Cange (1610–1688), a distinguished lexicographer who, besides writing a history of Byzantium, established many of the historical bases for the science of linguistics; his chief works are two vast dictionaries of medieval Latin and Greek, both of which were standard references for two centuries.

Borges's final literary reference, however, is apparently spurious. Neither in the National Union Catalog nor in several encyclopedias have I found any hint as to the existence of a "John of the Rood." I believe Borges here has set us all up for an elaborate joke by taking the celebrated mystic poet San Juan de la Cruz (i.e., St. John of the Cross) and anglicizing his name into the archaic-sounding "John of the Rood." ("Rood" was the Old English word for a crucifix.) Borges extends this literary prank by playing upon San Juan's reputation for describing mystical seizures in highly sexual language; hence the "quotation" from John compares the joys of communicating with God to the delights of "cork" or "mud," in sum, the pleasures of mattress and body.

Although the other names mentioned in the story are quite authentic, it is doubtful whether most (if any) of these authors ever made the statements attributed to them by Borges. Reading through the *Saturnalia* I find no reference to a People of the Custom (or of the "Secret" or of the Phoenix). Herodotus does have a paragraph (Book II, section 73) in which he discusses the appearance and breeding habits of the Phoenix bird (his information on the creature actually comes from sources in Heliopolis), but even this has no bearing on Borges's offhand inclusion of Herodotus among writers who have mentioned the cultists. In a broad sense, of course, these authors do speak of the People of the Custom, inasmuch as they all write about some ethnic group or other and thus indeed allude to the Greek or Roman or Persian offshoots of the Sect of the Phoenix. But it is doubtful that they employ precisely the same fanciful terms, the verbal conceits contrived by Borges for his mental amusement. My own suspicion is that anyone who might choose to set aside a year or two for the purpose of taking on the relevant writings of Flavius, Rabanus, du Cange, Gregorovius, and von Miklosich would draw mostly a blank with regard to these "Borgesian" allusions.

The spurious references nonetheless serve a legitimate aesthetic purpose. For one thing, they situate Borges's fanciful narrative within a seemingly objective and concrete historical reality; the erudite apparatus furnishes a structure both more solid and more global than could have been conjured out of an exclusively mental texture of conceits, ambiguities, and puns. Because almost all the authors listed by Borges deal in such realms as history, philology, and amateur ethnography, their writings endow the peoples of the Phoenix with depth in space as well as in time and document an existence stretching back to mankind's first literary records. The very first paragraph starts out with ancient Egypt and ranges rapidly and more or less chronologically through classical Greece (Herodotus), imperial Rome (Tacitus, Flavius Josephus), decadent Rome (Macrobius), the Carolingian Middle Ages (Rabanus Maurus), nineteenth-century Europe (Gregorovius, von Miklosich), and twentieth-century Judaism (Martin Buber); Borges's passing glances at du Cange further bring in the Renaissance and the Counter-Reformation. After arriving at the twentieth century, Borges mixes his heady esoterica with more immediate, strictly narrative material—recollections of chats with acquaintances, personal anecdotes about Geneva, and, closer to home, observations about assimilated sectarians in Uruguay. The "Secret" of sex is thus dealt with by Borges as a fact of both historical and everyday life.

No image could better evoke Borges's chosen reality than that of the once-revered Phoenix, the mythical bird that was annually consumed by flames and reborn from its own ashes. Significantly, the Egyptians— whose crucial role in the history of the sect has been noted—tended to associate the Phoenix with their worship of the sun as well as with human immortality. The bird thus symbolized both the life-giving forces of nature and the fact of biological propagation. Even without this specific knowledge in mind, however, the Phoenix immediately suggests the idea of heat and fire (passion) followed by regeneration, a natural cycle that repeats itself into eternity; on a less abstract plane, the bird corresponds by analogy to the male phallus.

"The Sect of the Phoenix" combines erudite esoterica, a Kafka sort of atmosphere, riddlelike hints, detective-fiction techniques, and informal anecdotalism, all of it vividly suggesting the ambivalence and awkwardness with which human beings of all ages and professions regard sex. In a curiously roundabout way (roughly paralleling the essential point made by the story), Borges shows how so many social activities of men and women are directed toward the concealment and denial or, on the contrary, toward the expression and celebration of this basic fact or, for that matter, toward the negation and glorification of the "Secret" at the same time. This effect Borges achieves without once employing the word "sex" (recalling T'sui Pen's huge novel dealing with time, in which the word "time" is studiously avoided). Borges even elevates coitus by endowing it with an aura of mystery; what a hypocritical Victorian society considered its "dirty little secret" (in D. H. Lawrence's phrase) here becomes an enigmatic people's undivulged "Secret," one that lives on through peace and war in all the members of a widespread yet elusive sect. Only in the last line of the story does Borges even mention biology, in his remark that "Someone has not hesitated to affirm that [the 'Secret'] is now instinctive" (L, 104; F, 185)—a bit of wry and outrageous understatement about one of the most ancient of instincts.

Borges was sometimes asked why his writings dealt so seldom with sex. His usual, evasive reply was that he thought too much about it and could never write about something so personal. As we saw in chapter 2, though, the author's own relationship to sexuality was a problematical one—his very knowledge of it was rather remote and abstract. Actually, a number of other Borges narratives do allot a significant role to sex, albeit the impression is never positive, let alone attractive. (The only exceptions appear in his very last volume of stories, *The Book of Sand*.) For example, the titulary protagonist of "Emma Zunz"—who resembles Polanski's heroine in *Repulsion* in her loathing of physical contact with men—utilizes sex as an instrument of revenge but also seeks revenge on sex. "The Intruder" portrays sex as a disruptive force that incites two loving brothers to murderous hate and brutality. In "The Dead Man" sex figures as part of the alluring but fatal machinery that entraps Otálora. In all these instances, sex is closely linked with violence and death. On the other hand, it is entirely in character that in "The Sect of the Phoenix" (Borges's one story focusing exclusively on the sex act) the matter should be discreetly veiled, cloaked in riddles and erudition, steeped in awe and mystery, and depicted by fantastic rather than realist means.

Two of the *Ficciones*—"The Lottery in Babylon" and "The Library of Babel"—are conscious homages to the type of narrative crystallized by Kafka in such stories as "The Great Wall of China" and "Josephine the Singer, or the Mouse-Folk," that is, the portrayal of a remote or imaginary society whose quaint absurdities dimly but unmistakably evoke our own. Borges makes particularly clear his debt to the Czech author when the narrator in "The Lottery in Babylon" alludes to "a sacred latrine called Qaphqa" (L, 33; F, 71); with this humorous, quasi–Middle East neologism, Borges pays his respects to the innovator who established the basic mold in which this parablelike story is cast.[3]

A Babylonian traveler, whose ship is about to set sail, supposedly informs an unnamed listener ashore about the vast workings of the lottery in Babylon. The traveler, who narrates the tale, has experienced every possible triumph or calamity, has known every conceivable situation high and low. These zigzags of fortune he owes to the Lottery Company, a mysterious but powerful entity that has institutionalized uncertainty and now touches on every aspect of human existence in Babylon. In a brief historical sketch we are informed about how the first lotteries, modest events held in barbershops, eventually lost money because they awarded desirable prizes only; these early lotteries, by appealing solely to people's hopes without arousing their fears, left the public unsatisfied. When penalties and harmful prizes were granted with the positive ones, however, many citizens found themselves pressured into buying tickets for fear of appearing cowardly. In the end, everyone was regularly affected by the lottery drawings and everyone was subjected to all kinds of punishments and rewards.

The Company, which came into being with the spread of the lottery among the masses, now runs the entire operation and, by extension, the whole of Babylon. Commanding total power, it shapes the most intimate destinies of all citizens. A citizen's every last move is steeped in chance; a Babylonian feels no great surprise if a wine jug he has bought contains a talisman or a snake; scribes routinely incorporate falsehoods in their writings, with no hint as to where. Nevertheless, the Company, the social force that makes all this possible, remains an enigma, mysterious and remote. Differing hypotheses as to the true nature of the Company are widely circulated as a result. Some thinkers believe the Company to be eternal; others feel that its power is exercised in trivial ways only; another sect sees the Company as a mere myth or fiction; yet another considers its existence ultimately unnecessary, since life in Babylon by itself is suffused with chance.

"The Lottery in Babylon" fancifully depicts a social nightmare, a civilization from which all semblance of order has been lost, one whose routines, hierarchies, and rituals (those mainstays of day-to-day stability) have been completely overturned by mass hysteria, an irrational process kept alive by vast forces living beyond individual control. Beyond individual understanding, too, are the very institutions regulating all this uncertainty; it is impossible to establish with any finality just what the Company is or, for that matter, whether it actually exists. Hence, the character of the ruling structures in one's own country has become fluid, unreliable, ridden with chance. Owing in part to the official policy of encouraging deliberate falsehood, the citizens have become totally disoriented in their perception of reality, a state of confusion to which apparently everyone has succumbed.

"The Lottery in Babylon" was written at a time when Axis power was at its height in Europe and when Argentine profascist military rumblings were first making themselves felt. The story thus reflects the climate of fear at that moment in history when right-wing totalitarianism was playing havoc with the established Western liberal order. "The Lottery in Babylon," in fact, has the aura—albeit somewhat abstract and "Borgesian"—of that specifically twentieth-century narrative genre: the dystopia, an account of life inside a fantastical corporate police state. Several of the elements that characterize both the factual and fictional versions of these political systems are here present: the control exerted by a single institution that is ubiquitous as well as elusive, the systematic and officially sanctioned lying, the covert use of informers and agents (for which the Company disclaims responsibility), the violent shifts in public and private fortune, the institutionalized insecurity and fear. (Some of Borges's descriptions of the *"Compañía"* [the word is abbreviated CIA in Spanish] read like curious but unintended foreshadowings of the Central Intelligence Agency, an invisible and omnipresent power, well known for destabilizing and dislocating the fortunes of many a remote republic.)

On a more ahistorical level, "The Lottery in Babylon" is a parable on politics and society in the abstract. It obliquely depicts the tendency of all powerful organizations to keep their people intimidated, the uses of planned confusion as an instrument of social control, the desperate need of individuals to disentangle in some way the multitude of facts in their environment and lives, and the conflicting ideas that emerge as to the nature of the larger forces presumably influencing one's destiny. Although the lottery clearly comes across as symbol for unspecified and sinister social mechanisms, the Company can be interpreted on something of a general metaphysical plane. Like the Chinese emperor and the massive construction projects vividly evoked by Kafka, Borges's Company could be anything—an economic entity, a governmental-sacerdotal organization, a divine power, even some god or gods. In effect, the disputes with which the story concludes are immediately recognizable as the various intellectual positions regarding religion: conventional Christianity, Enlightenment deism, the belief in an imperfect or even weak God, sophisticated agnosticism, and simple atheism.

"The Lottery in Babylon" is often mentioned in the same breath with "The Library of Babel," not only because of their echoing titles but also by reason of their common formal framework. Both stories create an ancient Middle Eastern cosmos in order to ponder certain social and metaphysical troubles of the present. Both center on a single corporate institution that dominates everyone's existence and suggests equivalent structures in our own world. Both depict the individual fully under the influence of these colossal organizations, impelled by forces that long predate the individual and that he or she never can hope to comprehend. Each story gives vivid examples of intellectual division among the thinking segments of the population, conflicts that arise precisely from the impossibility of any one person taking in the entire situation, let alone perceiving its more remote effects and causes.

Nevertheless, despite their obvious formal similarities, these two stories differ profoundly in aesthetic worth. Borges's portrait of the universal library in Babel stands among his greatest performances, one of the acknowledged high points of his art; "The Lottery in Babylon," by contrast, is something of a lesser work, one seldom invoked except by Borges specialists. This relative neglect is understandable, as the story has a certain unresolved, unsatisfying quality. For instance, the conceit around which Borges's narrative is built—the notion of a politically motivated, socially coercive, omnipresent game of chance ("aleatory totalitarianism," as it were)—seems forced and unconvincing. Actually, the idea lies quite outside the customary concerns of Borges, whose best work hinges on a hopeless clash between the higher-flown realms of mind and a harsher material world: for example, the clash between intellectual sleuthing and hard-boiled police ("Death and the Compass"), dreamy artistry and Nazi gunfire ("The Secret Miracle"), absolute memory and practical thought ("Funes"), mystical visions and banal reality ("The Aleph"), and, of course, a man's mental limits and an infinite library. The conceptual nucleus of "The Lottery in Babylon," on the other hand, holds no such potential contradictions between mind and matter and, as a result, no debates or major issues of significance are raised. Borges's habitual (and for him fruitful) preoccupations put in a brief appearance only in the last two paragraphs, where the reader encounters a description of the writing of Babylonian books and the final account of the discrepant hypotheses about the Company. Not surprisingly, these are some of the liveliest portions of the narrative; by then, however, it is too late and the learned musings seem like mere afterthoughts to the main drift of the story.

Over and beyond this questionable premise on which to construct a narrative, there are minor details that seem facile and even false. To say, for example, that those negative prizes "awoke, *as is natural,* the interest of the public" (L, 31; F, 69; emphasis added) and pushed all citizens into playing the lottery, seems an easy and arbitrary statement concerning what is "natural." (One detects here a glib and offhand use of that well-worn abstraction, "human nature.") In another instance, the narrator recounts that the masses imposed the lottery upon the rich—a curious social dynamic indeed, since in most actual dictatorships the rich and powerful utilize chosen popular sectors as a means of destroying political opposition (as was the case in Germany and Italy). Except for outright revolution, where the rich are simply tumbled down and dispossessed, the masses are not known historically for imposing their wills on their masters. (The distinct impression one gathers from this stray comment of Borges's is that of an old-fashioned, ill-formulated antipopulism.)

"The Library of Babel," by contrast, is tighter in argument, richer in suggestiveness, more vivid and exact in imagery, and, as narrative, more compassionate and exciting. Few tales can equal the immediate visual impact of Borges's opening sketch of the cosmic library, with its starkly uniform and seemingly infinite array of hallways, hexagons, spiral staircases, spherical lamps, bookshelves, and even water closets all spelled out with geometric precision by the narrator. It is a frightening landscape reminiscent of the awesome and enormous spaces of the painter Giorgio De Chirico. Here, together with countless other librarians, lives the aging narrator, at one time a traveler to other hexagons but now resigned to a peaceful death near the hexagon of his birth.

The library is traditionally assumed to be eternal, its very existence "the work of a god." The omnipresent hexagons lead philosophers to argue the impossibility of rooms of other shapes. On the shelves are evenly placed books, unvarying in their number of pages (410), lines per page (40), and spaces per line (80). The unit symbols are twenty-five—three punctuation marks and twenty-two letters. In actual combination these characters seldom make sense. One volume contains nothing but "MCV" repeated throughout; in another, "Oh time thy pyramids" pops up in a meaningless jumble. Numerous speculations have constantly sprung up to find order in this chaos. One decisive boost to understanding came when the twenty-five basic elements of print were fully established for the first time. From this discovery a thinker deduced that all possible letter combinations and all knowledge concerning the past and future of each individual—even the ultimate meaning of the cosmos—are to be found in the library.

In the wake of this discovery, there followed an exultant, feverish search by many a librarian for, on the one hand, *the* book dealing with himself ("Vindications," as these hypothetical entities were called) and, on the other, for a complete understanding of the universe. Depression inevitably ensued, however, with the realization that the sheer immensity of the library made it virtually impossible to find *one* single book among the billions of others. The tired narrator has been through all of this, but he cannot accept the ideas posed by recent skeptics who think of God's library as meaningless; nor does he relish the activities of some fanatics, known as "Purifiers," who burn supposedly useless books. Heavy of heart and spiritually exhausted, with a sense of everything having been said before, and bewildered by the waves of epidemics, heresies, and other social ills that intimate doom for all, the narrator takes resigned comfort in the library's endurance beyond the individual. He concludes his account with a speculation of his own, a vision of a library both infinite and cyclical, with its letter combinations endlessly repeating themselves in remote and inaccessible hexagons.

"The Library of Babel" is a virtuoso performance; no summary could convey the manifold suggestiveness, the heady sense of cosmic tragedy pervading this strange work. On one scale, it is a parable of human history since the Renaissance: the numerous enterprises and struggles cited by the narrator are said to span "four hundred years" and "five centuries" (L, 55; F, 91), precisely the commonly accepted length of the modern age in Europe. More pointedly, the story is an elaborately veiled, broodingly symbolic look at man's intellectual exertions; and the implied prospects, the ultimate hopes and significance that the story attaches to human knowledge and understanding are, to say the least, gloomy. Borges's librarians try pathetically to vindicate or disentangle their world; some of them narrowly universalize their immediate circumstances (arguing for the impossibility of nonhexagonal rooms, for instance); others infer the existence of God from the order of the library (an illogical presumption since, as David Hume would have noted, all one needs for a primal creator is a very smart, very powerful craftsman); still others deduce the presence within the library of all possible combinations of letters and thereby the existence of total truth (an inference that does not follow from the observed facts and one that can be safely entertained only if the library is unequivocally shown to be infinite in its extension). Most of the inhabitants in the library seek the book that will furnish self-understanding; others yearn for a "scientific" grasp (L, 53; F, 87) of the library-universe itself. Some, including the exhausted narrator, stoically and philosophically find solace in the library's ancient secular existence, consoling themselves with dreamy speculations as to its farther reaches and its future.

The deeper problem, as the story demonstrates, is not that absolutely no knowledge about the library is attainable. On the contrary, fundamental discoveries such as the principle of the twenty-five printed characters (analogous to the discovery of the atom in the physical sciences and of microorganisms in the biological sciences) are made. The trouble lies in the consequences of these finds: they arouse expectations, whet the appetite for still more knowledge, encourage dangerous illusions as to how much is truly knowable, and in the end bring even more unhappiness than was our lot under ignorance. The library (the universe) may be orderly, even rational, but its sheer size and complexity effectively militate against human comprehension. The library's surface order notwithstanding, no one can hope to grasp the totality, the overarching, all-embracing pattern. The result is that the "meaning" of the library and the lives of each individual librarian remain hopelessly elusive. "The Library of Babel" presents us with a pessimistic vision—rarefied, fragmentary, but no less tense and despairing for that—of the uses of science and philosophy. Ever the temperamental conservative, the skeptic as to human possibilities, Borges in this story takes a dim view of the scientific pursuit, whose very success and advances in the long run cause widespread discontent and frustration.

"The Library of Babel," with its multiple conceits and prolonged juggling with ideas, may on first impression strike the reader as a coldly intellectual piece, an extended variation on the old joke about those monkeys who, given sufficient time, eventually type out *Hamlet.* However, as Borges himself observed over French radio, the story has "a feeling of loneliness, of anguish, of uselessness, of the mysterious nature of the universe, of time, and, what is most important, of ourselves."[4] Indeed, throughout this "nightmare" (again Borges's word) there is, notably in the last few paragraphs, a sense of things long overripe and of a culture weary with itself, a feeling that everything has been tried and that nothing will ever work—all of it bringing a steady increase in madness, suicides, and physical violence among the librarians, a social landscape somewhat resembling the contemporary Western world.

Much of the literary power of "The Library of Babel" derives from a visual imagery breathtakingly vast but also rigorous and precise. There is no color, except for the black-on-white of trillions of printed pages and the "insufficient light" of spherical lamps; these imbue the overall narrative with a grayish cast, as befits an account about men struggling in a twilight zone between wisdom and ignorance. There is the library's combined spaciousness and coldly forbidding geometry, its staggering size accentuated by the regularly placed hexagons and bookshelves, as well as by the "polished surfaces" of the mirrors—all reinforcing the impression of library-dwellers trapped by both gigantism and rigidity.

It is overwhelming to speculate on the number of books housed in the library. As it happens, theoretical physicist George Gamow, in his scientific popularization *One two three . . . infinity* toys with much the same problem, in this case the combinatory possibilities available for fifty English symbols on a *single line* of sixty-five spaces. He computes the different possible sequences thus:

> The printed line can begin with any of these [50] signs so that we have here 50 possibilities. For *each* of these 50 possibilities there are 50 possibilities for the second place in the line; that is, altogether 50 X 50 = 2500 possibilities. But for each given combination of the first two letters we have the choice between 50 possible signs in the third place, and so forth. Altogether the number of possible arrangements in the entire line may be expressed as:
>
> $$65 \text{ times}$$
> $$50 \times 50 \times 50 \times \ldots \times 50$$
> $$\text{or } 50^{65}$$
> $$\text{which is equal to } 10^{110}$$
>
> To feel the immensity of that number assume that each atom in the universe represents a separate printing press, so that we have 3.10^{74} machines working simultaneously. Assume further that all these machines have been working continuously since the creation of the

universe, that is for the period of 3 billion years or 10^{74} seconds, printing at the rate of atomic vibrations, that is 10^{15} lines per second. By now they would have printed about

$$3.10^{74} \times 10^{17} \times 10^{15} = 3.10^{106}$$

lines—which is only about one thirtieth of 1 per cent of the total number required.[5]

This figure by itself staggers the imagination, but it applies *only to lines that differ*. Gamow's computation does not allow for repeated lines, which are a common occurrence in the Library of Babel, where whole books may vary by one letter. Hence, the number of volumes in the library, though not quite literally without limits, is a sum so unimaginably vast as to be infinite from any practical human perspective.

A t least five of the *Ficciones* exemplify Borges's best-known genre—the discussion of an invented book or author, usually in relation to larger human concerns. Other narratives in *Ficciones* ("The Garden of the Forking Paths," for instance) also make use of the device as a kind of subplot. As one might expect, those stories that dwell on fancied writers are cast in certain essayistic molds—the book review, the thumbnail biography, the posthumous appreciation or memoir. From a purely literary point of view, these book-within-book pieces are among the most innovative of Borges's works. Some of them, such as "Tlön, Uqbar, Orbis Tertius," have a monumental quality; in contrast, others, like "The Approach to Al'Mu-tasim," seem exclusively caught up in their novelties of structure and fail to excite the reader as a result.

"An Examination of the Work of Herbert Quain" is of interest chiefly because of its occasional epigrams and its provocative and forward-looking ideas for possible books. In its lack of significant narrative conflict and lesser intrinsic value, it somewhat resembles "The Approach to Al'Mu-tasim." The story does expand on the procedure earlier launched by "The Approach," insofar as it discusses not one but several books (in effect, the entire life's work of an invented author); and, as one normally does in such examinations, Borges's "essay" attempts to put "Quain" in historical perspective. Quain is even cited as saying he belongs not to art but to its history, an idea Borges was to explore more strikingly in his parable "A Yellow Rose" (in *Dreamtigers*).

Quain's writings are labeled, and today would still qualify as, "experimental"; fittingly, they all date from the era of proliferating "isms" between world wars. The story builds on the kind of casual speculation (for example, the assertion that street dialogue too is "literature") or the arty shoptalk about "new forms" sometimes overheard in Paris cafés. What gives Borges-Quain's speculations a certain interest is that they have since come true, taking shape at the hands of actual authors, including Borges himself. Quain's detective novel *The God of the Labyrinth,* with its erroneous solution and its prompting of the reader to deduce the correct one, somewhat recalls Borges's own "Streetcorner Man" (in which La Lujanera is briefly and wrongly blamed and a faint last clue turns the mindful reader back to the relevant data); *The God of the Labyrinth* also looks forward to "The Sect of the Phoenix," a story which, by planting misleading clues and furnishing no solution at all, obliges readers to function as their own best sleuths.

Quain's "novel" *April March* proceeds (as the title suggests) backwards; it also sets up for each given scene three possible antecedent episodes. This retrograde arrangement was later put to vivid use by Alejo Carpentier in his *Viaje a la semilla* (*Journey Back to the Source*), the biography of a Cuban-Spanish marquis, recounted inversely from death to birth; a more recent instance of reverse-fashion narrative is *Cadáver lleno de mundo* (1971) by the Mexican novelist Jorge Aguilar Mora. In addition, Quain's thrice-ramified mode of organization obviously brings to mind the labyrinthine book described in "The Garden of Forking Paths," a book that depicts not two or three but all possible outcomes (the bureaucrat T'sui Pen is thus even more experimental than man of letters Quain!). Certain novels of recent vintage also toy with the multiple-possibilities device: Bernard Malamud's *The Tenants* supplies two different endings; John Fowles's *The French Lieutenant's Woman,* three; and Julio Cortázar's *Hopscotch* presents to the reader a double option, either of stopping at chapter 56 with protagonist Oliveira poised for a plunge from a third-story window or of going on to the supplementary chapters that imply Oliveira's survival.

Again, Quain's play *The Secret Mirror* depicts in its first act some intrigues involving British lords and ladies, including the secret amours of the "haughty Amazon" Ulrica Thrale and a playwright named Quarles; but the second act exposes these dark goings-on as a drama conceived by Quigley, a commercial traveler who happens to worship from afar a real-life Miss Ulrica Thrale and who for his play has made her the heroine, converted his shabby rooming house into a country estate, and recast himself as "Quarles." A few years later, Borges's Hladík was to write a play in which the protagonist's delirium transforms his trivial life into high drama. Similar procedures are to be found in such recent products as Robert Coover's novel *The Universal Baseball Association,* whose protagonist fancies baseball games in his bedroom, and Julio Cortázar's story "La isla al mediodía" ("The Isle at Midday"), in which the vivid account of an airline steward emigrating to a Greek island turns out to be a wishful daydream. Luis Buñuel provides a spectacular instance of this device in *The Discreet Charm of the Bourgeoisie,* with its highly charged violent episodes time and again exposed as the absurd nightmares of the film's five bourgeois characters, while Alain Resnais's *Providence* presents a series of tense, emotionally wrought family dramas which, in the end, turn out to be a night of bad dreams in the mind of the paterfamilias.

As often happens, Borges puts much of himself in this little mock-essay. Like Borges, Quain in 1939 was forty years of age. Quain has just died; Borges recently had experienced a brush with death. The publication dates Borges gives for Quain's book closely coincide with those of his own prose works; Quain's list of titles, moreover, becomes increasingly "Borgesian." *The God of the Labyrinth* brandishes a familiar motif; *The Secret Mirror* resembles "The Secret Miracle" (by now presumably on Borges's mind) both in content and in name; and *Statements,* with its highly "original" and "secret" eight stories, inevitably brings to mind Borges's first major set of narratives, also eight in number, soon to be reissued under the distinctly contrary rubric *Ficciones.* Borges multiplies these oblique self-mirrorings in his final lines. An idea casually attributed to Quain—that "invention" is the greatest of all literary pleasures—is of course the very life-blood of Borges's aesthetic. All this self-referential tomfoolery is capped when Borges "confesses" having taken one of Quain's stories from *Statements* as the basis for "The Circular Ruins."

These private jokes, of course, do not necessarily add up to a good story. (Borges himself told me that he saw "An Examination of the Work of Herbert Quain" as little more than an exercise.) The piece exhibits many of the same faults earlier noted in "The Approach to Al'Mu-tasim"; it possesses a static quality and contains too many ideas passed in review, none of them heightened into thematic prominence. As a result, the story raises no problems and no issues of greater consequence—unlike "Three Versions of Judas," which indirectly questions Christian doctrine and by extension all religious doctrines, or "Tlön, Uqbar," a story that evokes nothing less than the global nightmare of the twentieth century.

"Three Versions of Judas" indeed stirs the intellect with the sheer novelty of its speculations. An understated parody of theological disputes, it gradually builds up to its bizarre hypothesis, one that is assuredly shocking within a Christian doctrinal context but, when seen from a larger perspective, is only slightly more so than various other heresies (or, for that matter, certain respectable orthodoxies).

Set around 1900 in Sweden—perhaps to convey an ambiance of cool and introspective taciturnity—it tells of Nils Runeberg, a deeply religious theologian who, in ascending order of outrageousness, formulates three possible explanations for Judas's deeds. First, Runeberg speculates that Judas's betrayal was superfluous, given Jesus's fame as a leader; hence, rather than an accident or a personal whim, Judas's act must have been predestined, a sacrifice of God-made-flesh by an apparent transgressor of flesh. Cast within the role of informer, Judas too traveled the path of self-denial. Second, Runeberg, under attack from his peers, asserts that, since Jesus himself appointed Iscariot and (being God) certainly must have known Judas's true character, the latter simply could not have acted from shallow greed. Moreover, Jesus, who had at his disposal boundless divine resources, would not have needed a mere mortal to carry out his will. Judas's true motive, Runeberg thereby argues, was not greed but a heroic asceticism. Third, in this "monstrous conclusion," rigorously argued and propped with biblical references, Runeberg announces that our sense of the Christian tragedy has been completely wrong: God did not assume the form of Christ, but—taking on the lowest possible identity—that of Judas himself. Runeberg now lives in hopeless isolation, his ideas disregarded or scorned. He wanders through the streets of the port city of Malmö, losing his mind and wishing he were in Hell with the Redeemer; he dies of broken health.

Through the conventional format of a scholarly article, with trappings such as footnotes, foreign language titles, recondite historical data, and authentic biblical citations, Borges makes ingenious use of some of the contradictions of church doctrine. Nearly every religiously trained person has on some occasion pondered the troublesome question, "If God is omnipotent as well as omniscient, how can man be considered free?" Borges's story plays on a specific variant of this dilemma by narrowing it to a concrete religious-historical problem, namely, "If Judas's eventual treachery was anticipated, even put in motion, by God the Father, how, then, can Judas be judged as a willful betrayer?" Or, from another perspective, "If Jesus was God and if Jehovah guided his actions, how, then, could the Deity in either form have appointed a traitor-to-be?" This thorny issue leads logically to one of two particularly vexatious possibilities: either Judas's betrayal was foreseen and even preordained by God (which automatically assuages Judas's guilt), or God (the Father or the Son) failed to apprehend Judas's true nature, which inevitably puts in doubt the absolute divinity of Jesus. Borges leaves out these questions, using them as the implicit basis for his intellectual drama; they are the starting point for his step-by-step exoneration of Judas, in which he presents the man first as God's unwitting tool, then as a free and voluntarily selfless individual, and finally as God himself. Needless to say, the novelty here is Borges's inversion of customary values as he argues on behalf of the traditional villain, just as in other stories he stands on its head the old narrative formula of cop and criminal.

As befits a supposedly learned article and literary biography, "Three Versions of Judas" flaunts a weighty apparatus of erudition—much of it concocted, we shall soon see. As in "The Sect of the Phoenix," the piece starts out with a forbidding array of archaic allusions and names from the early Christian era, thereby placing Nils Runeberg within a broad historical continuum. These obscure references (again, like the opening of "Phoenix") are all authentic. Basilides, Satornil, and Carpocrates were Gnostic thinkers who flourished in second-century Alexandria; their works, like those of virtually all such heretics, were destroyed by a Christianity triumphant, and their words survive only as quotations in Christian-inspired attacks on them. Borges alludes to a couple of these latter tracts: the apocryphal *Liber adversus omnes haereses* (*Book against All Heresies*) falsely attributed to Tertullian and not to be confused with Saint Irenaeus's more briefly named *Adversus haereses,* a standard historical work of reference; and the *Syntagma* (*syntagma* in Greek meaning any orderly listing of things), the title of two different compilations of heresies, one by Justin (ca. A.D. 150) and the other by Saint Hippolytus (ca. A.D. 200), with Borges not specifying which one is actually meant. Borges invokes these totally vanished antiheretical treatises not only to ponder the fate of Runeberg's writings had he lived in the second century, but also to set up a parallel between the intellectual lot of the Gnostic thinkers and that of a devout twentieth-century Swedish theologian who similarly endures orthodox attack and eventual oblivion. Early Christian intolerance, Borges dimly suggests, is repeating itself in the Runeberg case.

As the narrative proceeds, factual names begin to mingle with fictional ones—Borges's familiar trick. Hans Lassen Martensen is indeed listed in the *Encyclopaedia Britannica* (eleventh edition) as a "Danish divine (1808–1884)" and Martin Kemnitz as "German Lutheran theologian (1582–1586)"; also in that source are entries for two English divines named

Robertson—Frederick William (1816–1853) and William Bruce (1820–1886), either of whom may be the one mentioned in the story. From these real-life clergymen Borges "cites" certain speculations vaguely akin to those argued by Runeberg—philosophic allusions that, whether genuine or false, help give Runeberg's abstract ideas an impression of concrete ancestry. In contrast, those scholars directly connected with Runeberg (detractors such as "Lars Peter Engstrom," sympathizers such as "Erik Erfjord") originate either in Borges's mind or—in the case of Erfjord—with certain immigrant Buenos Aires families. Aside from not appearing in any standard reference works, their Nordic names are obvious stereotypes, much like the Ryans and Nolans in "Theme of the Traitor and the Hero." The same procedure can be observed in Borges's dizzying finale, where he mingles historical figures such as Isaiah and Saul with invented ones such as "John of Viterbo" and "Valerian Soranus." The *Midrashim* (from a Hebrew word signifying "investigation" or "study") designates not a religious sect but a rabbinical literary tradition that interprets the Scriptures for ethical or homiletic meanings (Borges thus grafts his own fanciful notions onto an authentic term). In addition, Borges takes a former classmate in Geneva, Maurice Abramowicz (who in the 1960s was a deputy for the Swiss Communist Party), and makes him a French religious scholar, even concocting for him an appropriately haughty bit of Gallic sarcasm. Borges's game is pretty much exposed, however, when he has "Erik Erfjord" cite the *Vindication of Eternity* by Jaromir Hladík, book and author both lifted straight out of "The Secret Miracle."

In addition Borges makes use of a Brazilian classic, *Os Sertões* (1902; translated into English as *Rebellion in the Backlands*), Euclides da Cunha's vivid account of a rural, religiously tinged, popular revolt against the Rio government and of the revolt's savage repression by the authorities. This work, translated into Spanish and published in Argentina in 1938, is briefly and accurately cited by Borges in a footnote to "Three Versions of Judas"; the phrase quoted is from a detailed summary of the bizarre and confused doctrine of Antonio Conselheiro, the visionary who believed, among other things, that "strength of character was something like a higher form of vanity, almost an impurity." [6]

Highlighted by Borges's footnote, this assertion is a rather casual statement in the original, with negligible import for da Cunha's line of argument, though of course it shows an obvious accidental resemblance to the fanciful conceits of Borges-Runeberg. Far more noteworthy are the extensive analogies da Cunha draws between the cult figure of the Brazilian backlands and certain early Christian heresies; he likens Antonio

Conselheiro to the Montanists, at one point even referring to him as a "crude Gnostic," the sect later used by Borges as focal point in "Three Versions." Thus Antonio, like Runeberg, is placed within a large and on-going tradition of religious dissidence. The doctrines of both these men, moreover, rise in the face of crisis to a pitch of millenarian, apocalyptic madness—with the obvious difference that the Wandering Brazilian always inspires his audience and infects them with enthusiasm, whereas the Swedish professor lives a solitary final three years, raving about divine ca-tastrophes to none but himself. Nevertheless, the numerous points of similarity (and contrast) between the two men suggest that Borges found in da Cunha's *Rebellion* some fruitful leads for the organization of "Three Versions of Judas."

Beyond the confines of this story lies the two-thousand-year-old de-bate, raging since the rise of Christianity, as to the true nature—human, divine, or both—of Jesus. The controversy is also a frequent target of satire, as in Luis Buñuel's film *The Milky Way,* which pokes fun at this and other issues by placing ancient doctrinal disputes into ordinary modern settings—a restaurant, an inn, a highway. Borges, by contrast, presents a dignified academic locale, into which Runeberg intrudes with the most farfetched arguments possible. Moreover, where Buñuel puts the church to obvious ridicule, Borges maintains a lofty objectivity by shunning any preconceived attitudes, leaving wide open such questions as whether Runeberg is a madman, an inspired fool, or a martyr to true intellect; whether his arguments per se are as good as, better or worse than, or simply outside those of the reigning orthodoxy; and, finally, whether the orthodox publicists are sincere defenders of the faith or merely intolerant reactionaries. Borges's narrative voice does make one positive remark about Runeberg's thinking—that it brought to an "exhausted" tradition the "complexities of evil and misfortune" (L, 100; F, 176), thus suggest-ing that the man's books possess the virtues and the energies of the new. At the same time, though, one must admit that Runeberg's ideas strain credibility and that, with their indulgence toward treachery, they could gain acceptance in no ethical or religious system, least of all in Christian-ity, inasmuch as they minimize the role of Jesus. For that matter, "Three Versions of Judas" could also be read as a view from the outside, a depic-tion of a tired and outdated subculture whose upholders as well as loyal dissenters exercise themselves over fine arguments and abstractions. All these are a few possible readings of a narrative in which no sides are taken. Borges instead gives dramatic shape to a fanciful and novel idea, one that is interesting to contemplate casually but obviously difficult to defend.

"Pierre Menard, Author of the *Quixote*" similarly deals with an invented intellectual, a minor Symbolist poet who, standing at the end of a tradition, also hits upon an elaborate and striking notion, one as novel as it is useless. As happens with Runeberg in his later years, Menard is totally taken up by his project, an obsession that might suggest madness were Menard depicted at closer quarters. Despite their differences—Runeberg is a somberly respectable academic, Menard a precious, turn-of-the-century decadent—both live single-mindedly for their manias: "writing" the *Quixote* in one instance, "rehabilitating" Judas in the other.

In format the story of Menard is a postmortem literary appreciation, an apology for his life written shortly after his funeral. The unnamed narrator who looks back upon Menard is a snobbish reactionary (his initial paragraph flaunts his aristocratic ties and snipes at Protestants, Masons, and Jews), a very French type of polemicist still found in the pages of the right-wing *Action Française*. The catalog he gives of Menard's published works (each item of which is a delight) furnishes what Borges called "a diagram of [Menard's] mental history."[7] Menard's mental spaces are conspicuously narrow, his subjects completely self-contained—pure poetry, symbolic logic (item f in the catalog), metrics (i, j), chess (e, g), even a project for an artificial poetic language (b). This introversion inevitably turns self-reflexive; for instance, the apocryphal retranslation into French of Quevedo's translation into Spanish of a devotional work originally in French (Borges's footnote), the study of metric patterns in French prose as evidenced in the prose of an author who had denied such patterns (j), and, of course, the revealing title *Les problèmes d'un problème* (m).

Indeed, much of Menard's work is so minute as to be pointless, for example, transposing Paul Valéry's greatest poem into a different meter (o) or improving the game of chess by eliminating one pawn (e) and then rejecting the proposal! Menard's "obstinate analysis" of poetry, his fascination with syntax (item n) and punctuation (s), and his concomitant belief that "censuring and praising" are merely "sentimental operations" that have "nothing to do with criticism" (n) all suggest a lifeless formalism, an effete nihilism in which basic questions of meaning and of value have lost their place. The one exception to this fine-grained claustrophobia is Menard's attack on his friend Valéry, a piece expressing the exact opposite of Menard's feelings—a rather primitive incursion into irony that later becomes a key to explicating and evaluating Menard's unpublished masterpiece.

The "masterpiece" happens to consist of two chapters from *Don Qui-*

xote, Menard's texts being identical to those of Cervantes, yet with not one copied word in them. The narrator now recalls the steps by which Menard arrived at this undertaking. Inspired by a casual idea of Novalis about achieving total identification with an author, Menard first considers reliving Cervantes's life and forgetting three hundred years of European history. This project he discards as too easy because his aim is to create his own *Quixote,* not as Cervantes but as Pierre Menard. He also contemplates the possibility of immortality, a situation that would inevitably result in his writing of the *Quixote* (another "Borgesian" play on that old fancy about monkeys, typewriters, and *Hamlet*). Menard eventually realizes that, having gone through *Don Quixote* at age twelve and knowing Cervantes's other works from more recent reading, his own mind perceives the *Quixote* in the same dim way that any author senses within himself a book yet to be written. This is Menard's point of departure; after thousands of drafts, most of them put to flames before the narrator's eyes, Pierre accomplishes a tiny fraction of his self-appointed task.

The narrator now builds a cunning edifice of evaluation. As he sees it, the *Quixote* is an achievement surpassing that of Cervantes. Unlike the latter, a Spaniard who simply relied on his national experience and native tongue, Menard was a twentieth-century Frenchman faced with an array of deceptively quaint stereotypes (conquistadors, gypsies, Carmen) and a seventeenth-century foreign language. Yet another difficulty overcome by Menard was the portrayal of the knight debating the question of arms versus letters. The original Don Quixote came down on the side of arms, an obvious and easy recourse for Cervantes, a seasoned ax-soldier. On the other hand, for a bookish man of letters like Menard to have so convincingly defended arms is (according to the narrator) an awe-inspiring feat. Menard's capacity for transcending personal limits and praising soldierly values has been attributed, among other things, to the influence of Nietzsche and especially to the penchant for stating opinions contrary to his own—the precedent of course being his "attack" on Valéry.

Now comes what may be Borges's most notorious conceit. The narrator quotes two long passages dealing with truth and history, one by Cervantes, another "by" Menard. These two passages are absolutely identical. Not so, this is but apparent, says the narrator, who dismisses Cervantes's words as empty rhetoric but extols Menard's as contemporary in their outlook and Jamesian in their pragmatism; he therefore judges Menard superior! (On the other hand, he praises Cervantes's prose style as natural and direct, but faults Menard's language as "affected" and "archaic"!)

After some further reminiscing on Menard's speculations, the narrator finishes his account by pondering a new technique of reading, one that employs "deliberate anachronism" and "erroneous attribution"—that is, disregarding history, conceiving the *Aeneid* as pre-Homeric and the *Imitation of Christ* as if written by Louis-Ferdinand Céline or James Joyce.

This literary mock-memoir was Borges's first major story; with its wealth of ideas and wit, it stands among his liveliest and best pieces. On one level, "Pierre Menard" is a clever parody of literary criticism and its sectarian debates, philosophical battles, and ardent attacks and vindications. (Borges himself, with his own aesthetic to uphold, was often a willing participant in such critical activity.) The unnamed narrator, an amateur critic, puts to work many forensic tools—learned allusion, sly sophistry, sarcasm, nostalgia—all with a view to explicating and indeed justifying the monumental but futile product of an eccentric précieux.

And yet, the story's levity notwithstanding, fundamental questions of aesthetics are raised by "Pierre Menard." One of these is suggested in the notion, posed by the snippy narrator, that Menard's *Quixote* improves upon Cervantes's by giving shape to the ideas of Menard's contemporaries. This sort of thing is a commonplace of literary journalism, but it points to one of the more troublesome problems of writing and judging both—the double but potentially conflicting loyalty of an author to the great works of the past and to the preoccupations of his time. Menard, of course, lives the two to an extreme degree; he transmits the past word for word, even as he reflects present-day thought.

Also at work in Borges's story is the thorny question of how much there remains to "say" in literature and how much material there is left with which to say it. Though Borges himself has never expressed doubts about the infinite possibilities of language and the imagination, his character Pierre Menard stands within a set of circumstances hardly favorable to newness and originality. As Borges observed over French radio, Menard suffers from "an excess of intelligence, a sense of the uselessness of literature, as well as the idea that there are too many books."[8] Coming as he does at the end of a literary period, Menard is weighed down by tiredness and skepticism. This is perfectly illustrated by his literary methods: his writings, which show no hint of any larger theme of his own, build exclusively upon the achievements of others. The *Quixote* project simply pushes his derivative tendencies to their ultimate conclusion.

Menard's friend and exegete, who is appropriately an aristocratic conservative whose sympathies are with the past, argues for the contemporary relevance of Menard's effort. This notion, plainly intended as a bit of a joke by Borges, was taken up for serious discussion by Alain Robbe-Grillet in *For a New Novel* and adopted as a key point of departure by John Barth in his well-known essay "The Literature of Exhaustion" (the title accurately describes Menard's own work).[9] Barth argued programmatically that, in the late 1960s, when many traditional themes and forms seemed to have played themselves out, the most promising and potentially fruitful literary procedure could well be the rewriting of older materials with an ironic perspective, the revival of dated, discarded, or otherwise lost forms through the medium of parody.

Actually, this aesthetic position is not new with Barth—Thomas Mann toyed with much the same idea in *Doktor Faustus*—or with Menard's apologist. The practice itself, minus the theory, has been in evidence in all the arts throughout this century. Joyce's *Ulysses* is an unheroic, contemporary recasting of Homer's *Odyssey* with close parallels in plot; one chapter consists almost exclusively of a series of parodies of English prose style, from the remotest forms of medieval Anglo-Saxon to Yankee snake-oil turn-of-the-century oratory. Playwright Christopher Fry was known for his five-act, blank-verse, Elizabethan-style comedies, an archaic form imbued by the author with a wit and irony highly modern in flavor. Barth himself wrote an eighteenth-century novel in the language and manner of Henry Fielding, *The Sot-Weed Factor*. In music, Stravinsky ingeniously worked out a neoclassical language and structure strangely reminiscent of Bach and Mozart; for his ballet *Pulcinella* he unabashedly lifted and spiced up entire pieces by Pergolesi, an eighteenth-century Italian composer; and in *The Fairy's Kiss* he similarly "modernized" Tchaikovsky.

In a more extreme vein, Marcel Duchamp brought a special emotion to visual art by simply putting a moustache on the Mona Lisa. Though his *visible* contribution to the new work might constitute only a tiny fraction of the material occupying the canvas, it could be argued by Menard's memoirist that Duchamp injects a typical formal portrait of the Italian Renaissance with contemporary irreverence and skepticism and that his work is therefore richer, more up-to-date than Leonardo's. Later instances of this type of artful buffoonery include Roy Lichtenstein's pictures of comic strips and, of course, Andy Warhol's proverbial Campbell soup cans. As film has developed into a more self-conscious medium, it too has made notable use of self-parody. One of the most striking instances of the "Pierre Menard effect" can be found in Woody Allen's *Play It Again, Sam,* which opens by showing in its entirety the closing scene from *Casablanca*. The relationship of that emotionally charged episode to Woody Allen's comic plot completely alters the meaning of the original Moroccan airport melodrama. The culminating point of a familiar Bogart-Bergman love-and-war saga is thereby transformed into the wistful and jocose opening scene of Woody Allen's bittersweet schlemiel satire.

In Borges's story, however, such practices and notions are carried to their ultimate and absurd extreme: the complete and unmodified reproduction of an earlier work. The idea is intriguing, though of course unrealizable in practice. To present as new art a moustachioed Mona Lisa or a giant soup can—artifacts which at least differ somewhat from their originals and whose natures are immediately evident to the naked eye— is one thing, but to pass off an entire preexisting novel as one's own requires an added measure of brazenness or naiveté. Borges, on the other hand, writes *about* someone actually doing this, comments on it with an implied aesthetic resembling the one formulated above, and, to cap the whole joke, defends an act of creation that is as admirable as it is useless. Although Pierre's own grandiose project is by itself a dead end (a fact aptly symbolized by the thousands of preliminary drafts he brought out and burned), "his" *Quixote* raises countless questions about the relationship between art, history, and originality, between received tradition and individual talent.

The arguments set forth by Menard's unnamed encomiast are a mixture of sound thinking and sophistry, but then, Borges's story is an extended satire of the intellectual patterns, formal subtypes, and sophistries of the genre of literary criticism. The opening paragraph, with its reactionary mumblings, captures the passions of ideologically motivated aesthetics. The narrator's personal praise for Menard is in the tradition of the posthumous literary eulogy often printed in small literary journals. The list of Menard's visible works recalls many a philological enumeration or catalogue raisonné. The account of how Menard came to write *Don Quixote* is a genetic explanation usually found in literary biographies. The suggestion that Menard glorifies war under the "influence" of Nietzsche is a recognizable critical commonplace. On the other hand, the assertion that Menard's prowar statements are ironic is itself an ironic imitation of a ruse by which a critic might justify works whose social doctrines make him uncomfortable (for example, Céline's anti-Semitic *Bagatelles pour un massacre* or Michael Cimino's anti-Asian *The Deer Hunter*). In the manner of historicist scholarship, the narrator finds in both Cervantes and Menard the philosophical ideas of their respective times. Last but not least, in his final paragraphs Borges prophetically satirizes the ahistorical structuralists of the future, with their synchronic and reversible perceptions of the entirety of world literature, their emphasis on reader rather than author, and their attraction for words like "palimpsest." (Critics like Gerard Genette, in apparent disregard of Borges's general spirit of humor and parody, have built entire theories on the fanciful notions played with in "Pierre Menard.")

Borges's utilization of the *Quixote* in this context is by no means accidental. Cervantes's masterpiece, itself one of the great parodies, has been called the "Rorschach blot" of art criticism, a work in which readers see what they want to see or what history conditions them to see. Literary commentators over the years have repeatedly read into *Don Quixote* the chief preoccupations of their own time and culture. Hence, eighteenth-century rationalists thought of Cervantes's would-be knight as an insensate fool; romantics esteemed him as a noble idealist fighting against an imperfect world; a religiously inclined Dostoevski saw in Don Quixote a figure of Christian purity and goodness; Marxists and other sociological critics see the knight as a representative of a decaying aristocracy clinging to superannuated feudal-chivalric values; Américo Castro, in his existentialist phase, saw Don Quixote as the individual who consciously and actively chooses to define himself and become a knight; and American interpreters, living in a world of relativistic uncertainty and flux, comb Cervantes's text for the finer ironies, the nuanced interplay between deceptive appearance and illusive reality. When Menard's commentator detects Jamesian pragmatism in Cervantes, he unwittingly falls in with a venerable old critical tradition.

A lthough "Tlön, Uqbar, Orbis Tertius" is the very first piece in *Ficciones,* discussion of this story has been left until last, since it is the longest and most complex as well as the most imposing of all the narratives gathered in this book. It is also one of Borges's most personal stories. It sets forth nearly all of his key ideas, preoccupations, mannerisms, stray notions, and conceits—and is therefore the most "Borgesian" of all of Borges's works. However, precisely because of this thorough identification of "Tlön, Uqbar," with the author's politics, aesthetics, philosophy, and personality, the meaning of the work may seem elusive to those not acquainted with other Borges writings.

The story opens with "Borges" having dinner at a rented villa with his friend and collaborator, Adolfo Bioy Casares. The latter cites a heretic from Uqbar whom he recently saw quoted in *The Anglo-American Cyclopaedia;* when they examine the house copy, however, they find no entry for "Uqbar." Some days later, they consult Bioy's personal set, volume forty-six of which contains a full four pages on Uqbar. There they read of a country in Asia Minor whose sole outstanding trait is its literature, which is invariably fantastic in mode and set always in "the imaginary regions of Mlejnas and Tlön" (L, 5; F, 16). That night Bioy and Borges ransack countless reference works at the National Library—but no sign of Uqbar. The narrative then leaps ahead two years to Herbert Ashe, a recently deceased British eccentric who left behind in a bar a mysterious object—volume eleven of *A First Encyclopedia of Tlön*. Its subject: the arts, myths, history, and philosophic debates of the peoples of a completely imagined planet. The perpetrators of this bizarre hoax remain unidentified.

The imaginary inhabitants of fancied Tlön have an intellectual peculiarity—they are all absolute idealists of the Berkeleian type. All life and activity on Tlön starts from the proposition that the universe, which is merely a subjective projection of the mind, has no material existence. Consequently, there are no nouns (words that presuppose a world of objects) in its languages, which instead make use of impersonal verbs or descriptive adjectives—not "the moon" but "to moonate" (verb) or the adjective "airy-clear-over-dark-round." (A Tlönese quotation here— *axaxaxas mlö* immediately stands out as one of the cryptic combinations cited in "The Library of Babel.") In the same way, since reality is strictly mental, the only legitimate science on Tlön is psychology; if seeming facts and events are really mind processes, then a lighted cigarette, some smoke, and a field in flames are not causal links but an instance of association of ideas. Like Ireneo Funes, the Tlönese do not reason about reality. Neither, however, do they recall the past, but instead engage in pure speculation, practicing a continual *Philosophie des Als Ob* ("Philosophy of As If," a fashionable German doctrine from the turn of the century, formulated by Ernst Vaihinger and frequently alluded to by Freud). As a result, there are numerous competing schools of metaphysics: one that negates time, another that thinks all existence a dream, another that conceives of life as a god's script (notions repeatedly toyed with by Borges in his writings).

The only philosophy that is unacceptable, indeed, inconceivable to the Tlönites is, predictably, materialism. One heretic attempted to illustrate the idea by venturing the example of a man who loses nine coins, which other individuals find some days later. Most Tlönites were baffled by the argument; those who took the trouble to confront it replied that "find" and "lose" are reckless neologisms, founded on the absurd presumption that an exact likeness might constitute identity. Tlön idealist thought thus denies the most basic of all mathematical axioms, that anything equals itself: $a = a$.

More description along these lines is followed by a "Postscript, 1947"—an elaborate joke, since the entire story, "Postscript" included, was written in 1940 and first published in 1941! This fabled sequel tells how a seventeenth-century secret society (among its members Bishop Berkeley) first planned an encyclopedia about a fictional country; how Ezra Buckley, an eccentric nineteenth-century American atheist tycoon, financed the project and broadened its designs to planetary scope in order to prove the sheer unnecessity of God the Creator; and how the grandiose project finally reached completion in 1914. Then, some years later, objects from Tlön begin to appear on Earth: an Argentine princess finds a compass inscribed with Tlön writing; in a Buenos Aires suburb, "Borges" comes upon a tiny but extremely heavy cone made from a mysterious substance—it is a Tlönese religious artifact.

The turning point is 1944, when a Tennessee journalist exhumes all forty volumes of the lost *Encyclopedia*. It fast becomes an international craze, with summaries, anthologies, and pirate editions sweeping across the globe. Writing as if these events were common knowledge, Borges now comes to the famous passage in which he remarks how, in the 1930s, "any symmetry with a semblance or order" could mislead the populace, which, confronted with an unfathomable universe, seeks out facile solutions and systems and is now under the seductive spell of a fanciful planet. People forget their national pasts, studying Tlön history, learning Tlön languages, giving over their very existences to Tlön. Eventually, in Borges's own apocalyptic words, "English and French and mere Spanish will disappear from the globe. The world will be Tlön" (L, 18; F, 34). Indifferent to all this hysteria, far from such madness, "Borges" works quietly on a Spanish version (not intended for publication, a fact emphasizing its marginality and futility) of Thomas Browne's *Urn Burial*—significantly, a work of antiquarianism that marvels wistfully at the ruins of ancient Greece and Rome.

"Tlön, Uqbar, Orbis Tertius" is a virtual compendium of Borges's most typical characteristics and themes; the story enjoys a special reputation as a result. Borges's partiality for philosophical idealism was a fascination that dated from childhood, when he talked at length about idealism with his father, and that he later made public in 1925, when he acknowledged (in the volume *Inquisitions*) Bishop Berkeley's crucial influence. In "Tlön, Uqbar" this fascination springs to artistic life via the depiction of an idealist planet, complete with the cultural and intellectual consequences thereof. The story's dark final observations, on the ultimate impossibility of human beings perceiving the order of the universe, bring to mind, of course, the epistemological nightmare of "The Library of Babel." The aesthetic doctrines and practices gleaned from volume nine of the *Encyclopedia of Tlön* also closely resemble those of Borges; for example, the idea of the unoriginality of all literature, the search not for truth but for "the astounding," the fictions that work solely within the multiple permutations of a single plot (*The Garden of Forking Paths* raised to planetary status), and the practice of inventing authors and attributing works to them. Such ideas and attitudes, employed piecemeal throughout Borges's poetry and prose, all fuse within the compact space of this story. Last but not least, "Tlön, Uqbar, Orbis Tertius" sums up Borges's two most celebrated formal procedures, the imagined antiworld and the invented book-within-a-book, both of them here converging in *A First Encyclopedia of Tlön.* This fabricated cosmos-in-forty-volumes not only reflects our situation, giving back an image of ourselves in reverse, it eventually intrudes into and *becomes* the entire world, the world we live in.

This "intrusion of the fantastic world into the real one" (L, 16; F, 31) is the very crux (indeed, the pivotal point) of most of Borges's major fiction. Whether the intrusion consists of an occult vision, a possibly subjective experience, or an odd conceit, most of Borges's stories build up to a disquieting irruption of unreality into ordinary, banal surroundings. "Tlön, Uqbar" differs significantly from its companions, however, in that the unreality—the strange apparition of an entry for "Uqbar" in one copy of *The Anglo-American Cyclopaedia*—intrudes from the very outset. (This supposedly pirated *Britannica,* incidentally, is yet another of Borges's spurious references.) Although the episode soon appears to drop out of sight unaccounted for, the "Uqbar" incident is indirectly explained by the intrusions that accumulate in the "Postscript." The "Uqbar" article, we are informed, makes brief mention of an "imaginary region" named Tlön; this seemingly casual allusion connects these baffling pages with the later discovery of the *Encyclopedia of Tlön* and, even more important, relates the Uqbar affair to the apparition of full-fledged Tlön artifacts and ultimately to the eventual takeover of the world by Tlön culture.

It is only after these mixed initial events that the full leap is made to an unreal cyclopedia and a completely unreal planet. Formal interests dictate that Borges not plunge outright into the matter of Tlön; the untimely exposure of Tlön would surely have weakened the theme's potential because the very idea is too monstrous, too fantastic for most readers to accept without some preparation. Instead, Borges establishes a series of credible contexts in which unreal events build up—that time-honored technique of detective and suspense fiction. Even though the word "Tlön" has a basis in wordly reality (a Tlen in Poland and a Tlos in Turkey), the name, according to Borges himself, was intended as an echo of *Traum* (German for "dream")—yet another unreal source.[10] The Tlönese "quotations" and the actual name, moreover, are suggestive of medieval Anglo-Saxon, an unreal world from a distant past that later became the aged Borges's dominant passion.

Todorov's "hesitation effect" has a special pertinence to this story. First-time readers of "Tlön, Uqbar" are often hard put to define the precise nature of the opening events, are initially unable to sift out the real from the fantastic, fact from fiction. Only some time later do they become aware that all of it is fiction, though some materials are even more fictional than others. In the same way, one "hesitates" between at least two explanations for the Tlönese items that turn up in Argentina; the magnetic compass and the heavy cone can certainly be construed magically (the sheer mental power of Tlön has acted upon and altered reality, something like the dreams of Pedro Damián in "The Other Death"), but a naturalistic interpretation can be ventured as well (the artifacts found are produced by artisans so much under the spell of Tlön that they adopt its metals, numerals, even religious symbols).

"Tlön, Uqbar" has the feeling of a slowly growing nightmare, of accumulating unrealities that become all-embracing in the last two paragraphs. First we read of an ordinary conversation in a real Buenos Aires suburb, and the discussion leads us to a nonexistent encyclopedia that is based on reality but once removed from its plagiarized source. Remoteness and exoticism are suggested by "Uqbar," supposedly an obscure Anatolian nation with a plausible Near Eastern name. Next, a very literal unreality intrudes with the fact of Uqbar's absence from other copies of the same edition of the same book, then from other books as well. A nonexistent country has now intruded, made itself felt in the antipodes, and then eluded its investigators.

Two things especially provide a sense of context in "Tlön, Uqbar": the detailed local geography and the characters taken from real life. Buenos Aires is a vivid presence throughout the piece; all episodes are set in well-defined places (a grocery store, an apartment, a bar) with the names of the streets and suburbs always spelled out. A still more striking device is the way in which Borges attributes spurious statements to genuine individuals—among them Néstor Ibarra (Borges's translator into French), Ezequiel Martínez Estrada (the respected Argentine essayist and social commentator), Carlos Mastronardi (a poet who was in the original *ultraísta* group and one of Borges's closest friends), Princess Faucigny Lucinge (an Argentine lady married to an irresponsible French aristocrat), Enrique Amorim (Borges's cousin-in-law), Alfonso Reyes (in 1940 the dean of Mexican letters), Drieu La Rochelle (the notorious French *littérateur,* right-winger, and eventual collaborator with the German occupation), and of course Borges and Bioy Casares. The Argentine readers who first encountered this story, with its allusions to well-known authors who may have been personal acquaintances, must have found themselves strangely disoriented and have felt some perplexity as to the truth of Borges's text, a certain hesitation, as it were. One critical work well characterizes the presence of these personages in "Tlön, Uqbar" as something "undigested." [11] It is as if a North American intellectual had casually picked up an issue of *The Nation* or *Partisan Review* and found him- or herself reading an ostensible essay containing opinions enunciated by Norman Mailer, Edmund Wilson, John Leonard, John Ashbery, Leslie Fiedler, Jacqueline Kennedy Onassis, and William F. Buckley, Jr., on the subject of a vast and puzzling, recently exhumed literary monster.

Borges applies these procedures on a grand global and historical scale as well. From the past he brings in real writings, bogus writings by real European authors, and some colorful but concocted personages. Among the concocted characters are the taciturn widower Herbert Ashe and the rich nineteenth-century atheist Ezra Buckley, vividly portrayed eccentrics whose quirkiness lends an air of authenticity to their Tlön-related acts. The Nashville *American,* by contrast, is a real newspaper. Equally authentic are the passing comparisons Borges makes to Schopenhauer and Russell, as is also "the lesser world of Meinong"—a reference to Alexius Meinong (1853–1920), a German logician and philosopher known for his studies in cognitive philosophy and whose theory of "unreal objects" is obliquely alluded to by Borges.

False attributions to real authors begin in the fourth paragraph of the narrative, where the two-line title of a German book by Johann Valentin Andreä with "Ukkbar" as its purported subject is "cited" in full. Though the volume, needless to say, is pure fiction, Andreä (1586–1654) did exist; he was a pietist theologian whose *Fama Fraternitatis* is considered the source book for the Rosicrucians, a historical secret society. Andreä also wrote something called the *Allgemeine General Reformation der ganzen weiten Welt* ("The Complete and General Reformation of the Whole Wide World"), which is almost an echo of Borges's mock-titles, resembling both Andreä's spurious study of Ukkbar and the grandiose projects dealt with in this narrative. In the same vein, among the original members of the fabled group that projected an imaginary world, Borges lists George Berkeley (partially because of the Irishman's idealist philosophy but perhaps because of his plans for starting a university in the American colonies) as well as one George Dalgarno, an English author (1626–1687) who devised sign languages for the deaf and also worked on a system for universal shorthand—activities that tie in neatly with the future devising of artificial languages for an invented planet.

This marriage between the factual and the fantastic, of course, is precisely what "Tlön, Uqbar" is about. Narrative procedure here thus corresponds closely to thematic meaning or, in more familiar terms, form adequately reflects content. Borges's account of a multivolume fiction so influential that virtually everyone ends up seizing it as a model of thought and action is in fact a parable about the lure of self-contained ideas, the destructive appeal of fabricated schemes and symmetries. Though the examples Borges cites side by side—Nazism and Marxism—tell us more about his politics than about baneful idealisms, the author's general insight has a larger relevance. The 1930s represent moments in history that are notorious for spawning idealized patterns that captivate the public imagination. The nineteenth century saw such grandiose social myths as the white man's burden, *mission civilisatrice,* manifest destiny, Sarmiento's "civilization-barbarism" dichotomy, and the Horatio Alger success fable. More recently, as American life becomes increasingly problematical, the turn of the century has seen a proliferation of instant-happiness therapies and pseudo-Oriental faiths, along with a hardened, rigid libertarianism. Borges himself, in his own occasional reflections on society, relies heavily on a nineteenth-century symmetry—"The State must be weak, the Individual strong"—a formula rooted in Spencerian ideology.

The quiet despair in the last few paragraphs of "Tlön, Uqbar" is, by Borges's own testimony, the real core of the story, for it reveals not only that Tlön has engulfed men's minds but also that a few individuals here and there have been completely left out. Borges once asserted to an interviewer that "the subject is neither Uqbar nor Orbis Tertius, but rather a man who is being drowned in a new and overwhelming world scarcely understood by him."[12] The twentieth-century dates cited in "Tlön, Uqbar" (1914, the 1930s, 1942) suggest a time of recognized crisis, a time of upheavals when people are cast adrift and, unable to accept their older beliefs, their history, or even their language, seek gratification (as is done on planet Tlön) in the amazing, the novel, and the bizarre. Tlön stands for the new ways of life that seize men's souls and violently sweep away the past. Far on the periphery of it all there lives a man of traditional culture who is skeptical of facile symmetries and fads, but feels too old to swim against the inexorable tide. Out of his element in a changed world, he hides alone amidst his ancient books on ancient subjects, resigned to his isolation.

That man we have seen identified in the narrative as Borges himself. And though "Tlön, Uqbar" undoubtedly is fiction, one cannot resist construing the final statements of the solitary Quevedian translator as an eloquent, highly distilled expression of Borges's own attitudes. It has been observed that this story is a compendium of Borges's leading philosophical and aesthetic preoccupations. At this point, one may remark that "Tlön, Uqbar" also furnishes a glimpse of Borges's political position—his aloof, traditional, centrist, elitist dislike of mass movements of either left or right. What gives these final paragraphs their narrative power are the anguished, even defensive personal convictions that lie imbedded in this ostensibly fictional reminiscence. The ending of "Tlön, Uqbar" comes as close to a political testament as Borges ever provided in his imaginative writing; his views of history, understated but impassioned, bring to a fitting climax the close of a gradually building literary "Borgesiana"—surely another reason why this story holds such a special place in the Borges canon.

It is curious that, for all its legend, "Tlön, Uqbar" is not among Borges's most accessible pieces. Besides requiring the reader's acquaintance with a certain philosophical school, and in addition setting up numerous corollaries and logical extensions to Bishop Berkeley, the story's protracted middle section—the somewhat static long summary of Tlönese thought and practice—is on the sluggish side. It is the "Postscript, 1947"—with its strange events, its evocation of a turbulent history, its hints of political hysteria, and its final sense of personal solitude—that pulls "Tlön, Uqbar" out from its temporary lapse into a rather abstract mentalism. These last pages rank among the greatest Borges ever wrote; without them, there would be no single locus of episodes that so well sums up Borges's art and outlook. It is not in vain that *Ficciones* starts out with "Tlön, Uqbar, Orbis Tertius."

7   *El Aleph* I

DOUBLES AND PUZZLES

Borges's other major collection of stories, *El Aleph,* first saw light in 1949. To its original fourteen narratives Borges added four in 1952. Ten of these stories can be found in the Irby-Yates anthology *Labyrinths;* the remainder are gathered in the Borges and di Giovanni collection, *The Aleph and Other Stories.*

The book contains numerous masterpieces, stories of breathtaking intellectual power that are haunting in their breadth and originality and easily the equals of any of the major narratives in *Ficciones.* On the whole, however, *El Aleph* lacks the impression of organic unity found in the earlier volume. *Ficciones* keeps an astounding variety of subjects, procedures, and genres in harmonious balance and can stand by itself as a unified entity (indeed is often referred to as such), but *El Aleph* has the slightly overall look of a patchwork anthology, a transition volume. There are a number of new emphases here, in formal treatment as well as in subject matter. Though Borges is customarily associated with invented books-within-books and elaborate symbolic-fantastic worlds, *El Aleph,* surprisingly enough, contains little of this sort of artifice. Instead of Borges himself dreaming up other kinds of cosmos, here his characters perceive a strange universe through magical and mystical means (as happens in the famous title story). Similarly, rather than set up halls of mirrors with fictive books, Borges now brings these duplications and reflections to bear upon his fictive persons; for example, an individual character finds out he is someone else or two different people turn out to be the same. This, needless to say, is that other well-known Borgesian theme, the Double. The motif is directly dealt with in only three of the *Ficciones,* whereas over half the stories in *El Aleph* play around with personal identity—stretching it, blurring it, or twisting it in some way. The most ambitious single narrative included in *El Aleph,* "The Immortal," tells of a universal man whose personality is constituted by all men in history. Because this narrative, as well as those stories that evoke mystical experiences, are the richest and most complex in *El Aleph,* I shall examine them in chapter 9.

Generally speaking, *El Aleph* is a volume in which, compared with *Ficciones,* characters matter relatively more than do books or ideas. In keeping with this shift in focus, there are in *El Aleph* a notable number of fast-moving narratives depicting rural or underworld toughs. These violent stories about knives and guns possibly reflect a change in the author's concerns, a movement away from the metaphysical anxieties of the Western world *entre deux guerres* to the more immediate social disruptions of Argentina in the 1940s and 1950s. (One might reiterate the fact that "The End" and "The South," though included in *Ficciones,* were also written during the Perón era.) Appropriately, in most of these action-packed narratives the fantasy is minimal, hardly more than a final mental twist (for example, "The Dead Man," "The Life of Tadeo Isidoro Cruz"); this tendency reaches its utmost expression in "The Intruder," a sex-and-violence yarn from which any "Borgesian" fancifulness is completely absent. The disquieting naturalism of this piece (which was written in 1966 and added to later editions of *El Aleph*) prefigures the straight blood-and-guts narratives that make up much of *Doctor Brodie's Report,* in which "The Intruder," significantly, is also included.

These glimmers of realism in *El Aleph* can sometimes take a turn that is atypical for Borges. "Emma Zunz" and "The Zahir," for instance, are studies in mental pathology that, were it not for their additional mixtures of fantasy and suspense, could well be classed as "psychological" literature. "Deutsches Requiem" is actually a portrait of so topical a kind of individual (for 1949) as a German Nazi officer. And yet, by a curious paradox, those tales from *El Aleph* that show Borges at his most fantastical—"Averroës's Search," "The Theologians," "The Immortal"—are far more bookish and abstract than any of their equivalents in *Ficciones.* As we can see, *El Aleph* presents, in somewhat uneasy company and in extreme form, the two opposite poles of Borges's fiction writing—on the one hand, a self-consciously mental and intellectual quality and on the other, an almost mindlessly unreflexive kind of action narrative.

One area in which *El Aleph* diverges from *Ficciones* is that of detective fiction. Strictly speaking, there are no true instances of the murder-mystery genre here, no narratives that combine the traditional enigmatic crime with the search, chase, capture, and resolution pulled off by a master sleuth or tough cop. However, several pieces in *El Aleph* ("Ibn-Hakkan," "The House of Asterion," "The Life of Tadeo Isidoro Cruz," "The Man on the Threshold," even "The Theologians") do present assemblages of clues, puzzles whose aim is to involve the alert reader. Of these, only the artfully clever "Ibn-Hakkan" and "Asterion" approximate the sleuth story somewhat, and they lack the richer suggestiveness of their *Ficciones* counterparts.

The narrative with the mock-overstated title "Ibn-Hakkan al-Bokhari, Dead in his Labyrinth" comes closest, at least in its raw materials, to the classic detective tale: it contains a crime, a sleuth of sorts, and a far-fetched solution that crops up some twenty-five years after the bizarre events. The story opens in Cornwall, where two young English friends visit an enormous red labyrinth by the sea. Poet Dunraven tells the mathematician Unwin of his earliest childhood memory—the arrival, in company with a pet lion and a black slave, of Ibn-Hakkan al-Bokhari, who forthwith ordered the construction of this vast maze. The Moor then visited Pastor Allaby and gave him the following account. Al-Bokhari and his cowardly cousin Zaid had long tyrannized a remote central African people. When an uprising took place, the two despots fled with much loot. Both reached safety in a desert cave, but cowardly Zaid's peaceful sleep so enraged al-Bokhari, who was troubled by nightmares, that he knifed his cousin to death. A few minutes later, Zaid's ghost appeared to him, vowing vengeance. Al-Bokhari then fled to Cornwall, where he proposed to elude his cousin's ghost by hiding in the labyrinth. Pastor Allaby, a scholarly man, later confirmed in back issues of the *Times* the story about two deposed African kings. One day al-Bokhari burst into Allaby's rectory and frantically blurted out that Zaid's ghost had just arrived and killed the slave and the lion; al-Bokhari begged for help but suddenly ran out. Puzzled that this frightened man could have terrorized an entire people, Allaby headed for the labyrinth, where he indeed found lion, slave, and master all dead, their faces smashed.

Unwin then notes a trapdoor in the labyrinth, ponders inconsistencies in Dunraven's often-told story, and pronounces it all a lie. Two nights later, in a London pub, Unwin explains to Dunraven what really had happened: no real fugitive would hide in something as obvious as a seaside labyrinth; a big city like London is a far more effective hideout. Unwin had also thought it odd that cowardly Zaid should sleep so soundly in the desert, but the case was actually the reverse—it was Zaid who couldn't sleep and, being too craven to murder the king, ran off with half the booty. Zaid then built the conspicuous labyrinth at a port city so as to lure his cousin, who inevitably had got wind of Zaid and his strange house. The real al-Bokhari then came for revenge but, underestimating his cowardly relative, entered unarmed. Zaid, from his trapdoor, then shot lion, slave, and king. Next he bashed in all their heads—a shrewd move, since one disfigured face might have raised doubts, but three equally deformed corpses would have the gruesomely persuasive power of a series. Zaid was understandably agitated when he saw Allaby because he had just finished off al-Bokhari and was headed back to Africa for the remaining loot. Zaid thus became the very man he was impersonating.

A parody of crime literature, "Ibn-Hakkan al-Bokhari" is reminiscent of "Death and the Compass," but the parody is now stretched to the point of pure caricature. Zaid's antics seem designed expressly to invite disbelief; the plot itself (a fraudulent Arab monarch, posing as the true king, who installs himself in a seaside labyrinth with a lion and a slave and sets up all this elaborate machinery to entrap his pursuer) is a scenario so marvelously far-fetched as to surpass Father Brown's most exotic escapades. This story, in fact, plays on a trick illustrated by G. K. Chesterton in "The Blast of the Book," a tongue-in-cheek entertainment depicting some spurious disappearances that are arranged as a regularly recurring series by a clever prankster, who thus gives the "crimes" an authentic air. "Ibn-Hakkan al-Bokhari," however, sets forth events so implausible that Borges seems to be lampooning Chesterton himself.

In addition, the noncriminal characters here are droll spoofs of detective-story stereotypes. The two young Englishmen serve as latter-day avatars (colorfully exaggerated, of course) of a binary opposition made famous by Dr. Watson and Sherlock Holmes. On the one hand, there is Dunraven, bearded and verbose, a garrulous, bad poet, who is so enamored of the bizarre that he swallows Zaid's story whole, never questioning its inconsistencies. On the other, there is Unwin, the reasoning and sober mathematician, laconic and wise, who smokes a pipe (like Sherlock Holmes) and who, in an extreme instance of mental sleuthing, with only the slightest contact with the elements of the problem at hand, solves a crime with scientific rigor at a distance of twenty-five years. Borges assigns this amateur detective some appropriate connections with his academic field. Unwin has published a paper on Pierre de Fermat, a French mathematician (1601–1655) who worked with Pascal and who established the foundations for the modern theory of numbers in the unusual form of personal jottings in his copy of the works of Diophantus (a Greek-Alexandrian algebraist). When first seeing the vast labyrinth, Unwin also reflects in passing on Nicholas of Cusa (1401–1464), a cardinal and theologian whose studies in physics and mathematics were far ahead of their time and who even formulated a hypothesis of a rotating earth.

The English names of the characters also hint lightheartedly at their respective roles. That poet Dunraven obscures things is intimated by "dun," while "raven" associates him with Poe. The word Unwin suggests "unwind"; indeed, this mentally active mathematician unwinds the tangled net handed down from Zaid to Pastor Allaby to credulous Dunraven. The bookish Reverend Allaby serves as Zaid's front man, an unwitting patsy whose very name reveals his function: he is the murderer's "alibi."

Still more hocus-pocus is at work in the formal structure of "Ibn-Hakkan al-Bokhari." To perhaps an even greater extent than "The Garden of Forking Paths," this story is an elaborate series of narratives-within-narratives, their characters and actions further linked by certain humorous parallelisms. Beginning with the outer frame of the story, there are: (1) the impersonal narrator's florid introduction to the two young Englishmen, (2) Dunraven's wide-eyed telling of al-Bokhari's arrival, (3) Pastor Allaby's account of al-Bokhari's visit to his rectory, and, at the exact center of the piece, (4) al-Bokhari's outlandish yarn about himself and his cousin. Then, in reverse, radiating outward from the center are: (4) "al-Bokhari's" phony tale of horror about the arrival of Zaid's ghost, (3) Pastor Allaby's account of his visit to "al-Bokhari's" labyrinth, (2) Unwin's spirited retelling of what really transpired between "al-Bokhari" and Zaid, and (1) the impersonal narrator's final look at the two young Englishmen. In addition, there is Allaby's sermon (printed elsewhere in the volume), entitled "The Two Kings and Their Two Labyrinths"—a whimsical and ironic two-page tale of an Arab monarch who avenges a former humiliation (a Babylonian king had mischievously dropped him in a labyrinth) by capturing his enemy and abandoning him in the deadliest "labyrinth" of them all, the desert. As if all this were not enough, there is yet another dose of story-within-story—Allaby's sermon does not recount the events directly but begins by invoking certain "chroniclers worthy of trust."

Further strengthening all this legerdemain are the numerous parallels and correspondences between the narratives. Allaby's sermon of the two kings contains in capsule form the conflict between al-Bokhari and Zaid and even matches the separate episodes of desert and labyrinth in Zaid's account. The contrast of intellects between Unwin and Dunraven parallels the opposition between tough al-Bokhari and cowardly Zaid; Unwin is tough-minded and sober, Dunraven excitable and soft. The sleepless night that Zaid spends with al-Bokhari in the desert cave has its corresponding episode in Dunraven's sleepless night with Unwin inside the labyrinth. A further parallel to the desert-labyrinth polarity that marks the two Arab narratives is the little adventure of Unwin and Dunraven, which begins on the sandy dunes of Cornwall and ends inside a pub somewhere in the maze of London. Their conversations take place in the summer of 1914, on the eve of England's great war; the story of al-Bokhari in turn begins on the eve of his overthrow. The humorously rhetorical tone that characterizes the entire story is established in the long and bombastic opening sentence, with its grandiose nature imagery, its pompous evocation of Dunraven's forebears, its mock-tragic observations on passing time.

Formally, as we have seen, "Ibn-Hakkan al-Bokhari" resembles the crime narratives in *Ficciones,* but it lacks their human depth and richness. There are no problems in "Ibn-Hakkan" other than the crime itself, no sense of tragedy similar to that underlying Lönnrot's actions, nothing like the tangled web of personal ties, ethnic loyalties, and family honor that helps give Yu Tsun's deposition its touching quality. Even the deliciously ridiculous use of parody here operates more at the surface level (the depiction of bizarre events and exaggeration of gestures and traits), in stark contrast to "Death and the Compass," which turns the entire detective genre inside-out. The latter further impresses us as a meditation on a way of life, an unsettling parable about the dangers accruing to intellect pursued for its own sake. "Ibn-Hakkan al-Bokhari, Dead in His Labyrinth" is one of Borges's wittiest pieces, but it does not go beyond its divertissement flavor, its humorous intent. This is skilled but lightweight Borges.

The three-page story "The House of Asterion" works in much the same way; it too is an ingenious literary puzzle concerning a labyrinth, the solution of which is spelled out at the very end. The bulk of the narrative consists of a monologue by aloof and proud Asterion, who lives without furniture in "a house like no other on the face of the earth." This utterly unique son of a queen insists that he is not a prisoner in his vast house but a willing resident who, during his one venture into the outside world, was terrified at the sight of human faces. And so, he spends his days wandering about, playing solitary games in the infinite galleries of his house, occasionally even imagining a visit by a second Asterion. Every nine years there is a ceremony in which nine men enter his house and fall without Asterion ever bloodying his hands. One of these men, before dying, had mentioned a "redeemer" for Asterion. Since that time, Asterion has expected this redeemer, wondering if its form will be that of bull, man, or some combination. Suddenly, in a brief four-line epilogue, Theseus appears on the scene, sword in hand, boasting that "the Minotaur scarcely defended himself" (L, 140; EA, 70).

The final sentence, then, reveals that "Asterion" is the Minotaur, his "house" the Cretan labyrinth, his "redeemer" the legendary hero Theseus. Borges obliquely shows his hand in his epigraph to the story, wherein he cites the *Bibliothiki*, a lengthy treatise dealing with the Greek heroes and gods that was written by Apollodorus, a prolific Athenian scholar who lived in the second century B.C. A Hellenist who happens to be well acquainted with this esoteric item will perhaps catch the name "Asterion" and follow from the outset the drift of Borges's narrative, but those readers who have forgotten the details of this particular myth may find useful my paraphrase of Apollodorus's account in *Bibliothèque*.

> When King Asterionus of Crete died, his stepson Minos claimed that the gods had chosen him for the throne. As proof, he publicly asked Neptune to make a bull spring out from the sea, promising the god a sacrificial tribute of the animal. A beautiful bull did emerge out of the ocean, and Minos was crowned King of Crete. But the bull was never sacrificed—Minos simply put the beast out to pasture. Angry at this breach of promise, Neptune made Minos's wife, Queen Pasiphae, fall madly in love with the bull. Through an elaborate ruse, Pasiphae lured and had sexual intercourse with the bull. From this union there was born Asterion, the Minotaur, who had a bull's head and a man's body. Minos then kept the Minotaur hidden away inside a labyrinth. In order to feed the monster, Minos demanded from the Athenians a periodic tribute of seven young men. Theseus, who was included in the third such group, resolved to put an end to this curse on his people. In Crete, Minos's daughter Ariadne fell in love with Theseus, furnished him a sword and a ball of string to help him find his way out. In a bloody battle, Theseus slew the Minotaur. After this he took Ariadne with him.

"The House of Asterion" indirectly hints at this myth by means of numerous clues. The "house," with its infinite doors, galleries, courtyards, and pools, is clearly labyrinthine in character. Asterion justifies the total absence of furnishings as a mark of his austerity, but actually one never thinks of labyrinths as having furniture. On two occasions Asterion alludes to the sea outside, which by this time the alert reader may have guessed is the Mediterranean surrounding Crete. Asterion's boasts about his royal mother—Queen Pasiphae—and his own singularity are obviously accurate. On the other hand, he exaggerates the uniqueness of his house, defensively dismissing rumors about a labyrinth in Egypt—a bit of a delusion, since Herodotus and Pliny indeed mention such an edifice, built by Amenemhe III of the twelfth dynasty, in about 2300 B.C.[1]

Asterion describes his activities, his surroundings, and himself in terms befitting a creature that is part animal. Needing no furniture, he instead possesses objects such as "mangers" and "drinking troughs," artifacts ordinarily not in human use. The games Asterion plays are notably animal-like—charging, running, crouching, jumping; he actually compares himself to a ram and thereby alerts readers to the fact that Asterion is *not* a ram. With no common experiences between humans and himself, Asterion has never bothered to learn to read or write. Human faces, "as discolored and flat as the palm of one's hand" (L, 138; EA, 67), understandably frighten a creature whose taurine face is rugged, snout-nosed, and brown colored; the quotation at the same time suggests that the narrator actually has hands. These hands Asterion never bloodies, for the simple reason that the dirty task of slaughtering the nine men is done by his horns. At the end of the monologue, Asterion all but gives away the story's secret when he asks himself whether his redeemer "will be a bull with the face of a man? Or will he be like me?" (L, 140; EA, 70).

All this is quite clever, Borges the puzzle maker at his best. What makes "The House of Asterion" so special, however, is the way in which a three-thousand-year-old myth is turned completely upside down, "revised" as it were. Where tradition evokes an epic battle to the death, Borges's version provides no struggle at all—no risk, no heroism, almost no blood. More important, the legendary Theseus—in standard renditions the brave hero of a cosmic drama—here gets short shrift; in lieu of a noble, godlike warrior performing courageous deeds and enunciating elevated words, we find an ordinary, slightly smug fellow, as suggested by his colloquial, somewhat prosaic remark, "Would you believe it . . . ?" What steals Theseus's thunder, of course, is the Minotaur, who is depicted as a more interesting and complex figure—pathetically lonely and proud, dangerous but also frightened and misunderstood; he even seems to kill without malice, as part of his assigned role. Aware that he inspires horror and disgust in humans, Asterion finds a defense in his blue-blooded ancestry (thereby placing himself above ordinary men) and makes his freakishness into a subjective asset, priding himself on being unique. Indeed, his own singularity he praises to an exaggerated degree, comparing himself to "the intricate sun" (L, 140; EA, 69) and going so far as to negate facts such as the existence of other labyrinths. At the same time, however, this unique being intensely craves companionship and plays fantastical games in which he imagines another creature exactly like himself. This is the inevitable wish of any singular creature; the realization of such a dream is the only possible cure for his loneliness (a Papagena for a Papageno) for, as Asterion so wistfully remarks, "the days and nights are long" (L, 139; EA, 68).

There are even biblical overtones in Asterion's monologue. His nine victims enter the house "so that I may deliver them from evil" (L, 140; EA, 69)—an echo of the Lord's Prayer. A more elaborate scriptural reference crops up when Asterion admits feeling no more sadness or pain, "because I know that my redeemer lives and will finally rise above the dust" (L, 140; EA 69). This is a verbatim allusion to Job 19:25—"For I know that my redeemer liveth, and that he shall stand at the latter day upon the earth." (The Portuguese, though not the Spanish, version of this passage speaks not of "earth" but, as Borges does, of "dust.") This particular reference hints at a parallel between Asterion's plight and Job's suffering, and both biblical allusions help place the Minotaur on a certain spiritual plane, in an eschatological context that transcends his beastly nature. In addition, the phrase "deliver from evil" (Asterion's euphemism for "to kill") gives a religious tinge to the slaughter of the nine men and suggests a basic naiveté in Asterion, who, much like a child, is unaware that his actions are looked upon as immoral. In similar fashion, the biblical word "redeemer" is not his misconstruction but appears to be his own oblique term for "executioner," the person or other such being who will finally deliver him from isolation.

The net effect of Borges's story is to reverse our habitual sympathies; we are made to feel something for the Minotaur while taking Theseus less seriously. Borges achieves this by restoring to the often-maligned beast such rightful facts as a royal ancestry and a proper name and by giving him a developed consciousness and a human share of existential anxieties— attributes not customarily associated with fabled monsters. The very beginning of Asterion's monologue ("I know they accuse me of ignorance" [L, 137; EA, 67]) is an original touch, for one never thinks of the Minotaur as knowing anything, much less as given to self-justification. Borges's story initiates a perspective that looks forward to certain revisionist literary works of recent vintage—for example, John Gardner's *Grendel,* which recounts the Beowulf saga from the monster's point of view and depicts Hrothgar's soldiers as less than noble; Aimé Césaire's *A Tempest* and Roberto Fernández Retamar's *Calibán,* respectively a play and an essay, both of which invert Shakespeare by portraying Caliban as victim, Prospero as oppressor; or the ironic Hollywood westerns of the 1970s (for example, *Blazing Saddles*), in which all the old cowboy conventions were mercilessly spoofed.

Borges once asserted that this story was polished off in a couple of days, prompted by three blank pages that were unexpectedly available in an issue of *Anales de Buenos Aires,* a literary magazine with which he was connected. It appears, however, that this erudite occasional piece went through more than a few days' gestation. In his epilogue to *El Aleph,* Borges traces his inspiration for "The House of Asterion" to a painting by G. F. Watts, a renowned Victorian artist who is today mostly forgotten. G. K. Chesterton included a reproduction of this painting, entitled "The Minotaur," in his critical study *G. F. Watts,* a book Borges cites a number of times in *Other Inquisitions.*[2] Watts's painting shows a wrinkled, lonesome, and rather pitiful creature leaning on his rooftop walls, staring out at a vast blue sea. Depicted as squashing a tiny bird (as naturally befits this savage beast), Watts's Minotaur nonetheless conveys a distinctly pathetic impression, even more so than does Borges's little story.

The story entitled "The Life of Tadeo Isidoro Cruz (1829–1874)" also recasts a myth, this time a local legend well known and beloved by Argentines. Here, however, Borges does not exactly invert the materials; he retells the myth not through the consciousness of the traditional villain but from the perspective of a lesser character whom the legendary hero befriends. The narrative sketches out a rapid outline of Cruz's life and touches upon such essential data as his being the illegitimate child of a gaucho soldier and a camp follower, his upbringing as a plains rustic, his marriage, and his murder of a taunting drover. This bloody incident brings about Cruz's flight to a thicket (where he takes on an entire police squadron), his violent capture, his sentencing to a term of frontier warfare against Indians, and his rise to the rank of sergeant. Above all, the narrative dwells on the decisive night when Cruz receives orders to capture a notorious outlaw. Here the situation does indeed reverse itself: when Cruz and his soldiers hunt down their man among some reeds, the man fights back so bravely and effectively that Sergeant Cruz, recognizing himself in the outlaw, cries out his solidarity with this man of courage. He turns against his own troops, fighting side by side with the deserter— Martín Fierro.

As in "The End" (in *Ficciones*), Borges saves for the last lines the fact that his story builds on *Martín Fierro,* José Hernández's nineteenth-century protest poem that quickly achieved the status of a kind of national epic. In contrast with "The End," however, this piece is not a sequel to Hernández's original but an elaboration of one of its episodes. A first-time reader who lacks a deep acquaintance with Hernández's celebrated work will come upon Borges's final revelation with some sense of surprise, but even to an Argentine reader (who presumably would have encountered *Martín Fierro* in school and would then have seen and heard references to the poem countless times since) the underlying link between Hernández and Borges may be less than obvious from the outset. To begin with, though Sergeant Cruz is Hernández's most important secondary character, in the poem he is always alluded to simply as "Cruz," without the Christian names here added by Borges.

This superimposition of concocted names upon a received one represents in microcosm the procedure by which Borges puts together a distinct life and personality for Cruz. As in "The House of Asterion," Borges takes the basic data of the original myth, rearranges them, and further combines them with materials of his own invention. From Hernández's account, Borges retains Cruz's lengthy spell as family man (I, 1741–1880; reduced by Borges to a single sentence), his stint as sergeant (I, 2053–2064), and his eventual death from smallpox (pt. II, line 907). Certain other facts are preserved but are altered by Borges for the sake of deeper significance. For example, in the original poem, Cruz is offered a military job, not punitively conscripted. He also never kills a heckler at a campsite; the only comparable incident is the occasion when Cruz cuts the strings on a wiseacre's guitar in a saloon.

On the other hand, Cruz's shift in loyalties is conveyed in a language extremely close to that of the original. Borges's Cruz discovers that his destiny is to be "a lone *wolf,* not a gregarious dog" (TA, 85; EA, 57). This apparently banal figure of speech is a telescoping of certain images invoked by Hernández in his account of the skirmish: Martín Fierro describes the death of one of Cruz's militiamen with the comparison "y ya salió como el *perro* / cuando le pisan la cola" ("away he went like a *dog* / whose tail's been stepped on" [pt. I, lines 1553–1554]). A few lines later, two other soldiers attack Fierro "lo mesmo que *perros* sueltos" (like a couple of *dogs* on the loose" [pt. I, line 1566]). These, then, are the "gregarious dogs" whom Tadeo Isidoro Cruz rejects. By contrast, when Hernández's Fierro characterizes the sergeant (who is now fighting on Fierro's side), he remarks that "y el Cruz era como *lobo* / que defiende su guarida" ("this guy Cruz fought like a *wolf* / defendin' his den" [pt. I, lines 1631–1632]), this being the wolf that Cruz, in Borges's narrative, has chosen to be.[3]

A yet lengthier allusion to the original text occurs when Borges says: "Cruz . . . called out that he would not be party to the crime of killing a brave man, and began fighting against his own soldiers, shoulder to shoulder with Martín Fierro, the deserter" (TA, 85; EA, 57). This passage is taken almost verbatim from Hernández, whose Fierro recites:

> un gaucho . . . pegó el grito
> y dijo "Cruz no consiente
> que se cometa el delito
> de mater ansí un valiente!"
> > Y ahí no más se me aparió
> > dentrándole a la partida. (pt. I, lines 1623–1628)

> (One of the gauchos . . . cried out
> and said, "Cruz won't stand
> for this! I won't let you bastards
> kill a brave man like this!"
> > And so then he joined with me
> > and fought against the police.)

(The reader will note that, in the Spanish, Cruz's speech is virtually identical in both works.) It is only appropriate that, at the high point of the story, when Sergeant Cruz is undergoing his *prise de conscience* (in Aristotelian terms both the recognition and the reversal of the drama), Borges should rely on the words composed by Hernández, words so much a part of their context and of the original myth that no other speech, even one penned by Borges, could hope to surpass them.

Most all the remaining facts of the life of Tadeo Isidoro Cruz—his conception in a shed, his work as a cattle drover, his military adventures— are invented by Borges. The aim of these added details, of course, is to drive home a larger and more essential truth—the social marginality of a drifter who ultimately sees himself in the loner Martín Fierro. Borges often makes this point indirectly, not by stating what Cruz actually *is* but by dwelling on precisely what Cruz is *not*. For example, in Hernández's narrative, Cruz's recollections make no mention of cities; from this lacuna, Borges ventures an observation that Cruz was to die without ever having seen a city, a point he then illustrates with an episode in which the gaucho refuses to move on to Buenos Aires. By this dialectical procedure, Borges emphasizes still more Cruz's rustic primitivism. In similar fashion, Borges contrasts Cruz's self-discovery with that of Alexander the Great and Charles XII of Sweden, only to mention that Cruz, who is an illiterate and basic sort of individual, learns not from books or from past models but from his own present experience. The perfunctory manner in which Borges reports the gaucho's military career subtly underlines Cruz's indifference to the national enterprise, his lack of any social or regional loyalties. Finally, Cruz's realization that his shoulder braid and uniform constrict him, together with his act of discarding his kepi as he joins Fierro, are details that spell out Cruz's effective rejection of all conventional ties. These and numerous other particulars in Borges's story help fill out Hernández's initial portrait of a man who stands completely outside established Argentine society.

Most significant of all of Borges's additions to Cruz's life, however, are certain actions and phrases that, in Hernández's poem, are attributed not to Cruz but to Martín Fierro. This transfer obviously emphasizes the sameness that brings the two men together in Borges's account. The incident that puts Cruz on the lam in Borges's story (the murder of the taunting drover) is akin to Fierro's own violent confrontation with a boastful tough (pt. I, line 1305). In Borges's narrative, shortly after the recounting of the murder, we read the following about Cruz as he hides from the law in the countryside: "A few nights later, the cries of a startled *plover* [*chajá* bird] warned him he had been ringed by the police. He tested his knife in a thick clump of grass and, to keep from entangling his feet, took off his spurs" (TA, 82; EA, 55). This passage consists of a cluster of sharply distinct allusions to what Martín Fierro, the original murderer fleeing the police, recounts in Hernández's poem. The cry of the bird is described by Fierro thus:

> Me encontraba, como digo,
> en aquella soledá,
> entre tanta escuridá,
> echando al viento mis quejas
> cuando el *grito del chajá*
> me hizo parer las orejas. (pt. I, lines 1469–1474)

> (Like I said, one night I was
> in that lonely place,
> with all that darkness.
> when a [*plover*] bird
> made me prick up my ears.[4])

Later in Borges's narrative, when Cruz is about to fight with Fierro, he once again hears a "startled plover" (TA, 84; EA, 56), a sound that makes him realize he had lived this moment before, when he too was an escaped criminal. This repeated phraseology makes especially evident the relationship between Cruz's earlier flight and Fierro's current escape.

In a stronger vein, Cruz's prebattle precautions as a lone fugitive are described with an extended quotation from Hernández; however, this quotation is from the account of *Fierro's* own preparations before engaging Cruz and the police. Borges's narrative, as we saw above, shows Cruz removing his spurs and testing his knife on the grass; similarly, Fierro states:

> Me refalé las espuelas,
> para no peliar con grillos; . . .
> y en una mate de paja
> probé el filo del cuchillo. (pt. I, lines 1499–1504)
>
> (I slipped off my spurs
> so I could fight easier; . . .
> and on a tuft of grass
> I tested the edge of my knife.)

As occurs in the case of Cruz's exalted cry of solidarity with Fierro, the language in this passage is virtually identical to that of the original, except that the action and many of the words are Fierro's. A reader of Borges's story who also knows the *Martín Fierro* will inevitably recognize these verbal fragments from Hernández's great gaucho myth.

Needless to say, the real purpose of this fast-moving series of episodes is to develop Borges's idea of the Double and to give tangible shape to his fanciful notion that, by virtue of their shared experiences, attitudes, and traits, Fierro and Cruz are essentially one. Borges's choice of characters here is hardly accidental; in the whole of Hernández's long poem, only Cruz brings to Fierro the precious companionship of an equal, the consolations of solidarity with a man much like himself. In Hernández's own sequel, the two gauchos actually stay together in Indian country for a number of years until Cruz's death. Hence, there is already present in Hernández's original poem an implied dynamic of the Double, that is, a relationship between two individuals who are simultaneously "the other" and "the same." Fierro himself acknowledges this fact when, following Cruz's autobiographical recollections, he remarks:

Ya veo que somos los dos
astilla del mesmo palo:
yo paso por gaucho malo
y usté anda del mesmo modo.... (pt. I, lines 2143–2146)

(I can see that the two of us
are chips off the same block.
I'm known as a gaucho outlaw
and you go around the same way.)

Borges's story simply pushes Fierro's observation to the limit by con-
densing and heightening it through Cruz's more dramatically fanciful realization that "the other man was himself" (TA, 85; EA, 56).

The likeness that Borges sets up between the two men, this "identity"
as it were, is enriched by the intermingling of another general idea present
throughout the story. Borges frequently interrupts his action-packed narrative to discourse abstractly on the notion that "any life . . . is made up
essentially of a *single moment*—the moment in which a man finds out,
once and for all, who he is" (TA, 83; EA, 55). This sententia, with its
wealth of underlying thought and experience, and the accompanying
theme of the Double are the two poles around which all of the action
revolves; without both of them, "The Life of Tadeo Isidoro Cruz" would
be little more than a conventional and well-written tale of adventure.

What gives this story its inherent interest is precisely those general reflections concerning personal existence (most everyone can look back at
some period when his or her essential self and authentic life-course became clear) that are singled out and concretely illustrated by Borges. With
surely intended irony, this idea flatly contradicts the title's use of the word
"life" (which in Borges's original Spanish was the even more pointed
term "Biografía"), for, to the reader's surprise, Cruz's "life" is not seen
as the aggregate of facts and dates that make up his existence, because
these are purely incidental to the special moment of self-discovery and
choice. As Borges's narrative asserts, that moment of self-awareness "ex-
hausts [Cruz's] story." On the other hand, the epigraph from Yeats—
"I'm looking for the face I had / Before the world was made"—hints
vividly, again in contradiction to the story's title, at an essential Cruz that
predates Cruz's own existence, an essence he paradoxically discovers
through the mediation of another. On the night he saw Fierro, Cruz
"glimpsed his own face . . . heard his own name" (TA, 83; EA, 55).

These thematic points are further emphasized by certain parallels within the narrative. Three bloody incidents punctuate Cruz's life, all of them occurring in nighttime darkness and all but the first one reaching their high point at dawn: the death of Cruz's unnamed father in 1829, Cruz's own act of violence and capture in 1849, and the encounter with Fierro in 1870. Cruz, who grows up an orphan, significantly discovers himself and joins Fierro in the very spot from which his unknown father had come. Borges thus hints at the idea of regeneration, a rebirth of Cruz's long-lost gaucho self, as well as suggesting a second adulthood, now beginning exactly twenty-one years after Cruz's own skirmish with the police.[5] (Borges makes use of his own family roots here: Cruz's father is killed fighting the liberal cavalry of Colonel Suárez, who happens to be Borges's great-grandfather, and whose name was actually Isidoro.)

"The Life of Tadeo Isidoro Cruz" is as tightly organized and richly textured as many of Borges's best stories; moreover, the idea it sets forth about the development of an individual is in itself interesting. In addition, the piece makes a compassionate and moving complement to *Martín Fierro;* one can no longer read the Cruz chapters in Hernández's masterpiece without bearing in mind their re-elaboration and enrichment at the hands of Borges. Nevertheless, there may be a problem of accessibility here, inasmuch as Borges builds his narrative with the materials of another literary work; much of the story's impact depends on the reader's knowledge of the original poem. In an earlier discussion of "The End," I noted the limitations of this approach, particularly when Hernández's poem, an Argentine cultural treasure, carries few resonances outside of Latin America's Southern Cone. Some critics would defend, even praise, this procedure on grounds of "intertextuality," but this strikes me merely as a way of justifying the "postmodern" aesthetic of literature-about-literature.[6] On the other hand, one could simply say that this is a story for Argentines, not for foreigners, and that is every bit as valid an argument as the "universalist" one.

The "Story of the Warrior and the Captive" also depicts, with somewhat greater depth of thought and feeling, the experience treated in "Cruz": an individual's radical shift in group loyalties. The piece opens with an account of Droctulft, a real-life Lombard warrior who (as Borges interprets it) found himself so taken by the complexity of sixth-century Ravenna, so moved by the grandeur of late imperial urban life, that he eventually changed sides and defended the city against his fellow tribesmen. The people of Ravenna in turn buried Droctulft in one of their temples and paid homage to the barbarians with a touching inscription in Latin verse. Droctulft was, to Borges, a man ahead of his times, an unwitting prophet whose conversion anticipates the eventual conversion of all Lombards, who soon adapted to Italian ways, as did many Germanic tribes.

Borges feels moved by what he sees of himself in this story, specifically by its resemblance to an anecdote he had often heard from his own grandmother, an Englishwoman, who now turns up as a character in "Story of the Warrior and the Captive." In the narrative, Señora de Borges bemoans (as she was wont to do in the 1870s) her fate as sole English lady on the pampas. One day the señora is taken to meet a blue-eyed Indian woman who is also of English birth. Perhaps expecting something, the two women feel a brief shudder of kinship, but the younger woman now speaks a halting English commingled with an Indian tongue. She explains how, following her arrival from Yorkshire fifteen years ago, her parents died in a raid by Indians; the Indians then raised the orphan child and one of the chieftains subsequently became her husband. Señora de Borges, horrified at the idea of an *Englishwoman* reduced to such barbarism, entreats her opposite number to abandon this tribal life. But the younger woman is happy as an Indian, and the two part company. A few years later, Señora de Borges, suddenly finding herself widowed, may have thought of the Indian-Englishwoman as "a monstrous mirror of her own destiny" (L, 130; EA, 51). Now, in the 1940s, her literary grandson dimly perceives, despite the enormous time and space between the two stories, a basic likeness and identity between the Lombard barbarian who chose the city and the young woman who opted for the desert. In their respective times, a comparable "secret impulse" (L, 131; EA, 52) drove these two individuals, worlds and cultures apart, to opposing ways of life.

The "Story of the Warrior and the Captive" is held together by an idea still more fanciful than the one Borges entertains in connection with Cruz: namely, that the particular situations of a Nordic warrior and a Victorian English girl over ten thousand miles and a thousand years apart—the former abandoning tribal "barbarism" in order to cast his lot with urban "civilization" and the latter rejecting her ties with "civilization" in order to live happily in a state of "barbarism"—constitute one story.

The narrative builds upon this dual opposition, now blurring it, now accentuating it, and in the long run doing both at once. This intellectual play of opposites and affinities begins with the title, in which the juxtaposition of "the Warrior and the Captive" inevitably suggests an action yarn about a rugged soldier and his female victim (the Spanish word employed here is *cautiva*). The reader of the piece eventually realizes that the two individuals have no direct relation, let alone contact, with each other. They are divided by time, distance, mode of behavior, type of cultural loyalties, and manner of historical transmissions (written versus oral); and—the supreme irony—the warrior of the narrative turns "soft," the captive woman "barbaric" and "hard." Moreover, the reader finds out that there is not one story here but two highly distinct *stories.* Yet in the end Borges applies his special talent for seeing unusual connections and convinces us that these two sets of events actually make up a single tale. In the grand scheme of things (at least to Borges's mind), it all amounts to one larger narrative.

The conceit of the Double, then, begins in the title. But in addition there is a subplot with a secondary fancy, a playing upon the identity of the two women who, their opposed cultural ties notwithstanding, are both English, both captives of the Argentine hinterland, and both married to men of arms. Hence, whereas the Lombard warrior and the Indian-Englishwoman are in a subtle way "philosophical" doubles of each other, the two women share a concrete and immediately discernible identity and thus form a second set of Doubles. The *cautiva* of the title could therefore be construed as referring either to the Indian-Englishwoman or to Señora de Borges, or even to both, since they after all embody the same problem. By the same token, the term "warrior" could include not only Droctulft but also the young woman's Indian husband and even Borges's grandfather, Colonel Borges. As it turns out, then, the "Story of the Warrior and the Captive" comprises as many as three stories working within its few pages.

These narratives are held together by an intricate network of resemblances and contrasts. Both Droctulft and the young Englishwoman come from the north and end up resettling someplace in the south. Both of them, at a certain point, choose to stay with their new circumstances. On the other hand, the two women find themselves forced to stay in Argentina because of the sudden deaths of immediate relatives. More telling, however, are the numerous differences that neatly set off warrior from captive. The Lombard forsakes a tribal past he had known in the wild lands lying between the Elbe and the Danube in order to take sides with a city in the vast Roman Empire. The young Englishwoman was from a province in the vast British Empire, yet she chose to remain in tribal life on the wild lands of the pampas. Droctulft (Borges speculates) did not understand the language of his adopted imperial home; in reverse fashion, the English girl living among the Indians can hardly speak the language of her former imperial home. Droctulft's epitaph points to

the contrast between his terrifying appearance and his simple good nature; on the other hand, the girl's blue eyes and lithe body, with their
suggestions of a quiet passivity, are vividly contradicted by her strong
hands and her involvement in bloody rituals. Droctulft, whose origins are
"the inextricable forests of the boar and the bison" (L, 128; EA, 48), is
dazzled by the complexity and grandeur of the organism of city life, with
its "statues, temples, gardens, rooms, amphitheaters, vases, columns"
(L, 128; EA, 48); the young Englishwoman, conversely, tells with loyal
detail of her life on the plains, with its "horsehide shelters, fires made of
dry manure, feasts of scorched meat" (L, 130; EA, 51). When she enters
the headquarters of Junín (not with amazement, as did Droctulft at
Ravenna, but with indifference and suspicion), the greater sense of scale
instilled in her by the desert makes "everything seem . . . too small for
her: doors, walls, furniture" (L, 129, EA, 50)—a marked contrast to
Droctulft's awed response before advanced material life in Ravenna.

The respective style and procedure of the two tales differ in accordance
with their subject matter. Because Droctulft moves from "barbarism" to
"civilization," the narrative texture is appropriately erudite. There are
quotations in Latin (including one from Spinoza, "sub specie aeterni-
tatis"), a biblical allusion, a footnoted reference to Gibbon's *Decline and
Fall,* and an acknowledgement of philosopher Benedetto Croce and ancient scribe Paul the Deacon as basic sources. As befits a narrative that
looks ahead to the assimilation of the Lombard tribe into Italic culture,
Borges's story of Droctulft culminates with a speculation about Dante—
the possible blood-tie between the greatest late medieval Italian poet and
an early medieval Lombard soldier. It is interesting to note that, beginning with the warrior's arrival in Ravenna, Borges narrates the remainder
of Droctulft's tale in the present tense, thereby giving the events a certain
immediate flavor and also anticipating Borges's final flourish about warrior and captive belonging to one timeless story.

In decided contrast, the encounter between the Indian-Englishwoman
and Señora de Borges is narrated in a direct, unadorned, and nonerudite
way, as befits an account of an incident in the wilds where a young British
girl has left behind European complexity and adapted to an allegedly
simple and barbaric life. No learned fancies, no names of authors are
brought to bear upon this portion of the story. Borges claims to have
written down the entire incident just as his grandmother had told it to
him[7]—an assertion that can be neither proved nor disproved today—but
the narrative manner is certainly conversational and anecdotal. As opposed to the stark classical grandeur that comes across in the Ravenna

episode, the story of the young woman on the pampas is almost naturalistic in its representation of physical detail. Without the Droctulft material, this story points to the unadorned realism of the later Borges style in
Doctor Brodie's Report.

Each of these episodes is rich in historical resonances. The Indian-
Englishwoman's story is set in the context of nineteenth-century Argentine westward expansion, an enterprise in which Borges's ancestors
actively participated. Indeed, the dates and place-names cited in the narrative relate exclusively to Colonel Borges's role in such national events
as the Indian wars and the suppression of the Mitre revolt in 1874. Borges
of course learned all of this at his father's knee; as a result, the scarcely
discernible historical elements in the second narrative function primarily
as background to the two women's experience. On the other hand,
Droctulft's conversion elicits from Borges a grand tapestry of historical
scenes gleaned from books, probably most of all from the *Encyclopaedia
Britannica.* The city of Ravenna, which so impresses Droctulft, occupied
a special place in the transition period from the Roman Empire to the
Middle Ages. Well known today for its numerous Roman and Byzantine
monuments and for its great wealth of early Christian art, the city played
a key role in the vicissitudes of Rome's long decline. It was capital of the
western empire in A.D. 402, and then was absorbed by the Ostrogoth
Kingdom in 476, brought into the Byzantine Empire in 540, and in 751
was finally seized by the Lombards, who made it the capital of their new
kingdom. The city later fell to the Franks, and then into papal hands.
Finally, that Dante's tomb is located in Ravenna also adds to the setting's
historical resonance.

Borges has thus chosen a place fraught with past significance and filled
with physical reminders of Italian political and cultural change. Ravenna
is a city that symbolizes the ongoing processes of civilization and the continual acculturation of new forces.

The Lombards are also accurately evoked by Borges, both as a historical entity and a physical people. Droctulft's Latin epitaph cites the
warrior's "long beard"—the most striking bodily trait of his fellow tribesmen, a fact that earned them their Roman appellation *langobardi* (long
beards). Borges speculates that Droctulft may have professed Arianism, a
famed heresy that denied the divinity of Christ and almost split the early
Christian Church. Despite its condemnation by the Council of Nicaea in
A.D. 325, Arianism attained a sizeable following among various Germanic
tribes until about the seventh century. At the same time, however, Borges
plays safe and imagines Droctulft in more likelihood a worshipper of

Hertha, the German earth goddess who, as Borges correctly notes, was borne from hut to hut by sacred cows. And the rapid "civilizing" of the Lombards to which Borges makes allusion is a fact examined with sympathy and depth in Gibbon's *Decline and Fall:*

> So rapid was the influence of climate and example that the Lombards of the fourth generation surveyed with curiosity and affright the portraits of their savage forefathers. Their heads were shaven behind, but the shaggy locks hung over their eyes and mouth, and a long beard represented the name and character of the nation. . . . The legs and feet were clothed in long hose and open sandals; and even in the security of peace a trusty sword was constantly girt to their sides. Yet this strange apparel and horrid aspect often concealed a gentle and generous disposition; and as soon as the rage of battle had subsided, the captives and subjects were sometimes surprised by the humanity of the victor.[8]

All of the learned references in the first part of the story are authentic—Croce, Gibbon, the Bible, and also Paul the Deacon, who was a Lombard man of letters (ca. A.D. 720–800) and author of the *Historia gentes Langobardorum,* a standard scholarly source. The lines from Droctulft's epitaph Borges cites just as he found them in Gibbon (the original poem, contained in Paul the Deacon's *Historia,* is twenty-six lines long). The one point on which Borges admits having strayed from his source is his conjecture about the warrior's motive for going over to the other side. In fact, Borges may not actually have read the *Historia,* which makes no mention of love for Ravenna on Droctulft's part. The change is described as occurring because Droctulft (who was held in captivity in Ravenna by imperial troops) desired revenge against his Lombard chieftains for their failure to rescue him (Paul the Deacon, Book 3, ch. 18). Another important item Borges omits is the fact that Droctulft was a Lombard duke; Borges clearly wished to present a portrait of an ordinary barbarian, a man like countless others who eventually followed in his wake. Droctulft thus comes across not as an individual with special leadership qualities or social standing, but as any acculturated barbarian, any warrior who was brought into the civilizing process.

These minor divergences aside, however, the bulk of Borges's text is historical, inasmuch as both episodes record actual incidents from the past. Borges tells the events basically as received, with fidelity to details of time and place and a bit of invented material brought in only to enhance theme and meaning. All of this inevitably raises a question of genre—namely, can a piece be considered fiction when its narrative plot is so predominantly factual? On the face of it, the "Story of the Warrior and the Captive" seems less a "story" than a highly fanciful personal essay of the sort found in his *Other Inquisitions.* It is certainly no accident that, in his epilogue to *El Aleph,* Borges himself specifically excludes "Story of the Warrior and the Captive" from the general rubric of fantastic literature. Perhaps, with a nod to Truman Capote, we might judge the piece a harbinger of the nonfiction novel—in this case, a nonfiction short story. Again, by analogy with the historical novel, "Story of the Warrior and the Captive" could be considered historical short fiction. In this regard, one should remark that the term *historia* (which in Spanish can signify either an invented "story" or factual "history") gives Borges's original title a richly suggestive ambiguity. Everything about "Story of the Warrior and the Captive"—title, form, content, discourse—vividly illustrates the degree to which Borges dissolves the established boundaries separating the various literary modes and genres.

Its dash of recondite erudition notwithstanding, this is one of Borges's most touching stories, a moving and unusually warm piece. The narrative genuinely evokes, in an immediate and personal way, the warrior's primitive awe, the Indian-Englishwoman's loyalty and suspicion, and Señora de Borges's bewilderment and isolation. Over and above this, a sweetly wistful nostalgia comes across in Borges's musings about the qualities irretrievably lost with the eventual disappearance or passing of each of these individuals. Perhaps the only problem with the story is its unstated but central dichotomy of civilized versus barbarian, today a somewhat dated view. Since about 1945, cultural relativism and similar ideas from anthropology have become so widely accepted that the basic polarity around which Borges's story is built might pass unnoticed or even be resisted by contemporary readers, who would tend to hold the more up-to-date belief that all cultures are equal and that no society is intrinsically more civilized than another. Borges's double narrative, by contrast, works within a nineteenth-century conception of culture, with European values the prevailing norm. Whatever its intellectual and cultural limitations, however, there are in "Story of the Warrior and the Captive" an uncommon depth of subjective feeling and a quiet amazement at the mysterious but inexorable forces that can bring about shifts in loyalty and changes of heart.

The narratives that oppose Cruz to Fierro or the warrior to the captive do so in order to reveal in the end that, in a manner of speaking, these contrasted individuals form one entity. "The Theologians" takes this conceit even further by asserting that, from a divine point of view, two men who work in personal opposition to each other are literally one person. The setting is the seventh century A.D. in Europe, the transition period to the Middle Ages. A politically fractured Roman Empire still lingers about as a geographical remnant and the officials of a young Christian Church are in the process of establishing doctrinal orthodoxy and crushing deviant sects. A recent heresy is that of the Monotones or Annulars, who hold that the same events keep repeating themselves in a ringlike cyclical history. Aurelian, the coadjutor of Aquileia, attacks the Monotones in an erudite treatise stuffed with fanciful comparisons and learned allusions. To Aurelian's humiliation, however, a highly regarded savant called John of Pannonia bests him by putting together a "limpid," "universal," "derisively brief," and hence much better refutation. Therefore John, not Aurelian, is summoned to the Council of Pergamum to impugn the Monotones and their leader Euphorbus. Thus begins a long rivalry between these two theologians—a purely personal battle, inasmuch as both men fight in the same camp, defend the same orthodoxy, and attack the very same heresies. It is also a rather one-sided struggle, for though everything Aurelian henceforth writes has the outdoing of John of Pannonia as its unstated goal, John himself (who scarcely appears in the narrative) does not seem much concerned with Aurelian's existence.

Some new heretics appear, known variously as Histriones, Speculars, or Abysmals. Spread out in numerous subcults, they share in common a consistently wild behavior and all manner of loose living, including incest, theft, and murder. Such dissipation is justified by the deviants in curious ways, notably: (1) the idea that evil here on earth is inversely reflected by good in heaven and, more important, (2) the bizarre notion that, since history never repeats itself, the commission of all possible horrendous acts today will preclude their occurrence in the future. Aurelian composes a report about the Histriones for the authorities in Rome; in trying to paraphrase the idea of the Histriones, he finds himself writing a twenty-word sentence that (Aurelian soon realizes) comes from John of Pannonia's earlier refutation of Monotone doctrine. John's refutation, in order to disprove the theory of cyclical time, had taken the logically antagonistic position of a history that never repeats itself. Aurelian then frames the sentence in such a way that it looks as if John had actually written statements dangerously resembling current Histriones doctrine. As a result, John is taken to trial, where he refuses to recant for fear of lending legitimacy to the older heresy of repetitions. John fails to realize that the affair of the Monotones no longer interests his judges, and he is thus condemned and burnt at the stake. Aurelian, seeing John on the stake, realizes that the doomed man's agonized face is vaguely familiar. Aurelian then undertakes a life of preaching and meditation throughout the empire. One day, in an Irish forest, lightning strikes the trees and Aurelian, like John, is burnt to death. In heaven, Aurelian realizes that, their enmity notwithstanding, he and John actually formed one person.

Rather than obliquely questioning personal identity, "The Theologians" roundly denies it, though Borges plays it safe by fusing the rival characters in a divine context. The narrative is studded, detective-story fashion, with clues that hint at the final disclosure. There are no social or doctrinal differences between Aurelian and John; both are priests who "served in the same army, coveted the same rewards, warred against the same Enemy" (L, 122; EA, 39). The similarities even extend to the sharing of scholarly specialties. John first attracts attention by publishing a treatise on the seventh attribute of God, Aurelian's very own field. Of John's works, only some twenty words now survive; Aurelian in turn happens to write a twenty-word sentence—presumably the surviving fragment—by John. John dies in a fire at midday just as, years later, Aurelian burns to death at noon. John of Pannonia's attack on Monotone doctrine seems written "by any man or, perhaps, by all men" (L, 121; EA, 38). In a Borges story this sort of observation, never casual, inevitably points to the possibility that John may indeed be any man, that he might be Aurelian, for instance. In another way, however, the remark signals the fact that throughout the narrative John remains an elusive figure, a kind of phantom. The intellectual and ideological rivalry around which the action revolves, after all, is a creation of Aurelian and his personal ambitions to such a degree that John at times seems little more than a projection of Aurelian's obsessed mind. Aurelian never meets John and he (as well as the reader) sees John but once—at the stake, where Aurelian actually sees his own face. John of Pannonia, moreover, is not once mentioned in the works of Aurelian preserved within the *Patrology* of Jacques-Paul Migne—an actual French priest, publisher, and editor (1800–1875) whose work is the most complete collection of writings of the church fathers in their original languages. (The idea of Aurelian's works being found in Migne is, of course, one of Borges's many concoctions in this narrative.)

On a more abstract level, the heretical doctrines summarized in the story anticipate the eventual fusion of two men into one and in addition provide a larger intellectual framework for Borges's final conceit. The sect of the Annulars preaches an endless series of repeating cycles, thereby foreshadowing the two theological refutations, the series of fires (the opening fire that consumes the monastery and the burnings of Euphorbus, John, and Aurelian), and the eventually converging lives of Aurelian and John. Even more important, a subsect of the Histriones interprets the actions composing a man's life in terms that the narrative will concretely show: "Perhaps contaminated by the Monotones, they imagined that all men are two men and that the real one is the other, the one in heaven. They also imagined that our acts project an inverted reflection, in such a way that if we are awake, the other sleeps, if we fornicate, the other is chaste, if we steal, the other is generous. When we die, we shall join the other and be him" (L, 123; EA, 41). Borges's story virtually demonstrates this general proposition: Aurelian, the abhorrer, the accuser on earth, has his "inverted reflection" in heaven, an abhorred and accused real self whom he joins upon dying. Significantly, the narrator describes these Histriones as being under Monotone influence, thus indirectly confirming the latter group's doctrine of continued repetition.

The passage from the Histriones also points to oppositions and contraries, polarities between doubles. And, despite Borges's insistence on the close similarities uniting Aurelian and John, the two churchmen are also divided by major personality differences. These are not the adversary positions manipulated into existence by Aurelian, but genuine contrasts in temperament that Borges, with his erudite arguments and subtleties, very nearly succeeds in obscuring. Aurelian is coadjutor of Aquileia and a powerful political administrator—in a word, a bureaucrat. Like most such bureaucrats, he knows how to use his professional contacts (the priests in Rome) and has enough savvy to twist facts to serve his ambitious designs. At the same time, he exhibits an appropriately pedestrian intellect—"laboriously trivial," as the narrative remarks (L, 120; EA, 37). His attack on Monotone doctrine consists chiefly of raids on the writings and materials of others. From his library he marshals a formidable heap of comparisons, quotations, and allusions, managing to throw into his refutation extensive references to Ixion, Prometheus, Sisyphus, Origen, Cicero, and Plutarch—a patently unoriginal approach, a kind of parody of scholarship.

While Aurelian comes across as a not very distinguished mind, John of Pannonia by contrast is a first-rate thinker. The narrative cites no specific occupation for John, but what matters is that he is a genuine intellect, a man capable of the most rigorous argumentation and lucidity of thought.

This is John's strength but also the weakness that brings his downfall. Like many intellectuals, his mind displays a certain inflexibility, an inability to adapt to changing circumstances, and an obsession with principle that is unrealistic and imprudent. Hence, rather than simply recant before his judges, John attempts to argue for the correctness of the views expressed by him *in the past,* a matter irrelevant to the business at hand. Moreover, he uses wit and irony, attitudes that notoriously irritate bureaucrats. Like detective Lönnrot, John thinks too much and is unable to deal directly with the prosaic world of the present. "The Theologians" thus deals fundamentally with the conflict between practical and mental temperaments, the administrator versus the intellectual, the politician versus the thinker. (A more modern reenactment of this conflict can be seen in the Russia of the 1930s, with Stalin playing the role of Aurelian, and with Trotsky and Bukharin as the real-life incarnations of John of Pannonia.)

Borges's two characters, of course, work within a larger context of Christian philosophizing, where discussing doctrine is a way of life— hence the multitude of theological allusions and respectable pagan literary names imbedded in the text. The ambiguous title of the story suggests not just two but a number of theologians; and indeed many church intellectuals from many ages are mentioned in the course of the narrative. These allusions are nearly all authentic and available in the cited sources (the obvious exceptions being the materials that relate to the fabled Monotones or Histriones), though even here Borges makes his accustomed bogus attributions to real scholars. The story opens with a reference to the greatest work of early medieval theology—*The City of God,* by Saint Augustine—specifically, a passage that in Aquileia has been incorrectly construed, read as if Augustine were propounding the idea of cyclical history and not, as was his intent, setting up the notion for the purposes of demolishing it. The text (in Book 12, ch. 13) reads as follows:

> According to some philosophers, the same periods and events of time are repeated; as if, for example, the philosopher Plato, having taught in the school at Athens, which is called the Academy, so, numberless ages before, at long but certain intervals, this Plato and the same school, and the same disciples existed, and so also are to be repeated during the countless cycles that are yet to be—far be it, I say, from us to believe this. For once Christ died for our sins; and, rising from the dead, he dieth no more.[9]

Borges remarks that the flames left this book of the *Civitas dei* "almost intact" (L, 119; EA, 35), an elliptical way of saying that the flames consumed Augustine's own repudiation ("far be it," etc.) but spared the heretical notion of cyclical history itself.

This episode concerning a passage from Augustine subtly foreshadows the ensuing events of the story. The flames that destroy the monastery library and most of Augustine's book will later consume Euphorbus, John of Pannonia, and Aurelian. Moreover, the destruction wrought by the Huns, Borges suggests, is impelled by religious intolerance, the driving force behind the emerging church. Even more important, the account of Augustine misinterpreted contains in a nutshell the fate that is to befall John of Pannonia; for, just as Augustine's presentation of cyclical time is purposely and reverently misread as a defense thereof, with the true context of the passage ignored, similarly, John's exposition of unrepeatable history as a means of refuting cyclical time is later purposely misconstrued as an early statement of a heretical doctrine, with obtuse disregard for the actual aims of the author. Borges's little story of the vicissitudes of a chapter from Augustine, as we can see, not only sets up a theological context but also establishes the essential drift and structure of the larger narrative to follow.

Once Borges has brought Augustine—the greatest of the church fathers and the only one known to today's general reader—into this theologic-fantastic fiction, he goes on to insert a host of secondary figures. The narrative alludes twice to Origen (A.D. 185–254), who, next to Augustine, was the most influential of the early theologians. Amazingly prolific, his only complete surviving work is the *De Principiis,* one of the cornerstones of early Christian thought and an attempt to construct a dogma both orthodox and scientific. (Legend has it that Origen castrated himself so that he could catechize women without having to undergo the hardships of temptation.) The *Zohar* (appropriately mentioned here in a heretical context) is one of the classics of cabbalist lore. The *Topographia Christiana,* to which both Aurelian and John adhere, is the work of one Cosmas of Alexandria, a sixth-century merchant and adventurer who, after traveling as far as Ethiopia, Persia, India, and Ceylon, became a monk and wrote the cited geography book; this work was an ambitious attempt to prove the earth rectangular and to thereby discredit the heathen notion of a world that is round. The disagreement between Bousset and Narnack on the origins of the Histriones is of course a fabrication of Borges, but the names belong to two highly regarded nineteenth-century German theologians—Wilhelm Bousset (1865–1920), a Protestant scholar of the New Testament, and Adolf von Harnack (1851–1930), a church historian and patrologist.

The biblical allusions in "The Theologians" are all authentic, as are most of the classical ones. For his refutation of the Monotones, Aurelian lifts from the *Academica Priora* (Cicero's bird's-eye survey of philosophical schools) a scornful sentence that mocks the idea of cyclical time. Actually, Aurelian (or perhaps Borges) brings together two such passages; moreover, Cicero makes references not to Lucullus but to his other interlocutor, Catullus. This fusion of two separate quotations and identities seems intended as yet another clue to the outcome of the story. The two quotations read as follows:

> Why indeed, you will say, should it be that in this world of ours, great as it is, a second Catullus cannot be produced, though out of all those atoms whence Democritus declares the universe to be constructed countless copies of Q. Lutatius Catullus not only may be formed but are in existence in the other worlds, which are countless in number? (Par. 17)

> Would you believe that there exist innumerable worlds, . . . some unlike this, some exactly like it, and that just as we are at this moment close to Bauli and are looking towards Puteoli, so there are countless persons in exactly similar spots with our names, our honors, our achievements, our minds, our shapes, our eyes, discussing the same subject? (Par. 40)[10]

The Plutarch passage that sparks Aurelian's imagination—a potshot at the Stoics and their notion of repeating time—is a dialogue from the *Moralia* (ch. 29) entitled "On the Obsolescence of Oracles": "If it is preposterous that there should be many supreme gods bearing one name, then surely these [Stoic] ideas will be far more preposterous; for they make an infinite number of Suns and Moons and Apollos and Artemises and Poseidons in the infinite cycle of worlds."[11] John in turn cites the reflection from Pliny's *Natural History* about there being no two human faces alike in the world: "And then, too, the human features and countenance, although composed of but some ten parts or little more, are so fashioned, that among so many thousands of men, there are no two in existence which cannot be distinguished from one another . . ." (Book 7, ch. 1).[12] The Greco-Latin passages utilized by Aurelian and John further reflect the temperamental and intellectual differences setting off one theologian from the other. Aurelian employs several such quotations; those cited, one might note, are long-winded, rhetorical, and, in their mockery and sarcasm, somewhat overstated—the appropriate expressions of Aurelian's unsubtle mind. On the other hand John, as befits the measured quality of his writing, makes use of a few laconic biblical verses and a classically concise sentence from Pliny. Moreover, whereas Aurelian simply expropriates and rattles off quotations without comment, John takes Pliny as a mere springboard toward his own special arguments concerning the nature of the human soul and human action.

These citations from classical authors, as we have seen, are authentic. The other names in "The Theologians" are compounds of fact and fiction. Except for the emperor Aurelian, who was born in A.D. 212 (coincidentally in Pannonia), there is no Aurelian in early church history. There actually was an author called Janus Pannonius (he lived much later, in 1434–1473), which is the Latin name of one Ivan Cesmicki or Janos Czesmiczei, a bishop in Croatia who distinguished himself as the first Hungarian poet ever to achieve foreign recognition for his Latin poetry. The heretic Euphorbus, burnt at the stake as a result of John's arguments, is also Borges's idea. There was, however, a celebrated Trojan warrior by that name who was slain by Menelaus. Indeed, the philosopher Pythagoras (who preached the transmigration of souls and is mentioned in that connection elsewhere in Borges's story) actually claimed to be a reincarnation of that same Euphorbus, all of which constitutes yet another clue to the true identity of John and Aurelian. Significantly, the Euphorbus of "The Theologians" accurately predicts that other fires will burn in the future. The narrative twice alludes to one "Erfjord"; readers will recognize him as the Scandinavian divine who prefaces Nils Runeberg's book on Judas.

The place-names, on the other hand, all refer to specific cities or regions of antiquity. Aquileia was a Roman frontier fortress at the head of the Adriatic, which, as Borges's story indirectly reports from the outset, was razed to the ground by Attila the Hun in A.D. 452. Pannonia was the ancient name for the area now comprising Hungary and lower Austria. Pergamum was a highly cultured city on the western coast of Asia Minor, the site of great libraries and of one of the seven original Christian churches. (The word "parchment"—in Spanish "pergamino"—stems ultimately from Pergamum.) At Nitria in Egypt there existed a monastery where monks lived without rules in a completely voluntary system. The Aventine, where a Histrione blacksmith crushes his own son in order that the boy's double might fly, is one of the seven hills of Rome. Late in his career, Aurelian does religious missionary work in Mauretania (the Roman term for Morocco), in Russadir (a Mauretanian city today known as the Spanish-Arab enclave Melilla), and in Hibernia (the Latin name for Ireland). As one can see, Aurelian, who comes from the eastern frontiers, eventually ranges into the westernmost corners of the old occidental empire. Borges's narrative in turn touches upon much of the empire's eastern peripheries—the Danube, Pannonia-Hungary, Asia Minor, and Egypt—and of course includes the city of Rome as well.

"The Theologians," with its ancient learning and exotic geography, gives an almost encyclopedic impression. The story attempts to re-create the intellectual texture of a time when the works of Augustine, Origen, and the Greco-Roman authors were recent enough for learned men to depend on them in their own writing. It is a narrative that seeks to re-create the postimperial order in Europe and to suggest the kinds of experience involved when a vigorous and confident (or, depending on one's viewpoint, aggressive and dogmatic) Catholic Church fills the political vacuum left behind by the decayed Roman Empire. That church imposes its authority upon other sects and wields an influence ranging from the river Danube to the deserts of North Africa, from the sunny coast of Anatolia to the dark forests of Ireland. Within this context, Borges's narrative skillfully reproduces the dialectical development of human thought, the unending clash between opposites and between entities that generate each other. He depicts the ongoing process of conflict that is always leading to new ideas, which are then opposed and brought down by new intellectual forces. The interplay of argument that essentially makes up the plot of "The Theologians" also furnishes an indirect illustration of the "Pierre Menard" effect: the same words that at one time earned John of Pannonia the respect of the church are at another time reread as heresy, construed and evaluated totally differently, and ultimately bring him to disgrace.

Unfortunately, Borges incorporates too much recondite erudition and old geography to make "The Theologians" very successful as a narrative. The heavy doses of book-learning (the only consistently concrete element in the story) seem to be an attempt at a kind of period color. In contrast to the bookish allusions in "The Sect of the Phoenix," where the scholarly names and references are part of the whole joke, and unlike Buñuel's *Milky Way,* a movie in which Christians come comically to blows over fine points of doctrine, the erudite apparatus in "The Theologians" seems ponderous and overly serious. And since the theses propounded are not so farfetched, so outré as those in Borges's other theological fantasy,

"Three Versions of Judas," the debates in the story take on a more abstract and scholastic, even slightly boring, cast. Borges deals here with an interesting conflict but, because of the means with which he depicts it, the conflict becomes lost in a tangle of obscure names and ideas. One is reminded of Henry James's later fiction, in which elaborately refined prose and excessive mental subtlety only succeed in undermining what little narrative interest there is. "The Theologians" is one of Borges's most admirably constructed pieces and, once we penetrate the scaffold of erudition, a disturbing story. In the end, however, too much is demanded from the reader for such meager results.

"Averroës's Search" somewhat resembles "The Theologians" in its awesome array of medieval erudition, its bookishly detailed flavor of period and place, its subtle personal conflicts and relationships, and its surprise ending. "Averroës's Search," however, is by far the fresher story. It is wittier and more ironic, and its final revelations are more striking than the somewhat predictable disclosure about double identity ending "The Theologians."

The opening paragraph finds the protagonist Averroës (1126–1198), the great Spanish-Arab scholar, at work in his library in Córdoba, composing an attack on a troublesome antirationalist treatise by a Persian mystic. Uppermost in his mind, however, is a problem related to his magnum opus, an extended commentary on the works of Aristotle—to wit, the elusive meaning of two curious words, "tragedy" and "comedy." As Averroës consults his learned tomes, he is distracted by the sound of three children playing a game in which they assume the roles of muezzin, minaret, and worshipper. Suddenly Averroës is reminded of a dinner invitation at the home of Farach, a Koran scholar, where a traveler named Abulkasim is to be present. At Farach's home the conversation centers chiefly on religion and scripture, but Abulkasim eventually talks about his trip to China. There, he recounts, he witnessed a bizarre spectacle: a house in which many people lived—most of them sitting in long rows, some sitting on balconies, and a few standing on an elevated terrace—where they played lutes, talked, and prayed. (The reader should bear in mind that the Islamic faith forbids all artistic representation of the human figure.) Abulkasim's Arab listeners consider these antics sheer madness. When he explains that, according to a Chinese guide, the people on stage were telling a story, his Arab interlocutors judge this a terrible waste, since one reciter could handle just as well what twenty such persons were doing. Following a lengthy discussion, Averroës returns to his home and then solves his enigma: he writes that tragedy means "panegyric," that comedy means "satire," and that the Koran furnishes numerous instances of both. Suddenly, without explanation, everything in the narrative—Averroës, his house, books, and slave girls, the birds and the river and Averroës's friends—disappears. In one long swoop, all vanishes into nothing.

Borges himself now intervenes with a separate postscript. He notes that, after narrating the defeat of Averroës, who was trapped within the limits of his culture and thus unable to grasp the concept of theater, he (Borges) at the same time realized that the defeat was also his own, that his attempt to re-create Averroës and his context was an undertaking no less absurd than Averroës's misguided grappling with tragedy and comedy. In Borges's final words, "The moment I cease to believe in him, 'Averroës' disappears" (L, 155; EA, 101).

This remarkable story is many things at once—a narrative about the nature of narrative (that is, aesthetics) and a reflection on the hazards of achieving workable knowledge (that is, epistemology). Less broad, however, is the problem at the thematic center of "Averroës's Search": namely, the degree to which any serious attempt to understand materials foreign to one's experience—whether the materials be an institution, an art form, or even an individual—will inevitably run up against the socially formed perceptions of the observer (an idea well known to anthropologists). Indeed, the narrative suggests, through Averroës as well as Borges, that such an enterprise is ultimately hopeless. Inevitably an observer relies on the artifacts and terms received from his or her own time and culture, and any "understanding" yielded by thought and research is only an approximate and partial view of the subject matter. It is not as if Averroës were absolutely off-target in his sense of dramatic genres. On the contrary, comedy (especially Aristophanic comedy) obviously resembles satire in spirit, while tragedies in some curious way do celebrate a noble hero even as they depict his downfall; these are no doubt important and fundamental traits. What Averroës has completely missed, of course, is the essential and primary experience, the material basis underlying the two terms: tragedy and comedy happen to be forms of drama, produced on the stage—a fact obvious to us but excluded from Islamic life.

The irony is that, during the brief course of the day, Averroës is subjected to casual but vivid hints as to the nature of drama. Toward the beginning, even as he leafs through learned dictionaries in search of a key to those baffling Greek words, Averroës hears children acting out the Moslem prayer rituals and improvising as protagonists, extras, and props—a crude form of theater that Averroës apparently ignores. The fact that the children speak in a Romance language and not in Arabic suggests that their incipient language and spontaneous game, both of which stand out-side the Islamic mainstream, represent an emergent Spain, a culture in which theater would eventually flourish. Even more striking is the way in which Abulkasim and his entire audience are unable to grasp what the Chinese actors and spectators were doing; reasonable explanations they summarily dismiss as ridiculous. In a crowning irony, Averroës, oblivious to these forceful clues as to the unstated assumptions in Aristotle's text, goes on to defend the traditions of the Koran and later misconstrues the meaning of the two theatrical terms. As happens with the investigators in Poe's "The Purloined Letter," Averroës fails to take note of the obvious, the experiences immediately at hand. (Averroës's and Abulkasim's cul-tural blinders bring to mind the case of Marco Polo, who, in his lengthy and detailed account of his travels in China, never once mentions the two most spectacular Chinese achievements: the Great Wall and, of all things, print! These phenomena were unassimilable, it seems, by Marco Polo's medieval European mind.)

The Koran and the way of life it represents are governing presences throughout "Averroës's Search." They orient virtually all thought and discourse, serving the Koran's adherents as intellectual refuge and prison house both. The words intoned by the play-acting boy, "There is no other god but God," are the opening line from a much-admired passage in the Koran; Moslems often recite it in their prayers. The passage reads as follows:

> God! There is no other god but He; the living, self-subsisting; neither slumber nor sleep seizeth him; to him belongeth whatsoever is in heaven, and on earth. Who is he that can intercede with Him, but through his good pleasure? He knoweth that which is past, and that which is to come unto them, and they shall not comprehend anything of his knowledge, but so far as he pleaseth.[13]

This poetic eulogy is also cited, in connection with a mythical scripture-bearing rose, at Farach's social gathering, where the scholars repeatedly invoke the Koran (its content and commentators both) as universal cri-terion of truth. When the traveler Abulkasim is put in a tough spot by a tricky question about that fabled rose—his answer could expose him ei-ther as a fraud or an infidel—he slips out by attributing only to God "the keys to occult things." This response is an allusion to the traditional Is-lamic conception of "five keys of secret knowledge," those things that only God can know.[14] Abulkasim also wards off this attack with a paraphrase from the Koran, "there is not a green or withered thing on earth which is not recorded in His Book" (L, 150; EA, 94), a counterargument that elicits "a reverent murmur" from his interlocutors. Borges probably has the following passage in mind: "There is no creature which creepeth on earth but God provideth its food. . . . The whole is written in the perspicuous book of his decrees."[15] Farach's guests also seriously discuss such points as the Koran's existence prior to the Creation, the Koran's capacity for assuming any possible animal form, the Koran as attribute of God, and the Koran's irrevocable and eternal character.

Into this closed universe, which is so steeped in tradition, religious dogma, and appeal to authority, Abulkasim's experience brings a glimpse of a world so utterly different that it falls flat and remains pathetically misunderstood even by Abulkasim himself—he still thinks of the theater audience as building residents! Petty sentiments such as envy can crop up, too. In a subtle but amusing sample of the illogic of xenophobia, Abulkasim's detractors deny that he was ever in China but also claim he blasphemed Allah's name over there. China is so, so far removed in experience that Farach and his guests cannot even conceive of its remoteness, cannot imagine anything beyond the outer limits of Alexander of Macedon's empire—an unwonted and vast distance terrifying even to Averroës.

Once the host and guests have ridiculed and rejected Chinese theater, they sing even more highly the praises of the Arab language, literature, and culture. Averroës, though obviously a more ecumenical sort in contact with Greek thinkers—the narrative remarks that he hoped to "interpret [Aristotle's] work as the ulema interpret the Koran"—nevertheless brings the evening to a climax when he delivers a long speech on the virtues of Arab literary traditions. He resoundingly asserts that pre-Islamic lyrics and the Koran hold all poetry of any worth, and he condemns all innovations as ignorant and vain. Averroës's loyalty to Islam is further upheld when he proceeds to find examples of Greek theatrical forms in the Koran. Despite an erudition greater than that of his Arab associates and a profound knowledge of foreign philosophers, Averroës can only yield, however unknowingly, to the pressures of his society. These are so much stronger than the influence of his studies of Greek thought that he eventually finds himself formulating a deeper, more learned, and animated defense of conservative Arabic literary values. In spite of, or perhaps precisely because of, his cosmopolitan perspective, Averroës in the end becomes a more committed and more eloquent spokesman for Islamic traditionalism in art.

The highlights and background of Averroës's life are accurately set up by Borges. Averroës, of course, was among the greatest and most erudite thinkers of the medieval Arab world. A judge in his native Córdoba, he wrote on astronomy, medicine, philosophy, and law. His chief independent philosophical work was the treatise that Borges depicts him composing—the *Tahafut-ul-Tahafut,* known in the West as the *Destructio Destructionis* ("Destruction of the Destruction"). It was written in reply to the *Tahafut-ul-Falasifa* (as the latter cognate suggests, a "Destruction of Philosophers"), by Muhammad ibn Muhammad Abu Hamid al-Ghazali (1058–1111). Al-Ghazali was a Persian mystic who gave up his professorship of philosophy in order to live the life of an ascetic and bring out works like the *Tahafut,* which is a polemic against reason, rationalism, and the belief in matter. As one might expect, the historical Averroës, a sober and practical man, took it upon himself to defend the rational faculty in his own *Destructio,* wherein he specifically invoked Aristotle.

Averroës's most important enterprise was the extensive commentary he wrote on the works of Aristotle. These writings (a monumental undertaking) were to exert a profound influence on the scholastic-Aristotelian synthesis later to arise in Europe. In order to re-create the circumstances in which Averroës wrote his exegeses, Borges provides him with certain secondary sources that the Arab scholar undoubtedly would have handled. Averroës frequently consults Alexander of Aphrodisias (A.D. 160–220), a Greek commentator who was Aristotle's first interpreter of stature and who is sometimes referred to as "the second Aristotle." Aphrodisias was a small, cultured city in Asia Minor. The Nestorian scholar Hunain ibn-Ishag (A.D. 808–873; known as Johannitius in Western sources) translated Aristotle into Syriac (a dialect of Aramaic spoken in Syria until the thirteenth century). Hunain's efforts were largely responsible for making the major works of Hellenic philosophy and science available to Arab scholars, most of whom, like Averroës, knew no Greek. The Nestorians were a splinter group of Christians who, in the wake of papal persecution, set up their own church in the Middle East, where, in small numbers, they survive today. Abu Bishr Matta ibn-Yanus (ca. A.D. 870–940) also translated Aristotle and wrote a treatise on the *Prior Analytics.*

In addition, Borges furnishes Averroës with the fundamental Arabic reference materials of his era. Ibn Sidah, a blind Andalusian scholar (d. 1066), compiled a dictionary entitled the *Mohkam,* which graces Averroës's shelf. Khalil Ibn Ahmad (A.D. 718–791), an Arabian philologist, put together the *Kitab-ul-Ain*—essentially the first complete Arabic lexicon. Averroës feels great pride in having in his possession the only copy of this book in all of Córdoba—a fictional situation derived by Borges from the fact that few copies of the *Kitab* actually circulated and none at all have survived to the present day. Averroës's own copy, the narrative says, was a gift sent him by Yacub Almansur, an emir whose real name was Abu Yusuf Almansur and who is known for defeating King Alfonso III of Spain in the battle of Alarcos.

In the background of the narrative (one could hardly speak of the "action") lingers Córdoba, capital of Moorish Spain after A.D. 756 and famous today as the site of a former mosque. Averroës lived almost all his life there, except for a few years spent in Morocco, where he had been exiled by certain political factions who considered him too liberal. This fact is obliquely alluded to toward the end of the story, when Averroës recalls having consoled himself in Africa with some Arabic verses addressed to a palm tree. Indeed, the conflict between the inflexible orthodoxy of medieval Islam and Averroës's more broadly ranging attitude is quietly played upon here and there in Borges's story. Averroës's arguments at the gathering are more subtle, complex, and profound than those of the others, who tend to rely on set phrases and received ideas. Averroës actually considers citing Plato at one point but restrains himself, well aware that the comparison would have no effect on Abulkasim; at another point, he anticipates the ideas of Hume. On the other hand, the personal reaction of Averroës to the Chinese theater episode is left prudently unreported by Borges, a lacuna by which he avoids having to depict Averroës's insensitivity to this foreign art form.

Averroës's knowledge of Arabic poetry, by contrast, is shown to be detailed and profound. This is precisely stated by Ernest Renan in his 1861 study, *Averroës et l'averroïsme* ("La paraphrase de la Poétique d'Aristote atteste, en effet, chez son auteur une grande conaissance de la littérature arabe, surtout de la poésie anté-islamique").[16] Renan's book, of course, furnishes the story's epigraph—and also its essential drift. The book even provides some of the story's obscure data (for example, the narrative opens with a philological outline of the development of Averroës's name, a subject to which Renan's study devotes an entire paragraph).[17] At the same time, Renan points out that Averroës's paraphrase of the *Poetics* evinces "a most profound ignorance of Greek Literature," with the observation that, though Arab scholars showed a clear grasp of Greek philosophy and science, figures such as Aeschylus and Sophocles simply remained outside their ken.[18] The full passage by Renan, from which

Borges extracts a few words, contains the kernel of the basic matter and the climax of "Averroës's Search." The passage reads as follows: "Averroës's blunders in matters of Greek literature cannot but make one smile. He imagines that tragedy is nothing more than the art of encomium, comedy the art of censure; he then claims to find tragedies and comedies in the Arabic panegyrics and satires, and even in the Koran!" [19] Borges's little narrative about Averroës is thus an extended imaginative reflection on this critical comment by Renan.

A major shift in the descriptive style of the story occurs just after the moment when Averroës tastes his illusory triumph. The remaining paragraphs allude to a harem, slave girls, a muezzin, and even a turban. Borges here deliberately adds some local color and lists picturesque artifacts of the kind typically associated with wall posters and travel lore. Lest the superficial reader be lulled into orientalist stereotypes, and lest sophisticated readers begin to ask why the great author suddenly succumbs to literary quaintness, Borges surprises us all by making the entire scene, with its trappings of exotica, simply disappear like a puff of smoke. This is not, however, that twentieth-century device by which the all-powerful author lords it over his characters, exposing their fictionality—but the opposite, an admission of authorial impotence. In his postscript Borges states that he wished to portray an intellectual defeat. The possibilities initially cited by him (squaring the circle, proving the existence of God, alchemy) are exercises in the unattainable and absurd; as such, these exercises tend to come off at best as pathetic (like Stephen Crane's glimpse of a man chasing the horizon) and at worst ridiculous (as in Swift's account of crackpot scientists). What is most ironic and sad is the unperceived situation of an intelligent man tackling a problem whose solution, though simply not at his disposal, is an elementary matter to other peoples—Greeks, Chinese, even local children.

More important, Averroës's search and failure are taken by Borges as symbolizing his (Borges's) own limitations, his ultimate failure as artist and intellect. For, just as Averroës tries to interpret an ancient Greek literary form by depending exclusively on recent Syriac or Arabic translations of Aristotle (who himself, let us recall, is a secondary source on Greek drama), Borges in turn attempts to evoke Averroës and his world by building exclusively on materials gleaned from a few recent European works of scholarship (again, secondary sources), such as the writings of Ernest Renan (1823–1892), renowned French critic and historian; Edward William Lane (1801–1876), an English Arab scholar who translated the

Arabian Nights and portions of the *Koran;* Miguel Asín Palacios (1871–
1945), Spanish orientalist; and (a key work not mentioned by Borges) the
eleventh edition of the *Encyclopaedia Britannica.*

Borges's games with mirrors are brought off with high skill in "Averroës Search." Just as an Arab-Hispanic scholar-philosopher misconstrues
ancient Greek aesthetic culture, in the same way an Anglo-Hispanic
philosophical writer misconstrues medieval Arab scholarly culture, even
to the point of using cliché descriptions thereof. There is also in this piece
a fully developed machinery of narratives-within-narratives. At the physical center of the story (and of course the thematic center as well) is
Abulkasim's account of a Chinese play; preceding and following this are
Averroës's preoccupations with Greek drama and Arabic literature; and
framing the Averroës plot are Renan, Borges's fancies, and the book-
learning from which the narrative is derived. In another way, the story
can be seen as a series of commentaries-upon-commentaries: Aristotle
had written a commentary on drama; Averroës later wrote a commentary
on Aristotle based almost exclusively on the scholarship and experience
of the medieval Arab world; Renan then wrote a commentary on Averroës
and his followers and commentators; and Borges now writes a fictional-
ized commentary on Averroës that is closely based on Renan and the
scholarship and experience of the modern European world. Both Averroës's and Borges's enterprises are doomed to failure, but Borges wisely
preempts his own forthcoming commentators by obliterating his creation before the reader's eyes and confessing his own errors.

Its formidable apparatus of esoteric erudition notwithstanding, "Averroës's Search" is a much more interesting and more readable story than
is "The Theologians." The almost forbidding plethora of quotations and
names in the latter piece seems too obviously brought in as background;
here, by contrast, all of Borges's applied encyclopedism turns out to be
part of a vast joke. Everything in the narrative, from the city of Córdoba
to Averroës's dictionaries, is set up before us only so that all may eventually vanish. Moreover, while "The Theologians" juggles throughout with
scholastic fine points and mental abstractions, "Averroës's Search" contains that marvelous episode in which Abulkasim and his compatriots
are confronted with the incomprehensible fact of theater—certainly one
of literature's finest, most striking depictions of the problems of being
culture-bound, a moment worthy of Swift. Even the scenery and setting
of this medieval Moorish *jeu d'esprit* have a more palpably vivid quality
than those in "The Theologians." Instead of the overabundance, in "The

Theologians," of ancient toponyms (none of which comes to life as a locality), "Averroës's Search" draws a smaller stage, with some sense of Córdoba as place, even with children at play. Although "Averroës's Search" is undoubtedly an instance of what we now see as postmodern fiction-about-fiction, it does not allow pure artifice and abstraction to dominate over concrete experience and clarity.

El Aleph II

TALES OF ACTION
AND VIOLENCE

More so than *Ficciones, El Aleph* contains a number of tales dealing with various types of physical violence—underworld executions, rustic machismo, political killings, even pathological revenge. Borges's famed erudition and fantasy tend to be absent from these stories, which are generally in the lean, unadorned, hard-boiled tradition. The only overt signs of Borgesian fancifulness in them are an occasional secondary conceit such as the blurred identities in "The Waiting" and "Emma Zunz" or the final play of contradiction in "The Dead Man." The one exception to this is "The Other Death," with its erudite and oneiric machinery every bit as elaborate as that in "Averroës's Search" or "The Secret Miracle." In "The Other Death," however, the narrative legerdemain is set, not in far exotic lands, but in twentieth-century Argentina and Uruguay. By contrast, "The Intruder" and "Deutsches Requiem" conspicuously avoid all fantasy and, surely not accidentally, these two stories are among the weakest in the volume.

On the other hand, Borges has given us one of his most powerful little tales in "The Waiting," a story about big-city gang executions, the kind of mobster bloodlettings one still reads about in American newspapers. In the tale, a man arrives early one morning by cab at a guesthouse in northeastern Buenos Aires. Clearly worried, he absent-mindedly pays the driver with a Uruguayan coin, regretting it immoderately. When the landlady asks his name, he replies "Villari" because nothing else comes to his mind. A simple man who is unaware of the artifice involved in having assumed his enemy's name, he lives from day to day, recalling youthful memories, receiving no mail, playing with a dog, and reading only one section of the newspapers (the obituaries, to see if by chance the real Villari may have died). Occasionally he goes to a nearby theater and watches gangster films, but they arouse in him no sense that he may be observing a fictional rendering of his own way of life. He treasures little things like tobacco and *maté* and tries to live purely in the present without thoughts of past or future. In a recurring dream he confronts Villari and actually shoots him down. One dark July (that is, winter) morning, two silent men—the real Alejandro Villari and a henchman—appear in his room and wake him. In a haunting gesture, the man asks them to wait and turns to the wall, hoping perhaps that they might be a dream. Then the two toughs blast him.

The protagonist of this story has chosen to wait or, as the title indicates, lives a life of "waiting." But unlike Samuel Beckett's tramps, who wait for a Godot that obviously will never come, Borges's gangster sits around waiting for the inevitable. Particularly striking is the banal and ordinary nature of "Villari" and his wait. Here we have what could be any middle-aged retired man living somewhere in seclusion—now indifferent to the loves and hates of his youth; killing time with books, movies, or pets; meeting dental appointments; and quietly waiting for the end—with the disquieting knowledge, cutting through all this everyday banality, that the end will be a violent one. In keeping with his ordinary quality, "Villari" lives in a remote niche of the sprawling Argentine metropolis, lost in urban anonymity in a quarter where there are no fellow Italians to remind him (or us) of his roots. Except for his Italian ancestry and his obvious gangster background, we know nothing of "Villari"—his looks, his temperament—other than the general remarks about his being neither more nor less courageous than anyone else. On top of this, Borges purposely blurs the identity of victim with that of victimizer, referring to the former throughout simply as Villari (never with quotation marks), while any critical discussion of Borges's story inevitably entails alluding to the protagonist as "Villari." Only at the end do we see the real Villari-the-victimizer (whose first name, we are casually reminded, is Alejandro), whereupon Villari-the-victim now reverts to his original identity of anonymous stranger.

Despite the story's surface realism, ruffled only by scattered hints of fantasy, "The Waiting" eludes all elementary analysis of actions or motives. It is true that "Villari" could have left town, hidden himself in disguise anywhere around Buenos Aires, or sought protection from cohorts of his own. He could have adopted any of a series of survival measures, ranging from flight to fighting back, for he obviously is neither a dunce nor a coward; indeed, he is rather quick to defend himself when someone jostles him on the street. Similarly, as regards the executioner, there are no reasons given for Villari's desire to eliminate the unnamed stranger, no explanations suggested as to how the bossman succeeds in tracking down a quasi-hermit who lives virtually sequestered in a remote guesthouse. In this special world of mysterious violence, where the usual real-life motives and explanations carry no weight and are without analytical value, both victim and victimizer ritually act out their predetermined roles. Villari-the-victim, who simply knows that someday he will be hunted down and shot, dedicates his remaining days to waiting for that moment; Villari-the-executioner simply finds his man one day—and that is all we are allowed to know. What is noteworthy about the plot, then, is what Borges leaves out. The entire drama is boiled down to the elemental experiences of pursuit, hiding, waiting, fear, and death. Even a precise sense of time is absent. While Borges vividly conveys the feeling of day-to-day monotony, there is no indication in the story as to just how many months or years actually have gone by in that rooming house.

On the other hand, one cannot but feel struck at the slight role played by the fantastic in so enigmatic, so dreamlike a narrative. Aside from the cautious use of the Double (in which the protagonist casually assumes the name of his victimizer-to-be), the only overt use of fantasy in "The Waiting" is be found in the few scattered references to dreams. When the man in the rooming house considers the off-chance that Alejandro Villari might already have died, he also infers from this the possibility that his own life might be a dream, a notion he quickly discards. More significantly, every night at the crack of dawn, the man has dreams (based, as usually is the case, on recent incidents and images) in which he successfully shoots it out with Villari and his henchmen; these dreams could be seen as a vivid imaginary fulfillment of the man's wishes. In a striking coincidence—striking not for reasons of meaning but because of its sheer eeriness—the two killers arrive at the identical hour during which the protagonist usually has his dreams. The stranger then turns to the wall, with the touching speculation ventured by Borges that "Villari" may have hoped to transform the killers into the accustomed dream of that hour of the morning.

But these dreams have no larger narrative aims, no effects other than atmospheric; if anything, "The Waiting" subtly highlights the powerlessness of the imagination, its lack of relationship and relevance to the prosaic, brutal world of daily survival in the city. Despite the protagonist's often-active dreaming, his life slouches quietly but inexorably on to the dread moment of cold, businesslike execution. In this story, its haunted air notwithstanding, the imagination and its uses are expressly played down. "Villari" adopts his singular alias not out of any love of artifice but because no other pseudonym occurs to him. When "Villari" watches gangster movies, he never thinks to note their connections to his own life. He reads Dante's *Divine Comedy* (proceeding through it in much the same meticulous way that Borges himself did during his worst days as a municipal librarian) and contemplates its punishments rather indifferently. Although he finds these horrors by no means farfetched, he apparently is not struck by their resemblance to human realities. "Villari" engages in these pursuits in all innocence, like an ordinary older man performing his daily chores, with no sense that popular films or high poetry possess any special significance, either in themselves or with regard to human existence. Art and artifice are, for any number of reasons, of little consequence to "Villari" and his precarious life situation.

Although "The Waiting" is in the gangster-story tradition, its atmosphere and meaning set it apart from that tradition. In this regard, one might compare Borges's piece with Hemingway's celebrated story "The Killers." Hemingway's victim Ole Andresson refuses to fight back, but he has a plausible motive: tiredness and old age. By contrast, as noted earlier, nothing about "Villari" can explain his passive resignation in the face of death. Moreover, Hemingway's narrative, as its title suggests, places far more emphasis on the callous cruelty of the unnamed killers and less on the victim, whose attitudes and feelings would necessarily be more complex and certainly more intense. Hemingway's concretely realistic piece—with its considerations of motive, its precise narrative point of view, and its portrayals of ordinary men who do exclusively ordinary kinds of things—contains none of the oblique hints, the brooding suggestiveness, the Kafkaesque overtones of Borges's story, where the surface events seem to stand dimly for something else. Borges's very title points to the ongoing situation rather than to any of the participants in the events. Indeed, despite its realistic trappings, "The Waiting" impresses one as being vaguely allegorical, a symbolic parable of the inevitability of dying. The elusiveness and banality of its setting and actors and the stereotyped quality of the two killers give an impression that one is observing more than a gangster yarn. One seems to witness an eternal drama in which Everyman awaits the onset of death. Despite its impression of brittle hardness, "The Waiting" is one of Borges's most provocative and pathetic little stories.

On the face of it, "The Dead Man" is a much simpler story, a fast-moving yarn of nineteenth-century frontier violence, capped with a surprise ending in which the discrepancy between Borges's stark title and Benjamín Otálora's feverish life is explained. Nevertheless, Borges's puzzles are subtly at work here and, as we shall see, there are even allegorical hints of the kind we saw in "The Waiting."

A nineteen-year-old Buenos Aires hoodlum named Otálora stabs a man and flees to Uruguay to meet with Azevedo Bandeira, an underworld boss. In Montevideo, during a drunken brawl, Otálora saves an old man from attack by a knife artist and finds out that the near-victim is Azevedo himself. Otálora, now in the good graces of the bossman, is engaged as an apprentice gaucho. Otálora fast learns rural skills and catches on to Azevedo's smuggling operations. Meanwhile, his sense of ambition grows. One afternoon at Azevedo's city house, the boss summons Otálora to bring him his *maté* tea. Otálora, as he looks at the legendary chieftain, who is sick in bed and fondling his redheaded mistress, is angered that this old geezer, whom he could kill at a blow, somehow enjoys such prestige. Later, at a desolate ranch called El Suspiro ("The Sigh"), Otálora launches a plot. He conspires with Azevedo's bodyguard Suárez, regularly disobeys Azevedo's orders, mounts Azevedo's horse, takes over the command (but retains Azevedo as figurehead), and beds down with Azevedo's redhead. Then the reversal: at a New Year's Eve celebration, just when a drunken Otálora is vaunting his power publicly, Azevedo and Suárez seize the redhead and hurl her at Otálora. In a sudden insight, Otálora realizes that his gains came about precisely because he had been sentenced to death, "that love and command and triumph have been accorded him because his companions already thought of him as a dead man" (TA, 99; EA, 33). Suárez disdainfully shoots the upstart boy.

"The Dead Man" tells a story, among other things, of inordinate political ambition and personal pride bringing about a man's own downfall—the theme of works as varied as Shakespeare's *Macbeth,* Werner Herzog's film *Aguirre,* the Renaissance treatise *De Cassibus Virorum Illustrum,* and the endless array of psycho-political studies dealing with such figures as Hitler. Otálora, of course, is quite ambitious and, more important, extremely brave—but he lacks all prudence. As Borges's Spanish version observes, he possesses "no virtue other than an infatuation with courage" (EA, 27), a physical daring uncomplemented by any deeper capacities or more lasting strengths, an amoral boldness that impels him to save Azevedo for nothing more than "the sheer taste of danger" (TA, 94; EA, 28). Otálora's courage is a raw, immature, and self-serving kind, a blind force that rushes on with no awareness of the importance of personal loyalties and group needs; thus, Otálora can simply tear up his letter of introduction or murder a fellow-smuggler, acts of self-reliance at its very starkest. This portrayal of Otálora's obliviousness to forces outside himself is another way of saying that he has absolutely no political savvy and no aptitude for the cool calculation necessary for the most violent power struggles. Only for the briefest spell can this brash and impetuous young man cover up, by means of simple audacity and force, his lack of those essential leadership qualities. Not accidentally has Borges depicted Otálora as only a couple of years into adulthood when he experiences both the pinnacle of power and a disgraceful death; his first name, Benjamín, with its biblical overtones, suggests a youthful leader who foolishly rebels against a Jacob who had so favored him.

In the end, Otálora—like a figure out of tragedy—receives the consolation prize of enlightenment, the realization that he was doomed from the start. Until then, Otálora never appears to take note of certain clues suggesting a set-up. For much of Otálora's story suggests that Azevedo's plot to do the boy in had existed from the very first encounter, that even the drunken brawl and the narrowly averted murder may have been a ruse. One is struck by the sudden return to normality immediately following the brawl and the rapid acceptance of Otálora within the next few hours. Moreover, the very same gaucho who had nearly knifed Azevedo sits afterward at the boss's right-hand side, joins in the men's reveling with no hint of disgrace, and the next day is sent to fetch Otálora—curious goings-on that a shrewder person would certainly have questioned. Later, when Otálora overhears laborers talking about "an outsider turned gaucho who's giving too many orders" (TA, 97; EA, 31), he takes this as a friendly joke, a sign of confidence, and not as an admonition. Otálora is so foolhardy as to plot with Azevedo's personal bodyguard, who has given him no initial signs of encouragement. Most absurd of all, after noting Azevedo's ability at "the art of slow intimidation . . . of leading a man on, step by step" (TA 98, 64; EA, 32), Otálora actually attempts to outdo the seasoned chieftain at this skill. Only at the last minute does Otálora discover that he had consistently misread all the signals in his own favor and that everything pointed to a trap. Azevedo's men had led *him* on, baited him, deluded him, filled his head with exaggerated notions of his own power, and crowned him king of fools, only to dispose of him thereafter. Hence Otálora is bold but obtuse, intrepid but not wise; he simply likes to fight and lord it over others, with no sense of the unwritten rules of authority and force. His deficiencies are not purely moral—though amoral he certainly is—but intellectual as well; he has an incapacity for understanding the relationship of others to him, plots included.

All of this unfolds within a formal framework with a surface simplicity as deceptive as the events encouraging Otálora's rise. Actually, throughout this fast-moving tale of the underworld, one finds present the hand of Borges the master. He starts out with a long opening sentence because, as he once noted to an interviewer, his aim was "to pull the reader out of his everyday concerns and introduce him quickly into the imaginary world set up by the story."[1] The entire story is told in the present tense, imparting a vivid immediacy to the reckless youth's headlong rush to power; by using the rather common device known as *presente histórico* (the customary Hispanic way of writing history and biography), Borges places "The Dead Man" within a familiar literary tradition. Borges's approach to Otálora's adventures also recalls the procedure he employed in "Theme of the Traitor and the Hero": the story we are to read, the author initially informs us, is not in its final definitive form, and other versions may exist. Hence, when we read of Otálora's success in taking Azevedo's horse and mistress the very same day, Borges goes on to mitigate the unlikely nature of these easy victories by invoking alleged accounts that claim greater time lapses between the two deeds. Borges thus gets the most out of fast action, but also soothes the incredulous reader by suggesting more believable alternatives. Above all, Borges never lets us lose sight of the fact that we are reading a story, a written object whose shape is contingent on the facts he chooses to tell and on the way he actually tells them. Much as in the above-mentioned Irish tale, where the narrative is presented as a general "theme" not bound to any single time or place, Borges sets forth the story of Otálora in mere outline, the details of which he will purportedly expand in the future.

In spite of Borges's modest apologies for the shortcomings of "The Dead Man," this piece is artfully structured for formal coherence and clarity. Otálora's first meeting with Azevedo and his gang is at a drunken free-for-all; he dies at the greatest brawl of them all, a New Year's Eve party in which the mobsters almost ritualistically eat freshly slaughtered meat. The death of Otálora, which takes place exactly at midnight, neatly rounds off a cycle and coincides with the end of the calendar year as well. Similarly, when Otálora first sees the redhead in Azevedo's room, she is "barefoot and half-dressed"; this illicit carnal appeal is accentuated in the dramatic closing scene when, as prelude to Otálora's execution, she is dragged out by force, once again "barefoot and half-dressed." The story is further built around a series of cultural oppositions such as city versus country (Otálora is a Buenos Aires tough who rises and falls in the countryside), Argentina versus Uruguay (Otálora, an Argentine intruder among Uruguayans, never misses his homeland), and Hispanic countries versus Brazil (there are gunfights with Brazilians; Azevedo and his morose bodyguard are of possible Brazilian origin). Significantly, though Azevedo Bandeira lives and works in Uruguay, his second surname, extremely common in Brazil, is obviously meant to suggest the *bandeirantes,* the legendary Brazilian frontiersmen of the nineteenth century.[2]

A marvelous little thriller, "The Dead Man" resembles "The Waiting" in its suggestion of forces standing beyond man's grasp and control. This is particularly brought out by the story's final little twist, the notion that Otálora has been considered a dead man all along (an idea that some readers may find hard to accept). After all, within the actual body of the narrative, Otálora is never dead; indeed, he only dies *after* the last line of the story. To Azevedo's men, however, Otálora is "dead" because from the very first encounter they have conspired to seduce him into dreams of grandeur and then shoot him. In a more metaphysical way, one could think of Otálora as dead because his brazen character and his paths of glory have led him inevitably to the grave. A marked man, condemned from the outset, Otálora's great success serves (in a kind of inverted Calvinism) as a harbinger of doom. Even his resonant name "Otálora" carries dark hints of predestination because it echoes the words *a tal hora* ("at such an hour"). His abandoning of home turf and urban roots to die in a more primitive land (the back country of Uruguay) brings to mind the way in which "Villari" readies himself to die in a remote corner of Buenos Aires; "Villari," however, dies in a resigned, accepting spirit in contrast to Otálora's intoxicated self-deception. "The Dead Man" is a thriller with parable overtones; it has the ring of those old moral fables in which the harshly sealed fate of one overly presumptuous individual seems to stand as a cautionary tale to us all. It demonstrates Lord Keynes's famed offhand witticism that "in the long run we are all dead."

The universal quality of the actions depicted here is further underlined by Borges's mentioning, in his epilogue to *El Aleph,* a Roman precedent to "The Dead Man." In a strikingly parallel account (*Decline and Fall,* ch. 29), Edward Gibbon tells of one Rufinus, an arrogant soldier-politician who, through a combination of craftiness and violence, succeeded in becoming right-hand man to the emperor. In that post Rufinus made many political and personal enemies. One day a monumentally impressive open-air military gathering takes place—a public ceremonial in his honor, Rufinus is led to believe. As it turns out Rufinus's rival Stillicho has fomented a plot against him, one involving thousands of troops. And so, at the very height of the ritual, the soldiers surround Rufinus and stab him with their swords. As Borges observes, Gibbon's account is a far "more grandiose and incredible" (EA, 177) study in ambition and defeat than is "The Dead Man"; but then, Borges's own narrative speaks of extraordinary forces only dimly hinted at by the intimate voices of suggestiveness and understatement.

Of all the stories in *El Aleph* that deal with criminal violence, "Emma Zunz" is the most accomplished, the most vivid and powerful, and by far the most moving. One summer evening, eighteen-year-old Emma arrives home from her factory job and finds a letter informing her of her father's suicide in Brazil. Caught in the complex web of shock, nostalgia, guilt, and fear, Emma recalls how the happier days of six years ago were shattered when Aaron Loewenthal (then manager of the factory and now owner) framed her father for embezzlement and forced him to flee the country. Reflecting upon this secret bond between herself and the deceased, Emma hatches a plan that same sleepless night. The next day she routinely goes to work, takes in strike rumors, chats with girl friends, and feels embarrassed when they talk of boys, for—an emotional idiosyncrasy that will color subsequent events—the opposite sex arouses in Emma "an almost pathological fear" (L, 133; EA, 61). Saturday morning Emma makes preparations for her plan: after verifying ship sailing dates, she telephones Loewenthal, poses as an informer, and sets an appointment for the evening. That afternoon she heads for the red-light district, picks up a coarse-looking Scandinavian seaman, follows him through a mazelike house of assignation, and—in a ritual that repels Emma, who feels horrified that her father could have so possessed her mother—goes to bed with the sailor.

Remaining alone, Emma tears up the money, gets dressed, leaves unnoticed, and takes a trolley through the dark streets. She heads for the factory, above which Loewenthal, a pious miser and widower, lives alone; he is protected by a dog outside and a revolver in his desk. Sitting in his presence, Emma stumbles through her informer act, naming a few names. Before her arrival, she had rehearsed at length the moment in which, after seizing his pistol, she would confront him, accuse him, extract a confession, and shoot him. But her fury over the physical outrage to which she has just been subjected virtually overwhelms her. As a result, Emma shoots the miser from behind at the first opportunity, too hastily for her speech to make any sense, and she thus never vindicates her father before a dying Loewenthal. Emma then makes a plausible mess of the room, picks up the telephone, and says what she was to say on countless future occasions—that Loewenthal had abused her and she killed him in self-defense. Her strange tale eventually convinces everyone because "substantially it was true. True was Emma Zunz's tone, true was her shame, true her hate. True also was the outrage she had suffered: only the circumstances were false, the time, and one or two proper names" (L, 137; EA, 65–66).

In that resounding final cadence (probably one of Borges's most perfect and beautiful single passages) there is a conceit fascinating in itself: that Emma's rage—against the sailor, against her father for having abused her mother, and even against men in general—could effectively and justly override circumstantial falsehoods of time, persons, and place. Emma's deposition contains details that are fictional, but, in a more significant way, her claims are true to a larger reality, true to the strength of her conviction, and above all true to the passionate and righteous anger brought on by those who had, however unknowingly, wronged her.

Emma's explanation of the murder arises out of a situation fraught with ironies. Emma does achieve her purpose of liquidating Loewenthal, but, when she actually shoots him, her act of violence takes on a meaning totally different from that which she had had in mind. What was first conceived as a vendetta for her father turns quite unexpectedly into a vindication of herself, her revenge against the sailor, and more. Hence, although Emma does avenge her father on the face of it, at the moment of execution the issue of filial vengeance has dwindled in importance. Similarly, Emma plots her crime in such a way as not to be found out and succeeds to a degree beyond reckoning. With utmost calculation she tears up all incriminating papers, tells no one (not even friends) about her father, sleeps with a sailor who knows no Spanish and will leave town shortly, has herself deflowered in case medical examiners are summoned, makes herself inconspicuous at the hotel and on the trolley, and disarranges Loewenthal's living room—making everything as air-tight as possible. What is even more ironic, over and above such careful planning for the perfect crime, Emma escapes censure and prison because of an unforeseen emotion—her fury at having been used and victimized by a man (albeit not the same one); this feeling gives her added energy and heightened powers of persuasion. The only gap in her deeds is the fact that Loewenthal is never informed about her prime motive because at that very moment Emma shoots him for more complex grounds of feminine honor. (One might say that Emma has transferred her anger from sailor to factory-owner.) In another sense, however, this renders her crime still more perfect, since not even her victim finds out about the threat to his life.

This remarkable little narrative stands out because of its special differences from the rest of Borges's oeuvre. "Emma Zunz" is the only major

Borges story in which the chief character is a factory employee and, more important, a woman. Owing perhaps to this central circumstance, the piece conveys a sense of everyday life too often missing in his work. Through such key facts as the protagonist's five-and-a-half-day work-week, her leisure activities at a women's gymnasium, her companions' talk of boyfriends, and her Sunday afternoon strolls with friends (to this day the preferred weekend pastime of Buenos Aires inhabitants), the story of Emma Zunz's brief spell as avenger and outlaw neatly sketches for us the daily existence of a first-generation working-class *porteña* of the 1920s. It might be noted here that "Emma Zunz" is perhaps the only Borges work in which an ordinary character prepares and eats an ordinary meal ("tapioca soup and a few vegetables" L, 133; EA, 61).

In addition, "Emma Zunz" is one of the few great Borges stories in which the decisive factor is not an abstraction, not a bookish or mental pattern, but the forces of sheer passion, albeit passion slightly twisted. This is a story that, to an astounding degree, peers into the depths of a simple human heart. On one hand, we are witness to Emma's fear of the male sex, a condition attributable to anything from psychological damage or frigidity to immaturity or mere shyness. Borges, however, is concerned not with etiology but with the manifestations and consequences of this young woman's disorder. Thus the narrative successively mentions Emma's exclusion from the boy talk of her girlfriends, her picture of movie actor Milton Sills (Emma's way of dealing safely with sex—a man remote and unattainable), her indifference to her father when bedding with the sailor (an episode that causes in her an onrush of "disconnected and atrocious sensations"), the "grief of her body" and the "nausea" (L, 135; "*tristeza*" in the original) that besiege her when she puts on her clothes, and her urge to punish Loewenthal for "the outrage she had suffered" (L, 136; EA, 64).

All of this inner sexual turmoil Borges conveys as vividly as Roman Polanski does in his renowned film *Repulsion,* but with far more empathy than one finds in the work of the icy, clinically minded Polish director. Surely one reason for the compassion that underlies this story is the fact that "Emma Zunz" deals with basic human feelings. For example, when Emma learns of her father's death, Borges's prose, with its references to her burden of sensations and her subsequent weeping, suggests all the confused pain common to the recently bereaved. Equally strong in its emotional impact is the scene at the hotel, particularly when, after the sailor is gone, Emma tears up his money and then regrets it; about this subtle ambivalence the narrative laconically remarks, "An act of pride and on that day . . ." (L, 135; EA, 63). In spite of Borges's own confessed dislike for psychological art and science, "Emma Zunz" focuses with a rare intensity, a rich sympathy and authenticity, upon the psychologies of loss, unformed sexuality, and resentment—all in the space of some eight pages.

Two things in particular help make "Emma Zunz" a uniquely powerful story: its density of urban images, feelings, and atmosphere, and its varying shades of darkness. Emma's childhood remembrances excepted, the narrative is filled with people, places, objects, and activities that are typically urban—a textile mill, a woman's club, workers' strikes, a port (with its customary red-light district and cheap hotels), sailors and prostitutes, streetcars, and telephones. More important than this cityscape, however, is its relationship to the orphaned protagonist, a late adolescent who is alienated in some degree from her surroundings. From Borges's description we gather that Emma lives in a rooming house, though her neighbors are mentioned only obliquely as potential readers of the fatal letter—for this reason, she tears it up. Two extended passages depict Emma lying in her bed, alone; later we read of her lying alone and grief stricken in the hotel room. She chooses a foreign sailor in order to avoid any incriminating personal conversation, but this linguistic distance emphasizes all the more her separateness from men. Emma's walk through the brothel area has an unreal, almost hallucinatory character; there she sees herself "multiplied by mirrors, revealed by lights, and undressed by hungry eyes" (L, 134; EA, 62). In similar fashion, the house of assignation is described as a series of receding depths, successive doors and galleries, a long labyrinth both dwarfing and intimidating her. Afterward she sits up front in a streetcar and is seen by Loewenthal walking across the gloomy courtyard—as always, alone. When she makes her statement over the telephone (a coldly technological artifact), her interlocutor remains unidentified by Borges, an omission further underscoring Emma's isolation. The watchdog, furiously barking outside in the dark patio of the empty factory, is a perfect capstone image to a story pervaded by that peculiarly modern sense of urban loneliness and anonymity. Finally, the fact that the action unfolds in an enclave of first-generation Argentine Jews gives "Emma Zunz" a special quality, the Ashkenazim names accentuating the marginality of virtually all the actors, above all Emma's, in what is an ethnically Latin city. (In a late interview, the author himself explained why he had made the characters in this story Jewish: "Since the plot is strange and occurs in Buenos Aires, the reader will accept something strange more readily if he is told it takes place among Jews."[3])

Throughout "Emma Zunz" there prevails a somber feeling of night, a look of blacks and grays. The story covers three calendar days, with the greater part of the action occurring at or after sundown. The narrative opens with Emma arriving home late on a Thursday in January; in the enveloping summer darkness she nurtures her pain and spends the entire night in anxiety, weeping but also scheming. Borges summarizes Emma's Friday rather perfunctorily, focusing on her social life after work and her modest meal, with their nuances of alienation and uneasiness. Saturday afternoon is the only daytime period in which much is made to happen. That day's summer sunlight is quite eclipsed, however, by the feverish unreality of the brothel district, by Emma's lying in bed (first at home, pensively; later at the hotel, in fear and trembling), and above all by Emma's tortuous sexual encounter. The dark visual character of the story is further reinforced by its setting in the industrial suburbs of Buenos Aires, an area of predominantly gray hues.

Correspondingly few direct references to color or light appear in "Emma Zunz"—four of them, to be exact. The first is Emma's memory of the yellow lozenge-shaped windows in her childhood home, a bit of nostalgia later undercut by the presence of the identical sort of windows at the cheap hotel; the bright lights of the brothels only underline the sleaziness of the surroundings. The one positive use of light in the story occurs on the morning after the arrival of the letter, when "the first light of dawn defined the rectangle of the window" (L, 133; EA, 60), the very moment at which Emma has perfected her ingenious crime plot. This haunting combination of darkness, personal isolation, and urban bleakness suggests those novels of contemporary loneliness (the best-known of them being Sartre's *Nausea*) or the somber desolation of certain black-and-white movies, such as Antonioni's *Eclipse*. "Emma Zunz" does seem a natural for the cinema; in fact, the Argentine director Leopoldo Torre-Nilsson made a film based on the story early in the 1970s, entitled *Days of Rage*.

Paradoxically, despite the gloom and darkness pervading "Emma Zunz," it is considerably more optimistic a piece than are most of Borges's writings. Unlike other Borges thrillers, the protagonist here is less an unwitting pawn of circumstances than a thinking being who creates her own circumstances, painful and sordid though these may be. If Emma in the end is driven by emotion, it is at least her own emotion and not that of others. Moreover, she succeeds in her enterprise, even though (as often occurs in real life) its realization works out rather differently from what was first planned. As if this were not enough, Emma persuades others of the rightness of her act by the sheer force of her personal conviction; as implied in a stray reference in the sixth paragraph of the narrative ("that brief chaos which today the memory of Emma Zunz repudiates and confuses" [L, 134; EA, 62]), Emma is still alive at the time of the story's telling.

Borges's characters are usually depicted as tossed about and deceived by outside forces. In "Emma Zunz," by contrast, a person can choose a course of action, and the difficulties that present themselves may even fuel one's will to take action. It might be additionally noted here that "Emma Zunz," besides being a superb instance of the psychological thriller, has the makings as well of a classic women's story. Despite Borges's own problems with the opposite sex, he manages to write with great empathy, without a hint of condescension, about the inner plight of a shy and sexually troubled young woman and about her ingenious vendetta as well. "Emma Zunz" is a story in which a woman triumphs, as does the justice that its female protagonist creates.

On the other hand, the remaining three stories that deal with criminal violence ("The Intruder," "The Man on the Threshold," "Deutsches Requiem") are the least satisfactory of all the pieces gathered in *El Aleph.* It seems odd that the same man who created "Emma Zunz" could also have written "The Intruder," a disturbing tale of jealousy and frontier violence, set in the 1890s, that implicitly celebrates a male companionship strengthened by misogyny. The story's two roustabout protagonists, brothers Cristián and Eduardo Nilsen, are always together as teamsters, gamblers, rustlers, cop-killers, brothel frequenters, and drunkards. Their intimate bond is threatened when Cristián, the elder of the two, brings home an attractive, dark woman named Juliana Burgos. In the ensuing narrative both men use her as a live-in servant, share her body, fall in love with her, quarrel repeatedly over her (without acknowledging her as cause), attempt to rid themselves of her by selling her to a brothel, and eventually bring her back. Finally, Cristián solves their problem by murdering her, offstage. Moved by all that they had experienced, the two brothers embrace in tears.

"The Intruder" contains no mental fancies, no magic, and no significant formal novelties; its direct, simple, if beautifully cadenced prose exhibits no apparent ironies, ambiguities, or artful rhetoric. This is perhaps Borges's only foray into the psychology of adult interpersonal relationships and their attendant emotions. Love and jealousy, family, and the precarious ties of friendship are themes notably absent from Borges's tales. In this story, however, he touches upon such matters as suppressed love changing to anger or to third-party jealousy and the subjective struggle against it—glimpses of a realm not customarily found in Borges. The tie stressed here, of course, is of a rather archaic sort, the macho bonds between men in the wilderness, a relationship of the kind one might encounter at all-male clubs, on athletic teams, or in men's-magazine stories about hunting. In an interview, Borges recalled first having heard a similar account in the 1920s from Nicolás Paredes, the mafioso who had inspired "Streetcorner Man." He quotes Paredes as having observed, in this connection, "Any man who thinks about a woman for five minutes straight isn't a man, he's a queer." In the world of male bonding, friendship is stronger than love.[4]

Alas, Borges's sketchy presentation of his materials does not allow for the development of the subject. The two brothers are virtually indistinguishable except by obvious tags, such as names and relative age, and by the admittedly ingenious device of having only the elder of the two ever speak. Worse still, Juliana Burgos comes across as little more than a vague shadow; indeed, her presence is felt only via Borges's brief first introduction and later by the indirect medium of the Nilsens's behavior. Otherwise she remains an invisible abstraction throughout, without emotions, reactions, changes, or traits of her own. (Granted, to the brothers, through whom all of the action is seen, she is "no more than an object," "era una cosa"—TA, 64; EA, 173.) Because of this serious lacuna, one finds no psychological enlightenment as to why the Nilsens should have taken any real interest in this particular woman, let alone fallen in love with her. On Juliana's own side, we find not the slightest hint of why she accepts such brutal treatment. As a result, she never comes to life, be it as repressed rebel, beguiled lover, willing slave, or some combination of these. Even Chaucer, in his equally disturbing "Clerk's Tale," gave patient Griselda a more-than-equal say in her loyal bondage and depicted her expressions of personal acceptance of her lover's depredations.

One is thus forced to conclude that "The Intruder," in spite of its careful understatement, suspenseful buildup, and polished prose, is a rather shallow story that moreover strikes negative chords at this moment in history. Not surprisingly, so traditional a lady as Doña Leonor Azevedo de Borges (the author's own mother and loyal reader) found the piece not at all to her liking. Oddly enough, though, Borges consistently singled out "The Intruder" as one of his two or three best works.

Still less convincing is "The Man on the Threshold," a Kiplingesque tale of exotic violence. Set in colonial India, the plot centers around the mysterious kidnapping of a hated British judge named Glencairn.

Charged with the task of finding Glencairn, the narrator (one Dewey) combs the unnamed city in vain, asks countless natives about Glencairn, and, to his anger and dismay, gets nothing but false answers. When he addresses a ragged old beggar seen sitting on a threshold, the latter delivers an endless yarn about a tyrannical British official from the nineteenth century who, after being kidnapped, was taken before a people's tribunal and sentenced to death. During and after the beggar's lengthy narrative, hordes of people continually swarm out of the house. Dewey now enters, makes his way through the onrushing crowds, finds a naked man holding a bloody sword, and sees Glencairn's bloody corpse in the back.

"The Man on the Threshold" is a more clever story than "The Intruder." Some passages have a lively immediacy, in particular Dewey's feverish account of his innumerable interrogations and false leads. At the same time, the idea of the colonial government assigning as investigator an unaccompanied Englishman (instead of a group of native informers) rings a trifle inauthentic. More important, the story's formal core, its basic trick—the beggar holding off Dewey by reminiscing about the remote execution of an English official, even as a like vendetta takes place only a few yards away—is a narrative-within-narrative that smacks of contrivance. A key problem here is one we saw in connection with "The Intruder," that of insufficiently profiled characters. Dewey is colorless and unmemorable, and the wrinkled old beggar, who exhibits no magical aura, concrete social resonances, or distinctive personal traits, comes across as an easy stereotype. A closely related difficulty is that, of all the stories found in *Ficciones* and *El Aleph,* only "The Man on the Threshold" attempts to draw a specific and recent oriental locality instead of inventing a fictional Eastern realm. Not surprisingly, the exotic mise-en-scène never comes to life, largely because, in contrast to the situation in "Averroës's Search," the local color in "The Man on the Threshold" is set up unquestioningly, with no hint of irony. Written in conscious emulation of Kipling (with precise echoes of *Kim* in the references to "Nikal Seyn"), Borges's story exhibits many of the faults of that Anglo-Indian minor author, without the strengths of Kipling's own experientially derived perceptions. "The Man on the Threshold" would undoubtedly have come off somewhat better had Borges set the action in a Buenos Aires slum.

"Deutsches Requiem" is a great deal more complex and ambitious, but, as we shall see, these traits succeed only in making the story that much more flawed. The resonantly named narrator, Otto Dietrich zur Linde, first introduces himself by listing his distinguished military ancestors. Pleading guilty in an unspecified war-crimes trial to charges of torture and murder, zur Linde feels no remorse and seeks no pardon; rather, he hopes his own statement will help to elucidate the nightmarish history of Germany. Though basically a nonviolent person, he had during his youth read fashionably apocalyptic authors such as Nietzsche and Spengler. Under their spell he joined the Nazi party, yearning thenceforth for world war and the New Order. In 1939 he was seriously wounded during an obscure anti-Semitic riot at Tilsit, and his leg was amputated as a result. Finally, in 1941, Otto zur Linde was assigned to head a concentration camp at Tarnowitz, Poland. From that vantage point of power, he made every effort to avoid committing the capital "crime of mercy." He almost succumbed to this unthinkable sin when one David Jerusalem was added to his roster of prisoners. Jerusalem was a purportedly renowned poet whose Whitmanesque verses celebrated human existence so much that Otto zur Linde was nearly moved by him. Eventually, due to zur Linde's exertions, the poet went mad and killed himself. The accused now explains this sordid incident; it was motivated not out of racism but out of a personal need to destroy his own sense of compassion, "a detested area of my soul." Formerly jubilant at the victories of the Nazi Reich, zur Linde is aroused to a like exultation by the defeat of his homeland. Beyond the hell-fire of the war just finished, he perceives a hidden continuity; for, as long as there is violence (even Allied violence against Germany), as long as everyone rejects "servile Christian timidity," there is satisfaction in Otto zur Linde's heart.

"Deutsches Requiem" is Borges's only extended attempt at "political fiction." Strictly speaking, however, the narrative deals not with Nazi politics as such but with a species of intellect and personality, a cultural type. This limited focus is of a piece with Borges's own political strengths and weaknesses, for though he consistently opposed Nazism and its local Argentine offshoots, he never demonstrated the slightest historical understanding of how a collective phenomenon such as the Third Reich can arise. Hence, while Borges's joyous essay about the liberation of Paris, "A Comment on August 23, 1944," can still move readers with its flights of eloquent lyricism, the article nevertheless formulates no significant political concepts. Indeed, the essay suggests fantastic literature in its observation that "to be a Nazi . . . is . . . a mental and moral impossibility" (OI, 141; OI, 185). This is a curious assertion in light of the fact that many former Nazis went on to lead comfortable lives in South America, Africa, the United States, and Germany (some of them actually working for national governments), and also that, beginning in the late 1980s, neo-

Nazism would once again be on the rise. More curious still is Borges's offhand suggestion that "Hitler wants to be defeated" (OI, 142; OI; 185), a wishful fancy rather than a logical argument. Hitler may have imprudently overextended himself, but to say that this betrays a yearning for defeat resembles those "death wish" speculations entertained by the aging Freud, a thinker whom Borges frankly disliked. This essay, with its stretches of idle metaphysics, with its precious and inadequate comparison of Hitler to the classical dragon and of the Allies to Hercules, exhibits Borges's literary genius in evoking the collective joy of liberation, but it hints at no larger grasp of the social conflicts involved in Nazism other than tired platitudes about the oneness of Western civilization. "Deutsches Requiem," as we shall see, suffers from a similarly lopsided quality.

The protagonist of "Deutsches Requiem" suggests that his life and testimony could shed light on German history. Borges's avowed aim with zur Linde, then, resembles that of Thomas Mann with his composer Adrian Leverkühn in *Doktor Faustus;* in both works one man embodies those aspects of German culture and character that may have led to Nazism. From the outset we read that Otto zur Linde descends from an illustrious line of military men. A remote ancestor of his died in the battle of Zorndorf (1758), a key moment in the Seven Years' War when Frederick the Great routed Muscovite troops through the use of massed cavalry charges; zur Linde's great-grandfather was killed in action in the forest of Marchenoir, one of the major battles of the Franco-Prussian War of 1870; and his own father distinguished himself in Namur, a Belgian fortress town that fell to a four-day German siege in 1914. These are all critical moments in the rise of German military might. The Seven Years' War established Prussia as the chief Continental power of its time; the Franco-Prussian War was the beginning of German ascendancy over France; and, despite the final defeat in 1918, the Great War began as a series of German triumphs. In any case, the events cited by Otto zur Linde are all field victories, themselves associated with Germany's best-known expansionist leaders—Frederick the Great, Bismarck, Kaiser Wilhelm, and of course Hitler. Another fact of interest is zur Linde's birth in Marienburg, a town known today as Malbork. Malbork is located in present-day Poland but was held by Prussia from 1772 to 1945; hence, from his very birth zur Linde is associated with German imperialism in the east. The protagonist's name means literally "at the linden tree"; this may be a suggestion of Unter den Linden boulevard in Berlin, where numerous Nazi rallies were staged. In addition there was a German Expressionist poet named

Otto zur Linde, whose work Borges certainly encountered in the 1910s, and who is "sometimes credited with coining the [Expressionist] movement's name."[5]

Otto zur Linde's own mental portrait is sketched out via his artistic and literary preferences. In his early youth he liked Brahms, Shakespeare, and Schopenhauer but later he fell under the spell of Nietzsche and Spengler. These tastes are in keeping with a well-known paradox: that, in addition to the military realm, German culture has distinguished itself above all in two of the most otherworldly activities—metaphysics and music. Brahms in particular represents an old-fashioned and abstract approach to music making and is in fact the composer of the long, brooding oratorio entitled *Deutsches Requiem*. Shakespeare, whom zur Linde considers a fellow Teuton, is probably included here because he has long been the favorite foreign author in Germany. Vastly more important in this regard, however, are zur Linde's favorite thinkers. Though Schopenhauer belongs to that long tradition of German Idealist philosophers, he stands out because he has a completely pessimistic outlook about the worth of any social reform, an attitude with underlying fascist implications. More important, Schopenhauer's antirational and antidemocratic ideas were to exert a prime influence on Nietzsche, a thinker notorious for his consistent idealization of aristocratic warrior races, his contempt for ordinary human beings, and of course his status as semi-official philosopher for the Nazi regime. Nietzsche was seen at the time as the most eloquent modern spokesman for warlike values and ruthlessness. His theories of culture in turn profoundly influenced Oswald Spengler, who wrote *The Decline of the West,* a kind of literary monstrosity, an overwrought and encyclopedic system of historical development. The second volume of Spengler's work contains—buried amid the esoteric allusions and heady conceptualizing—cynical comments about the decay of democracy, sinister pronouncements that *"War is the creator . . . of all great things"* (emphasis in original), and hushed battle cries about "race-quality," "master-natures," and the rise of "our Germanic world."

These twin materials, the German militarist past and the prowar, antidemocratic, apocalyptic strain in German philosophy, are presented as key elements in the making of Nazism. Unfortunately, as an accounting for the rise of Nazi power, such tags as "German militarism" and "Nietzsche" are rather conventional explanations, ready-made formulas one encounters in casual street-corner talk about the whys and wherefores of German fascism. Static clichés, they convey no specific sense of the historical development of German society. As such, they leave vast areas of experience unresolved—for example, why England and France, with militarist and reactionary traditions of their own, did not succumb to native fascisms. Similarly, to link so directly the ascendancy of Nazism with the writings of Nietzsche and Spengler is to attribute to books a disproportionate role in bringing about political events. "Deutsches Requiem," despite its artful literary trappings, treads a much-beaten path.

The one notable strong point of "Deutsches Requiem" is its highlighting of certain notorious Nazi traits: namely, the rejection of mercy (even mercy that is politically useful), the unquestioning submission to higher authority, and a dizzy taste for apocalypse and hyperbole. The second- and third-named qualities permeate zur Linde's exultant rhetoric when he speaks joyfully of destruction and yields to Allied orders as readily as he once did to Nazi rule. Most important of all, however, is his confrontation with the poet David Jerusalem. We have here a fundamental clash of values between the Nazi convert's studied brutality and the lyric poet's spontaneous warmth. Zur Linde had once read the man's verses and even enjoyed them, but he makes it his current business to destroy (there is no specific indication how) their author. This he does without bigotry or hate. If anything, zur Linde loathes the vestiges of tenderness within himself. The larger motive, however, is a coldhearted destructiveness, cruelty for its own sake. This aspect of Nazi ideology and practice takes distinctly Nietzschean overtones when, toward the end of his statement, zur Linde expresses "faith in the sword" and hopes that what is to reign will be "violence, not servile Christian timidity" (L, 147; EA, 89). The thinking here closely parallels that "spiritualizing and intensifying of *cruelty*" extolled by Nietzsche as the necessary alternative to Christian meekness and nonviolence.[6] Otto zur Linde, neither a killer by nature nor insane, is actually the dutiful follower of a principle, "an ethic of infamy," as Borges called it in an interview.[7] Neither cynical nor corrupt, zur Linde is presented as a very special sort of individual, "a saint who is unpleasant and stupid."[8] He is the devout believer of a quasi-religious creed that hails cruelty as its prime virtue.

None of this intellectual scaffolding appears ample or adequate enough for the vast and recent subject taken on by Borges. The stark historical reality looms far too large behind Borges's cerebrations. To present Nazi cruelty by way of mental conceits and Nietzschean phraseology is simply to put us at too great a distance from the physical, moral horror of the real-life events. Nazism is dealt with on the same plane as a metaphysical problem, which it obviously is not. In the same way, Borges resorts to his familiar apparatus of scholarly footnotes; he mixes authentic and invented literary allusions and mingles historical references with phony ones. Although this technique is a reliable and fruitful resource for his fantastical fables, in this story it seems woefully inappropriate to the sheer enormity of the topic. The net result is an ostensibly political narrative that is bookish and abstract, even precious; it is almost a scholar's remote appreciation of Nazism but without the factual utility of ordinary scholarship. The Nietzschean snippets in particular seem a formal contrivance, a mental construction deliberately brought in to give shape to Otto's ravings. Indeed, zur Linde's personality seems vaguely modeled after Nietzsche's— for example, his presumable sexual impotence (brought on by his leg wound), his philosophical inclinations combined with his romanticizing of war, and his nonviolent disposition reshaped by a militarist metaphysic. (There is also a facile hint of psychological "compensation" in the idea of a labor camp boss being sexually impotent.)

Throughout "Deutsches Requiem," therefore, Borges applies readymade outside schemes that cannot cope with the inordinate monstrosity under examination. One of these outside schemes happens to be nothing less than the author's own temperament and background. A reader casually acquainted with Borges's history and tastes will take note of such "Borgesian" details as Otto zur Linde's military ancestry, his hospitalization in 1939, his predilection for Schopenhauer, his sententia about all men being either Platonists or Aristotelians—all among Borges's pet items of conversation. The narrative result is a troublesome confusion of voices. One virtually *hears* Borges reciting his life and loves to an interviewer, autobiographical tidbits that sadly interfere with his portrait of a Nazi and rob it of autonomy and objectivity. Some of these personal congruences are disquietingly intimate: an ancestor of zur Linde's led a decisive cavalry charge, as did a great-grandfather of Borges's; Brahms is included among Otto's favorites for no apparent reason other than the fact that Brahms is about the only classical composer Borges actually knows. Otto zur Linde therefore comes across not only as an intellectual mouthpiece for Nietzschean slogans but also as a very close replica of Borges's personality and preferences. He is a dim shadow of his literary progenitor. These procedures (the grafting of the author's own traits and interests onto an unsympathetic character, and the excess philosophical baggage brought to bear upon an experience that is fundamentally sociopolitical in nature) make "Deutsches Requiem" one of Borges's least satisfying narrative creations. Although trick stories like "The Shape of the

Sword" can be read as animated if flawed trifles, the weightiness and solemnity of "Deutsches Requiem" render the piece not only off-target intellectually but artistically static and opaque as well.

T he most complex and ingenious of all of Borges's tales of violence is also one of the best stories in the book—"The Other
Death," a magic thriller set in Argentina and Uruguay in 1946.
Its narrator (named "Borges") reads in a letter from his friend Patricio
Gannon that Don Pedro Damián, after having relived in a final delirium
the bloody battle of Masoller, has just died. A volunteer in the gaucho
army during the 1904 Uruguayan uprising, Damián returned afterward
to his sheep-shearing job in northern Argentina and lived a quiet forty
years; that brief war was his one special moment. "Borges," who met
Damián briefly in 1942 and found him taciturn and dull, now seeks data
on Masoller and obtains from Emir Rodríguez Monegal a letter of introduction to Dionisio Tabares, a colonel in that battle. The colonel feverishly narrates the bloody events but, to "Borges's" surprise, remembers
Damián as a braggart who lost his nerve at the high point of combat.
Disgruntled by this toppling of one of his lesser idols, "Borges" attempts
ineffectively to justify Damián's cowardice. Some months later, "Borges"
returns to Montevideo for additional details from the colonel, in whose
company he finds a Dr. Amaro, another Masoller veteran. When "Borges" bitterly recalls Damián as the half-breed who cowered before the
bullets, both men stare at him in perplexity: the colonel is unable to remember Damián, and the doctor asserts that the boy actually died a heroic
death, heading a battle charge. This bizarre contradiction is later upheld
and compounded in a letter to "Borges" by the colonel himself! Further
complicating all the mystery, Patricio Gannon later insists to "Borges"
that he never wrote a letter about this Damián, whose name means nothing to him. Later, when "Borges" heads north to make on-the-spot in-
quiries, Damián's ranch has vanished, none of the villagers recognizes
the name, and one Abaroa, who witnessed Damián's death, just recently
breathed his last. As if this did not suffice, a photograph of the man "Borges" thought was Damián turns out to be that of an Italian tenor.

A bewildered "Borges" now plays with three conjectures: (1) that there
are two Pedro Damiáns (a hypothesis that still fails to explain the colonel's triply varied responses), (2) a speculation, ventured by one of
"Borges's" female friends, that Damián may have returned as a ghost, and

(3) "Borges's" own grand leap that starts from the assumption of Damián's original cowardice and survival. This last fact was so shameful to the young man, however, that he thereafter set out to strengthen his resolve in preparation for the moment when he could once again prove his courage. And the time did come (in the form of a last-minute hallucination in Damián's head) during which the battle of Masoller repeated itself in all its destructive glory and Don Pedro Damián went back in history to die a hero's death. The sheer power of Damián's willful dying vision thus brought about the radically shifting assessments of Colonel Tabares (who recapitulates Damián's successive identities), Gannon's amnesia about his letter (this document went against the backward revision of the reality of Damián's death in 1904), the convenient passing away of Abaroa (who, possessing the contradictory and damaging knowledge of Damián's ensuing existence, simply had to go), "Borges's" "misplacing" of the Gannon letter (a fact alluded to in the story's opening line), and much more.

This remarkable piece depicts the classically "Borgesian" type of action—the irruption of fantastic, miraculous, or otherwise unreal elements into the ordinary, everyday world of reality. The fantastical source here is not an encyclopedia but a dream, a wishful delirium that imposes itself upon the world and, in the process, modifies the sense of the past hitherto held by all concerned. The story takes as its intellectual point of departure a theological question as to whether God's powers include the capacity to undo and remake past events. Ever since the time of Thomas Aquinas, it has been the standard church line to negate this possibility; the argument is that "God's power cannot reverse His eternal decrees, for this implies change of intention or new knowledge, both of which are impossible in a perfect God."⁹ But a celebrated eleventh-century churchman named Pietro Damiani (St. Peter Damian in English), known mostly for his monastic reforms, did toy with this notion in his minor treatise *De omnipotentia*.¹⁰ Borges's "The Other Death," however, shows the feat being performed not by God (at least not seemingly so) but by agency of the powerful imagination of a determined, courageous individual. Moreover, the material *events* of forty years ago are not erased or altered, much less the entire ensuing historical fabric, but the *memory* of these slight events and the *idea* of Damián entertained by other people are obliterated, as are a few vestigial items (a picture, a ranch, a friend) associated with him, these last two being virtually exorcised out of existence. In short, what changes is the private and public identity of Damián, who evolves from a surviving onetime coward to a hero dying young; who, in an eleventh-hour act of the will, wipes clean his cowardly past; who, in so doing, transforms what little remaining historical record there is of that past.

The turn-of-the-century world within which Pedro Damián's dream operates, one might emphasize, is a concretely real if distant one. The political context of his personal adventures happens to have been one of the major crises in Uruguayan history. When the renowned reformist José Batllé y Ordoñez was elected to the presidency in 1903, a gaucho nationalist uprising broke out, led by the flamboyant military-political caudillo of the Blanco party, Aparicio Saravia. Most of the year 1904 was taken up by a bloody civil war, with fierce battles at Illescas, Tupambaé, and Masoller (all mentioned by Colonel Tabares in "The Other Death") and with a rebel approach toward the capital city—a planned attack unexpectedly called back by Saravia because of ammunition shortages (a legendary fact also cited, with scorn, by Borges's colonel). The horrific battle of Masoller was the decisive encounter of the conflict: it decimated the nationalist ranks and killed off most of its leadership, including Saravia himself. Hence, Masoller (as of this writing the last remembered full-scale military clash in the River Plate region before the 1960s) is a major event, as awesome to Uruguayans and Argentinians as the battle of Gettysburg is to North Americans. Even more important, the revolution of 1904 was the last time the rural gauchos, with their traditional values of manly courage and machismo, acted as a major political force in the Plate region. The defeat at Masoller is thus a milestone, a moment of special historical significance to antigaucho liberals like Borges; it signals the end of one era and the beginning of a very different one. Needless to say, there is a profound irony in Pedro Damián's waiting for another gaucho war in which to prove himself, inasmuch as the rural values he continued to live for had become irrelevant in an era of relative social peace.

The history in "The Other Death," then, is a very real if remote entity; to mid-twentieth-century inhabitants of the Plate region it is a vivid remembrance of other worlds past. The geographic setting here is comparably real but of a special sort, an alternative kind. The action takes place chiefly in Uruguay (to Argentines, I should reiterate, a more primitive country). Much of it occurs not in Montevideo but far off in the rural backlands, almost at the border of Brazil. The story also contains several references to the Argentine northern provinces, with their rugged lifestyle. For example, Gualeguaychú, cited in line two of the piece, is a commercial port town in the province of Entre Ríos; not too far away is

Paysandú, a river port in Uruguay. Similarly, in a procedure familiar from "Tlön, Uqbar, Orbis Tertius," Borges peoples his fantastical text with real-life individuals. Patricio Gannon, who first informs "Borges" of Pedro Damián, is an occasional writer, scion of a rich Anglo-Argentine ranching family in Entre Ríos. At the time of Borges's writing "The Other Death," Emir Rodríguez Monegal was a promising young man of Uruguayan letters; later he became a leading critic of Latin American literature, the author of a more or less official biography of Borges, and, until his death in 1985, a Yale University professor. The aristocratic-sounding "Ulrike von Kuhlmann" is either a fanciful pseudonym coined by the author for an unidentified upper-class Argentine lady quite close to him, or a real-life German adventuress, the daughter of a diplomat and the possessor of Valkyrian good looks, who lived in Argentina in the 1950s.[11] The narrative also mentions a photograph of Enrico Tamberlik (1820–1889), a famed Italian tenor who spent much of his life in Madrid and was particularly renowned for his high notes.

The plot of "The Other Death" develops around an intellectual contradiction and moves from a well-established axiom to its unsettling logical opposite. It starts with Emerson's poem "The Past," which emphatically asserts time's irreversible nature, and ends with Pier Damiani's stray notion that God can undo what has passed. The relevant opening portion of the poem, initially mentioned by Gannon with regard to his translation into the Spanish, reads as follows:

> The debt is paid,
> The verdict said,
> The Furies laid,
> All fortunes made;
> Turn the key and bolt the door,
> Sweet is death forevermore.
> No haughty hope, nor smart chagrin,
> No murdering hate, can enter in.
> All is now secure and fast;
> *Not the gods can shake the Past.* (Emphasis added.)[12]

Emerson's lines express one of mankind's oldest thoughts. The concept of the inviolate past is commonsense wisdom, orthodox philosophy, even basic science. The poem, immediately associated with Gannon's first report of Damián's recent death, thus appears as something that is about to be refuted, neutralized, canceled out, challenged by events. As is therefore appropriate, when Gannon unknowingly feels the effects of the other death (Damián's past remade by what Emerson calls "haughty hope") and forgets about the old soldier, his former interest in Emerson's unshakable past equally eludes him. As the narrative proceeds to demonstrate the possible truth in Pier Damiani's speculation, the ironclad, absolute statements of Emerson's poem recede from Gannon's as well as from the reader's memory. Even as triumph in battle belongs to Pedro Damián, so does the triumph of an idea redound to Pier Damiani.

"The Other Death," permeated by a factual reality that it later partly negates, works precisely by a dialectical interplay between opposing forces: real, objectively known history versus Damián's elusively subjective history; real-life palpable individuals versus the slippery identity of one man; frozen past versus changeable past (or the memory thereof); Emerson versus Damián. In addition to all this, Borges himself intrudes in the penultimate paragraph and compounds the confusion by casting doubt on the dependability of what we have just read. As he confronts the curious fact that only he and "Ulrike von Kuhlmann" seem aware of the mysterious upsets going on in the world about them, he inevitably wonders if his own imagination might have invented some of it, if the old gaucho really was called Pedro Damián, if the name was perhaps unconsciously prompted by his reading of Pier Damiani, or for that matter if Pedro Damián ever existed at all. Moreover, perhaps he (Borges) has written a true story that he now believes is just a fantasy, a fantasy that he now finds truthful, or a fiction that his readers (paralleling the shifting conceptions held by Damián's detractors) will eventually perceive as factual. The degree of reality of Borges's protagonist and even of his entire narrative is thereby rendered as hopelessly uncertain as was Pedro's death. The result of such juggling and mental mystification (dazzling artistry and delicious humor aside) is that it softens the effect of the actions depicted and counteracts the sheer far-fetchedness of the ideas set forth. Obviously, a dying man's delirium could never erase public memories of his past nor cause relevant physical objects to disappear, though the possibility of such extraordinary powers is interesting to contemplate. Borges, however, preempts readers' resistance and incredulity by stating that, actually, some or much or even all of "The Other Death" may be false.

In addition to these lighthearted mystifications played in public, Borges's narrative contains a subtle but significant revision of historical reality in the photograph of Tamberlik, who is portrayed "in the part of Otello" (TA, 108; EA, 76); this photograph is an impossibility, inasmuch as Tamberlik had retired from the stage in 1878, while the world premiere of Verdi's *Otello* took place in 1887, a scant two years before Tamberlik's own death. This concealed contradiction, however minor, reproduces in miniature the ambiguities of Damián's own career; a portrait of Tamberlik in a concocted situation furnishes yet another instance of possibilities not fully actualized, of "what-might-have-been" in history. Tamberlik certainly could have done the role of *Otello* had he remained active through old age (or had Verdi written *Otello* some twenty years earlier), but the picture, itself a metamorphosis of a former Damián photo, depicts an act that is purely imaginary.

Indeed, one of the themes implicitly dealt with in "The Other Death" is the thorny problem of what elements can constitute a man's final and definitive biography. In 1904, Pedro Damián acted like a coward; in the forty-odd years that followed, however, he lived poised for his moment of heroism. Had Damián been granted a second opportunity for combat, he would have fought bravely and perhaps died a hero's death. The fact that the occasion presented itself only in dreams does not vitiate Damián's potential for courage, though there does remain the dilemma of the "real" past versus his merely possible present. One might venture to say that Borges's story reverses the well-known Sartrean idea by suggesting that an individual's life can be judged as the sum total of his *potential* acts, which could even cancel out what he had previously and palpably done. In dreams begin our personal identities.

"The Other Death" is many things at once. On one level, it is a playful parable on the nature of the past or on how individuals look upon the past. For, although it is true that events of the past remain unmovable, nonetheless the knowledge and interpretation thereof can vary widely according to individual, group, and epoch; indeed, events can be altered or suppressed if someone possesses such power and has a stake in doing so. In García Márquez's *One Hundred Years of Solitude,* to cite a celebrated instance, the banana company can expunge from public memory the ruthless slaughter of three thousand plantation workers. Borges's story takes this idea even farther and shows how forces such as subjective desires, dreams, and inner strengths might erase the memory of one's own cowardice. Finally, it must be noted that, philosophical dalliances aside, "The Other Death" is a most amusing story because of the pranks it plays on the objective world and above all those it plays on Borges's fictional self. Especially entertaining are the two successive scenes in which Colonel Tabares topples the narrator's preconceptions about Pedro Damián's moral fiber. There is a vivid immediacy to these dialogues, a colloquial, conversational, almost auditory quality to the language employed. All these elements—the philosophical-parable overtones, the identity theme, the use of fantasy, the evasive formal trickery, and the humor—combine to form a story that stands unmistakably among Borges's five or six richest.

9 *El Aleph* III

THE VISIONARY EXPERIENCE

T he volume *El Aleph* contains a handful of formidable, imposing and somewhat longer stories that depict holistic experiences and convey a vivid glimpse of grand totalities, be these the mystical, unitary revelations of "The God's Script," "The Zahir," and "The Aleph" or the multitudinous adventures, attitudes, and personalities of a universal wanderer in "The Immortal." The first three of these stories divide neatly into Hindu, Islamic, and Hebrew mysticisms, according to their choice of lexicon and imagery, while "The Immortal" complements these Eastern-tinged artifacts with its 3000-year patchwork of European authors from Homer to Shaw.

This group of narratives has been accorded special attention by Borges scholars, whose expert exegeses are a virtual necessity in sorting out the vast array of formal intricacies and recondite learning. Without the guiding hand of a seasoned explorer, the uninitiated reader is apt to founder in Borges's erudite tangle of metaphors, ellipses, obliquities, religious references, and obscure proper names. Mysticism, of course, is a notoriously difficult, perhaps impossible, subject to write about. The most celebrated mystics, without reservations or irony, have defended the substantiality of their visions yet have also insisted on the essential incommunicability of their experience. In his stories, by contrast, Borges sets forth cosmic seizures through a highly sophisticated and ironic objectivity. Whether this is done by means of the vagueness of setting and the narrator's delusions in "The God's Script," the dense book-learning in "The Zahir," or the counterweight of love and satire in "The Aleph," Borges's elaborate literary apparatus serves to keep his explosive subject matter at arm's length, to give it outer density via his thick verbal-cognitive texture.

The mystical tales appear to have an autobiographical basis. In 1928, Borges published in his collection *El idioma de los argentinos* a little five-page essay entitled "Sentirse en muerte" (literally, "Feeling Oneself in Death").[1] Highly subjective and personal, with no bookish references, the piece tells of an uncanny sensation Borges experienced "a few nights ago" while strolling idly in Barracas, a poor neighborhood with which he is relatively unfamiliar. As he ambles about the muddy roads and craggy sidewalks, he approaches an alley bordering on the pampas and sees a rose-colored wall that seems to radiate its own "intimate light" rather than that of the moon. Staring amid the nocturnal silence, he feels transported twenty years into the past. "I felt dead, like an abstract perceiver of the world," says the twenty-nine-year-old author. "Or rather, I suspected myself of possessing the meaning—reluctant or absent—of the word *eternity*" (IA, 149–150).

Being on the edge of the city, facing a moonlit wall, hearing no sounds save perhaps a few crickets: the set of conditions is just right to prompt such a seizure in a young man then predisposed to transcendent sorts of knowledge. Nighttime, aloneness, minimal sensory stimuli—these in fact constitute the initial stages for such visions, as reported by the great mystic writers.

Borges would later exclude this hauntingly beautiful piece from collections of his work. Still, he was not averse to discussing the topic. In a conversation with Willis Barnstone, he reminisces:

> In my life I had only two mystical experiences and I can't tell them because what happened is not to be put into words, since words, after all, stand for shared experience. Twice in my life I had a feeling, a feeling rather agreeable than otherwise. It was astonishing, astounding, I was overwhelmed, taken aback. I had the feeling of living not in time but outside time. It may have been a minute or so, it may have been longer. But I know I had that feeling in Buenos Aires, twice in my life. Once I had it on the South side, near the railroad station Constitución. Somehow the feeling came over me that I was living beyond time.

Putting that moment into perspective, Borges further elaborates:

> I felt very grateful for it. I know people who've never had it, and I know people who are having it all the time. My friend, a mystic, abounds in ecstasies. I don't. I've only had two experiences of timeless time in eighty years.[2]

The involuntary rapture by which Borges was twice overcome—so powerful that it inspired in his younger self a desire to evoke it in a confessional narrative—also remained vividly enough with the writer over the years to induce from him an eloquent recollection in his eighties. One can understand, then, that Borges would have wished, at the height of his creative powers, to capture a like transport through the medium of his fantastic fiction.

The simplest of the three mystical tales in *El Aleph* is "The God's Script." As its title suggests, it is the narrative most specifically focused on a religious vision. The narrator, Tzinacán, is a former Mayan priest who had sacrificed victims atop his pyramid before the Spanish invasion. Now he languishes in a vast semicircular cell, a dark, deep pit where light enters only briefly at noon when a jailer opens a trapdoor to lower him food and drink. In the neighboring cell, the other half of the circle, there is a caged jaguar that Tzinacán can see momentarily at noon through the bars of a window. To pass the time, Tzinacán tries recalling everything he knows, from statues of serpents to the shapes of trees. Eventually he remembers a tradition of his god—the magical sentence that at the end of time would appear somewhere and, after being read by a chosen one, would halt the tide of evil and destruction.

Time being at an end for his own people and he being their last priest, Tzinacán comes to believe that the man chosen to read the god's script is himself. Recalling that one of the god's attributes is the jaguar, he concludes that the formula must lie hidden in its spots. So Tzinacán racks his brains, first learning the precise configuration of those bodily marks, then seeking the secret pattern. After much effort and frustration, and an almost infinite nightmare about infinite grains of sand, Tzinacán rediscovers his condition as prisoner and blesses his immediate surroundings. Suddenly he experiences "union with the divinity, with the universe" (L, 172; EA, 180). He sees the entire cosmos—its origins, its present, its gods, his own enemies—and feels himself part of the whole. Moreover, as an incidental by-product of his cosmic vision, Tzinacán has divined the magical sentence in the jaguar's fur, fourteen words that, were he to pronounce them, would destroy the prison, crush the Spaniards, and restore Maya independence with Tzinacán as ruler. Yet, after such knowledge, he "cannot think in terms of one man" (L, 173; EA, 121), even if this means saving and avenging himself. He decides on silence, resolves not to employ the secret formula, and dies humbly with his might and omniscience in his cell.

"The God's Script" depicts one of the two most dramatic types of subjective conversions found in the literature of imprisonment. This case involves not the awakening to active political opposition but the obverse, the reconciliation through religious ecstasy, the acceptance of one's plight through direct apprehension of a supernatural order, and the serene sense that in the divine scheme of things one's physical sufferings are of slight import. Borges makes his prisoner the personal victim of Pedro de Alvarado, who was the first Spanish mayor of Mexico City, the subsequent ravager and ruler of Central America, and one of imperial Spain's most bloodthirsty leaders. This extreme relationship between the last pagan priest and the cruelest Catholic conqueror heightens the pivotal contrast between the oppressor and oppressed; similarly, the jaguar (an entity as important to the plot as Alvarado) is the bearer of instinctive violence and divine wisdom and unites the opposites that, in Tzinacán's final vision, become one. The prisoner himself is the pre-Columbian equivalent of an intellectual, a man most apt to fill out his long and lonely days with mental activity; he is at the same time a man of religion and is predisposed to conceiving of himself as someone favored by the gods. Most important of all, however, Borges sets his narrative in conquered Maya lands in order to avoid problems of cultural association both in his writing and in our reading of the story. Our relative lack of knowledge about that vanished world (in particular our ignorance about its mystical traditions) helps make us more open, more "innocent" observers of Borges's chosen subject matter, whereas, were the narrative set in Europe or Asia, an informed reader would inevitably expect a more historical, even realistic use of language and imagery.[3]

The story of Tzinacán contains in outline the basic steps common to most mystical experience (with the important difference, it should be remarked, that Tzinacán's rapture comes to him by accident, without conscious intent on his part). He lives, first of all, in a state of chronic sensory deprivation, with essentially no visual, human, or (save for the jaguar's presumed noises) aural stimuli and with no noteworthy changes in the tactile realm. It is precisely this sort of stark, cloistered isolation that Spanish, Islamic, and Indian mystics have customarily inflicted upon their bodies in their preparatory rites. Rather than engage in selfless prayer or meditation, however, Tzinacán concentrates his mental energies upon the jaguar's spots for strictly worldly purposes of physical escape. This practice is his personal equivalent, albeit unknown to him, of that fundamental technique of mysticism: the fixing of one's attentions upon a single point in space, with the aim of removing from one's mind all else that is earthly. Tzinacán obsessively focuses his every waking thought upon those spots, though what actually does result is a negative mystical experience, a "bad trip"—his recurring nightmare of the grains of sand.

It is at this juncture that Tzinacán accepts his humble condition as prisoner; on everything that belongs in his environment—the dampness, the jaguar, his own decrepit body, the darkness, the stones—he confers his deepest blessing. This decisive act springs from an attitude corresponding to detachment; detachment represents a key moment in the mystical path when a subject sheds all selfish desires and attains a rarefied feeling (vaguely comparable to what is sometimes indicated by our tired word "love"), a pure state deeply infused with a sense of the divine. Directly following this particular moment, Tzinacán, as happens with other mystics, succumbs to his seizure.[4]

Tzinacán's moment of high rapture comprises elements typical of the kind of religious ecstasy whose essence is "the apprehension of *an ultimate nonsensuous unity in all things,* a oneness or a One to which neither the senses nor the reason can penetrate."[5] Hence, the vision of Tzinacán shows such traits as union with the deity and the universe; an oceanic feeling of infinity; seemingly contradictory sensations (fire and water); the annulment of ordinary oppositions and of temporary, earthly enmities (Tzinacán and Alvarado are revealed as belonging to a vast, single fabric); and the obliteration of the sense of time (Tzinacán sees "all things that are, were, and shall be" and grasps "the causes and the effects" [L, 172; EA, 119]). Tzinacán remarks that the wheel vividly perceived by him differs from the metaphors previously cited by men who have seen God. As one scholar has observed, mystics often distinguish between "the ineffable Reality and the symbols they use."[6] The almost incantatory lilt of the anaphora "I saw . . . I saw . . ." suggests the exalted rhythms of mystic prose, even its concrete wordings; from the *Bhagavad-Gita* to Rimbaud's *Drunken Boat,* the formulaic repetition of "I saw" has been a basic literary device. "All mystics speak the same language, for they come from the same country," the French visionary Saint-Martin once noted.[7]

Nevertheless, while Borges does set forth the procedures common to most mystics and also echoes their language and style, his poetic imagery seems borrowed from specifically Asian traditions—notably but not exclusively those of India. For example, Tzinacán states that "God has been seen in a blazing light, in a sword, or in the circles of a rose" (L, 172; EA, 119). God as light, of course, is a commonplace, even universal symbol, but the image in particular serves as a verse refrain in the *Upanishads* ("The whole world is illumined with his light"). The likening of God to a rose is frequent in Persian Sufism, and legend also has it that Muhammad considered the red rose a primal manifestation of the glory of God.[8]

The Buddhist Tai-hui has compared Zen to "a sword about to be drawn." [9]
Above all, however, much of the content of Tzinacán's experience (including the preparations and the aftermath) Borges appears to have gleaned
from two classic works of Hindu mysticism: the *Upanishads,* a series of
treatises dealing with spiritual enlightenment that were composed mostly
between 800 and 400 B.C., and the *Bhagavad-Gita,* a self-contained set
of episodes from the *Mahabharata* epic (200 B.C.–A.D. 200) in which the
divinity Krishna stands as Supreme Being before the warrior Arjuna. [10] On
the other hand, there is no discernible evidence in "The God's Script" of
features from Christian mysticism—the affective quality, the personifi-
cation of God, the use of sexual or matrimonial imagery, or the avoidance
of pantheism.

When Tzinacán begins to study the jaguar, he philosophizes that "to
say the *tiger* is to say the tiger that begot it, the deer and the turtles devoured by it, the grass on which the deer fed, the earth that was mother
to the grass, the heaven from which the earth was born" (L, 171; EA, 118).
This infusion of holistic meaning into a single word, followed by Tzinacán's speculations about the inadequacy of ordinary speech, is a train of
thought closely akin to what the father tells his spiritually impatient son
in the *Chandogya Upanishad:* "My child, as by knowing one lump of clay,
all things made of clay are known, the difference being only in name and
arising from speech, and the truth being that all are clay; as by knowing a
nugget of gold, all things made of gold are known, the difference being
only in name and arising from speech, and the truth being that all are
gold—exactly so is that knowledge, knowing which we know all." [11] The
knowledge to which the father alludes, of course, is something possessed
by a god only; but again, the Hindu disciple and Tzinacán both find out
that this higher knowledge can be reached through communion with
such a god. Then, after having attained divine understanding, Tzinacán
ceases to bemoan his fate or death; the *Isha Upanishad* describes a comparable serenity in a wise man who has had his vision:

> Who sees all beings in his own self, and his own self in all beings,
> loses all fear.
> When a sage sees this great Unity, and his self has become all
> being—what delusion and sorrow can be near him? [12]

By far the greatest points of contact between "The God's Script" and
Hindu mysticism, however, are to be found in Tzinacán's account of his

dazzling ecstasy, a passage highly reminiscent of the *Bhagavad-Gita,* chapter 11.

KRISHNA

7   See now the whole universe with all things that move and move
        not. . . . See it all as One in me.

SANJAYA

9   When Krishna, the God of Yoga, had thus spoken, he appeared to
        Arjuna in his supreme divine form.
10   And Arjuna saw in that form countless visions of wonder. . . .
12   If the light of a thousand suns suddenly arose in the sky, that splendor
        might be compared to the radiance of the Supreme Spirit. And
        Arjuna saw in that radiance the whole universe in its variety, stand-
        ing in a vast unity in the body of the God of gods.

ARJUNA

15   I see thee in all the gods, O my God; and the infinity of the beings of
        thy creation. . . .
16   All around I behold thy infinity. . . . Nowhere I see a beginning or
        middle or end of thee, O God of all, Form Infinite!
17   I see the splendour of an infinite beauty, which illumines the whole
        universe. It is thee! with thy crown and sceptre and circle. How
        difficult thou art to see! But I see thee: as fire, as sun, blinding,
        incomprehensible.
19   I see thee without beginning, middle, or end; I behold thy infinite
        power. . . . And I see thy face as a sacred fire that gives light to the
        whole universe.
20   Heaven and earth and all the infinite spaces are filled with thy spirit.[13]

It would be impossible not to take immediate note, in Tzinacán's and Arjuna's respective mystical experiences, of such close parallels as the sudden and vast light; the sense of infinite variety, space, and power contained within a vast oneness; the pantheistic indistinguishability between God and the cosmos; the elimination of time sequence; and the stock phrase "I see."

Hovering over Tzinacán's exalted vision is the symbol of a boundless and omnipresent wheel. To Western readers, the most familiar use of this image is found in the book of Ezekiel in which the captive prophet sees four winged monsters accompanied by as many wheels, "so high that they were dreadful" (1:18). But it is in India that the wheel functions as a dominant religious and cultural motif: in Vedic rites it stands for the sun; in Hinduism it is one of the weapons of the solar god Vishnu; in Buddhism it figures as a basic symbol in the Wheel of the Law; and the circle that graces the Indian national flag stands for Gandhi's spinning wheel, which was to smash the British cotton factories. Most important for Borges, however, the mystical wheel recurs here and there in various *Upanishads;* it comes up briefly in the *Brihadaranyaka* where the spirit, or oversoul, is compared to the hub of a vast wheel from which there emanate numberless spokes: "as all the spokes are held together in the hub and felly of a wheel, just so in the Soul all things, all gods, all worlds, all breathing things, all souls are held together!"[14] Most striking of all is the extended mention of the wheel in the *Shevashvatara Upanishad,* in which the lovers of Brahman behold the power of God and speak of him as follows:

> We understand him as a wheel with one felly, with a triple tire. . . .
> In this Brahma-wheel the soul flutters about, thinking that itself and the Actuator are different.
> It is the greatness of God in the world by which the Brahma-wheel is caused to revolve.[15]

In addition to these elements clearly derived from Hindu mystical literature, Borges uses materials and vocabulary taken from the Maya epic poem and book of creation, the *Popol Vuh.* The work mentions a historical Tzinacán—who was "the ruler of the Cakchiquels at Iximché"—within a discussion of language differences between rival Cakchiquel and Quiché groups.[16] Tzinacán's god Qaholom (actually the word for "father" in the Quiché tongue) refers from the outset of the poem not to a fixed and precise deity but to a kind of unnamed primary spirit that had preceded all earthly creation. Borges's choice of the figure of the jaguar is by no means arbitrary; among the names of the first men in the *Popol Vuh* are three heroes named Jaguar Quiché, Jaguar Night, and Wind Jaguar. A scholar and translator of the work points out that the Maya word *balam* ("jaguar") strongly suggests "magical powers and is one of the words for 'witch.' It appears to be used in the *Popol Vuh* as an epithet, almost as a title, and can be interpreted as something like 'mighty.'" [17] Hence, even though the close association between jaguar and god appears to be something invented by Borges for the narrative aims of his story, the tigerlike animal symbolizes certain legendary glories and strengths in Quiché-Maya mythology.

In addition to his vision of a wheel, Tzinacán reports having perceived the origins of the universe narrated in "the Book of the Commons"—a code title employed by Borges for the *Popol Vuh*, which, in its story of the creation, treats at length the points briefly cited in "The God's Script." Tzinacán alludes to "mountains that rose out of the water"; the Maya book correspondingly says, "Then the mountains [were] asked to come from the water, / straight way there were great mountains" (223–224). [18] The first men of wood mentioned by Tzinacán figure prominently during the first episodes of the *Popol Vuh* as a group of tentative and unsuccessful creatures, the first humanoids to walk upon the earth.

> At a stroke the dolls were made
>   Carved of wood.
> They looked like people
>   And they talked like people. . . . (623–626)
> They were the first numerous people
>   Who came to be here on earth. (666–667)

Tzinacán's reference to the verbal violence of the cisterns and to the dogs that ravaged the wooden dolls' faces is exactly as it appears in various moments of the Mayan poem:

> And there spoke up all their jars
>   Their griddles
> Their plates
>   Their pots. . . . (721–724)
>
>   Everything
> Abused their faces. (728–729)
>
>   "Pain you have caused us
> You have eaten us,
>   And now we are going to eat you back,"
> Said their dogs to them. (730–733)
>
> "So now you can try
>   Our bones

That are in our mouths;
    We shall eat,"
And their faces were destroyed. (769–774)

By employing material from Mayan tradition, Borges gives to his narrative a concrete historical texture and a content that nevertheless avoids the easy evocations of local color. Similarly, Tzinacán's vision has taken on universal resonances through its Far Eastern imagery and style.

In "The God's Script," Borges has put together a typical mystical experience, a kind of exemplary model for such unitary seizures the world over; and the resemblances among these are often striking. A real-life instance comes from the novelist and scientific publicist Arthur Koestler, who, in his autobiography *The Invisible Writing* (the title is significant), recounts his experiences as a prisoner of the Francoist forces during the Spanish civil war. Koestler spent hours scratching mathematical and geometrical formulas on his cell wall—a "finite means," as he put it, of arriving at a "comprehensive statement about the infinite." This activity is akin to Tzinacán's extended focusing upon the jaguar's spots. Later, after much brooding on the grim fact that he might be shot, Koestler was invaded with a feeling of reconciliation that led him to reflect: "So what? is that all? have you got nothing more serious to worry about?—an answer so spontaneous, fresh and amused as if the intruding annoyance had been the loss of a collar stud."[19] These musings are the psychological equivalent of that moment when Tzinacán serenely blesses his circumstances. It is at this point that Koestler found himself swept away by his mystical vision: "Then I was floating on my back in a river of peace. . . . Then there was no river and no I. The I had ceased to exist, . . . [had] established communication with, and been dissolved in, the universal pool."[20] Koestler, of course, employs the more common archetypal metaphor of water, in contrast with Borges's more culturally bound image of the wheel; but the purpose of both motifs is identical, to convey the sensation that the speaker has fused with a vast oneness. Finally, in a notable parallel to Tzinacán's search for the god's script, Koestler becomes aware of an "invisible text" in this universe although, unlike Tzinacán, he does not feel personally empowered to decipher it.[21]

Borges in "The God's Script" reconstructs a profoundly universal sort of human experience. A possible flaw, however, is its lack of a precise sense of how we are to respond to Tzinacán's concluding attitude. To take a contrasting instance: Hladík in "The Secret Miracle" may or may not have had a full year of grace, but at least in his mind he finished writing his play—a positive feat with which the reader can immediately sympathize. Tzinacán on the other hand believes himself endowed with enormous supernatural powers that he chooses not to utilize, and whether his self-conception is admirable or pathetic remains, in the end, impossible to determine. Self-delusion of this sort is normally viewed as foolish or at best sad, yet there is nothing ridiculous or pitiful in Tzinacán, whose situation combines the tragic and the exalted. Another problem is the unspecific setting; there is nothing particularly "Mayan" about Tzinacán, and one can easily imagine the plot unfolding someplace else. As if to further complicate matters, this "Mayan" priest cites symbols from foreign religions and even echoes Ortega y Gasset when he muses that "a man is, by and large, his circumstances" (L, 172; EA, 119); as a result, Tzinacán comes off less the prerational sorcerer and more the cosmopolitan, Westernized, mid-twentieth-century intellectual. One also finds it difficult to reconcile Tzinacán's vision of an enormous wheel with the fact that pre-Columbian material culture did not know and exploit this technical artifact. These are problems of focus in what is otherwise a dazzlingly constructed narrative.

"The Zahir" (pronounced *zah-HEER*) is arguably a better story—more intensely feverish but also more palpable and concrete. It is also uncommonly dense, even for Borges. The enigmatic first paragraph, for example, includes a description of a twenty-centavo coin, a list of former entities that functioned previously as Zahir, and an ominous indication that the narrator (named "Borges") is losing his mind. The opening four sentences thus present in miniature the three key elements of the plot as well as its general narrative drift. It all began on 6 June with the death of Teodelina Villar,[22] a professional model whose pretty face had once bedecked many car and cold-cream advertisements and who had suffered deeply during the Nazi occupation of Paris because, alas, "how could one follow the fashions?" (L, 157; EA, 104). With religious fervor this little soubrette lived by the dictates of *porteño* sociability, French clothing, and Hollywood tastes. Consumed by an inner despair, she was given to changing her coiffure with alarming frequency. Now, after a decline in the family fortune, she is dead, and "Borges" (who was deeply in love with her) attends the wake, finding her face more beautiful than ever. The narrator then goes to a cheap store, gulps down a brandy, receives a twenty-cent coin in change, and stares at it, mentally listing numerous legendary and literary coins. He later catalogues some of the infinite possibilities of money, and still later dreams he is the gold coins being guarded by the griffin, the mythical animal with the body of a lion and the head and wings of an eagle. Determined to be rid of this metallic obsession, "Borges" the next morning finds an ordinary bar, pays for a brandy with the coin, and, with the help of a tranquilizer, sleeps well that night.

Still haunted by the coin, "Borges" attempts to distract himself by writing a fantastic tale, a monologue by a monster who turns out to be Fafnir, the dragon and gold hoarder of the Nibelung legend. "Borges" also tries to switch obsessions by staring upon other coins; he even visits a psychiatrist. Then, after reading a German monograph casually picked up at a used bookstore, "Borges" finds out that what is troubling him is a "Zahir." The word, which in Arabic means "visible" and is used for evoking one of Allah's ninety-nine attributes, also denotes any single physical object that takes on the mysterious property of being unforgettable, the image thereby driving its victim mad. The book cites examples: an astrolabe in Persia that had to be thrown into the sea, a man in India who saw and drew tigers everywhere—much to the envy of "Borges," stuck with his banal coin. Later, in October, he hears from a friend that Teodelina's sister Juliana as well as a family's chauffeur have taken to raving incessantly about some coin; Juliana has even been put away in an asylum, where she is spoon-fed. With this sinister intimation of his own future, "Borges" realizes that before long his own identity will be totally dominated by the Zahir. He wanders about Buenos Aires, hoping in vain that the obsession will fade away or that "behind the coin I shall find God" (L, 164; EA, 114).

The experience depicted in "The Zahir," despite its exotic flavor and its obvious congruences with that of mystical illumination, differs markedly from the exalted visions described in the other two related stories by Borges. Where Tzinacán's religious ecstasy and "Borges's" encounter with the Aleph are unmistakably positive, in this story what the protagonist "sees" and "knows" is a disturbance, a source of mental anguish and eventual insanity. Moreover, while "The God's Script" and "The Aleph" evoke an infinite sensation of a large and organic oneness, a cosmic totality, the vision of the Zahir imposes itself as a continued and almost cancerlike growth, a proliferating multiplicity in the narrowest realms, a vision that excludes rather than embraces all else. A Zahir intensifies and specializes perception and knowledge, instead of widening them. It may also be remarked in passing that, of these three mystical tales, "The Zahir" is the one most likely to lend itself to purely psychological readings of the Freudian type. "Borges's" obsession could be interpreted as enormously exaggerated guilt feelings projected onto the coin, the physical object that was closely associated with what the narrator himself acknowledges as a coarse act—his going to a dive and having a drink directly after Teodelina's wake. This attractive but shallow woman would inevitably arouse in the love-struck narrator a great deal of ambivalence, which is, according to Freud, a prime source of obsessional guilt in neurotics. (There are some difficulties with this interpretation, as I shall show promptly.) In another sense, "Borges's" seeing the coin everywhere at all times corresponds to his formerly encountering Teodelina's face in all the newspapers and magazines.

One distinguishing feature of the Zahir experience is that it does not descend upon the protagonist in one grand swoop but slowly invades and engulfs "Borges's" spirit, without his realizing at first what is happening. This failure of realization occurs even though the obsession begins when he senses "the beginnings of a fever" after receiving the coin (L, 158; EA, 106), a feeling that, we understand in retrospect, is by no means physiological in origin. It is then that his mind takes off on a curious train of thought, successively citing eleven renowned examples of coins ranging from the Greek myths to Joyce's *Ulysses*. This state of consciousness is so self-absorbed that, after he has roamed the city streets (in a movement that is circular, like the coin), the narrator ends up back at the store where he had started from. "Borges" next reflects upon the numerous unforeseeable (basically infinite) things that money can represent (Brahms, maps, chess, coffee, books by Epictetus, and so forth). Later, in bed, "Borges" feels "sleepless, obsessed, almost happy," a deceptive quasi-euphoria soon overcome by dreams about his being a pile of coins. The irony of it all is that these thoughts creep up on "Borges" without his being aware that they constitute the beginnings of a long-term disaster. Only next morning does he realize that the coin is doing something of more than casual significance to him, though he has yet to gauge its overwhelming influence and waits two months before consulting a psychiatrist. As a further irony, his discovery of Julius Barlach's learned treatise (the archly Teutonic title means *Documents Pertaining to the History of the Legend of the Zahir*) only aggravates "Borges's" troubled spirits, inasmuch as he now realizes that his condition has no cure and will, in view of historical precedents, become much worse. Hence, unlike the note of inner acceptance and contemplative peace on which "The God's Script" ends, "The Zahir" presents an open-ended structure beyond which the empathetic reader can imagine "Borges" succumbing, as did Juliana, to a state of absolute paralysis.

The mysterious force of the Zahir, with its exotic examples purportedly gleaned from the German scholarly book, provides a magical rather than psychological explanation for the narrator's slow mental collapse. After much library sleuthing and personal interviewing, however, I have concluded that the mystical entity "Zahir" is an invention of Borges. Although the Arabic word does signify "visible" (as he indicates in the story), there appears to be no such occult phenomenon by that name in Islamic lore. A medieval sect known as the "Zahirites" actually flourished, but their doctrines were precisely the reverse of what is conveyed by Borges's use of the term—they believed in a strict, unmetaphorical interpretation of the Koran. (The group was named after its founder, Daud uz-Zahiri, "David the Literal.") To add to the suspicion, nowhere in various encyclopedias or in other reference volumes do I find listings for a Julius Barlach, a Zotenberg, a Persian scholar named Lutf Ali Azur, or an archive at Habicht (a real mountain in the Swiss Alps). Abulfeda (1273–1332) did exist, but his times and his fields of knowledge show no connection with mysticism or madness (he was a rather conventional Arabian historian and geographer). Borges included him, it seems, simply to enhance the Islamic atmosphere of his narrative. This also appears to be the case with Colonel Philip Meadows Taylor (1809–1876), an actual Anglo-Indian judge, engineer, and administrator who wrote highly successful potboiler novels about his Asian experiences, including the one mentioned by Borges in "The Zahir." Taylor's own posthumously published memoir (*Story of My Life*, 1920) makes no mention of Zahir; in fact, there is no entry in his book for 1832, the year cited by Borges!

Borges, then, dreams up an elusive Islamic icon, a bit of underground popular necromancy that serves to infuse this narrative of mental derangement—hardly a new subject—with a freshly magical, oriental aura. On the other hand, the intellectual germ for Borges's story seems to have been a conception that does exist in Islam, a trance state referred to as *qabd* (literally "contraction") by Muslim mystics. The following description of *qabd* by a Western scholar cites those very characteristics experienced and brought out by the narrator of "The Zahir."

> Those who experience . . . contraction are . . . prisoners of an overwhelming obsession. . . . There are contracted men who have no appetite whatever for anything except their obsession, for they are

> devoted to it to the exclusion of everything else. . . . One of the proximate causes of contraction . . . is the presentiment of damnation and a mysterious intuition that such punishment is deserved. Inevitably contraction will gain possession of the mind. . . .
>
> The only remedy for this condition is complete submission until the mood passes. For if the sufferer exerts his will in a wild effort to shake himself of it, . . . the contraction will only increase. . . .[23]

Borges's story obviously portrays the "overwhelming obsession" here described, but it also suggests a particular detail, the sense of "damnation," of a "punishment" that is "deserved;" this sentiment is touched upon in connection with Teodelina's death and the narrator's improper act. Beyond this, "Borges's" active efforts to rid himself of the obsession only bring on a worsening of his state, just as happens to the sufferer in the above passages. Hence, "The Zahir" actually does evoke a disturbance of the soul recognized and dealt with by Islamic thinkers. What Borges seems to have conjured up is the ever-shifting Zahir, a physical artifact that in this story unites the prosaic and the portentous, the local and the exotic, the metallic and the metaphysical, the slight and the sublime; the twenty-cent coin, an immeasurably powerful talisman, provides this subjective narrative with a specific material focus, a basis in the historical, the commonplace, and the concrete.

"The Zahir" forcefully exemplifies Borges's best-known narrative procedure, an irruption of magic into the world of reality. The outside setting and circumstances are realistic enough, even banal: a fluffy-headed but charming lady and the city of Buenos Aires, almost as omnipresent as the coin itself; the neighborhoods, parks, railroad stations (Constitución), subway train system, and a great many of the streets in the Argentine metropolis are alluded to by name as the narrator wanders about them, mysteriously possessed by a bizarre spirit from the East. Through "Borges's" consciousness, this intrusive Arabian presence lingers above the winter of the South American urban landscape, casting an Eastern shadow over the narrative and transforming it into a kind of perfervid oriental fantasia on Islamic themes. Side by side with the Hispanic geography, Borges sets up a multitude of proper names and tales from the vast Islamic world ranging from West Africa to Indonesia. In the very first paragraph the narrator rattles off Gujarat, a city in India; Surakarta, a large town in Java; Nadir Shah (1736–1817), a robber turned warrior who became a notoriously harsh ruler of Persia; Rudolf Carl von Slatin (1857–1932), an Anglo-Austrian adventurer and administrator in British Egypt who also spent ten years imprisoned by the fanatical Mahdi sect in the Sudan; and Tetuan, a city in southern Morocco.

This onrush of personalities and places at the very outset of the piece (information garnered, one later realizes, from "Borges's" countless re-readings of Barlach) represents the narrator's overactive, uncontrolled mind. Later, when the Barlach treatise is actually being discussed, "Bor-ges" casually drops names of still more Asiatic persons and places—Bhuj, an Indian town, again in the Gujarat area; Mysore, the name of an Indian state and its capital city; Shiraz, a provincial capital of Persia; Khorasan, a northeastern province of Persia; and Farid Ud-din Attar (1119–1229), a widely read Persian mystic poet, most famous for his *Colloquy of the Birds* (familiar to Borges readers from the "Approach to Al'Mu-tasim"). Attar's work *Asrar Nama* ("Book of Things Unknown"), mentioned twice in "The Zahir," Borges seems to have quite unabashedly invented.

"The Zahir" confronts the reader with a heady mixture of factual eru-dition and mock-learned flimflam. Amidst the plethora of authentic ref-erences to genuine authors, there also can be found spurious attributions to real literati as well as to purely invented writers and personalities. In the realm of fact, for example, the coins recalled mentally by "Borges" after receiving the Zahir are cited exactly as reported in their original sources. Here follows a brief elucidation of these numismatic references:

> Charon the boatman used to receive an obolus (Greek penny) in pay-ment for each soul he ferried across the Styx toward Hades. Belisarius, the famed Byzantine general, fell into disgrace with Emperor Justinian and (legend has it) took to begging for pennies.[24] Laïs, a legendary Greek courtesan, became so unattractive in old age that she would "accept a sovereign or threepence and submit to old men and young alike."[25] The Seven Sleepers of Ephesus were fabled Christian youths who hid in a cave during Emperor Decius's persecutions (A.D. 250); two centuries later they awoke and sent one of their own to purchase food—he aroused suspicion when he tendered a coin from Decius's era; he then led the authorities to the cave, where the seven youths exhibited a holy aura—after which all of them went back to sleep. Isaac Laquedem is one of the names given to the Wandering Jew. The Persian poet Firdusi (b. A.D. 941) received from the emperor an offer of one thousand gold coins for each thousand verses of his very famous poem (a work still read in Iran) but, as Borges says, returned all the money because it was tendered in silver. Ahab in *Moby Dick* rivets upon the *Pequod's* mainmast an Ecuadorian gold doubloon, the reward for the

first crew member who harpoons the white whale.[26] Mr. Bloom in
Joyce's *Ulysses* carries in his pocket a notched Dutch Florin. King Louis
XVI, fleeing in a carriage for Varennes in 1791, was spotted when the
postmaster of Ste. Menehould noticed his resemblance to the royal
portrait on an *assignat* bill (not on a *louis* coin, as "Borges" states).[27]

Similarly, the story-within-a-story that the narrator composes in order
to steer his mind away from the Zahir is closely based on a set of episodes
from a medieval Icelandic work of old Norse, the *Volsungsaga* (known
also as the *Prose Edda*). Parricide, treasure, Gram the sword, and heroic
Sigurd are all preserved intact from the original, though in this case the
action is seen from the perspective of the scaly monster (as in "The
House of Asterion"). The *Fafnismal*, from which the narrator claims to
have extracted this Nordic trifle, is a minor old Icelandic poem that indeed deals (not sympathetically) with the titular dragon made famous by
Wagner's *Ring* opera cycle.[28]

Closely paralleling the infiltration of the Zahir into a clearly identifiable urban setting, Borges inserts into this solid context of authentic erudition an unreal world of imaginary authors and historical figures (Julius
Barlach, Lutf Ali Azur, Al-Yemeni, Yauq) or assigns unreal writings to real
writers. Moreover, pushing all these literary-historical games to their utmost limit, he dreams up an entire occult tradition and gives it a global
sweep, unabashedly locating it in genuine places across Asia, the Middle
East, Africa, and even Spain. From a strictly technical point of view, "The
Zahir" exhibits a formal virtuosity seldom equaled by Borges in his career
as a writer of fiction.

The erudition in this story has a formal and structural purpose; it informs (in both senses of the word) the narrator's mysterious obsession,
gives it specific origins and substance, and helps narrator and reader understand what is happening. Both find out from Barlach that the situation of "Borges" is beyond all hope, that his mind is no longer his own.
Nevertheless, one must regretfully conclude that the erudition becomes
excessive and that the many esoteric books and proper names become
serious obstacles to the narrative flow. For example, why does Borges
allude to *two* non-Western social manuals—the Hebrew *Mishnah* and
the Chinese *LiChi* ("Book of Rites")—simply to characterize Teodelina
Villar's own exaggerated concern for etiquette? It could be argued that
these non-Islamic allusions help set Teodelina apart from the Moslem
materials that dominate the remainder of the narrative, but this seems an
oversubtle rationalization after the fact. The section on Fafnir seems par-

ticularly gratuitous; it impresses one as a stray idea that Borges wished to utilize and so worked into "The Zahir." Admittedly there is some thematic relation to the outer narrative: just as Fafnir guards a valuable treasure, "Borges" in his dream has been turned into gold and is watched over by the griffin. The irony of course is that "Borges," though composing the piece in order to forget about coins, finds himself unintentionally replicating the substance of his nightmare. These two paragraphs, however, appear to be needless impediments to the cumulative rhythms and tensions of the larger narrative.

"The Zahir" takes up a worthy idea—individual depression in the modern city. Unfortunately, Borges overburdens his text and thickens his prose with so many bookish ingredients that they obscure the story's central action, namely, the increasing derangement of the protagonist. Most of the allusiveness in "The Zahir" has an admittedly ironic significance inasmuch as it inadvertently results from the narrator's researches into his mental state, a condition that is in turn intensified by the new knowledge. The entire ensemble of erudition, however, lacks the crackling wit and playful quality that make some of Borges's other bookish pieces ("Pierre Menard," for instance) so appealing.[29]

Borges's humor gives an indispensable freshness to "The Aleph," for the lighthearted and mischievous irony of this piece enables it to overcome those problems of focus and proportion seen in "The God's Script" and "The Zahir." The story opens in 1941 when "Borges" (again narrator and protagonist) recalls the remote death of Beatriz Viterbo (1929), with whom he had been in love. Every year since, on her birthday, he has nourished his affections by visiting her house and family. One unpleasant result of this yearly rite has been his acquaintance with Beatriz's cousin, Carlos Argentino Daneri, an aggressively verbose library employee who entertains flatulent theories about the glories of twentieth-century man. Carlos's overblown pomposity has found a perfect vehicle in *The Earth*, a vast and ever-growing poem in which he hopes to describe the entire globe, country by country—its rivers, resorts, buildings (for example, gas stations in Veracruz), and much geographical trivia all singled out somewhere in his overwrought alexandrines. One day he invites "Borges" over to hear samplings of this monstrosity. It is marvelously bad poetry and its grandiose foolishness is further compounded by liberal sprinklings of foreign phrases, long words, and much name-dropping. Carlos's declamatory performance is capped with an explication de texte, in which the rhymes, metrical patterns, and obscure references of his *Earth* are all examined in excessive detail.

Some unspecified time later, Carlos Argentino telephones "Borges," much upset about the landlords' plans to demolish his family house. Such an act would destroy Carlos's treasure: the Aleph he keeps hidden in his basement. This mysterious item—as he explains it, a point in space containing all other points—is his sole source of information for *The Earth*. "Borges" now thinks the man quite mad, but he nevertheless drops by the house. Carlos takes him down a trapdoor into the cellar, gives him a makeshift pillow, instructs him to lie flat and to fix his gaze upon the nineteenth stair, heads back upstairs, and shuts the door, leaving "Borges" terrified that he may be at the mercy of a lunatic. Suddenly he sees the Aleph, a tiny sphere alive with the image of everything that exists upon the planet. Here follows Borges's celebrated list of what the narrator saw there: the churning sea, deserts and their grains of sand, an Inverness woman, the reader's face, "Borges's" bedroom, obscene letters written by Beatriz to Carlos, and Beatriz's house. However, the catalog must be savored in its entirety by the reader for its evocative rhythms and imagery. "Borges" continues to lie there, genuinely awed, until Argentino suddenly breaks in on this high contemplation and prattles away about the Aleph. Our hero wickedly deflates the poetaster by amicably suggesting a cure in the countryside. Outside again on the street, everything appears strangely familiar to "Borges." Then, in a 1943 postscript, the narrator complains that, although Carlos Argentino's hack epic has just received the second national literary prize, his own book of verse did not even attain nomination. The story ends with a complicated hint that Carlos's Aleph may be false, that the Hebrew term he uses may be cribbed from the many books found in his Aleph!

"The Aleph" is one of Borges's most memorable creations. It ably synthesizes a set of disparate elements in addition to developing each one in its own right. Besides the vision of the Aleph (a moment of astounding poetical radiance and beauty, easily one of Borges's loveliest prose passages), the story brings in such seemingly unrelated matters as the deeply felt attachment of the narrator to the memory of Beatriz; a hilarious caricature of verbosity in Carlos; a parody of bad poetry via *The Earth;* the comic spectacle of "Borges's" endurance of Carlos and his prolixities (out of love for Beatriz); and, for the concluding paragraphs, a dose of "Borgesian" bookishness. Throughout the piece an elegiacally wistful quality prevails, a unifying sentiment that further sharpens the focus of the story. No single component is allowed to predominate at the expense of the others, a structural accomplishment that gives "The Aleph" a balance and perfection not found in Borges's other narratives of mystical understanding.

Of course the centerpiece of all this, the climactic moment of the story, is the narrator's overwhelming vision, in a basement on Garay Street, of the thing Carlos Argentino calls an Aleph. The special potency of "Borges's" account of his experience stems from the elementary simplicity of the Aleph's form as well as from the directness and immediacy of its content. As regards the latter, what "Borges" sees consists chiefly of everyday objects; it is a *physical* catalogue, as sensuous and visual as anything found in Whitman or Neruda, with just enough esoterica to spice it up and with delicious surprises—Beatriz's obscenities, for instance. The common artifacts constituting this vision, moreover, ultimately determine the manner of its presentation. Where Tzinacán's ecstasy seems somewhat contrived and arranged according to outside religious schemes, and where "The Zahir" multiplies entities of a rather bookish and exotic kind, the visual images of "The Aleph," by contrast, shine forth with no discernible effort. They are concrete and unique, precisely profiled yet related to a larger whole, a whole that nonetheless manifests itself with ease and grace and with no apparent signs of library footwork or intellectual strain.[30]

Equally important for the convincing nature of "Borges's" vision is the fact that the Aleph has an objective existence within the confines of the story. Instead of being a possibly subjective mental illusion, the Aleph is something that actually exists as a presence dazzling to its viewers. There is no doubt that a man of sound mind and sensitive makeup named "Borges" is actually witnessing, with judicious detachment and wisdom, an entity awesome in its significance. The author Borges succeeds in devising an object that is both magical and realistic; though built from the ordinary world, it is cosmically inspired as well.

What especially lends credibility to "Borges's" account of the Aleph (visual clarity and seductive rhythms aside), is the highly ironic nature of the narrative context in which the experience occurs. The Aleph itself, needless to say, is an instance of the pure sublime, yet everything connected with it is questionable, even ridiculous. The immediate circumstances of the vision are downright comical: "Borges" spread out flat on a tile floor with a burlap bag for a pillow, lying in "something of a pit" with empty bottles, piles of burlap bags, and mice, and on the stairway the microcosm and macrocosm of the Aleph—all of this under a condemned house in a run-down urban neighborhood. Framing this unique experience is the person of Carlos Argentino, with his overblown pre-liminary instructions (more ridiculous in the original Spanish, where he bandies puffed-up phrases like *decúbito dorsal* [EA, 162]). Afterward, fol-lowing hard upon the narrator's perfect and laconic observation ("I felt infinite wonder, infinite pity" [TA, 28; EA, 166]), Carlos intrudes with his hilariously boorish cracks about being cockeyed (*tarumba* [EA, 166]), seeing the Aleph in color, and "one hell of an observatory, eh Borges?" (TA, 15; EA, 166). The humor here is further enhanced when "Borges" thanks the old windbag for his basement hospitality and earnestly sug-gests quiet and fresh air.

Though in this story the author inexplicably has Carlos speak with the Castillian *tú* instead of the Argentinian *vos,* there is a genuinely oral character to the vulgar poetaster's speechifying—he sounds like many a *porteño* hustler on the make. In addition, at an early point in the story, Carlos humorously anticipates "Borges's" own catalogue when he ex-tols twentieth-century man and goes on to list numerous modern arti-facts: "telephones, telegraphs, phonographs, wireless sets, motion picture screens, slide projectors, glossaries, timetables, handbooks, bulletins . . ." (TA, 17; EA, 153). A larger irony here (one of the most important in the piece) is that, despite privileged and repeated access to one of the absolute wonders of the universe, Carlos Argentino remains a bad poet. Contact with an infinite number of facts cannot make up for Carlos's inadequate sense of form.

Beyond all this comic absurdity, "The Aleph" is composed of a rich tissue of interconnecting ironies that are clear in intent and embodied in concrete entities. The most salient of these ironies is brought about by the humorous foil, posed by Carlos Argentino, to all that is positive about Beatriz. The story plays on such contradictions as the sanctity of Beatriz's house and Carlos's presence therein; Beatriz's svelte grace and frailty and Carlos's "pink-faced, overweight, gray-haired" look (TA, 16; EA, 152); the intense earnestness of "Borges's" love for Beatriz and the sheer silliness of Carlos's behavior; the telephone that at one time conveyed Beatriz's sweet voice and now transmits that of Carlos Argentino. The poetaster thus serves as an indispensable link to the subplot of Beatriz, who, though long dead biologically, remains alive in the loving memory of "Borges" and in his less-than-willing ties to her cousin.

In addition, "The Aleph" strongly suggests an ironic relationship be-tween its fondly remembered Beatriz and her renowned namesake Beat-rice Portinari, celebrated by Dante in the *Vita Nuova* and the *Paradiso* (Beatriz's Italian surname, Viterbo, heightens this intimation).[31] Indeed,

Borges's story is cleverly constructed as a parody of Dante's works. Before the writing of the *Vita Nuova* and of "The Aleph," the respective Beatrice in each work has long been dead; these literary works serve as elegies for the lost love. In Dante's *Vita Nuova* the narrator has dealings with a dear friend who is closely related to Beatrice (section 32); sees a vision of the young lady's former beauty (section 39); intersperses the prose narrative with some of his finest poems; and follows each of the latter with formal explications and analyses. In "The Aleph," on the other hand, the narrator has dealings not with a dear friend but with a boor who happens to be Beatriz's cousin. This cousin, moreover, intersperses "Borges's" prose narrative with some of the worst poetry imaginable and follows each verse with presumptuous explications and analyses. In similar fashion, Beatrice serves as Dante's guide in *Paradiso*, leading him ever upward to a joyous and highly contemplative union with God, the cosmos, and herself. In "The Aleph," by contrast, "Borges's" guiding hand is not Beatriz but a tenth-rate Vergil named Carlos Argentino, who leads the narrator downward into a pitlike cellar. Perhaps the ultimate irony is that, where the *Vita Nuova* reveals Beatrice in all her living beauty and the *Paradiso* leads the poet to a joyous, highly contemplative reunion with his beloved, "Borges's" vision reveals nothing more than the stark reality of her bones and the bizarre fact of the obscene letters. Hence, "Borges's" memory of Beatriz and the multiple photographs that he wistfully stares at actually preserve an infinitely more attractive image of the dearly departed than does "Borges's" grand mystical vision; the vision, after all, captures not the past but the present.

Other ironic discrepancies at work in "The Aleph" include, for example, the national literary prize received by Carlos Argentino for his horrendous long poem, or "Borges's" twin recollection of his grief and of the changed cigarette advertisements at Constitución station. Even the twin epigraphs to the story have a deeply ironic significance. The Shakespeare quotation comes from a conversation in which Hamlet complains to Rosencrantz and Guildenstern that Denmark is a prison; the intense desire expressed in the epigraph to Borges's story is swiftly undercut in the Shakespeare play by the ugly reality apprehended by Prince Hamlet (act 2, sc. 2):

> HAMLET: What have you, my friends, deserved at the hands of Fortune, that she sends you to prison hither?
> GUILDENSTERN: Prison, my lord!
> H: Denmark's a prison.

ROSENCRANTZ: Then is the world one.

H: A goodly one, in which there are many confines, wards, and dun-
geons, Denmark being one o' the worst.

R: We think not so, my lord.

H: Why then, 'tis none to you, for there is nothing good or bad but
thinking makes it so. To me it is a prison.

R: Why, then your ambition makes it one. 'Tis too narrow for your
mind.

H: *Oh, God, I could be bounded in a nutshell and count myself a king of infinite
space were it not that I have bad dreams.* (Emphasis added.)

The lines from Hobbes take Borges's intent still further, for their context is openly hostile to certain notions of infinity; in one of his final chapters, the British thinker attacks, on numerous grounds, the arid, tired
Aristotelianism of the still-dominant scholastic philosophy of his time.
Hobbes in particular takes to task the Aristotelians ("they" in the extract
Borges cites) for defining eternity as the endless survival of the present
moment, an obviously static conception of the universe. Since Borges's
narrative deals with passing time and the inexorable process of endless
change, and since even an Aleph, with its infinite powers of seeing, cannot
recapture Beatriz's face, Hobbes's sharply worded objection has a precise
relevance to the fantastic-realist fiction that follows.

All these interrelated ironies gain focus through Borges's mastery of
form, the story's almost classical balance of structure. "The Aleph" is
built as a series of concentric narratives: its opening and its concluding
outer edges have as their subject the narrator's wistful memory of Beatriz;
directly within this outer frame we have Carlos Argentino and his ele-
phantine encyclopedism (geographical in the first part of the story, literary in the postscript); and at the very center of the narrative stands the
Aleph itself. Another cyclical presence framing the events is the Plaza
Constitución. After Beatriz's death, "Borges" initially recalls that the
publicity posters at Constitución station flaunted their indifference to his
bereavement by advertising a new brand of cigarettes; by contrast, following his experience with the Aleph near the end of the story, all the human
faces at Constitución seem strangely familiar to "Borges" because they
now belong to his recently attained knowledge and vision. Humorously
opposing Argentino and his Aleph (two A's) are three Z's (the landlords
Zunino and Zangri, and the lawyer Zunni). Within this well-planned architectural scaffold there is a unity in the incidents, most of which concern irretrievable loss—the death of Beatriz, the progressive fading of her

image, the demolition of the house where she lived, the destruction of the Aleph, and of course "Borges's" loss of the national literary prize. Corresponding to this unity in mode of action is a profound unity of feeling, with an elegiac, nostalgic quality prevailing throughout, a sentiment emphasized at various points by the narrator's melancholy references to the pictures of Beatriz, by the Proustian association of the telephone receiver with her voice, and by his remark (on learning that Beatriz's house is about to be destroyed) that "after the age of fifty [forty in the original], all change becomes a hateful symbol of the passing of time" (TA, 22; EA, 160).

The story is also highly persuasive because the experience of the Aleph and the enveloping narrative both bristle with facts—historical, literary, even everyday. Buenos Aires is a vividly felt presence, not only through its geography (Garay Street, Constitución station, Chacarita cemetery), but also through its daily rituals and ordinary population (cafés, lawyers, landlords, train commuters, the writers' club). The global geography is no less authentic. Carlos Argentino's vision may be an undisciplined garbage heap, but it is composed of real places— Queensland, the northeastern tropical state in Australia; the Ob River, running from the Urals to the Arctic; Veracruz, the large port city on the Gulf of Mexico. "Borges" too sees and cites specific locations—Fray Bentos, Querétaro, Mirzapur (towns in Uruguay, Mexico, and India), and Alkmaar, a town in northern Holland where "Borges" sees a globe, that favorite Dutch domestic artifact.

Genuine literary texts and historical figures also have their role in "The Aleph." The early comparison of Carlos's *The Earth* to the *Poly-Olbion* of Michael Drayton (1563–1631) is perfectly appropriate; in that fifteen-thousand-line monstrosity, Drayton took up the task of describing every nook and cranny of England and Wales in (of all things) alexandrine tetrameters. To this text he appended a running commentary by his friend Jeffrey Selden, much as Carlos explicates his own alexandrine verses. The Captain Burton paraphrased in the story's "postscript" is no less than Sir Richard Burton (1821–1890), the renowned Victorian linguist, orientalist, translator of the *Arabian Nights,* and adventurer-at-large. Burton (as the narrative notes) really served as British consul from 1865 to 1869 in the southeastern Brazilian town of Santos, later writing a book (*Highlands of Brazil*) about his experiences. All titles listed in Burton's purported manuscript are perfectly authentic, and the discoverer of this "lost text," Pedro Henríquez Ureña (1884–1946), is the eminent scholar and critic from the Dominican Republic who, fleeing the Trujillo dictatorship, went on to spend most of his productive life in Argentina. Even *The Sharper's Cards* (the "Borges" work that fails to attain nomination for the national prize) is a genuine title; it was the first book-length attempt of Borges himself, who wrote it in Spain about 1920 and, following failure to find a publisher, destroyed it. In a sense, the characters in "The Aleph" also are real, for Beatriz is presumably a composite of several of the tall, regal ladies once loved by Borges, and Carlos Argentino is a portrait of a reportedly bad poet who wrote in a style much resembling that of the fictional character.[32]

Broadly speaking, then, there are only two absolute inventions in this narrative. One of these is the manuscript listing Aleph-like phenomena, which is attributed by the narrator "Borges" to Captain Burton. The other concocted entity here is the Aleph itself. The term "Aleph," signifying a single point in space that holds images of all other points in space, comes from Borges's literary imagination. In the earlier works listed in the "postscript," man-made artifacts such as all-seeing mirrors appear, but this small, inexplicable, mysterious, cosmological sphere we owe to Borges. The idea of using the Hebrew letter "Aleph" to denote this elusive entity seems to be taken from two rather disparate sources: an underground cabbalistic tract and a twentieth-century mathematical concept. The cabbalistic roots of the term are found in the *Sepher Yetsirah* (the "Book of Formation"), which is a brief, anonymous, enigmatic, early medieval work of Judaic mysticism that interprets God's entire creation as having been effected by the numbers "1" to "10" and by the twenty-two letters of the Hebrew alphabet: "God drew them, hewed them, combined them, weighed them, interchanged them, and through them produced the whole creation."[33] In this system (vast in implications but laconically sketched out in the original), "Aleph" is one of the three "mother" letters and contains all of the remaining twenty-one. A European scholar makes the following remarks about this character: "The first nine letters are the archetypes of numbers from 1–9. Aleph, number 1, is the unthinkable life-death, abstract principle for all that is and all that is not. It lives and is timeless, yet all time is in it. It is beyond measure, beyond understanding, yet all measures and all understanding have their roots in it."[34]

The vision in Borges's story is an extrapolation from something merely implied in the *Sepher Yetsirah:* if the letters of the Hebrew alphabet have a primordial relationship to the whole of creation and if "Aleph" in turn contains all of these letters, it follows then that "Aleph" by itself has a special relationship to all of creation. From here it is a perfectly conceivable step to place "Aleph" in the outside world and to transform this mystical-linguistic idea into an entity observable in space; in the Cabbalah, however, one must emphasize that it decidedly is not an object. On the other hand, one might note that "Borges's" detached contemplation of the Aleph belongs to the Judaic tradition, for ecstatic unions are rare with Hebrew mystics, who customarily stress objectivity over personal feeling.[35]

The other source of Borges's Aleph (acknowledged by the author in an interview)[36] is Bertrand Russell and, thus, ultimately the German mathematician, Georg Cantor (1848–1918), whose *Mengenlehre* ("theory of sets") is even alluded to in the story (TA, 29; EA, 168). Cantor is also known in his field for having formulated the notion of "transfinite" cardinals, that is, numbers that are not altered by the addition of one. In order to designate these transfinites, Cantor adopted the Hebrew letter "Aleph." Bertrand Russell, who gives the various types of infinite numbers a detailed look in his *Introduction to Mathematical Philosophy*, describes transfinites as "the smallest of the infinite cardinals, which have other suffixes. Thus the name of the smallest of infinite cardinals is $\aleph$."[37] The number so signified is "the limit (in order of magnitude) of the cardinal numbers 1,2,3, . . . n . . . , although the numerical differences between $\aleph$ and a finite cardinal is constant and infinite."[38] What concerns us, however, is not the fine distinctions of a highly specialized field but the fact that there actually do exist mathematical entities termed "Alephs," which are infinite and serve as a theoretical limit to all preceding finite numbers. Here again, as one observed with the *Sepher Yetsirah*, one can see the inferential genesis of Borges's imaginative idea. Just as Cantor's "Aleph" contains all previously existent numbers plus itself, similarly, the Aleph planted by Borges in Carlos Argentino's basement contains all existent points plus itself.

I have shown how Borges invented a point in space and called it Aleph. In the actual story, however, Borges gets himself off the hook by having his narrator impishly suggest that Carlos Argentino may have appropriated the term from elsewhere and attached it to whatever that thing was in his basement (hence, the narrator's dismissal of a "false Aleph"). After all, "Borges" speculates, Carlos may well have seen the name employed in certain texts found (with everything else) in his Aleph; he could thus have read the word in the *Sepher Yetsirah,* in Georg Cantor's theory, or in

Burton's manuscript and then so labeled the astonishing phenomenon. The suggestion is that Carlos may have possessed nothing more than an optical instrument of the kind cited in Burton's list of human artifacts. The genuine Aleph is "really" hidden deep inside a column of the Mosque of Amr near Cairo, one of Islam's oldest existing temples.

In order to give this falsely attributed observation of Burton's a touch of authenticity, Borges cites Ibn-Khaldun (1332–1406), an Arab scholar and man of politics whose extensive writings in philosophy and history are among the greatest works of early social theory; his works are veritable forerunners of the modern human sciences.[39] The citation given by Borges comes from the Muqaddimah ("prologue") to Ibn-Khaldun's history of the Berbers, in a section where he examines the development of architecture and related skills in Arab lands: "At the beginning the dynasty is a Bedouin one, and therefore needs for its construction activities the help of other regions."[40] Borges's text purposely gives the impression that Ibn-Khaldun is discussing the Amr Mosque, its columns, and possibly even its hidden Aleph, but there is no mention of these matters in the original context. Borges cites Ibn-Khaldun above all to lend an impression of authority to the Aleph he has seen and to deflect the reader's disbelief by raising the possibility of yet another Aleph, remote and virtually inaccessible in the Middle East.

These scholarly references, though they appear at the end, nevertheless perform an essential narrative function for the story. By adducing concrete precedents to the Aleph, these recollections of older texts enhance verisimilitude; at the same time, by diminishing Carlos's claims, they furnish us a necessary irony with which to think about that visionary experience. What is most satisfying about these learned materials is that, by arising almost as a casual afterthought, they seem incidental and as such do not obscure Borges's narrative. In "The Zahir," however, the allusive apparatus badly overloads the style and the plot. Borges's last-minute bookishness in "The Aleph," by contrast, heightens and strengthens his preceding central story line without eclipsing it. The comical Carlos, the memory of Beatriz, the contrasted feelings of "Borges" toward each of them, and his exalted vision in the cellar remain far more in the foreground than does any recondite esoterica. Basic human sentiments such as nostalgia, love, bereavement, petty irritation, resignation, and awe—all subtly evoked and kept in delicate balance—are aspects of "The Aleph" far more memorable than its artifice and intertextuality. These personal feelings, with their twin context of urban landscape and mystical contemplation, are the key concerns in one of Borges's finest pieces, a narrative that is touching, amusing, and inspiring all at the same time.

"T he Immortal," Borges's longest and most ambitious story, also depicts a grand holistic experience. Here, however, the wisdom is achieved not in a single moment of dazzling insight but during the slow accumulation of thousands of years. This piece, moreover, takes the cult of bookishness to a degree that is extreme even for Borges. Indeed, "The Immortal" has as its implied theme the essential value (both as personal solace and historical residue) of literary texts.

The narrative opens with a note on Joseph Cartaphilus, an aged, worn-out antique dealer who has recently sold the Princess Lucinge an original edition of Pope's translation of the *Iliad*. Inside the book she discovers a mysterious manuscript—the story we are about to read. The first-person narrator of that text, one Marcus Flaminius Rufus, who is an army officer posted in Asia Minor during the reign of Emperor Diocletian, heeds an inner impulse to seek out the River of Immortality and the celebrated City of Immortals. After traversing many strange east African lands and cultures and after enduring much hardship, he is abandoned by his expeditionary force. One day he awakes and finds himself on the slope of a mountain, hands tied. Down below he espies a tribe of mute troglodytes (cave dwellers) and, on the opposite bank of a filthy stream, the sumptuous city of legend. After vainly awaiting help for several days, he recklessly leaps down, drinks from the stream, and walks toward the city (followed by a stray troglodyte). The city, however, turns out to be a bizarre architectural monstrosity without a trace of human life.

Disappointed, Rufus leaves the place and tries to teach language to the lingering troglodyte, whom he calls "Argos" because of his hangdog quality. One day, during a rainstorm that provokes wild ecstasy among the cave dwellers, "Argos" groans. Rufus, moved, cries out the troglodyte's nickname. Suddenly Argos stammers a line out of the *Odyssey* (book 17), "Argos, Ulysses's dog." When an astounded Rufus asks him how well he knows the *Odyssey,* the once mute troglodyte admits to being no less than Homer himself—"It must be a thousand and one hundred years since I invented it" (L, 113; EA, 18). Homer now informs Rufus that the filthy stream is the renowned river and the troglodyte tribe that of the Immortals, who long ago abandoned the city and resolved to ignore the physical world and to live in pure thought. Rufus now joins with them and reflects upon the consequences of immortality, a condition under which one can experience all and be all. At different moments in his eternal life, an Immortal can be perverse or kind, evil or virtuous. An Immortal, moreover, neither feels pity for nor furnishes help to others; with eons of time standing before and after him, he knows everything will happen again and therefore has no use for the elegiacal or for any reminder of death or mutability. However, the Immortals are also not preoccupied with their own comfort because the well-being of the body is of no ultimate consequence.

In the tenth century, it occurs to the Immortals that there must also exist a river of mortality, and they go on their separate quests. Rufus wanders far and wide—he fights in England in 1066, transcribes Sinbad's adventures (in Arabic), purchases Pope's *Iliad* in 1716 (the volume with which Borges's story opens), converses with Vico, sails on the Patna (the boat in Conrad's *Lord Jim*), and so forth. One day in Eritrea he drinks from a spring and, with relief, senses pain: he has tasted the water of death. At this point Cartaphilus interrupts Rufus's narrative to clarify some curious facts. He singles out specifically Homeric phrases in Rufus's prose and remarks on the Roman soldier's shift from military activities to sedentary ones such as transcribing Sinbad's voyages; such activity is understandable if we think of Homer the poet writing out a kind of Arabian *Odyssey*. The dizzying impression conveyed by this enigmatic page is that Homer, Rufus, and Cartaphilus all form one and the same person. (Borges never states this too baldly, holding the idea aloft as an ambiguous hint—somewhat as Alain Resnais does in his haunting film *Last Year at Marienbad*.)

Following Cartaphilus's pinpointing of Homeric phrases, "Borges" adds a 1950 postscript wherein he cites a book by one Nahum Cordovero, who situates Cartaphilus's manuscript in the tradition of literary patchwork from the Greek *centos* to the poetry of T. S. Eliot. Noting snippets from Pliny, Descartes, De Quincey, and Shaw, Cordovero pronounces the manuscript a hoax. Not so, says "Borges," who defends the authenticity of the work and argues that, when a wasted Cartaphilus took pen in hand and composed his astounding memoir, those words and phrases from literary history were the only reality remaining to him.

"The Immortal" posits and develops a typical "Borgesian" speculation: what would it be like if a man or a group of men were immortal? Section four of the story furnishes us a concrete illustration. There we read of the absolute tolerance (or perhaps nihilistic indifference) of the Immortals toward whatever happens. The reason for this detachment is that anything worthwhile in the present is offset by something calamitous in the future and vice-versa. In a famous moment in Dostoevski, it will be recalled, Ivan Karamazov argues that if God does not exist there are no absolute moral laws and thus everything is permitted. In a community of Immortals everything also is permitted because, from a standpoint of eternity, everything happens anyway. Everything, moreover, will happen again sometime; thus, in the worldview of the Immortals, nothing is unique and nothing has value in itself, because any event inevitably echoes the past and foreshadows the future. As a result, the Immortals, who live without fear of personal death, are both too privileged and too wise. Like many old men, they know too much and are therefore jaded and desensitized; but, like children, they are untroubled by the possibility of death and unconcerned with the fate of other individuals.

Because experience of the new is unknown to the Immortals, because ethical distinctions for them carry no weight or meaning, and because death by inanition, disease, or other causes is an impossibility, there are no legitimate grounds for action among the Immortals. There is no "deadline" before which something needs to be done. Seldom do the Immortals even speak, for everything has been said and they have heard everything. In a world without death, nothing is of immediate or ultimate necessity and quietism is an inevitable result. Paradoxically, the Immortals are spurred to action only because they realize that somewhere a river of death must flow.

An immortal existence, furthermore, has special consequences for personal identity. Having literally all time in which to develop, travel, and even take action, an Immortal's personality has no final limits. He can eventually experience all situations, play all roles—in a word, *be* everyone. He may be a warrior at one stage of his life, a man of letters at another. If he is old enough, he may have met Homer; with world enough and time he can eventually become Homer as well; and if he happens to have been the original Homer, he can develop into other individuals but also encounter the Immortal who has become Homer! This partly explains the utter ambiguity as to who is saying what about whom in the last two pages of the main narrative.

The Homeric and other literary citations in "Rufus's" text could be explained by any or all of the following: (1) they were uttered because Rufus-Cartaphilus was once truly Homer; (2) they evolved naturally and coincidentally out of Cartaphilus's own language, with its wealth of experience and exposure; and (3) they were expressed as intended allusions to Homer and to other authors on his part—a common literary device.

After all, the prose of any typical English writer at the green age of forty will doubtless exhibit its share of biblical or Shakespearian phraseology, as well as snatches from writings currently fashionable. Cartaphilus, by extension, has at his disposal the entire body of Western literature beginning with Homer—something he has lived and experienced directly in his travels, not to mention the direct contact with famous writers. Because he is utterly alone on earth and knows not a soul with whom he may share his past, Cartaphilus has nothing left to draw from in his efforts to communicate, save what Yeats called "monuments of unaging intellect," the literary record of Europe's past.

Joseph Cartaphilus, the Princess of Lucinge reports, seems "wasted" (understandable, given his thousands of years of age). His gray look and vague features befit a man who has been all men; since he has seen artifacts from all times and places, it is quite appropriate that his business be antiques. His surname, however, has special implications and a lengthy history, for "Cartaphilus" happens to be one of the numerous designations once applied to the Wandering Jew. This mythical story is a kind of anti-Semitic equivalent to the legend of the Flying Dutchman. The first recorded mention of the name appears in the *Flores Historiarum,* by Roger Wendover; this thirteenth-century chronicler tells of a porter in the employment of Pontius Pilate whose name was Cartaphilus. The latter reportedly slapped Jesus, who then replied to the porter, "I am going, and you will wait till I return." As punishment, Cartaphilus was condemned to live until the age of one hundred years and then revert to age thirty—a cycle that would repeat itself until the end of time. According to Wendover, Cartaphilus has since wandered the earth, talking with casual listeners about the dawn of Christianity.[41]

What clearly seems to have been an antecedent for "The Immortal," however, is a book whose title tells all—*Chronicles Selected from the Originals of Cartaphilus, the Wandering Jew, Embracing a Period of Nearly XIX Centuries.* This literary curiosity was penned by David Hoffman, an eccentric nineteenth-century jurist from Baltimore, Maryland. George Anderson, the author of an impressive study of the Wandering Jew legend, appears to have waded through Hoffman's huge three-volume work and notes that "Cartaphilus assumes a bewildering number of names, characteristics, and intellectual and philosophical postures."[42] Hoffman's Cartaphilus also travels far and wide, meeting all manner of celebrities, including Cornelius Agrippa (whom Borges's story mentions). Whether Borges read David Hoffman's *Chronicles of Cartaphilus* could only have been ascertained by asking him directly, but the coincidences of range, fact, and even names seem proof enough. (It happens to be just the kind of book Borges would have liked to read.) Whatever the degree of Borges's acquaintance with Hoffman's strange opus, the artistic method employed in "The Immortal" is entirely his own; he boils down the materials of a vast book and a two-thousand-year legend to twenty-odd pages.

The use of the name Cartaphilus, Borges once told an interviewer, actually figured in his first drafts for a story dealing specifically with the Wandering Jew. This germ of an idea Borges then expanded to that of a more ecumenical Immortal, though of course he retained Cartaphilus, mentioning the name in the initial paragraph of the narrative as "a clue, to let you know what the story is about."[43] The possibility of using Homer, on the other hand, came to Borges as almost an afterthought during his composing of the piece. He said: "I asked myself, What would the epic of an immortal man be? I took up the theme of an immortal among immortals. . . . I thought of a very ancient person and hit upon the prototype of an ancient man, Homer, a Homer who continues to live and evolve, who forgets Greek, who in the end has been all men."[44] Here we see the beginning of those strong intimations, discussed above, that the protagonist of "The Immortal" is a Homer who has become Rufus and later Cartaphilus. Borges in fact demonstrated to the same interviewer how this use of Homer was precisely his intent: "I began with a soldier who has forgotten he had been Homer, a Homer who first constructed the ordered edifice of the *Iliad* and afterwards the chaotic edifice of the City. . . . If a man is immortal, after centuries he will be all men. At the end of the story one suspects that the narrator is Homer."[45]

Even though Borges did come much later to the idea of Homer as protagonist, the Greek poet figures quite early in the finished narrative. Cartaphilus reportedly comes from Smyrna (traditionally regarded as Homer's birthplace) and is buried on the isle of Ios (where Homer's remains, legend has it, are to be found). This choice of Homer as a kind of governing presence throughout has special thematic significance for "The Immortal." Homer is the oldest of the "immortal" poets and ultimately the father of all Western literature; he can be said to live on today through the power of his poetic language and the freshness of his storytelling.

The literary allusiveness of "The Immortal" has both formal and thematic interest; its vast range of references, its echoes from other works, are also chosen for precise thematic reasons. For a detailed look at this matter, I refer the reader to *The Narrow Act: Borges' Art of Allusion,* a pioneering work by Ronald Christ, who dedicates his final thirty-five pages to identifying, citing, comparing, and explicating the sources and raw materials which go into the making of this story. I can only touch very briefly on what Christ demonstrates in great detail. The passage from Pliny (singled out by Nahum Cordovero in the "postscript") is a description of various peoples of central Africa (the Troglodytae, the Garamantes, the Argilae) in terms virtually identical to those of Rufus. Descartes's epistle offers a speculation, similar to that ventured in "The Immortal," as to why monkeys never speak; Thomas De Quincey is mined for basic imagery. Shaw's *Back to Methuselah* is a play that deals with longevity and its consequences; its fifth act, entitled "As Far as Thought Can Reach," is filled with reflections of the kind found in "The Immortal" (for example, "any fool can play the flute, or play anything, if he practices enough"; or "everything happens to everybody sooner or later if there is time enough"). The passages from Homer are accurately pinpointed by Cartaphilus. Among unacknowledged sources for "The Immortal," one might remark a parallel in *The Time Machine* to Borges's troglodytes and their lofty indifference; in a passage strikingly similar to the moment when Rufus cries out in vain for help, Wells's fantastical Eloi make not the slightest effort to save the nearly drowning time traveler.

"The Immortal," with its allusive texture and its overt singling out of this allusiveness, invites comparison with T. S. Eliot's *The Waste Land*. Nevertheless, the fundamental reasons for identifying allusion in Borges and Eliot show a world of difference. Eliot publicly admitted late in life that he appended his scholarly materials quite simply because the poem was considered too short for publication as a book! Hence, for all their imposing aspect, the famous "Notes to *The Waste Land*" were mostly a pragmatic affair, concocted with the express aim of filling up additional pages.[46] In "The Immortal," by contrast, the actual set of notes (the "postscript") takes up very little space. Moreover, while Eliot's "Notes" are an entity quite separate from *The Waste Land* itself, Borges's own acknowledgment of sources exhibits demonstrable formal and thematic functions within the body of the narrative.

There is, to begin with, an obvious hall-of-mirrors effect in Borges's narrative: Cartaphilus explicates his own text, which in turn is examined and criticized by Cordovero, who is in turn refuted by Borges—commentary about commentary about commentary. The "postscript" also contains its own hidden plays of meaning in, for example, Cordovero's reported study of the tradition of literary patchwork. The technical name for this latter genre is *cento*, based on a Latin word signifying "a garment made up of several pieces" and related to the Greek *kentron*, "cloak of rags." The title of Cordovero's study, *A Coat of Many Colors,* reflects these diverse meanings. The book's length of one hundred pages may signify little in English, but Spanish *cien* derives from Latin *centum,* thus further echoing *cento* in concealed word play. Cordovero happens to be the surname of Moses Cordovero, the greatest writer of the Jewish mystical tradition, but the name also suggests the Greek word for "yarn" and various modern cognates; here Cordovero is the yarn holding together the patchwork that makes up "The Immortal."[47]

The many fragments from past literature, from Homer to Shaw, that go into the making of "The Immortal" also constitute the key to its larger meaning. First, the numerous allusions are perfectly justifiable, given Cartaphilus's long life. Since he has done all manner of things—fight wars, write poems, travel, meet celebrities—he has also conceivably read all kinds of texts and absorbed their influences. On the other hand, in view of his countless years and experiences, there is a high probability that Cartaphilus would independently hit upon certain ideas and images employed by other authors, a common real-life occurrence. Ultimately, of course, one might say that external influences as well as individual tendency are simultaneously at work.

And yet, however much he may have seen and done in the past, in the end a wizened Cartaphilus touchingly writes, "There no longer remain any remembered images; only words remain" (L, 118; EA, 25). One can understand how, in his three thousand years, this wanderer would forget most facts and most images from the past. Indeed, the Immortal's text bristles with apologies for his unsure memory—"As far as I can recall" (the manuscript thus begins), "I do not remember my return," or "later events have inextricably distorted the memory of . . . our journey." In contrast to Funes and his incapacity to forget, Cartaphilus is unable to retain even the basic facts of his identity, a matter which is never clarified for the reader. Just as the narrator of Eliot's *The Waste Land* shores a few literary fragments against a world in ruins, those literary words from the past serve Cartaphilus as his sole meaningful grasp on an infinitely long and elusive reality.

Cartaphilus's suggested triple identity of Greek poet, Roman soldier, and Jewish wanderer implicitly situates him within those ancient civilizational forms—Greek literature, Roman imperialism, Judaic religion and intellectuality—out of which Western culture was to develop. Going beyond antiquity, the Immortal ranges through the literature and culture of England, France, Italy, Germany, Czechoslovakia, Hungary, Samarkand, and India. The soldier Rufus journeys from Persia westward through Asia Minor to some point east of the Sahara (where the City of Immortals appears to be located). In the final analysis, "The Immortal" is a parable about the tenuous survival of this broad range of human experience and historical grandeur through "words of others." The writings of great authors, if only a "poor pittance," are nonetheless our sole meaningful contact with a past that lingers on, vaguely and imperfectly, in the present.

Borges later regretted most of what he does in this story, finding it too long and, with its "baroque" and "luxuriant" prose, overwritten.[48] He is on record as wishing that he had completely redone the piece and reduced it to one-fifth its actual length.[49] There is a point to Borges's harsh self-criticism. "The Immortal" has an awkward, unwieldy quality, and, except for the pathos in the third-person accounts of Cartaphilus, one notes a certain flatness, a curious lack of meaningful irony and emotion in the narrative. On one hand, there is a richly suggestive ambiguity in our never being told exactly how Homer, Rufus, and Cartaphilus form one person; on the other hand, Borges does carry this indirection to excess, making the story needlessly vague and confusing toward the end. Of all Borges's ambitious works, this one is by far the least successful. Certainly it cannot compare favorably to "The Library of Babel" or "Tlön, Uqbar, Orbis Tertius," with their brooding sense of a cosmos beyond human control. Though not a simple exercise on the order of "Herbert Quain," "The Immortal" is an unfortunate instance of possibilities not fully realized. What the story above all lacks is a central image like the library or the encyclopedia, for far too many ideas and incidents are at work within these twenty pages. Unlike "The Aleph" or "The God's Script," where the whole of experience appears simultaneously in a single place and moment, the holistic understanding in this work comes from slow accumulation and extensive travel through several millennia. For subject matter of this sort, a sense of development is necessary; perhaps such development is impossible within the confines of a short story. Because of the notions it suggests, "The Immortal" is an interesting but ultimately static effort, too abstract and mental for the type of vital experience it sets out to depict. By no means beginners' Borges, "The Immortal" is the very last of his stories a reader should attempt to tackle.

Part III

BORGES'S PLACE
IN LITERATURE

10   *Dreamtigers* and Later Works

A TENTATIVE SUMMATION

Borges's output in prose fiction after *El Aleph,* though abundant, presents a somewhat changed picture. Of five subsequent gatherings, only *El hacedor* (literally "The Maker," but retitled *Dreamtigers* in the English translation),[1] a thin opus first issued in 1960, is unmistakably of major artistic importance. The other collections— *Crónicas de Bustos Domecq* (1967; *Chronicles of Bustos Domecq,* 1976), *El libro de los seres imaginarios* (1967; *The Book of Imaginary Beings,* 1969), *El informe de Brodie* (1970; *Doctor Brodie's Report,* 1972), and *El libro de arena* (1975; *The Book of Sand,* 1978)—all pose troublesome aesthetic limitations that I shall discuss in the proper place.

Any reader taking up these volumes must bear in mind an awesome fact: they are the work of a man almost completely blind. Composed mentally, then dictated to various personal friends and amanuenses, Borges's later stories came into being unaided by direct authorial contact with the page. In chapter 3, I noted how, in his mature years, Borges used to work over his prose, writing and rewriting each paragraph until it would assume precisely the shape he desired; this craftsman's procedure was denied him when creating the stories found in *Doctor Brodie's Report* and *The Book of Sand.* It was not accidental that, after the loss of his eyesight, Borges came back to poetry following a prolonged absence and produced some fine volumes of verse. (The poetic medium, of course, afforded him those age-old and ever-useful writer's aids: brevity, prosody, and rhyme.) This later poetry, much of it the equal of his earlier lyrics from the 1920s, often deals touchingly with the subject of his blindness. One of Borges's collections of poems bears the resonantly suggestive title *Elogio de la sombra* (1969; *In Praise of Darkness,* 1973).On through his final years, poems by Borges continued to appear with regularity in the pages of news dailies such as *La Nación.*

The volume from Borges's later phase that offers the greatest interest, however, is *Dreamtigers*. As a book it is an unusual artifact, resembling a miscellany with its grab bag of prose parables, political meditations, short-short stories, and a comparable amount of verse (some of it among Borges's best). There is also a kind of appendix that consists of fanciful passages purportedly quoted from old books but all invented by Borges. The exception is "H. Gering," who was a real-life Icelandic scholar (1874–1925); the book attributed to Gering, however, is quite spurious. Later Spanish editions of *El hacedor* also included a prose poem, dedicated to the slain John F. Kennedy, on the subject of political assassination throughout the course of history.

From the brevity of *Dreamtigers's* fictions, a first-time reader might be led to conclude that its parables were (like the later stories of Borges) written mentally after the author had gone blind. In reality a good deal of these materials predate the actual conception of *El hacedor* as a book. For example, the sketches entitled "Dreamtigers" and "My Toenails" appeared in the newspaper *Crítica* as far back as 1934. Other pieces exhibit preoccupations closely akin to those developed in *El Aleph*. "The Captive" reproduces in part the story of the Indian-Englishwoman and Borges's grandmother, with the blonde, gray-eyed, Argentine "Indian" woman here becoming a knife-obsessed male, and with numerous parallels in language between the two narratives. "Everything and Nothing" plays with the central idea, dwelled upon in "The Immortal," of an individual who is all men. "The Draped Mirrors" sets up the same basic plot as "The Zahir" (a banal physical object that drives someone to madness), but actually this brief sketch, with its directness and its absence of esoteric baggage, carries far more dramatic impact than does Borges's overwrought Islamic fantasy. The bitterness and immediacy of those sketches portraying aspects of the Rosas and Perón dictatorships suggest that the Perón regime either was still in effect or had only recently been overthrown.

There are thus sufficient indications that certain portions of *Dreamtigers* were in existence some time before they were bound together into a single volume. What made the book possible was a request from his publisher, Emecé, for a new full-length manuscript. When Borges protested that he had no written book immediately handy, his editor, Carlos Frías, urged him to go nosing about in shelves and drawers where he would surely hit upon some forgotten materials and early drafts. For a year or so Borges and his mother Leonor did exactly that, and the end result of this process was *El hacedor*.[2]

Given the almost occasional origins of the volume, it is not surprising that *Dreamtigers* should present no common thread—no largely recurring theme or subject, not even a genre—holding much of its disparate contents together. Yet to Borges it was his most personal book, and it has also remained a favorite of many of its readers.[3] Granted, the artistic quality is somewhat uneven, more so than is usual in collections of short texts. Some of the parables are little more than clever games, intellectual juggling with ideas. In this category belong "Dialogue on a Dialogue" and "Argumentum Ornithologicum," early pieces that lightly spoof the ontological argument and other notions from metaphysics. The explicitly political commentaries ("The Sham," "Dialogue of the Dead") share the limitations noted earlier in "Deutsches Requiem," namely, excessive fancy at the expense of concrete knowledge and wisdom.

Other more effective pieces deal with the sense of human loss as passing time and inevitable death take their toll; as such, these sketches radiate a profoundly infectious nostalgia. "Mutations" wistfully remarks on how certain objects—arrows, lassoes, crosses—in distant times were basic tools of existence and a source of genuine awe but today are innocuous symbols, artifacts of everyday décor. "The Witness" speculates fictionally upon the death, sometime in the High Middle Ages, of the very last Saxon, the final remaining relic of an older culture that the Normans and their descendants have pitilessly displaced (an emotionally charged sort of situation well known to anthropologists and some linguists). One of Borges's most intensely soulful compositions bears a woman's name, "Delia Elena San Marco"; it concerns a casual good-bye that is transformed by Delia's unexpected death into a farewell, with a flow of city traffic across which the two friends wave now becoming the Acheron river, and with the narrator skeptically speculating on immortality and a possible future farewell—all kept in a perfect, harmonious balance.

The richest stories in *Dreamtigers* give us inventive, imaginative portraits of great authors from the past—Homer, Dante, Marini, Shakespeare. Such figures fascinate Borges because, although he himself sees literature as a means of masking private situations, he paradoxically sees literature as something produced by living people, by conscious individuals with personal histories and temperaments. To write, as Borges sees it, is no less an activity than being, say, a soldier or a mystic. Writing is, in his unashamed phrase, "one of the many destinies of man."[4] As is fitting, then, some of these sketches of grand old poets deal in great degree with possible reasons why they (or by extension any author) might feel compelled or destined to write.

In "The Maker," an unnamed protagonist with some past record of heroic action goes through life more or less indifferent to the multifarious phenomena around him (Borges here inserts one of his dazzling catalogues) and with no great desire to register "memory's delights." One day he realizes he is going blind. Desperate, he descends mentally into his past and recalls two incidents, one a childhood moment of anger against another boy (after which his father had given him a knife to encourage his manhood), the other a dim recollection of his first amorous experience. It is at the moment of remembrance when he recognizes that it is his destiny to sing the *Iliad* and the *Odyssey*.

What is novel about this sketch is that Borges conjures up a real-life, flesh-and-blood Homer (an individual whose historical existence is hardly beyond dispute); moreover, the man's epic poems here are not (as they were in "The Immortal") inevitable facts in a grand time scheme but, instead, the result of a specific person's conscious choice within a situation. Homer in "The Maker" decides to compose poetry not only because he is gifted with special powers of observation and sensitivity but also because, later in life, private misfortune spurs him to artistry and furnishes him the need and the will to create.

Borges himself once remarked in an interview that writers write because basically they are unhappy,[5] a casual suggestion that surprisingly resembles Freud's idea of aesthetic creativity. Freud's theory states that artists are individuals who, owing to some physical or psychological difficulty, are excluded from the normal activities of society and seek in art a compensatory means to (in Freud's memorable phrase) "power, money, and the love of women." In the case of "The Maker," Homer formerly had known normal life but now, with his handicap, stands excluded from war and from love (from "power" and from "women"); he will instead sing of them ("Ares and Aphrodite") in his verse. Of course, "The Maker" is not a thesis-narrative written and filtered through a preconceived idea. It aims to evoke a vital experience and seeks to convey that special moment of truth when a man understands himself and his fate, when an individual (who happens to be Homer) becomes aware of the poet and senses the epic poems that are growing inside of him. Borges's Homer thus discovers that he is a "maker," that his artistic identity and inchoate art must be fashioned and "made"—a notion, implicit in the title, suggestive of existentialist kinds of thinking fashionable at the time the sketch was written.

The best-known of all the literary parables in *Dreamtigers* bears as its original title an English phrase, "Everything and Nothing." This provocative little vignette is the thumbnail biography of an Englishman who feels curiously empty, who lacks a set personality. In order to feign a personality, the man becomes an actor and then writes plays to create individuals that he might become—characters with names like Julius Caesar, Juliet, and Macbeth. Wearying of this unreal world, he assumes the dry role of businessman and thus takes on yet another personality. On his deathbed, he prays to God and asks the Lord to allow him, just once, to be one and himself. But from the whirlwind a voice replies that "my Shakespeare" was intended to be, like God, "many persons—and no one."

The immediate source of inspiration for this piece seems to be a letter from George Bernard Shaw to Frank Harris that actually contains the remark, "I understand everything and everyone, and am nobody and nothing"; the remark is quoted by Borges in his essay on Shaw (OI, 173; OI, 220). The resulting vignette is the most concise, direct, and unadorned expression of the "Borgesian" subject running through the tortuous prose of "The Immortal" and casually recurring in many of the author's other narratives—the idea that any man is potentially all men. There is also the slightest hint of a literary doctrine here, one variously put forth by Keats, Eliot, and Borges himself, to the effect that, inasmuch as literature has as its ultimate aim to share in the language, attitudes, and experiences of all other men, to write literature is, by its very nature, a denial of personality.

No historical figure would have been more appropriate for the imaginative treatment of this theme than Shakespeare. The gaps in the biography of the poet, coupled with the sheer power of his work, all constitute one of the strangest contradictions in literary history. No single writer is more responsible for so large a cast of memorable characters, so vividly drawn that they have become and will long remain an indispensable part of our language and our everyday stock of images, ideas, and types. At the same time, although official documentation concerning the raw data of Shakespeare's fifty-two years of life—numerous materials confirming his birth, baptism, marriage, parenthood, residence, career, lawsuits, business transactions, last will and testament, death and burial—has come down to us, we have absolutely no hint about what Shakespeare may have been like as a man, an individual person. Because there are no letters or private papers extant and no surviving accounts of his conduct from the pens of friends or enemies, nothing is really known of Shakespeare's manner, his temperament, his likes and dislikes, his strengths and weaknesses, his feelings vis-à-vis others. Curiously, we know a considerable amount about the personal side of ancient authors such as Euripides or Vergil, and the colorful idiosyncrasies of Christopher Marlowe and Ben Jonson have preserved for us a distant memory of Shakespeare's most notable fellow contemporaries. To compound the frustration, despite the powerful emotions present in his works, Shakespeare in his art remains steadfastly impersonal. From the poetry and plays it is impossible to infer *anything* about their creator's own preferences and beliefs, as could be done with Pope or Dostoevski, men whose writings always show a strong commitment to particular kinds of values.

This lack of personal information is troubling to all who love Shakespeare. He thus is seen literally as "everything and nothing": the greatest author of them all, his poetry the richest and most abundant, his many tragic and comic characters still alive in our minds today—and yet his own qualities as a human being and real-life character are an absolute, unmitigated blank. The frustrating vacuum has led numerous authors to speculate imaginatively on Shakespeare's life and temperament. One speculation has been that he may have been an ordinary man with no salient, immediately discernible idiosyncrasies, perhaps even undistinctive and uninteresting. Borges's parable, then, concretely dramatizes that possibility: the great playwright and poet may have fashioned so many individuals because of his own absence of a well-defined individuality. Thus avoiding the old platitudes, tired rhetoric, and awed servility that constitute the perils of writing appreciations of Shakespeare, Borges in "Everything and Nothing" pays a moving tribute to this most astounding of all literary figures.

It seems only fitting that those parables in *Dreamtigers* dealing fancifully with the elusive identities of various poets and writers should have, as the final entry, a meditation on the author himself, the quite famous "Borges and I." The vignette focuses upon two separate persons: the narrator "I" who has personal tastes (for example, hourglasses, maps, coffee) and the "Borges" who shares these tastes but "in a vain way," posturing with them like an author. Meanwhile, the narrator reads of "Borges" in reference works, receives mail addressed to the writer, feels uneasy with "the other one," and sadly realizes that he lives on, thanks to "him." Despite "Borges's" achievements, however, those works now belong neither to the shy narrator nor to the famous author but to tradition. It ends with one of Borges's most celebrated single sentences, "I do not know which of us is writing this page."

This little parable (considered by some critics to be the most perfect page of Spanish prose)[6] analyzes its subject through two differing yet coexistent personalities: Borges the public author and Borges the private individual. The private man has a taste for simple delights (coffee) and older things (those etymologies, hourglasses, and eighteenth-century typefaces), but the public man makes a calculated show of, brings artifice to, these tastes. The private man has experiences of his own, the public man poeticizes them, and the private man is thereby fulfilled. What the public man wrote in the past, however, now eludes each of them, because those works find their place as the collective property of all readers; moreover, when the private man dies, only some stray facts of himself will survive in the public legacy of the other. That is why the private man now recognizes himself less "in [Borges's] books than in others or in the laborious strumming of a guitar" (L, 246; H, 51). The private person understandably can better identify with books that speak to his immediate situation or with the immediate sentiments of folk music than with stories composed two decades ago by his other self. Nevertheless, despite the copresence of these two entities, it is difficult to distinguish between them, hard to discern where one ends and the other begins. Hence, the narrator's uncertainty as to who writes the page, the ordinary man or the author. The immediate and obvious impression, of course, is that the private person is musing on the fact of two Borgeses, but the writer of the page could really be the author Borges *posing* as the private man and thus casting a complicating light on the entire passage one has read. If "the other one" did produce this page, then "Borges and I" is yet another public pose worked out by the vain, theatrical Borges.

The story, then, dwells on a problematic split familiar to anyone studying a public figure—the simplified image of a man or woman who is in the collective public's eye and, underneath that, the more subtle and complex private person who lives from minute to minute, day by day. (Borges himself once asserted that fame is another form of incomprehension; in other words, the elements that make up anyone's fame are but a fraction of his or her full identity.) More broadly, however, "Borges and I" develops a theme that touches us all, for every one of us is conscious of a public image that we project at work and in group play, and a private person who, in varying degrees, differs from the somewhat artificial persona created by us for public appearance. By the same token, the public acts of our earlier years also eventually seem to us the conduct of someone else; those experiences now belong not to ourselves but to the shared memories of our former classmates or fellow employees. However, our private activities can be transformed into public business, and not by high art alone (as any casual survey of the mass media will show). Borges's example of liking coffee is revealing in this regard. Most of us take a cup of coffee in the morning, a harmless enough private deed. Yet our attitude would differ markedly were we to drink coffee in the presence of (in ascending order of publicness) a new lover, an enemy, a journalist, a photographer, or a TV cameraman from network news. It is a common occurrence to see—in gossip magazines, for instance—pictures underscored with captions such as "Borges at home, sipping coffee" or "Borges examining his hourglass"—images that are, in fact, staged by media men. In such a situation, a love for coffee and old artifacts does indeed become the pose of an actor.

"Borges and I" rounds off with a personal touch the most impressive phase of its Argentine author's literary growth. It is a sweetly subjective meditation in, again, what is a highly personal book that Borges repeatedly singled out as his favorite. Other readers may not concur with these preferences. For example, the collection has been judged "overrated" by the Anglo-American critic Michael Wood,[7] and certainly the prose parables in *Dreamtigers* lack the darker power of the *Ficciones*. The fact that these little sketches, written purely for the amusement of their author, are so predominantly "literary" in their focus, is especially significant, inasmuch as they reveal just how much Borges's most intimate concerns revolve around books and bookmen. They are parables for readers who share Borges's love of pondering over strictly literary problems and literary people. Consequently, the pieces have none of the unforgettable nightmarishness or inspired force of the parables of Franz Kafka, whose visionary miniatures evoke not poetic mysteries but the absurdities and irrationalities of everyday life. Borges has often been termed a "writer's writer"; of all his works, *Dreamtigers* best illustrates this common reservation.

Besides summing up a creative period, "Borges and I" hints at a new future direction for its author. The piece alludes, with just a trace of self-deprecation, to "games with time and infinity" that now belong to the past and speaks of a need to conceive something else. One indication of the new paths Borges would soon explore was his cooperative effort with Margarita Guerrero, the work that in English bears the title *The Book of Imaginary Beings* (1969). The first version of this anthology appeared in 1954 under the name *Manual de zoología fantástica,* with eighty-two vignettes; thirty-four more pieces were added in 1967, when it was published under its current title, *El libro de los seres imaginarios.* To the English version, four more pieces were added.

This delightful little volume gathers creatures from all manner of times and places, arranges them in alphabetical order, vividly and amusedly describes them, and, when the ultimate sources are literary, identifies and often fully quotes pertinent passages from the work in which the imaginary being originates. Here we encounter old standbys such as the minotaur, the unicorn, the chimera, assorted dragons, and the biblical behemoth; we see real animals (the panther, the pelican) in the curious shapes with which sundry Europeans were wont to imagine them; we find fanciful monsters fabricated by Kafka and Poe, and fantastic fauna of Chilean, Chinese, and Yankee folklore; we wonder at esoteric beasts that bear unlikely names such as humbaba, burak, and squonk. From the "A Bao A Qui" to "Zaratan," Borges's and Guerrero's catalog will bring un-alloyed pleasure to many a browser or fantastical-zoological researcher. *The Book of Imaginary Beings* has no high literary aims or functions be-yond what its original title states: to be a manual. The book thus makes a worthy companion to such classic works as Bullfinch's and Edith Hamil-ton's Greco-Roman compendia; it can serve as a modest complement to the global reach of the *Larousse Encyclopedia of Mythology* and is also ac-cessible to scholars who happen to be of grammar-school age. Borges's literary art here loses nothing for the very reason that it pretends to very little. Unlike the *Cronopios and Famas* of Julio Cortázar, whose invented creatures touch upon deeper human feelings and suggest specific human types, *The Book of Imaginary Beings* is, as Borges himself puts it, simply a bit of fun, a "sideshow." [8]

In the mid-1960s, Borges brought out another group of vignettes in collaboration with his close friend Adolfo Bioy Casares. This more so-phisticated set of entertainments was entitled *Crónicas de Bustos Domecq* (1967, issued in English as *Chronicles of Bustos Domecq*). For this volume, Borges and Bioy created an eccentric, peripatetic journalist-aesthete,[9] a highbrow gossip columnist who has spent a lifetime reporting on the world of avant-garde art and its practitioners in and about Buenos Aires. Here, for example, is César Paladión, who has written word-for-word remakes of such works as Goethe's *Egmont,* Rousseau's *Emile,* Conan Doyle's *The Hound of the Baskervilles,* Stowe's *Uncle Tom's Cabin,* and even (in Latin!) Cicero's *De divinatione;* the literary justification ten-dered by critics is that, since poets like Eliot and Pound built their poems from the fragments of others, Paladión carries this to the logical extreme and simply appropriates complete opuses. Here is Ramón Bonavena, founder of "descriptionism," a school that consists simply of describing, in multi-volume works, such slices of life as the north-northeast corner of the author's desk. Here is the Uruguayan-Jewish poet Nierenstein Sonza, who habitually sends for publication not his final, polished poems but their much cruder original versions, with the theory that oral traditions will eventually improve his germinal drafts. Naturalism is turned on its head when one author submits to a literary contest (requiring poetry about the venerated subject of roses) not a poem but a real-life rose. Here is F. J. Loomis, whose "novels" consist solely of one word repeated throughout, thereby reducing literature to its essentials. Here we find architects who design nonfunctional buildings; a poet, Santiago Ginsberg, who employs words in total disregard for their meaning but with much concern for their purely private associations and emotions; another writer, Tulio Herrera, whose poetry leaves out all those boring connectives that provide basic information and whose novels never bring in the protagonists; an artist who, after painting realistic cityscapes, covers them with black shoe polish; and a dandy who was wont to stroll all day around a seaside resort with clothes meticulously painted onto his naked body—until the police got wise and arrested him.

Bustos Domecq's reportage spans most of this century up to the time of the publication of his *Chronicles* (from 1908 to the mid-1960s), but the bulk of the artists and "works" discussed belong to the period between 1910 and 1940, when the avant-garde experience and idea, and the Bohemian enclaves that nourished them, were at their creative height. Many great paintings, poems, and novels came out of that milieu, but much nonsense also was peddled under its name. This collection lightly mocks the more crack-brained manifestations of self-deluded avant-garde hacks and clever con-men; it also spoofs the gullible hangers-on, the socially ambitious art watchers such as Honorio Bustos Domecq himself.

Readers will inevitably spot some of the targets, the general artistic procedures, the movements, and even the men (many of them respectable today) lampooned in these sketches. Cesar Paladión, who simply copies other men's works is, of course, a less subtle version of Pierre Menard, discussed in chapter 6. (In the 1980s, an artist named Sherry Levine took pre-existent photographs by Walker Evans and simply exhibited them with her own name—allegedly her way of protesting against patriarchy.) The so-called descriptionism of Ramón Bonavena appears to be an unloving jab at the ultra-objectivity and *chosisme* of French novelists such as Robbe-Grillet. The poet who leaves out essential connectives has simply pushed to an absurd degree of brevity the penchant of twentieth-century poets for maximum obliqueness and compression. The painter who blacks over his meticulously realistic canvasses has a real-life counterpart in the American abstractionist, Ad Reinhardt, whose morose paintings consist exclusively of various shades of black. The novelist whose novels consist of one single repeated word has a close equivalent in Andy Warhol's films and in some of the music of John Cage. One also finds in this volume occasional potshots at *ultraísmo* and its adherents—Borges's way of expiating his youthful sin as active crusader for that particular Modernist sect.

Though some of the stories gathered in *Bustos Domecq* are amusing, a good many of them are not. One often finds oneself smiling at the intention behind the squib but not at whatever wit may be imbedded in the vignette itself. Some of it is repetitive: "The Multifaceted Vilaseco" and "Homage to César Paladión" both play upon the notion of fruitful plagiarism, with nothing much being gained by the overlap in subject matter. Some of the humor of Borges and Bioy is forced; "Sartorial Revolution II" tells of a fashion designer who has devised a special glove, one on which each finger comes equipped with a different mechanical gadget—an old comedian's routine that is not very funny.

A couple of the more effective pieces attributed to Señor Bustos Domecq not only succeed in their humor but manage to transcend their condition of parody. For example, "A Brand-New Approach" is a pseudo-report, an intellectual fantasy about historical revisionism and mythmaking gone mad. It is a world in which France celebrates Waterloo as a French victory, the American South glorifies Appomatox, Mexico includes Texas in its national maps, Tunis regularly observes the razing of Rome by Carthaginian conquerors, and Argentine schools hark back to heroic times when Argentina annexed Spain, "a truth backed by a fine." The vignette is a witty reflection on the extremes to which any national entity will go for the sake of enhancing its historical self-image. On the whole, however, even the strong sketches exhibit only those strengths peculiar to the lampoon genre; they are pure parody with all its limitations—single-issue focus, endless verbal razzle-dazzle, muscle-flexing cerebralism, and a narrow gamut of emotion. Although most of these pieces probably elicited knowing chuckles from the readers who first encountered them in magazines, several in succession do not make an especially rewarding experience. One becomes too much aware of the tricks and formulas being repeatedly trotted out for use. Unlike *The Book of Imaginary Beings,* this volume offers no factual information that might compensate for its general lack of larger artistic significance. (Borges himself admitted to me in conversation that he considered parody "contemptible"—*"despreciable"*—as a genre.)

Unfortunately, unlike Borges's other prose works, *Chronicles of Bustos Domecq* loses far too much in translation. For instance, the text is filled with local references (places, public personalities, institutions) that carry no weight outside Argentina. (The di Giovanni translation attempts to solve this by changing those proper names to northern entities such as academic critics Frank Kermode and Carter Wheelock or institutions like the AFL-CIO.) Another problem is the virtuoso language woven by these two Argentine artificers; the texture is thick and busy with colorful colloquialisms, serpentine syntax, and humorously recherché big words, a medium that would require equivalent verbal virtuosity in English. In the end, however, the delightfully mannered prose of Borges and Bioy may resist all efforts at anglicizing. Pedantic as well as precious, Señor Bustos Domecq's style lies not too far from the flowery rhetoric of a Hispanic arts columnist and full-time aesthete, a colorful sort of figure often seen gracing the periodicals of South America but practically nonexistent in North America, where arts reportage customarily strives for an informal, bouncy flavor—even when the language is dense (John Leonard, for instance). Perhaps a closer equivalent would be the baroque prose of certain American conservatives such as William Buckley or William Safire, but even in their case the tone and manner taken are a bantamlike petulance, not arty, florid foppishness. Style, normally unobtrusive in Borges's fiction, is here essential to the whole overstated joke. I'm afraid this aspect falls completely by the wayside when Bustos Domecq's writings travel north. *Chronicles* is a divertissement more complicated in form than *The Book of Imaginary Beings,* and the Argentine local color and lexical spice brought into play in this volume happen to be among its chief complicating factors.

M any of Borges's admirers were quite puzzled by his two collections of short stories from the 1970s—*Doctor Brodie's Report* and *The Book of Sand.* In the late 1960s, it should be mentioned, Borges was feeling creatively spent. The combination of his unhappy marriage and the sense that he could never replicate the high achievements of his middle phase had brought about in him a case of writer's block. This is not an uncommon experience among writers who have been fortunate enough to produce a masterpiece or two and to attract admiring readers into the bargain. One factor can be the possibility of repeating oneself, which is a temptation to be studiously avoided by any seriously committed artist. Some, like Forster or Salinger, simply stop practicing their art altogether. Others, like Joyce after *Ulysses* or Nabokov after *Pale Fire,* keep up their experiments, though with some loss of proportion or authenticity. Then there is the case of Faulkner, who, following the exhaustion induced in him by the monumental labors involved in writing *Absalom, Absalom!,* moved to a more traditional sort of storytelling in his Snopes trilogy. Norman Mailer, for his part, took decades in matching, with *The Executioner's Song*—in which the journalist, the stylist, and the imaginer all succeed in coming magically together—the novelistic greatness that he had attained as a twenty-five-year-old beginner with *The Naked and the Dead.* Relatively few are writers like García Márquez, who, in the intimidating wake of *One Hundred Years of Solitude,* demonstrates a capacity for reinventing himself as literary artist with each new book he has written.

Borges found himself in a comparable situation in his late sixties. And it was his then-amanuensis and translator, Norman Thomas di Giovanni, who managed to persuade him that he should write—or, now, dictate—fiction once again, based on the author's special experiences and knowledge of an earlier Argentina. The result was the collection *Doctor Brodie's Report.*

Brodie's Report has some special significance in Borges's oeuvre because of its preface, a key document in which the writer declares that "now, having passed seventy, I believe I have found my own voice" (DBR, 11; IB, 10). He specifically employs the term "realistic" in characterizing these pieces. The author thereby sets aside, unequivocally if gently, his celebrated fantastical ways and adopts a diametrically opposed type of narrative writing. Indeed, in *Brodie's Report* there are, with a couple of exceptions, no signs of the labyrinths, magical mirrors, or human doubles of another era; those exotic or imaginary places and the journeys through time that seemed to be the very mark of the real Borges, are now mostly gone. On the contrary, these stories plainly set out to depict recognizable, credible sorts of people in places familiar to their author and his Argentine contemporaries (the action of the pieces unfolds mostly in the early twentieth century, when the author was a growing boy). Over and beyond matters of approach and content, Borges also admits to giving up "the surprises inherent in a baroque style" (DBR, 11; IB, 9), a change that stayed with him in his subsequent work. For, together with what he saw as a cleaning up of his narrator's workshop, there also was an astounding process of simplification, a scaling down of language. The reader will find no "Whitmanesque" catalogues of unlike objects here, no parenthetical ambiguities or skewed expressions of sentiment, no mock-scholarly disputes or droll footnotes, no re-sounding parallelisms or hidden repetitions—the stylistic devices that at one time gave Borges's prose its haunting and otherworldly quality.

To most (though not all) readers the net result of Borges's change of tactics is an unfortunate impoverishment of the texture (the intellectual content, structural solidity, high wit, and linguistic density) of his art. Curiously, both here and in *The Book of Sand,* Borges retains many of his better-known narrative tricks; for example, the "found" manuscripts and the seeming apologies for omitted or incomplete materials. Within the rather reduced literary forces put into play by the author, however, these techniques stand out more than is necessary and draw to themselves an attention somewhat disproportionate to their simple surroundings. In the worst cases, provocative epigrams about the narrator's uncertainty or the fictive illusion tend to take on an uncomfortably sententious flavor in this fragile context. Hence, a passing paradox like "I no longer know whether the events I am about to relate are effects or causes" (DBR, 46; IB, 103) leaps out at the reader and has the effect of a facile and gratuitous mannerism with no justifiably organic relationship to the violent action piece within which it arises.

Because none of the material in *Doctor Brodie's Report* even ap-proaches the level of the *Ficciones* or the stories in *El Aleph,* there is little reason to discuss any one piece in detail. "The Gospel According to Mark" and "Guayaquil" are perhaps the most interesting tales, both of them dealing with latter-day repetitions of historical events—the Cruci-fixion in the former, the mysterious private meeting between the two great South American liberators San Martín and Bolívar in the latter. In both stories, the vital role of power and coercion pervades the histori-cal reenactment—brute violence without religious feeling or divine re-demption in "The Gospel," sheer personal will without social basis in "Guayaquil." (However, in the latter story Borges fails to demonstrate convincingly how Zimmerman, the short, homely central European émi-gré, actually succeeds in besting the wealthy scion of a grand old family; simply to say that greater will is at work is insufficient). "The Elder Lady" is about an aristocratic Argentinian señora, the daughter of a minor hero of the nineteenth-century independence wars, a widow (perhaps a com-posite of the author's own mother and grandmother) who lives far be-yond her times until quietly breathing her last at age one hundred in 1941. It is a touchingly pathetic picture of old age, with its remoteness from present-day circumstance and its stronger memories of the past.

The remaining stories in this book are, for the most part, rather slight.

They deal either with gratuitous violence or interpersonal fine points; they contain no larger thematic or formal elements to infuse the narratives with substance and lack the wit or irony to make them at least amusing. The title piece is surely one of Borges's weakest single works. Purportedly a found manuscript in which a Scottish missionary named Brodie tells of his years with the Yahoo tribe, the story inevitably comes off as a pale reflection of "Tlön, Uqbar, Orbis Tertius," which in framework and procedure it superficially resembles but without the global human concerns and disquieting fear that make Borges's encyclopedic fantasy so great a story. One could never say, as Borges did about "Tlön," that the Yahoos in "Doctor Brodie's Report" are really a pretext for conveying the anguish and confusion of an isolated individual. Though the story obviously takes its terms and part of its plot from Swift, little else seems to have been transmitted from the great satirist, for "Doctor Brodie's Report" fails to suggest any specific, strongly felt notions about non-Yahoo peoples.

Doctor Brodie's Report, it should be observed, is a work of considerable literary maturity. By comparison with the early *Universal History of Infamy,* the craft in these narratives is completely under control and sure of its aims and procedures; its smooth prose is seldom ruffled by unassimilable or extraneous elements. Yet Borges's very first stories, with all their youthful experimentalism and awkward energy, have an original spark, the germs of things to come. The fundamental problem with *Brodie's Report,* however, is its lack of personal virtues commonly expected from the work of elder artists. It shows resignation without deep serenity, acceptance without great wisdom (unlike what we find in the later Shakespeare or an aged Cervantes), sober realism without a Pablo Neruda's joy in physical reality, awareness of human conflict without the inspired vitalism of the 70-year-old Yeats. *Doctor Brodie's Report* is, on first and final analysis, one of master Borges's least appealing efforts.

T *he Book of Sand* is a curious collection. Unlike *Doctor Brodie's Report,* which presents a uniform tone throughout and visible continuity in plots, themes, language, and even lengths of the narratives, this later book shows no discernible pattern. It contains some completely fantastical tales ("Utopia of a Tired Man," "There Are More Things," and the title story), while one piece ("The Bribe") deals with a rather trivial, if quirky, aspect of U.S. academic life. A few stories actually come close to Borges's earlier achievements ("The Congress," "The

Night of the Gifts," "Avelino Arredondo"), but some are surprisingly slight, especially "The Other." There are no overarching concerns, thematic or otherwise, in *The Book of Sand*. Although certain subjects do recur, they do not add up to any systematic set of preoccupations. Reflecting Borges's old-age hobby, his personal affair with old Norse and its cultural kin, a few stories are medieval fantasies located in northern Europe ("Undr," "The Mirror and the Mask," "The Disk"); still other narratives carry Nordic trappings of imagery and vocabulary.

If there is anything strikingly new about this volume, it is the fact that, for the first time in Borges's career with fiction, he depicts in positive terms (without erstwhile associations of danger or destructiveness) the experience of physical love between man and woman. "Ulrike" builds up to nothing less than an erotic scene in a darkened, red-wallpapered hotel bedroom in the medieval town of York; it is a romantic anecdote, the story of a South American professor's casual encounter and night of sweet love with a lady from Norway who, like himself, happens to be touring England by train. "The Congress" also interpolates a lengthy amorous episode—this time with one Beatrice—originating in the reading room of the British Museum. (Perhaps some future biographer of Borges will explain the author's predilection for the female name Ulrike.[10]) "The Night of the Gifts" tells of an old man's vivid memory of his first sexual experience with an Indian girl in a brothel. This initiation coincides with a gunfight on the premises between a legendary Argentine bandit and the police; thus, the narrator knows love and death the very same night, the bedroom shielding him from the bullets.

As suggested above, *The Book of Sand* is extremely uneven in its artistry. On the negative side, one finds too many pale echoes of Borges at his best. "The Other," essentially a "Borges and I" that is diluted and spread thin, depicts the elder author seated on a bench by the Charles River in Cambridge, Massachusetts, where he comes across an earlier Genevan version of himself; the two Doubles engage in uninteresting chit-chat, bandying personal and political topics that uneasily recall Borges's interviews. Similarly, "Undr," a Nordic fantasy about a powerful poem whose one chosen word evokes all experience, will seem familiar to a reader who knows the briefer, more dramatic "Parable of the Palace" in *Dreamtigers*. In a like vein, "The Sect of the Thirty" is a mock-historical Christian and Roman fable along the lines of "The Theologians"; it too contains concocted references to Gibbon, but the old magic is now gone and the performance is mechanical and perfunctory. "Avelino Arredondo," though not a bad story, is clearly "The Waiting" remade in mirror image; based on a historical incident, it tells of an ordinary Uruguayan who completely isolates himself from everyone in order to prepare for his culminating act—the successful assassination of his country's president.

The formal roughness of *The Book of Sand* makes itself evident within individual narratives as well. "There Are More Things," of course, takes its title from the famous lines, "There are more things on heaven and earth, Horatio / Than are dreamt of in your philosophy," addressed by Hamlet to an astonished Horatio who has just seen and heard the ghost (act 1, sc. 5). Dedicated to H. P. Lovecraft, whose grotesque fantasies it resembles, the piece takes us inside a mysterious country house where the furnishings have utterly monstrous sizes and shapes; a horrified narrator realizes that they fit some strange creature, whose footsteps can be heard coming toward the house. This episode, which comes during the final two pages, is truly spine-chilling, but unfortunately Borges takes up eight pages of complicated subplots before getting there and so spoils a basically sound idea.

The only narrative in *The Book of Sand that* comes close to the level of Borges's middle phase is "The Congress." Unlike other stories gathered here, this rather long piece actually improves upon an earlier work. In *Chronicles of Bustos Domecq,* Borges and Bioy spoke with engaging wit of a "Brotherhood movement" (*gremialismo*), the brainchild of an attorney named G. A. Baralt who perceives in the world "a multitude of secret societies, or brotherhoods, whose members are not only unknown to each other but who may, at any given moment, change their status" (CBD, 67; CBD, 64). Some of these brotherhoods might be composed of "individuals sporting Catalan surnames, or surnames that begin with the letter G," or even so ephemeral a group as "persons attacked by a cigarette cough who, at the same time, may also be wearing baggy trousers or be sprinting along on ten-speed bicycles" (CBD, 68; CBD, 65). It is a bright and sparkling piece that can bear at least one amused reading.

"The Congress" goes beyond this idle sort of spoof and tells of an odd assortment of Argentines who, funded and presided over by a rich Uruguayan rancher named Alejandro Glencoe, secretly band together to form "the Congress of the World," which represents the entire human race in all its diverse subgroups and sects. They make written and personal contact with interested individuals from all over the planet; Glencoe himself is seen representing such groups as men with red beards, men sitting in armchairs, and of course Uruguayans and ranchers too. Eventually, because "everything gives witness," they begin to buy all kinds of books and periodicals, even Ph.D. theses and theater programs. One day, when the

Congress is into its fourth year, Glencoe suddenly shows up and orders that all those piles of printed matter be put to the flames. He has finally realized the futility of a project that would embrace absolutely everything on the globe, which happens to be before their eyes all around them, and he thereby formally dissolves the group. The narrator now looks back on the long night of the book burning with some sense of loss but has few distinct reminders of the Congress, most of whose members he has never encountered again.

Though not so richly textured as "Funes the Memorious" and "The Library of Babel" (stories whose underlying philosophical themes Borges once again treats here), "The Congress" is certainly the worthiest of the author's later narrative products. Borges ably captures the commanding figure of an ambitious landowner-philanthropist; he evokes Buenos Aires street life, the social peculiarities of dwelling on a ranch, and the ambiance of the British Museum reading room, where the narrator is sent to do research. Most important, Borges gives a convincing picture of a covey of misguided crackpots and slick opportunists. This is a memorable portrait of those dreamy enterprises that either collapse dramatically or fizzle into nothingness. Sadly, there are still spots where Borges gratuitously repeats himself—when he attributes to the narrator, Alejandro Ferri, one of his very own esoteric dabblings ("The Analytical Language of John Wilkins"), when Ferri solemnly declares that "words are symbols that assume a shared destiny" (BS, 48; LA, 61), or when a knife fight suddenly flares up in a bar. In the balance, however, "The Congress" is a skillfully paced, transparently constructed story; in a weak volume like *The Book of Sand,* such relatively superior work inevitably draws attention to itself. Probably one reason for the greater strength of "The Congress" is that Borges had the initial idea for it during the 1940s, though he did no serious work on the narrative until some thirty years later, in the early 1970s.

A lthough the bulk of his later fiction is disappointing, only Borges could have produced it. Any reader who knows the Argentine author at his best will immediately take note of certain procedures, preoccupations, or stray thoughts that no one except Borges would ever think to bring up, much less dwell upon. Moreover, the narrative modes and genres employed by the elder Borges are precisely those he once made into a high and fine art. Thus, *Brodie's Report* gives us more adventure yarns and thrillers; *Bustos Domecq* bristles with parody and satire; and fantasy is the essential lifeblood of the *Imaginary Beings* bestiary. And in *The Book of Sand* Borges again employs fantasy and builds stories around mental abstractions—esoteric philosophies and arcane theological turns of mind.

Despite continuities with the more familiar, mature Borges, however, these stories have a rather thin quality and a cramped, confining feel. They tend to stay strictly within conventional generic boundaries and seldom spill over beyond the accepted limits of their particular narrative mode. For example, "The End of the Duel" in *Brodie's Report* tells of an ongoing enmity between two rural types and terminates with their bizarre deaths; after such elementary form and content, the bloody finale seems merely shocking, theatrical at best, with the impression being one of mindless violence. In Borges's mature phase, by contrast, such genres and procedures are expertly combined and intermingled in fruitful ways. "Death and the Compass," which is a great detective story, also parodies the genre; it builds solidly but ironically on some mock-Hebraic mystic lore and includes a structural-numerological game, all within a single piece. Similarly, "The Dead Man" is a thriller about adventures in gangland, a study in youthful ambition, a moral-political fable, and an intellectual paradox and jigsaw puzzle in one; the hard-boiled underworld plot of "The Waiting" is much enriched by fantastical materials such as the Double, blurred identities, and dreams.

In the same way, *The Book of Imaginary Beings* is a delightful compilation of self-contained fantasies, and most stories in *The Book of Sand* deal in magical events. In almost none of these pieces, however, does fantasy fuse with other narrative means. On the other hand, "Tlön, Uqbar, Orbis Tertius" depicts sinister objects bobbing up in the modern world, summarizes mysterious texts-within-texts, discourses on Idealist philosophy, contains creditable elements of suspense, and starkly conveys a sense of global evils encroaching upon the individual mind. Several of the late stories exclusively evoke interpersonal relations and rivalries ("The Duel," "The Bribe") in the same way that "The Sect of the Thirty" focuses solely on religious fanaticism and eccentricity. "The Theologians," by contrast, weaves a rich verbal texture around the rivalry between Aurelian and John, presents several (not just one) heretical sects as well as some dialectical interplay among their doctrines, and sets up clues that, detective-style, lead up to the final fantasy of the Double. Hence, Borges's greatest works do not simply relate one story but integrate and *inter*relate several types of narrative. In fact, the reason why "The Congress" is a considerably better story than its companions is that Borges brings in more than one single theme, one plot, or one sort of action; alongside its central plot are other materials such as the knife fight, the incidents on the ranch, the love affair with Beatrice, and a study of power relations and authority figures.

The pivotal difference between the mature and the elder Borges, then, is that the story-telling art of *Ficciones* and *El Aleph* comes out of a larger, unified narrative practice that synthesizes disparate elements, transcends the usually discrete divisions, and disregards generic categories and customs. In his later work, however, though retaining those same genres and procedures, Borges keeps each field separate and works mostly within its given guidelines; he rarely goes beyond or bridges the traditional boundaries and familiar narrative spaces. It is this fragmented approach to fiction (not necessarily blindness and biology, as many commentators, including Borges himself, are wont to claim) that lies behind the wispy, lightweight quality of Borges's late prose products. These stories are so hidebound by convention that the result is conventional writing, albeit somewhat redeemed by that unmistakable "Borgesian" intelligence and glow.

Also missing in Borges's late prose is a certain grand theme that gives his middle stories their disturbing atmosphere of tragedy and gloom (even, paradoxically, when the tone is light and humorous). Unlike most of the later work, virtually all of Borges's major stories show the aims, ambitions, desires, and ideals of the human mind that enters into ineluctable and hopeless conflict with a wider social or natural world and its indifferent ways. This contradiction takes on many forms in as many narratives. One finds in *Ficciones* and *El Aleph* conflicts between the desire for scientific understanding and the sheer vastness of the universe ("The Library of Babel"); between the desire for intercultural knowledge and the limits imposed by one's own culture ("Averroës's Search"); between the desire for satisfying symmetries and the role of mindless chance ("Death and the Compass"); between the clarity, richness, and originality of a thinker's work and the narrow intolerance of his colleagues ("Three Versions of Judas," "The Theologians"); between gentle literary talent and military might ("The Secret Miracle"); between a former coward's newly acquired courage and a lack of opportunities in which to test that courage ("The Other Death"); between a boss's perception of his political power and the manipulations of his cohorts ("The Dead Man"); between mystic awe and the less-than-inspiring everyday life ("The Aleph"); between wishful dreams and murderous brutality ("The Waiting"); between carefully worked out plans and intentions, and eventual results and significance ("Emma Zunz"); and between a man's attachment to traditional cultural values and the inexorable tide of fashion ("Tlön, Uqbar, Orbis Tertius").

In these and other stories the mind is depicted as vigorous and alive, brimming with inspiration and creativity; yet, in the end, it is outdone by exterior forces immensely more powerful though less wondrous than itself. Needless to say, this is Borges's profoundly pessimistic view of the long-range strengths and capabilities of human thought, a precious, wondrous gift—floating in a vast and impenetrable cosmos, and situated in a social universe where group rules and collective cohesion take priority over independent thought—that is as puny and impotent as it is admirable and complex. The dominant presence of this larger theme in Borges's writings from the 1940s no doubt reflects his own situation during that decade when, following years of living solely for his ideas and by his pen, the author found himself plunged into the most difficult and painful time of his life (see chapter 11). In contrast, when Borges gained international fame and prestige, when his own belief in mind was no longer being questioned, and when his existence ceased being one of major personal and political conflict, he seems to have put behind him this dark picture of human intelligence trapped in its highest aspirations, dwarfed, frustrated, beleaguered, or otherwise set upon by forces outside itself— and his art subsequently lost all depth of feeling as well. Without this organic narrative pattern, this deeply tragic sense of the role and uses of mind, Borges's stories inevitably took on their look of artful dabbling and superior amusement. Borges's later stories are an unfortunate instance of genius no longer animated by a grander conception of life and no longer holding a vital link with common experience. A mind completely free to spin its fancies can fall prey to the lure of whimsical complacency; it needs reminders of its limits in order that it may strive to overcome the traditional limits of literature itself.

11 Literature and Politics
North and South

Surveying the sum total of Borges's works, one is struck by a kind of "bulge" at approximately the middle of his career. This bulge constitutes the relatively brief spell (1939 to the middle 1950s) during which he produced the stories gathered in *Ficciones* and *El Aleph,* as well as the prose parables in *Dreamtigers.* Until then, Borges had brought out many of his strangely provocative essays and some lovely books of verse, but little as yet of universal import. During the 1960s and 1970s, well after his writing career had peaked, he reaped the benefits of his sudden and deserved fame, living the life of a much-esteemed public figure and journeying from podium to podium, prize to prize. In these years, as we have seen, he wrote the anticlimactic narratives of *Doctor Brodie's Report* or playful trifles like *Chronicles of Bustos Domecq.* What is noteworthy about those luminous fifteen years—the *Ficciones* and *El Aleph* years—is that they closely coincide with a biographical and historical moment, a specific period of acute crisis in Borges's life as well as in the larger world itself.

Let us recapitulate the facts. In 1937, at age thirty-eight, Borges started work as a cataloguer in a dreary suburban library. Borges somehow spent nine years in that shabby place, earning very little and doing pointless tasks among what he always remembered as an unpleasant crew of philistines. It was Borges's first regular job and his only extended encounter with the coarse nonliterary world. But his troubles had only begun; in February 1938, Borges's father died. In December, Borges hit his head on an open window casement while climbing a stairway. The wound became seriously infected, and he nearly died of blood poisoning. While recovering, Borges began to write his greatest works; ironically, these works were largely unrecognized for more than a decade, and the annual prizes regularly went to authors far below his level. Borges never was to forgive or forget this last fact (though he did conceal it under the venerable public persona he adopted in the mid-1960s).

Beyond these personal troubles, there was the growing sociopolitical nightmare. From 1930 onward, the fascist wave abroad—in itself distressing for a Borges sympathetic to liberal Europe—had set in motion a number of local equivalents. In contrast to the rest of Spanish America, which was passively in favor of the Allies, an idiosyncratic political militarism arose in Argentina. Perhaps less pro-German than it was anti-English, it was in some degree brought slowly to power by widespread anti-imperialist (that is, anti-British) sentiment, culminating finally in the right-wing military populism of Perón. Though the political outlook of the Peronistas and other nationalist sects of the time was more or less right-wing corporativist rather than left-wing socialist, they drew a significant amount of support by their opposition to British capitalism, a key issue in a country long dominated by English finance.

A brief look at Peronism is perhaps called for. This strangely contradictory sociopolitical phenomenon has not been well understood, especially outside Argentina. The Andrew Lloyd Weber musical *Evita* has compounded the incomprehension by personalizing an entire history in the figure of one woman, while scanting the larger economic bases and historical context of the Peronist era. Distortion has been the norm rather than the exception.[1]

The conditions leading up to Perón's rise to power go back to 1930, when massive emigration from Europe to Argentina had come to a halt. During what later became known as the "decade of infamy," a series of conservative governments, determined to put an end to the popular gains made previously under the Radicales, kept themselves in power through a subtle system of electoral fraud. Then, as a result of the Second World War and its immediate aftermath, Argentina experienced a dramatic internal change. The catastrophic events in Europe led to an enormous leap in the demand for Argentina's food exports. In addition, with Old World and U.S. manufactures geared in great measure toward military production, and with European factories destroyed, the lack of available imports from overseas made for rapid growth in small industries in Argentina. Remote though it may seem now, as a consequence of global destruction, the Argentine economy in 1946 was one of the wealthiest in the world.

Because of the incremental surplus in both primary products and manufactured goods, Buenos Aires saw an enormous expansion in its working-class sectors, made up of poor, dark-skinned workers who had moved from the countryside to take jobs in the city. Directionless, with-

out much political experience, they were ripe for agitation. The traditional, left-wing union activists were unable to speak the popular language of these Hispanic-style, Catholic migrants. Moreover, communist
organizers, because of their principle of solidarity with the Soviet struggle
against the Nazis, had decided not to encourage strikes among Argentina's more militant workers.

An ambitious Colonel Perón, seeing his main chance in these toiling
masses, moved into the influential cabinet position of Secretary of Labor
in 1943 and quickly began winning over his constituents with mass rallies
and social promises, while simultaneously undercutting socialist and communist unions. Eventually, with a great deal of help from his shrewd wife
Eva—herself of humble origins—he won the presidency both in 1946
and in 1952, in what historians generally concede to have been fair and
democratic elections.

Perón's political triumphs cannot be blithely dismissed as being the
result of mere mysticism or demagogy. On the contrary, the social and
economic rights gained by Argentine workers during the 1946–1955 period—rising wages, job security, health clubs, gymnasiums, and a voice
in government—went well beyond the status of token gains. (In addition, under Perón, women first received the right to vote.) Still, what
ultimately allowed for these advances was the absolute size of Argentine
output and its strength relative to overseas economies that had been leveled by war. Once Europe began its inevitable recovery, Argentina's
comparative advantage (which was largely accidental, conjunctural) necessarily began shrinking, and there was much less to go around. The national pie had become smaller, as had the available pieces.

The question inevitably arises as to whether the Perón regime was fascist. Any thoughtful answer is inevitably complex and ambiguous. Perón
of course picked up many of his grandiose, theatrical tactics from Mussolini and Hitler, whose organizing methods he admired. This alone,
however, is not enough to make the label stick. After all, the Nazi leaders
borrowed many of their propaganda methods from American advertising
techniques and from college football-game practices; and yet that sort of
cultural borrowing does not ipso facto make U.S. folkways retrospectively
fascist. There is also the matter of Perón's unique demographic base:
whereas Nazism appealed mainly to the unemployed *lumpen* and to those
disaffected petit-bourgeois elements who, if anything, feared being reduced to proletarian status, Perón built his foundations among the very
proletariat whose militant rise had frightened conservatives and fascists in
Europe. In a similar contrast, whereas in Europe the landed aristocracies

tended to favor fascism, in Argentina the oligarchy hated Perón and his wife, both of whom liked publicly taunting the big landowning classes. Moreover, the Jew-baiting that had at first characterized some of Perón's allies eventually was abandoned, and "under Perón Argentine Jews made strides towards greater political and social equality."[2]

Ironically, one major point of similarity between European fascism and Argentine Peronism is the fact that the Perón administration scarcely reformed or modified the nation's social structure. Surprising though it may seem, not an inch of land or capital goods was expropriated from the old oligarchy for redistribution among Argentina's less advantaged. The heated attacks on the nation's economic elites were largely rhetorical (if certainly voluminous and large-scale), or they took the form of such symbolic acts as eliminating second-class carriages on the trains. In addition, the British-owned railway was nationalized on terms that were quite generous to its former English masters. Finally, the small-manufacturing enterprises, whose goods had substituted European imports, tended to favor Perón, inasmuch as his economic policies generally favored national industry.

How dictatorial was the regime? No doubt the government frequently violated freedom of speech and of the press, and subjected the opposition parties to enormous pressures and occasional arrests. This sort of thing, however, is common throughout Latin America, even under civilian, democratic administrations. Curiously, under Perón, the Argentine parliament continued to function as a deliberative body, and the intellectuals, though certainly harassed, were neither murdered, "disappeared," nor sent to rot in solitary-confinement cells. Perón's strength derived not so much from brute force as from his electoral support among the masses, from the absolute majority he enjoyed at the legislative level, and from the strength-in-numbers that this generated.

Following the ouster of Perón in 1955, his followers were banned from public office. During the leader's long exile in Spain, Peronist organizations remained active as a kind of illegal labor party. With the subsequent rise of the Latin American guerrilla left, many socialists as well as Peronists began claiming him as a fellow comrade in the anti-imperialist struggle. Meanwhile, in the late 1960s and early 1970s, Argentina became embroiled in its own bizarre and uncontrolled brand of civil strife, with some half-dozen armed groups taking on the military government. The Peronists themselves divided into left- and right-wing factions, oftentimes expending their ammunition on each other as much as on their nation's salaried troops.

Faced by rising chaos, in 1973 the reigning military junta finally decided it was time to legalize the Peronists, in the hope that the aging leader could control his own wayward forces. Elections were held that year. As expected, Perón once again won at the polls. Tragically, what he did once in power was to make war on his own left-wing insurgents and on the Marxist guerrillas, producing further political and economic chaos. The tired and ineffectual man died in 1974; his widow, Isabelita, lacked any political skills or authority; and the more old-fashioned, revolving-door military governments that seized state power a couple of years afterward proved to be unimaginably more repressive, earning a distinction as the most brutal dictatorship in Argentina's history. Their downfall came in 1982 when the armed forces—in a blatant bid to drum up patriotic fervor among the populace—invaded and occupied the Falkland-Malvinas islands, declaring them national territory. The ruse worked briefly, until Britain's technically superior naval operatives quickly routed the youthful and inexperienced Argentine recruits. The Argentine officers, accustomed to making war on their own people, were incapable of waging a real war on the battlefield.

After the astonishingly stupid military junta fell in disgrace, democratic elections followed. In a surprise upset, the Peronistas—now known as the Justicialistas—lost to the Radicales. Though the Perón party did win later, in 1988, its leadership soon embraced free-market principles. As of this writing, the Peronists are not so much the party of Argentina's laboring classes as simply another neo-liberal government, more or less along lines that have become the global norm since 1989.

Back in 1946, however, Peronism was a new, aggressively confident force in Argentina, with a mission to fulfill. And, as was inevitable under a nationalist regime, those mildly liberal, pro-English (the labels closely overlap) sectors of Argentine society were subjected to cultural isolation and political harassment. At the outset of Perón's presidency, as we saw in chapter 2, Borges was purged from his library post and shadowed by the police (a fate endured by thousands of his compatriots). In 1948, Borges's mother, Leonor, his sister, Norah, and their friend Adela Grandona were involved in a street demonstration; the police arrived and arrested several women, including these three, on charges of disturbing the peace. Mrs. Borges spent a month under house arrest; Norah and Adela served their term at a cellblock for prostitutes at the Buen Pastor prison.

Borges understandably was to look back on the 1938–1955 years as his worst. The events must have seemed shocking to a fortyish man of letters, one whose pleasant existence hitherto had seldom been ruffled by cares

other than literary. As late as age thirty-four, Borges could accurately remark, "Death and life have been lacking in my life," for clashes with his
environment, whether with immediate surroundings or society at large,
were as yet unknown to him. Then came boring work and bad company,
bereavement and a brush with death, forced cultural isolation, and political persecution. The piling up of disagreeable experiences no doubt appeared to him irrational and beyond comprehension.

As a refined and hypersensitive individual totally lacking in vulgarity,
Borges inevitably felt discomfited and threatened by the spectacle of the
great unwashed masses, with their populist emotions and styles, taking
over the public arena under the guidance of their despicable leaders, General and Mrs. Perón. It should nonetheless be noted that Borges's understanding of Peronism was and remained extremely limited and elementary. His interpretation essentially boils down to a kind of schoolboy
view, which we might paraphrase roughly as follows: "That evil man
named Perón, a Nazi, imposed his will on Argentina, bringing along with
him his cheap little floozy of a wife, the former streetwalker Eva Duarte."
(That Eva had been a streetwalker, a commonplace accusation, actually
has no basis in fact.) "Besides, Perón took away my job, and arrested my
relatives." This personalizing of the phenomenon is arguably as myopic
and mythological as the all-too-familiar version set forth in the musical
Evita. The larger socioeconomic picture, and the interclass politics of
Peronism, simply lay beyond Borges's ken. Even his semi-official biographer, Emir Rodríguez Monegal, tactfully admits, in so many words,
that the author's hatred of Perón was overstated and naive.[3]

Such, then, were the circumstances under which Borges brought out
his greatest stories. From his vantage point of chaos—his altered family
situation, a miserable job, and the rise of an antiliberal regime—the creation of fantastic stories served him as a concrete means of organized
defense. The act of writing the *Ficciones* and *El Aleph* thus constitutes a
classic instance of literature thriving in an adversary role, nourished by a
struggle against untoward personal and political conditions. The subjective stance of Borges the man is of course a complex matter, but in its
literary version there are two noteworthy components: a nostalgia for
combat in the past and a learned, urbane liberalism vis-à-vis the present.
It is highly significant that Borges's knife stories, with nineteenth-century
heroism as their subjects, were written at the height of military-populist
dictatorship in Argentina. In such a context the stories assume a character
of subtle protest, of opposition through counterexample: the true courage of the days of republican Argentina (a time when the Borges family

and its values were at their peak of class prestige) stands in implicit contrast to the shabby, dictatorial 1940s (when the economically ruined Borges family, together with its social allies, was politically deprived). As Borges once said in an interview, "in the case of the rural tough, the *compadrito,* his courage was selfless, disinterested . . . ; if he had a religion, it was this: a man should never be fainthearted."[4] By so projecting this ideal of personal courage onto isolated individuals, onto nineteenth-century men standing alone, Borges in his stories recalls the times when the rural knife-wielder knew his place in Argentine society, unlike the 1940s, when these rustics were to become a collective entity, serving as shock troops and ideological cannon fodder for the anti-oligarchical, antiliberal, anti-British rhetoric and actions of Perón. (One is reminded of Sarmiento, the nineteenth-century activist, author, and eventually president of Argentina, who, while condemning the gauchos morally and politically in his classic tract *Facundo,* also expressed a civilized admiration for their survival techniques and picturesque arts.)

Far better known is the opposition stance exemplified by Borges in his richest, most celebrated tales of fantasy. In "Tlön, Uqbar, Orbis Tertius" the narrator looks back on the lure during the 1930s of such false and facile symmetries as (in his words) "dialectical materialism, anti-Semitism, Nazism," all of which have culminated in the reigning hysteria over planet Tlön. Impervious to but alone among these omnipresent idealisms, the narrator finds silent refuge in Sir Thomas Browne's *Urn Burial,* an evocatively nostalgic work on classical archaeology. (The easy juxtaposition of Nazism with Marxism may suggest the extent of Borges's acquaintance with the latter.)

This essentially is the apology of the civilized man of letters, the cultivated gentleman who, in a time of social upheaval, can side neither with the rebels nor the reactionaries. Experientially removed from the arena of social battles and lacking even the political information available in books, he dismisses left and right as equally false and is unaware of the untenability of his stance (though well realizing his irrelevance) in a crumbling social panorama. Ironically, Borges's fanciful view of the Hitler decade is itself an idealist intellectual's interpretation; it sees political turmoil being brought about not by economic dislocations but by the mass appeal of a few seductive ideas—recalling those old-fashioned historians who believed that the French Revolution was "caused" by the writings of Voltaire and Rousseau. For all of Borges's artfulness and sophistication, the dizzying final paragraphs of "Tlön, Uqbar, Orbis Tertius" ultimately reflect the bewildered middle-way position of certain 1930s moderates, who, though fearful of the Axis, for ideological reasons had been unwilling to make common cause with the antifascist left, tending instead to brush off both sides and label them fanatics.[5]

Much the same spirit informs the last few pages of "The Library of Babel." There the narrator-librarian surveys a universe beset by ignorance, violence, and plagues, by ideological splintering and a tired sense that all has been said—much as Europe and Argentina must have appeared to Borges in 1941. The story, unlike "Tlön, Uqbar," avoids any explicit social or political judgments but focuses instead on an epistemological question. Rather than attack the right and the left as equally and hopelessly utopian, it depicts the scientific search for knowledge as futile and pointless. Though certain fundamental truths about the library-universe are occasionally hit upon (such as the decisive discovery that twenty-five letters form the basic components of all the books), these only whet people's appetites, giving rise to feverish quests for more knowledge about one's self and the cosmos, and finally generate social division and personal despair. The truth seekers, unfortunately, cannot grasp what the narrator knows: that the universe, and by extension any ultimate knowledge thereof, is "infinite," "useless," and "secret." The note on which the story ends is thus a scientific quietism rather than a social conservatism. But then, because in this story the library is the world, to cease seeking to uncover its laws does correspond to social withdrawal.

This is the muted agony of an essentially traditionalist intellectual, a nostalgic man of letters whose old world has become opaque and incomprehensible, and whose accumulated readings (the cultural heritage of a happier, more stable past) furnish him no concrete hold on the present, when things crumble; he then projects his own historical bewilderment onto others. Borges's bleak philosophical nihilism, however, by no means enjoys universal acceptance. Such views are hardly conceivable, and would be less than absolute, from the pen of a practicing politician or a research scientist, both of whom accept a body of knowledge and its uses. The fact looms large that Borges, his celebrated erudition notwithstanding, scarcely knew the natural sciences—their mode of knowing, their praxis—while his sense of twentieth-century social thought was particularly limited. Even Freud's discoveries Borges once shrugged off as the ravings of "a kind of madman," and in a 1945 essay on Valéry (in *Other Inquisitions*) Borges actually puts Freud in the same camp with Nazis and assorted modern barbarians. For his nonliterary readings, Borges amused himself with mystic writers, dabbled in Jung, and loved Schopenhauer, speculative thinkers who spin highly provocative fancies and conceits, but whose contributions to fruitful, significant knowledge are in the end rather limited.

T hese and other darkly brooding tales, written during a time of personal torment for Borges and a time of political struggles in Europe and Argentina, exist in part due to the prompting of these larger crises. The proof of this is that, when Borges finally emerged from his woes in 1955, his work began losing its textural and philosophic richness. By the same token, little of Borges's output before 1938 suggests the writer of fiction of worldwide and revolutionary impact, other than retrospectively. It is entirely probable that, had Borges not been compelled to undergo these unsettling experiences, he would have remained what he had been until his middle thirties: a good and fairly interesting poet and a talented literary gentleman much like others of his kind, those numerous Latin American men of letters from the old elites, who write a certain amount of excellent verse and seldom attain major stature. And though the earlier essays are filled with fresh insights and conceits, they are still the work of an eccentric genius who has not yet hit upon his most fitting medium and subject matter.

Borges's sudden leap into literary greatness around 1940, then, appears to have been catalyzed by a special situation, the unique congruence of his personal crisis with an unusual moment in Latin American history: that period during the 1930s and 1940s when the liberal, Anglophile sectors in Argentina were under siege by a mass movement of the right, much as the liberal antifascist forces were in Europe. When, with the anti-Perón coup of 1955, the struggle against the populist right came to an end, those old elites reverted to a simplistic anticommunism. Borges himself shared in the political crudities of that social nucleus through the early 1980s, and so he signed petitions favoring the Bay of Pigs invaders, pleaded for the execution of Régis Debray in Bolivia, dedicated the first copy of his translation of *Leaves of Grass* to none other than Richard Nixon, quietly supported the Onganía dictatorship in the 1960s, and asserted repeatedly that Blacks and Indians were inferior to whites. Moreover, because, for Borges, there was nothing worse than Marxism or Peronism, it followed that the anti-Peronist dictatorship that followed in 1976 was in itself a good thing. Hence, for several years Borges defended the military juntas, openly praising Generals Videla in Argentina and Pinochet in Chile as "gentlemen," and making a number of like statements that would alienate and sadden many of his admirers world-wide.

To his credit, Borges in his final years underwent a change of heart. In 1980, returning from a trip to Spain, he gave an interview with *La Prensa* and said, "I cannot remain silent in the face of so many deaths and disappearances." He also signed, along with his fellow writer Ernesto Sábato, an open letter in the daily *Clarín* concerning the fate of the disappeared.[6] In one of his lengthy published conversations with María Esther Vázquez, he grudgingly acknowledged the grief of the famous mothers of the disappeared victims: "Some may have been histrionic, but I felt that a lot of them were crying because you can sense their genuineness. Poor women, so unfortunate they were! That doesn't mean their children were all innocent, but no matter. Anyone accused of a crime has the right to a prosecutor, not to mention a defender."[7] Finally, in 1982, Borges protested the Falklands war, characterizing the action with a metaphor so vivid it was cited in the international media: "Two bald men fighting over a comb."

At the same time that Borges's best work initiates a new literary period, it also signals a culmination of an earlier, lengthier social and cultural era, that of the domination of Latin America by Europhile, moderately liberal upper classes. It is one of those ironies of history that this social milieu—so often subjected to legitimate criticism, so remote from basic human concerns and from those larger struggles that can nourish great art—accidentally found itself during the 1930s and 1940s in a position of active opposition to the international right, and holding the view that that force, more than any other, constituted the greatest effective threat to civilization. It was the first time since the days of the Rosas dictatorship that Argentina's pro-English liberals had been politically victimized and thereby drawn into the broad arena of their nation's conflicts. As in the Rosas days, the so-called second dictatorship gave rise to a formidable, impressive literature from the opposition. Borges's greatest stories, which exalt the old Europe of humane letters and evoke a lost, courageous nineteenth-century Argentina, are the greatest literary works to emerge from the historical myths and longings of that nation's old Anglophile elite.

Significantly, the novelists that followed in Borges's wake had no personal links with, and no stake in, his preferred social arrangements, values, and practices. Products of the urban middle class rather than of the patrician creole sectors, they depended not so much on family money or aristocratic patronage as on full-time work in such fields as teaching, translating, clerking, journalism, and diplomacy. Their literary sources and subjects also differ substantially from those familiar "Borgesian" themes—on the one hand, gaucho wistfulness; on the other, Western culture under siege by barbarians, by raiders of libraries, by vandals under the spell of Nazism, Marxism, Freudism, Peronism, or Tlönism. Julio Cortázar, for example, drew freely on French thought and surrealism, on anthropology and jazz. In another vein, Manuel Puig, Cabrera Infante, and the younger Mexicans were to find a locus of their own in films and pop culture, while García Márquez, Fuentes, and the early Vargas Llosa were varyingly influenced by Faulkner, Spanish American regionalism, and Marx. Borges's urbane, erudite concern for minor Edwardians and the glories of Western civilization inevitably appeared slightly quaint and irrelevant to these novelists, however much they admired his literary achievement.

The impact of Borges on the U.S. writing scene was in some ways as powerful as was his earlier influence on Latin America. The American 1950s were a desert, a bleak stretch relieved only by one or two entertainments by Nabokov; for barrenness, few literary epochs can match the Cold War years. The quiet arrival of Borges's Englished fiction was to make a key difference for the 1960s; his dreamlike artifices helped stimulate a writing culture that had been all too steeped in WASP suburban metaphysics and Jewish-novel neorealism. The Argentine master reawakened for us the possibilities of far-fetched fancy, of formal exploration, of parody, intellectuality, and wit. There are fantasies by Robert Coover and Donald Barthelme scarcely conceivable without the originating presence of Borges, an allusion to the Argentine writer actually appears in Thomas Pynchon's *Gravity's Rainbow,* and the longer novels of John Barth are shaped in great degree by a theory of parody derived from Borges.

Without going so far as to argue direct influence, one can ultimately discern Borges's hand in Barthelme's "Paraguay," a story about a fantastical realm that reflects in distorted ways certain aspects of this world. Borges's central use of dreams was picked up by Coover; the hero of his novel *The Universal Baseball Association* has set up an entire baseball league in his head, an unreal world that governs his private life. Borges's distillation of the lowly genre of parody came as a refreshing antidote to the heavy moralism and solemn religiosity of American Cold War fiction. Thus, Pynchon includes a masterful spoof of Jacobean drama in *The Crying of Lot 49,* while Barthelme lampoons the interview format in "The Explanation" and in "City Life" comically recasts the old yarn about a country bumpkin who arrives in the metropolis. Finally, those novels by Coover *(The Public Burning)*, Doctorow *(Ragtime)*, and Ishmael Reed *(Flight to Canada)* in which personages from real life are brought in to play key roles have their pioneering precedents in "Tlön, Uqbar, Orbis Tertius," "Story of the Warrior and the Captive," and "The Other Death," narratives that artfully disregard traditional distinctions between factual and fictive characters.

In addition, Borges's expert rehabilitation of the detective story (a genre once considered artistically substandard) had its visible repercussions on the American literary scene. In the realm of creative fiction, Ishmael Reed and Thomas Pynchon have constructed some of their best work around the recognizable format of a mystery under investigation by a sleuth protagonist (with sometimes curious solutions). In the world of critical opinion, it has become increasingly acceptable to name Dashiell Hammett and Raymond Chandler along with the major American authors of the twentieth century. Chandler's novels are now included in the *Library of America* series of classics, and his life and work have been studied by Professor Frank MacShane.[8] Before the 1970s one could scarcely have imagined a critical biography of this or any maker of thrillers, written by a Columbia University academic, and with aid from the Guggenheim Foundation. It is Borges's own magisterial contribution to the literature of crime—in the form of such texts as "Death and the Compass," "The Garden of Forking Paths," "The Waiting," and "Emma Zunz"—that to a large degree has made possible this latter-day reassessment of a fictional mode formerly thought of as subliterary.

Though "influence" is a thorny area in which it is notoriously dangerous to tread, Borges's work definitely appears to have served as the immediate model for two American works of fiction from the 1960s. One of these is John Gardner's novella *Grendel,* which retells the story of Beowulf from the view of the titular monster, who in the process becomes the real hero of the book. Borges's readers, of course, will inevitably be reminded of "The House of Asterion"; prior to Borges's little fable, there is no instance of a major author so inverting the hero-monster relationship. It seems unlikely that, before writing *Grendel,* Gardner (a learned man but also a fairly traditional novelist) could have been unaware of Borges's revisionist myth. Any casual examination of the two works, moreover, will reveal numerous similarities. The soldiers in the Gardner book are boorish drunks, rather crude and unappealing figures, as is Borges's Theseus; Grendel, on the other hand, is portrayed as a lonely creature with unappreciated metaphysical depths, as is the Minotaur; and, just as Asterion criticizes the Cretans for their flat and pale faces, Gardner's Grendel similarly speaks ill of the soldiers and their pale faces—in all, a series of resemblances too close to be merely coincidental.[9]

The other American novel from the 1960s in which Borges's influence seems evident is *The Crying of Lot 49,* by Thomas Pynchon (who has lived in Mexico and shows a good knowledge of Spanish). In this book—one of the most interesting American novels of Post-Modern vintage—the heroine, Oedipa Maas, casually stumbles upon a vast global conspiracy called Tristero, a clandestine postal network that secretly rivals the U.S. Post Office. After going through various European wars and revolutions over the centuries, Tristero has come to establish itself in the underworld of alienated dropouts in (of all places) suburban Los Angeles. Already this kind of paranoid historical fantasy resembles "Tlön, Uqbar, Orbis Tertius," but at one point Pynchon actually employs the very language of Borges's story. In an important scene, Oedipa encounters a Mexican anarchist named Jesús Arrabal, who makes the following cryptic remark: "You know what a miracle is. Not what Bakunin said. But another world's intrusion into this one."[10] Readers of Borges's encyclopedic fantasia will doubtless recall the moment when objects from Tlön start appearing in Buenos Aires; this phenomenon elicits from Borges's narrator the observation that "such was the first intrusion of the fantastic world into the world of reality." In this case, the carryover of ideas and vocabulary from Borges to Pynchon is unmistakable.

The ending of Pynchon's novel suggests yet another debt to Borges—specifically, the device of presenting events that, as in "The South" and "The Secret Miracle," can be construed either as subjective hallucinations or as real happenings. Pynchon takes this narrative tool to further lengths and still greater sophistication in *The Crying of Lot 49,* where toward the end Oedipa ponders as many as three possible interpretations of her bizarre experiences: (1) that the Tristero conspiracy really exists, (2) that the Tristero and its related events have been a series of hallucinations in her own mind, and (3) that a California tycoon named Pierce Inverarity, formerly Oedipa's lover and now dead, had set up the entire Tristero apparatus as a grand hoax, a posthumous joke being played on the heroine from his grave. In a very specific sense, then, the last few pages of Pynchon's book are among Borges's Yankee offspring, the northern children of *Ficciones.*

These are only a few instances of what Borges has made possible for Post-Modern fiction in the United States. Perhaps Barthelme, Pynchon, Gardner, and Coover would have come to these ideas by other means had Borges not inaugurated them, though without Borges the task would have been more difficult, the process of discovery more circuitous and demanding. The very fact of the availability of Borges's narrative art had a determining role in shaping American fiction in the waning days of the Cold War. Borges facilitated things for North American fantasists; he put at their disposal an entire set of genres and procedures, a common property that Pynchon and other fiction writers were thence able to adopt and later develop in their own personal ways.

Still, the peculiar shape and nature of Borges's public fame in the United States shows nuances that differ from his reputation in Latin America. His standing in these parts has been much higher, both in relative and absolute terms. While most North American literary people at least know of Borges, fewer have heard of Cortázar, Carpentier, Fuentes, or Vargas Llosa, and even García Márquez's fame has had its detractors. It is an added irony, moreover, that the peak of the Borges cult on the American campus came at a time (the late 1960s and early 1970s) when the younger authors of the Hispanic world had, for more than a decade, simply assumed the existence of Borges and gone beyond him—indeed, when Borges's work had become less of a revolution, an innovation, a surprise, and had assumed its rightful and relative place in the Latin American literary landscape.

There are identifiable reasons for the somewhat lopsided quality of Borges's American fame—some purely circumstantial, others profoundly historical and political. Among the former reasons one must note Borges's simple physical presence in the 1960s. During these years he delivered literally hundreds of lectures across the land, in fine English, with a fluency equaled by few Latin American authors of his generation, whose second language was more often French. It is a reasonable guess that most of Borges's serious U.S. readers have actually experienced the fulfillment of their wish to hear him speak on some occasion, a wish that cannot be realized by Cortázar or Beckett devotees. Similarly, Borges's willingness to talk with all kinds of interviewers gave him further visibility, planting his name in national weeklies and newspapers as well as in drugstore paperbacks and little magazines. All of this stimulated interest, and it gave Borges fans some sense of having concrete ties with him, of knowing him as more than an authorial abstraction. At the same time, people who had not read Borges found their curiosity aroused by these reminders of his existence. Before Borges, probably no other non-English-language author had been given so much direct exposure to the American limelight. Finally, Borges's childlike pro-Americanism inevitably flattered his audiences and enhanced his acceptability to those Americans easily discomfited by the anti-imperialism of most other South American authors.

But there are social facts and institutional forces that contributed just as significantly to Borges's influence in America. Among these is the vastness of the North American academic subculture; there are more colleges and universities in the United States than in all of Europe, let alone in Latin America. Many of these schools were quite rich during the 1960s and could pay Borges substantial fees for the myriad seminars and lectures (so many talks, in fact, that he inevitably repeated himself). Even more important, here was a bookish author with a great deal of obscure erudition, an Argentinian Eliot-Pound-Joyce whom several hundred Spanish professors could carefully explicate in their classes and about whom they would weave a network of articles in two or three dozen special-interest journals. These articles, in turn, were read by thousands of graduate students, who then wrote papers derived from the articles and found themselves setting their sights on being future authors of articles on Borges. The nature of the Argentine author's oeuvre is such that it generated a whole profession and came to play a well-established part in the American publishing machine, like Chaucer editions or Chinese cookbooks.

Aside from the decisive boost given Borges by academia, however, there is the deeper role of the stories and the broad uses to which their meanings lend themselves. While the stylistic and formal manner of Borges gave the literary professionals a task to perform, at the same time the specific content of *Ficciones* supplied his readers with a precise political optics, a cluster of historical attitudes, and a mode of social feeling that helped strengthen and define their ideological posture. During the 1960s the United States was torn by social conflict: riots in the ghettos, a seemingly endless war in Asia, and the campus revolts ultimately sparked by that war. In this disorderly picture (comparable to that of Europe in the 1930s or Argentina in the 1940s) Borges's artifices provided a defense for those American academics who were as confused by the whole spectacle as our informant on Tlön or the librarian at Babel are bewildered by the sinister forces they evoke. Chairmen of literature departments, professors still pushing the New Criticism, and apolitical novelists like John Updike roughly shared a vague, inarticulate opposition to the war in Indochina, an opposition that was combined with an inability to sympathize with (indeed, a marked hostility toward) the highly vocal antiwar left. They found in Borges's nightmares a sophisticated, inspired, vividly argued affirmation of their own stance: that is, an urbane aloofness, a middle-way quietism, a studied, even-handed, occasionally snobbish indifference to right and left, in this case to the physical slaughter of the war and to the moral anger of the opposition activists. Borges gave aesthetic shape and justification to the politics of loftiness of those literary people who, in their alienation from and ignorance of the political situation, carved out for themselves (as do Borges's raconteurs) a refuge in seminars and old books, in the monumental libraries of the American university system. Just as the narrator shuts his eyes to politics and hides in his Quevedian translation of Sir Thomas Browne at the end of "Tlön, Uqbar, Orbis Tertius," in like manner some professors of the 1960s took their stand in the past, in the great traditions of the West, which irate radicals and Blacks on the one hand and weekly body counts and B-52 strikes on the other seemed to have rendered marginal, useless, invalid, "irrelevant."

That our literary milieu found in Borges's fiction not only a peculiar artistic greatness but a useful social content as well becomes clearer when one considers the lesser following thus far gained in U.S. literary circles by other Latin Americans. Though Cortázar, Carpentier, and the early Vargas Llosa are comparably major artists—whose novels are read throughout the Spanish-speaking world, well-received by North American reviewers, and intensely examined by professional Hispanists (who often as not miss the social meaning of their books)—they did not generate the intellectual cult, let alone the academic market, enjoyed here by Borges.

Part of the explanation for this must lie in the unsettling tone and content of these authors' works. The atmosphere of threat in Borges's tales comes off as bookish and abstract when contrasted with the more concretely physical horrors in the stories of Julio Cortázar (who, let it be said, is every bit as great a writer of short fiction as his elder compatriot). Cortázar's novel *Hopscotch* puts into question the very value of European thought and learning, and his dadaistic *Cronopios and Famas* (a commercial failure here) tweaks the nose of bourgeois respectability by disrupting routine. Alejo Carpentier's close affiliation with the Castro government could hardly have promoted his standing in the United States. His best-known novel, *The Lost Steps,* is built on a suggestion that Europeans, for all their rich culture, may have been far more barbaric than the indigenous peoples of Venezuela—a notion contemplated by only a fringe of educated Americans. Another of his novels, *Explosion in a Cathedral,* pins down the various ideological nuances and posturings brought into being by revolution, an experience that is too remote for most American liberals, who, with their relatively conflict-free internal history, tend toward political consensus and compromise.

Similarly, although García Márquez's *One Hundred Years of Solitude* has enjoyed good sales on the American market, that novel has yet to attain the full academic, canonical respectability of Borges's work. Again, however, the politics (anti-imperialism, prorevolutionism) embedded within the texture of García Márquez's books probably puts off a fair portion of the American readership. The attacks on him in the 1980s by conservatives such as Anthony Burgess and John Simon, for instance, seemed ideologically rather than artistically motivated. Moreover, García Márquez's warmly humane, understanding portraits of his characters, so unlike the literary aura surrounding Borges's gauchos and hoods, probably meets with a certain amount of incomprehension, even condescension, from the many American readers still tinged with attitudes of cultural superiority toward Hispanics.[11] And of course, the Colombian author's prolonged presence on the U.S. immigration "blacklist" has put him beyond the reach of his *yanqui* fans; by contrast with Borges, there have been no American lecture tours or talk-show appearances for García Márquez. Finally, the novels of Fuentes and the early Vargas Llosa, steeped as they are in Marxist concepts, inevitably fall on deaf ears with an American public largely hostile or indifferent to, or—perhaps worse yet—utterly ignorant of, the cluster of issues raised by that strand of thought.

N one of this diminishes Borges's stature as a literary artist. There were aspects both modish and ideological to his fame in the American 1960s, but the intrinsic worth of his contribution is now an accepted fact. His stories, moreover, have a special significance in that they cleared the way for numerous literary trends on both American continents and determined the shape of much fiction to come. In his part of the world, Borges's meticulous approach to language—his careful construction of each sentence, his strict avoidance of Hispanic bombast, his cool understatement—succeeded in revolutionizing Spanish prose writing. As the Argentine novelist Alberto Vanasco once told me, "Before Borges one could write sloppily. Not any more, though." Borges thus stands in the same relation to current Latin novelists as Flaubert, who launched the ideal of a perfectly sculpted prose page, once did to numerous authors in Europe. At the same time, by rejecting realism and psychologism, he opened up to our northern writers a virgin field and led them to a wealth of new subjects and procedures—in a word, provided an alternative to Updike and Bellow. In successfully transcending the old modes of representation and discourse, Borges accidentally did for us a job previously performed elsewhere by Poe, the fantast from a "barbarous," backward land who, by way of Baudelaire, freed French verse from its classic and romantic dead weights.

The art of every author also has its social origins and functions, however, and the content of some of Borges's best stories expressed in their time the antifascism, anticommunism, and antipopulism of the older liberal, Anglophile elites of Argentina. This outlook, masterfully given shape in Borges's best books, furnished artistic fuel for the supine antiwar and hostile antileft politics of our 1960s liberal literati. Hence, besides being a catalyst, a Poe to our new fiction writers, Borges's work took on a conserving function, one that was previously allotted—during those innocently anxious, quietly haunted 1950s—to Camus, who deemed life absurd, history a nightmare, and action meaningless, and who preached that man's sole path to salvation was an indulgent metaphysics of subjectivity. The 1960s were too angry, too rough to be soothed by so callow and wispy a pessimism; Borges furnished a more concrete and objective stance, one built on more than personal feeling. To what Camus and others perceived as a mindless left, to a knowledge and history without hope or meaning, Borges gallantly counterpoised a consolation through books, through the verbal treasures of the past.

The 1970s were a rather different matter, what with universities in the doldrums, collegiate enthusiasm for "pure" learning on the wane, students shying away from literary study, and a widespread skepticism about personal salvation through Art. There was no war, no strife, but the status quo, after the defeat in Vietnam and the Watergate scandals, had become a great deal less persuasive than it had been some years previously and needed a more fitting advocate to prop up its image. After being badly bruised in Asia, the antileft American reader wanted a less sophisticated, less urbane, less witty anticommunism, one that did not cloud things up with mental fancies or old books, one that wasted no time on right-wing threats and was even antiliberal in tendency. The system needed a sterner, more openly political conservatism that would drown out the din of American violence abroad and proffer arguments against the political disillusionment back home. That function seems to have been assigned, through 1989, to Solzhenitsyn.

12   Borges as Argentine Author

AND OTHER SELF-EVIDENT
(IF OFTEN IGNORED) TRUTHS

I n a polemical essay first published in *Salmagundi* in 1980, George Steiner unfavorably compared the intellectual scene in the United States with that of Europe. And twice in that controversial piece Steiner referred incidentally to Borges, mentioning him in the same breath with European figures such as Heidegger, Wittgenstein, Webern, Joyce.[1] The context and the tone were both highly flattering to Borges. Now, Borges was scarcely the focal point of Steiner's reflections, and obviously the eminent critic would know that Borges writes not in Europe but from the remote latitudes of Argentina, in South America. Nevertheless, there is something symptomatic in George Steiner's casually listing Borges in his European line-up. Behind such an offhand inclusion there lies a received idea, an established judgment that, in routinely seeing Borges as a European sort of artist, suggests either passive ignorance or willful disregard of his origins, life, and work as an Argentine.

There is a neat political logic to the way in which this judgment emerged and became standard, even commonplace. On the one hand, the traditional, Hispanophile, Catholic old right could find nothing positive in Borges's secular individualism, his attachment to liberal European values, his indifference to the culture of Spain, his skepticism, agnosticism, and philo-Semitism. On the other hand, the Latin American Marxist sectors have only begun to reconcile themselves to Borges's taste for mental amusement, his love of metaphysics, his wholehearted defense of Western cultural values, his libertarianism, anticommunism, and Anglophilia. Finally, in the middle, are the educated Western (or Westernized) liberals who stand on Euro-American universalism, who live for the spiritual riches of the European past, and who profess a civilized and centrist, tolerant but skeptical attitude toward what they see as the extremes of left and right. Such liberals inevitably find in Borges a kindred spirit who treasures their own values and sees the world much as they themselves do—or at least as they did from 1940 to 1970.

These differing perspectives, however, do have one thing in common: they all deny Borges any local roots, any Argentine preoccupations or content, any relationship with the national past or present. In so doing, they overlook entire blocks of elementary fact, such as Borges's youthful years as a fervent literary nationalist, the reasons for his breaking away from nationalism after 1930, and the substantial amount of Argentine material still present in his later work as storyteller and as cosmopolitan.

In order to address this issue I would like to do a number of things together. First, I will take another look at Borges's fascinating volume of essays from 1926, *El tamaño de mi esperanza (The Extent of My Hope)*, and then relate the book to the times during which it appeared. Next, I will briefly survey the political landscape of the 1930s and take stock of Borges's writing situation in that decade. Finally, I will be taking one more bird's-eye glance at the entire body of Borges's major fictions, noting the Argentine and River Plate elements that, not withstanding Borges's "Europhile" and "universalist" stance, are a significant part of his output as narrative artist.

The Extent of My Hope is a remarkable gathering, in some ways typical for Borges, yet in other respects unique, distinctive.[2] It exhibits his now-familiar ecumenicism, his interest in a wide range of European writings as well as in general questions of poetics and aesthetics. Among the book's essays one finds a favorable review of Bernard Shaw's *Saint Joan;* an appreciation of Oscar Wilde's *Ballad of Reading Gaol;* a speculative commentary on a well-known line of verse by Apollinaire; theoretical articles on the lexicon of poetry; a critique of rhyme, which in those days Borges actually deemed useless; and a rapid history of the subject of angels in literature.

None of this is surprising—it is the Borges we all know today. But there is more. Borges, we might recall, had recently spent some time in Spain, where he had been keeping company with young avant-garde poets and intellectuals. And so, in *The Extent of My Hope* there are allusions to Medieval and Golden Age Spanish authors such as Góngora, Quevedo, Gracián, Lope de Vega, Juan de Mena, and Jorge Manrique; there is also a long study of Spanish ballads (*romances*) and the metamorphoses they undergo when transplanted to Argentina. These Peninsular opuses and names would appear but seldom in the later Borges, who would come to regard Spain's literature as of lesser interest and moreover,

when compared to French or English authors, as an acquired and secondary taste for the typical Argentine reader.

What is most striking about *The Extent of My Hope,* however, is its cultural nationalism, its programmatic advocacy of homegrown products and
cultural values, its pleas directed to the Argentinian reader, and in particular its warm, romantic enthusiasm for the city of Buenos Aires. Borges's
stance and intent are spelled out in the opening lines of the book:

> I want to speak to the natives: to the men who experience life and
> death here in this land, not to those who think the sun and moon are
> in Europe. This is a land of born expatriates, of men who long for
> things foreign and faraway; *gringos* they truly are, whether justified
> by their blood or not, and my pen doesn't speak to them. I want to
> converse with the others, with our younger homebodies who don't
> go belittling the ways of this country. Today my argument is the
> fatherland and what it has of past, present, and to come. (TE, 5)[3]

These first lines, with their glowing and inspired nativism, set the tone
for the book and also hint at Borges's specific aim—namely, to help create a culture that will bring glory to the Argentinian capital. As he says
later in that piece: "More than a city, Buenos Aires is now a country,
and it must be discovered by the poetry and music, the painting and religion and metaphysic which accord with its greatness. That is the extent
of my hope, which invites us all to be gods and to labor in its incarnation" (TE, 8).[4] And in the next-to-last essay, Borges rhapsodizes lyri-
cally around this expectation that his hometown someday will be duly
celebrated:

> How lovely it is to be the inhabitants of a city that has been com-
> mended by a great verse! Buenos Aires is a spectacle forever. . . . But
> Buenos Aires, packed though it is with two million individual destinies,
> may remain deserted and without any voice so long as some symbol
> fails to settle within it. . . . The provinces are populated, [but] . . . the
> city still awaits its poeticization. (TE, 143)

Oftentimes in this volume Borges announces his intention to roam about
the city and explore its working-class outskirts. As he says at one point,
"More than a hundred outlying streets await me, with their moonlight
and solitude and a glass of sweet rum" (TE, 87). On the very last page of
the book, Borges even forges a principle, a requirement out of such direct

experience of Buenos Aires: "Let no one venture to write *slum* without having strolled leisurely on its raised sidewalks; without having desired it and suffered it as one does a lover; without having felt its adobe walls, its small fields, its moon shining just around the corner grocery store" (TE, 153).

One reason why Borges advocates a poetry for the urban center is that, as he sees it, the Argentine countryside already has in its gaucho poems a literature worthy of admiration and respect. He unabashedly asserts that the humorous gaucho narrative *Fausto*, by Estanislao del Campo, is "a mi entender, la mejor [poesía] que ha dicho nuestra América" ("to my view, the best [poetry] ever to be spoken by our America" [TE, 13]). The use of the expression "nuestra América" stands out and, of course, makes sense in the light of Borges's nationalism in the 1920s, though admittedly the juxtaposition may be a matter of casual happenstance. And yet, many will recognize it as a term first given cultural and ideological significance by the great Cuban poet and freedom fighter José Martí, and as a set phrase commonly invoked in the twentieth century by Third World–style nationalists from Latin America.

At the same time, Borges in *The Extent of My Hope* advocates not a narrow and parochial kind of nationalism, but rather one that will address broad human experiences and concerns as well. What he envisions is "Criollismo, pues, pero un criollismo que sea conversador del mundo y del yo, de Dios y de la muerte. A ver si alguien me ayuda a buscarlo." ("Nativism, then, but a nativism conversant with the world and with the ego, with God and with death. Let's see if someone can help me find it" [TE, 10].) Hence even at its most passionate, Borges's nativist ideal shows as it were transnational horizons, displays universalist and indeed metaphysical aspirations. In this way he looks forward to his well-known talk "The Argentine Writer and Tradition," in which he was to single out "all of Western culture" as the most suitable Argentine literary terrain and would assert with utmost confidence that "our patrimony is the universe" (L, 184, 185; D, 160, 162).

In keeping with the book's nativist content and cultural ideals, the language and style employed in *The Extent of My Hope* show a correspondingly Buenos Aires character and flavor. On repeated occasions Borges speaks to the reader not with the Castillian *tú* but with that distinctively River Plate pronoun *vos*—for example he says "vos y él y yo, lector amigo" (TE, 14). He also reproduces phonetically the everyday pronunciation of certain Spanish common nouns—he writes "la realidá, la ciudá, la voluntá," and so forth, without the final d's, somewhat as if

T. S. Eliot had in one of his early essays spelled the present-participle forms "reading" and "writing" without their final g's.

Reading some of these pieces, one may be struck by the degree to which they are composed in what seems to be a kind of literary *porteño*, an artfully distilled version of the oral and informal Spanish of Buenos Aires. A couple of passages should simply be read aloud, savored for their musicality. I ask those who have no Spanish to bear with me for a moment, and as Borges himself says when quoting a gaucho poet, "Aquí va un manojito" (TE, 19).

On the first page of the book, Borges says,

> Quiero conversar con . . . los muchachos querencieros y nuestros que no le achican la realidá a este país. Mi argumento de hoy es la patria: lo que hay en ella de presente, de pasado y de venidero. Y conste que lo venidero nunca se anima a ser presente del todo sin antes ensayarse y que ese ensayo es la esperanza. ¡Bendita seas, esperanza, memoria del futuro, olorcito de lo por venir, palote de Dios! (TE, 5)

Similarly, on the occasion of the folding of *Proa* magazine, Borges nostalgically recalls, in an open letter, the friendship of his fellow editors:

> Brandán, Ricardo: Voy a orejear un aniversario teológico. Lejos, aun más lejos, quince cuadras después del lejos, por escampados y terceros y pasos a nivel, nos arrearán hasta un campito al que miren grandes gasómetros (que harán oficio de tambores) y almacenes dorados, cuya pinta será la de los ángeles que se desmoronarán desde el cielo. . . . Eso será el Juicio Final . . . y se verá que no hay ningún Infierno, pero sí muchos Cielos. En uno de ellos . . . empezará una suelta tertulia, una inmortal conversación sin brindis ni apuros, donde se tutearán los corazones y en el que cada cual se oirá vivir en millares de otras conciencias, todas de buena voluntá y alegrísimas. . . .
>
> ¡Qué lindas tenidas las nuestras! Güiraldes, por el boquete de su austera guitarra, por ese negro redondelito o ventana que da de juro a San Antonio de Areco, habla muy bien la lejanía. Brandán parece petisón, pero es que siempre está parado a la otra punta de un verso. . . . (TE, 85–86)

And so forth. Much in these passages is virtually untranslatable. Besides their vision of the future, what they both offer is their inspired prose poetry—the rhythms, the suffixes, the consciously Argentine lexicon, the implied inflections of melody, the rhetoric in the best sense of that word. (This stylistic impression was completely intended. Borges later observed, with irony, that in the book "I tried to be as Argentine as possible. I got hold of Lisandro Segovia's dictionary of Argentinisms and introduced so many localisms that a lot of Argentines found it hard to understand. Given that I've since lost the dictionary, I'm not sure that I even understand it myself."[5]) There is simply no non-Spanish or even non-Argentine equivalent for this sort of prose, and it is therefore not surprising that *The Extent of My Hope* should have remained among the least recognized of Borges's earlier volumes outside his native land.

Borges's literary nationalism in *The Extent of My Hope* is of a piece with his general outlook at the time. During the 1920s he had consciously set out to be the poet of his native city, a *porteño* Walt Whitman, and his first published book bears the appropriate title *Fervor of Buenos Aires*. A close and intimate involvement with the urban landscape is the most telling trait of the poetry from this period—one piece, "Vanilocuencia," begins "La ciudad está en mí como un poema" ("The city is within me like a poem"). With their tone of delicate, subdued, romantic melancholy, these early verses quietly conjure up the cobblestoned streets, back alleys, quiet plazas, and cemeteries; the patios and gardens, the upper-class neighborhoods and interiors; the daylight, the sunsets, and the working-class districts of Buenos Aires. One of Borges's most beautiful and celebrated poems from this decade is entitled "Fundación mítica de Buenos Aires" ("On the Mythical Founding of Buenos Aires"); it ends by judging the town "tan eterna como el agua y el aire" ("as eternal as air and water"). So wistfully evocative of the old city's moods are these lyrics that I have encountered a good number of Argentine literati who, in spite of serious reservations about Borges himself, can nevertheless recite much of his *porteño* poetry by heart, and who have casually declaimed stanza after stanza to me over beefsteak dinners or coffee.

In similar fashion, Borges's 1920s verse shows a profound preoccupation with matters Argentine. The title of one book, *Cuaderno San Martín*, alludes obliquely to the Argentine national hero. Several poems from the decade deal with the author's own ancestors and their political or military role in the Republic's heroic past—a reminder to us of Borges's patrician origins, of the part played by his forebears in shaping liberal

Argentina. Some of the streets walked by the twenty-seven-year-old poet may in fact have borne the very names of Borges's illustrious forefathers. On the other hand, Borges was not above devoting some attention to the ideological enemies of his tribe, as in "Rosas," a meditative poem dealing with the nineteenth-century conservative dictator of that name.

Borges's efforts at literary Argentinism during the 1920s, we saw earlier, reflect his personal aim of reintegration after having spent seven years as a youthful expatriate with his family in Europe. The time of his return, moreover, was one of the happiest moments in Argentina's general history. There was a world economic boom, and Argentina, then the wealthiest country in Latin America, shared in the global prosperity through massive food exports, which at the time were reaching their highest percentage to date of foreign trade.[6] The Unión Cívica Radical was firmly in power, with strong support from the middle class as well as the sons of immigrant workers. Among those supporters was Borges himself, who, as we noted in chapter 2, was a member of the Radical Party. He became mildly active in the 1928 presidential candidacy of Radical boss Hipólito Yrigoyen and actually alludes to Yrigoyen in the poem "On the Mythical Founding of Buenos Aires."

This harmony of economic, political, cultural, and personal interests came to an abrupt end with the crash of 1929. The ensuing business slump in turn triggered the adventurist action of General José Félix Uriburu, who on 6 September 1930 sent tanks into the streets, deposed President Yrigoyen, and seized state power. Though civilian rule was restored in 1932, Uriburu's move signaled the rise of an Argentine nationalist, and more or less fascist, wave.[7] Throughout the 1930s, right-wing sects were to proliferate under names like Legion of Mars, Argentine Nationalist Action, Argentine Guard, Nationalist Civic Militia, and Argentine Civic Legion.[8] They shared anti-immigrant and anti-Semitic attitudes and were also anti-British, a fact that, in a country long dominated by British imperialism, could appeal to the patriotic reflexes of otherwise unsympathetic Argentinians. To these perceived foreign ills the nationalists counterposed their model of Hispanic traditionalism and a nostalgic, idealized vision of Catholic Spain.

The overall reactionary thrust eventuated into openly pro-Axis governments and activities in the early 1940s. One Argentine daily, *El Pampero,* was frankly pro-Nazi, and the short-lived dictatorship of General Pedro Pablo Ramírez had as its minister of education none other than Gustavo Martínez Zubiría, well known for publishing viciously anti-

Semitic novels under the pseudonym Hugo Wast. The culmination of this entire dynamic was the Perón presidency of 1946. Perón's mass movement and government administration developed into a strange species all its own, but he began with the blessing of the church, the army, and the police, and he started out by "implementing the old aspirations of the nationalist groups."[9] Among the first victims of Perón's nationalism was Borges, who, for having backed the Allies in World War II, found himself purged from his low-paying library job.

Ideologically, the nationalist groups were antiliberal, anti-Radical, and antileft. Under General Uriburu, for instance, the national police inaugurated the Special Section for the Repression of Communism. So widespread and notorious were to become the abuses of this organism that a Radical deputy once characterized it as the agency that "formerly persecuted communists and now devotes itself to persecuting pedestrians."[10] As a result of this right-wing upsurge, the moderates, liberals, Radicals, socialists, and Communists now found themselves thrown together as allies in the opposition. This historical accident would give rise to such curiosities as the March for the Constitution and Liberty, on 19 September 1945, when conservative landowners, former socialist deputies, and communist activists marched side by side against the nationalist military dictatorship.

An inevitable cultural consequence of the political drift that began in 1930 was that nationalistic sentiments, ideals, and aims had lost their credibility and legitimacy with anyone not situated on the far right. The distinguished novelist Ernesto Sábato once recalled how, during his days as a young communist student between 1930 and 1935, "we were ashamed to invoke big words like Fatherland (*patria*) and Liberty, especially with a capital F or L, so often had we heard them prostituted on the lips of public crooks."[11] Similarly, in a 1930 pamphlet, the Communist Party boss Rodolfo Ghioldi said, "In Argentina we have oppression by the landlords, the imperialists, and the bourgeoisie; to defend the fatherland here is to defend the landlords, the imperialists, and the bourgeoisie."[12]

Borges seldom stood on more than the sidelines of political thought or action, and of course a man of the left he never was. And yet he too would fall in with the new set of political configurations. His civilized, tender-minded, affective nativism from the Radical 1920s, for one, had nothing to say to the harsh and bellicose nationalism of the fascistic 1930s. His ecumenical attachment to British, European, and Jewish high culture inevitably put him at odds with the xenophobic anti-Semitism and Anglophobia of the nationalist sects. He personally protested against an anti-Semitic group's outrageous statements, even belonging to an ad hoc committee designed specifically for such protests.

Against his earlier desires Borges now found himself in the antinationalist camp, sharing terrain with center and left forces and also fitting in with the larger shape of international politics, including quiet sympathy for the Republican side in the Spanish Civil War. Now, Borges to this day is attacked for his cosmopolitan ethos and his pro-European values. For example, the Cuban poet and essayist Roberto Fernández Retamar, in his highly influential book-length essay *Calibán*, finds serious fault with Borges for having repudiated the nationalism of *The Extent of My Hope*, and for saying in 1951 that "our tradition is Europe."[13] By citing these sources outside of their organic, temporal context, however, Fernández Retamar grants Borges neither a part in history nor a history of his own.

The conjunction of factors that helped encourage Borges's early nationalism, I think, are clear. Less clear is the fact that, during the 1930s and 1940s, when Borges turned universalist and cosmopolitan, in all the advanced nations at the time, nationalism served as the ideology and rhetoric of the far right. The Spanish Falange, the German Nazis, the Action Française, the diverse Argentine sects, and a large proportion of the U.S. advocates of "Isolationism" (as they liked calling themselves) were uniformly characterized by a provincial, strident nationalism combined with aggressive antiliberal and antileft attitudes. By contrast, liberalism and the left were internationalist or cosmopolitan in outlook and posture. Nationalism bore a bad name before 1945: it is only after World War II, with decolonization and the emergence of the Third World, that left-wing thought begins fusing with nationalist action.

Significantly, the opposition politics of the 1860–1940 period had been dominated by entities known as the First, Second, Third, and Fourth *Internationals*, whereas a distinctive revolutionary feature since 1950 has been a succession of resistance groups named "*National* Liberation Front." Ironically, among the reasons for the Argentine Communist Party's failure to gain local followers was, precisely, its abstract internationalism, its excessive loyalty to European and Soviet struggles that, to the ordinary Argentine migrant worker, seemed as remote as the moon. It took a skilled tactician like Perón to speak to the Argentinian proletariat in national terms, however opportunistic and perverted those terms were. Not accidentally, Borges's defense of European culture was written at the very height of Perón's nationalist regime.

The 1930s show Borges groping for usable materials, domestic and especially foreign, and also seeking new forms as a writer. He was publishing almost no poetry, having given up on being the native singer of Buenos Aires. Aside from some now-classic essays, the only substantial imaginative work he produced before 1939 was the *Universal History of Infamy,* a collection of experimental tales. These sketches—highly original but still inchoate in form, lively but awkward in their rhythms—are the product of a mature author then experiencing a mid-life career change and apprenticing himself to a new literary craft. As we all know, the apprentice grew, became a master of the art, and, as the expression goes, the rest is history.

Borges's reputation rests overwhelmingly on the stories contained in *Ficciones* and *El Aleph.* A good many of those pieces are indeed universalist and cosmopolitan, set as they are in London or Prague, in imaginary Babels or Babylon. Borges's detractors commonly cite this as proof of his indifference to Latin American realities. And yet, in his defense one could just as easily mention Borges's two retellings of the *Martín Fierro* gaucho classic, or those narratives depicting Argentine hoods and gangsters, or the stories dealing with the late-nineteenth-century Argentine frontier ("The Dead Man") and the 1904 gaucho uprising in Uruguay ("The Other Death"), or the touching portraits of a working-class *porteña* ("Emma Zunz"), of a Mayan priest ("The God's Script"), or of an unforgetful—and unforgettable—Uruguayan peasant boy ("Funes the Memorious"). But then, such glaring omissions are typical of all charges that Borges is, as it were, un-Argentine. The Germanness of Brecht, after all, is never questioned on grounds that his plays are set in exotic realms like China or Chicago; nor is Flaubert's having produced Carthaginian or Biblical fictions, and a novel about infinite books, ever raised as evidence of his being un-French. I'm being obvious and simple, but the obvious has long been shunned, and one explanation for this blind spot on the part of the anti-Borgesians may be equally simple—they have not read him very much. They know him mostly through the prism of the media and via the universalist image constructed of him by his liberal, Europhile devotees. Ultimately, however, Borges's mind, output, and history are too encompassing, too broad for the neat, closed schemes of theoreticians, be they of the "nationalist" or "universalist" persuasion.

A poet from St. Louis, Missouri, who later emigrated to Europe once made a profound observation concerning the matter of local versus universal. In his essay "American Literature and the American Language," T. S. Eliot observes, "Universality can never come except through writing about what one knows thoroughly. . . . And, though it is only too easy for a writer to be local without being universal, I doubt whether a poet or novelist can be universal without being local too."[14] Borges, we have seen, began his career as an intensely local poet, writing about what he knew thoroughly—the old-time Buenos Aires cityscape. Later, driven into cosmopolitanism by the narrow, sterile chauvinism of the far right, he nonetheless was to retain local roots even during his most universalist phase. The cosmic experience of the Aleph takes place in a Buenos Aires basement, in a street named after Juan de Garay, an ancestor of Borges who founded the city in 1580.

In 1971 an American student at New York University asked Borges if his work is "escapist," "anti-realist," and ignores "Argentine reality." Borges's telling riposte was, "I may be allowed to say something that smacks of vanity—I am a part of Argentine reality."[15] Borges's family background, nationalist years, antifascist cosmopolitanism, and narrative use of Argentine subjects all clearly sustain his counterargument. Allied and attached to a liberal Argentinian and world-historical project that appears to have run its best course and, in our time, has turned increasingly and harshly conservative, Borges may not have been part of the Argentina desired by the Hispanophile old right or the nationalist new left, but Argentine it was. The anti-Borgesians as well as the European admirers like George Steiner, both of whom claim Borges for Europe, need to revise their mental charts and literary maps. It seems embarrassingly self-evident to say so, but Borges is an Argentine author.

Abbreviations

I n this list of abbreviations, English translations are indicated as such only where some confusion with the Spanish title might arise. For lists of English translations and Spanish editions of Borges's works, see the note on page references and the bibliography.

BS	*The Book of Sand* (1978)
CBD	*Crónicas de Bustos Domecq* (1967) / *Chronicles of Bustos Domecq* (1976)
DBR	*Doctor Brodie's Report* (1972)
EA	*El Aleph* (1968)
D	*Dreamtigers* (1964)
F	*Ficciones* (1962) / *Ficciones* (English translation, 1966)
H	*El hacedor* (1971)
HUI	*Historia universal de la infamia* (1971)
IA	*El idioma de los argentinos* (1928)
IB	*El informe de Brodie* (1971)
L	*Labyrinths* (1962)
LA	*El libro de arena* (1975)
OI	*Otras inquisiciones* (1966) / *Other Inquisitions* (English translation, 1966)
TA	*The Aleph and Other Stories, 1933–1969* (1978)
UHI	*A Universal History of Infamy* (1972)

Notes

Chapter 1. Buenos Aires and Beyond

1. Genette, "L'utopie littéraire," pp. 123–132.
2. Chao and Ramonet, "Entretien," p. 3.
3. Interview with Borges in *La Nación,* 27 April 1976.
4. Kovacs, "Borges on the Right," p. 23.
5. Barnatán, *Borges: Biografía,* p. 102.
6. A well-known Argentine joke articulates this national difference with self-effacing humor: "Mexicans descend from the Aztecs, Peruvians descend from the Incas, and we Argentines descended from the boats."
7. Another illuminating joke about Argentine identity: Q. "What is an Argentine?" A. "A Spaniard who fancies himself a Frenchman and speaks like an Italian."
8. Literally, "from the port," the generic term used for designating natives of the port city of Buenos Aires.
9. Some of these reviews were gathered by Sacerio-Garí and Rodríguez Monegal in their collection of Borges pieces, *Textos cautivos.*
10. Interview with Borges in *La Opinión,* 13 September 1974.
11. See, for example, Sorrentino, *Siete conversaciones,* passim.
12. Gilio, interview with Borges in *Borges,* p. 15.

Chapter 2. A Sort of Life, a Special Mind

1. This profile of Borges is based chiefly on the following sources: Borges, "Autobiographical Essay," *The Aleph;* Barnatán, *Borges: Biografía;* Bosco, *Borges;* Burgin, *Conversations;* Canto, *Borges a contraluz;* Ibarra, *Borges;* Jurado, *Genio y figura;* Olea Franco, *El otro Borges;* Rodríguez Monegal, *Jorge Luis Borges;* Sorrentino, *Siete conversaciones;* Stabb, *Jorge Luis Borges;* Vaccaro, *Georgie;* Vázquez, *Bor-*

ges: Esplendor; Woodall, *Borges;* and many interviews with Borges found scattered in magazines and newspapers, too numerous to be itemized within this note.

2. Interview with Borges in *La Opinión,* 9 May 1976.

3. Barnatán, *Borges,* p. 77.

4. Vázquez, *Borges: Esplendor,* p. 63.

5. Linda S. Maier, *Borges and the European Avant-garde,* p. 10.

6. For a personal account of Argentine *ultraísmo,* with some of the details relating to Borges's involvement in that movement, see Torre, *Literaturas de van-guardia,* pp. 582–585.

7. Roberto Alifano, *Últimas conversaciones,* p. 43.

8. Quoted in Barnatán, *Borges: Biografía,* p. 161.

9. Ibid, p. 164. See also Rodríguez Monegal, *Jorge Luis Borges,* pp. 171–172.

10. See Olea Franco, *El otro Borges,* pp. 23–76.

11. Canto, *Borges a contraluz,* p. 34.

12. The quotation and discussion by Luna are cited in Barnatán, *Borges: Biografía,* p. 167.

13. Olea Franco, *El otro Borges,* p. 138.

14. Borges, *El tamaño de mi esperanza,* p. 5. Cited in Christ, *The Narrow Act,* p. 49.

15. For a fuller examination of this volume, see chapter 12.

16. In Argentina as in the rest of Latin America, the poorer urban neighborhoods tend to be on the outer edges of the city—the "suburbs"—rather than in the inner core (as is the case in the United States).

17. Bosco, *Borges,* p. 71. See also Gerassi, *Los nacionalistas,* passim.

18. Borges, "Nuestras imposibilidades," in *Discusión,* 1932 edition. This essay was suppressed in later reprintings of the book.

19. "Desagravio a Borges," pp. 7–33.

20. For an extended look at the interplay between Borges's financial woes and the political situation, see chapter 11.

21. Canto, in *Borges a contraluz,* p. 245, notes that the author had not "the slightest idea" about administration, a lack that was further compounded by his blindness.

22. Vázquez, *Borges: Esplendor,* p. 23.

23. Woodall, *Borges,* pp. 140–142, 203–208.

24. Canto, *Borges a contraluz,* p. 17.

25. Ibid, p. 98.

26. Ibid, p. 83.

27. Ibid., p. 98.

28. Barnatán, *Borges: Biografía,* pp., 88–89; Vázquez, *Borges: Esplendor,* pp. 49–50; Woodall, *Borges,* pp. 32–33.

29. Canto, *Borges a contraluz,* p. 117.

30. Ibid, p. 114.

31. Vázquez, *Borges: Esplendor,* p. 267.

32. Ibid., p. 179.

33. Canto, *Borges a contraluz,* p. 262.

34. For a fuller account of this episode, see Woodall, *Borges,* pp. 229–231.

35. Canto, *Borges a contraluz,* p. 279.

36. Barnstone, *With Borges,* p. 178.

37. Woodall, *Borges,* p. 256.

38. Alazraki, *Borges and the Kabbalah,* p. 177.

39. Barnatán, *Borges: Biografía,* p. 335.

40. Barnstone, *With Borges,* pp. 183–184; Woodall, *Borges,* p. 262–264.

41. Cañeque, interview, in *Conversaciones sobre Borges,* p. 376.

42. Vázquez, *Borges,* p. 41.

43. Jurado, *Genio y figura,* p. 15.

44. Charbonnier, *El escritor,* p. 21.

45. Burgin, *Conversations,* p. 137.

46. Barnatán, *Borges: Biografía,* p. 84.

47. Ibarra, *Borges,* p. 114.

48. Burgin, *Conversations,* p. 114.

49. Gass, "Imaginary Borges," p. 6.

50. Christ, *Narrow Act,* p. 43.

51. Botsford, "About Borges," p. 725.

52. Stevenson, *Dr. Jekyll and Mr. Hyde,* p. 99.

53. For an examination of Stevenson's influence on Borges, see Balderston, *El precursor velado.*

54. Esslin, *Theater of the Absurd,* p. 20.

55. Burgin, *Conversations,* p. 156.

56. Ibid, p. 125. Ironically, Borges had his own "sexual obsession," as we have seen, and he benefited considerably from psychoanalytic treatment under Dr. Cohen-Miller.

Chapter 3. What Borges Did for Prose Fiction

1. Guibert, interview with Neruda, *Seven Voices,* p. 30.

2. Schneider, "Julio Cortázar," p. 24.

3. García Márquez and Vargas Llosa, *Diálogo,* pp. 53–54.

4. Ibid., p. 59.

5. Fuentes, *La nueva novela,* p. 25.

6. Santana, "La vida y la brújula" (interview with Borges), p. 4.

7. Cortázar, *La vuelta al día,* pp. 32–33.

8. Forster, *Aspects of the Novel,* p. 108.

9. Ibid., p. 111.

10. Olea Franco, in *El otro Borges,* p. 239, also interprets the absence of moralization in the *Infamy* stories as Borges's conscious way of *not* writing like a social realist.

11. Todorov, *Introduction,* p. 116.

12. Summarized in Rodríguez Monegal, *Borges par lui-même,* p. 61; also in Irby, introduction to *Labyrinths,* p. xvii. According to Irby (private communication), Borges destroyed his notes immediately after delivering the lecture.

13. Christ, *Narrow Act,* p. 15.

14. Christ, interview with Borges, p. 160.

15. Christ, *Narrow Act,* p. 98.

Chapter 4. The Apprentice Fiction Maker

1. Charbonnier, *El escritor,* p. 64.

2. Rodríguez Monegal, "Borges, Lector Britannicae," p. 34.

3. di Giovanni, "Borges' Infamy," p. 9.

4. Ibid., p. 10.

5. Rodríguez Monegal, "Borges, Lector Britannicae," p. 35.

6. Canto, in a revealing observation, notes that, during their many conversations, Borges displayed utter indifference to the social texture and apparatus of the great nineteenth-century novels. The only aspect of them that interested him was their narrative climaxes. Canto, *Borges a contraluz,* pp. 78–79.

7. Burgin, *Conversations,* p. 29.

8. A full photograph of Orton is included in Rodríguez Monegal, "Borges, Lector Britannicae," p. 35.

9. Olea Franco, *El otro Borges,* p. 249.

10. Barnatán, *Borges: Biografía,* pp. 229–231.

Chapter 5. *Ficciones* I: Doubles, Dreamers, and Detectives

1. The matter of traitors is discussed at length in Tamayo and Ruiz-Díaz, *Borges,* p. 62.

2. Burgin, *Conversations,* p. 145.

3. Hernández, *The Gaucho Martín Fierro,* trans. by Carrino, Carlos, and Mangouni (1974 ed.).

4. Some of the insights here discussed I owe originally to Enrico Mario Santí, "Escritura y tradición."

5. Irby, "Encuentro," p. 8.

6. Todorov, *Introduction,* p. 36 ff.

7. Burgin, *Conversations,* p. 53.

8. Christ, interview with Borges, p. 158.

9. Irby, "Encuentro," p. 7.

10. Canto, *Borges a contraluz,* p. 164.

11. Borges, "Nota sobre Joyce," pp. 60–62. For this reference I am indebted to Irby, *Structure of the Stories.*

12. Charbonnier, *El escritor,* p. 79.

13. As quoted in a review by D. W. Harding, *New York Review of Books,* 9 May 1968, p. 10.

Chapter 6. *Ficciones* II: The World within a Book

1. Christ, *Narrow Act,* p. 190.

2. Cirlot, *Dictionary of Symbols,* p. 134. I am indebted to Audrey Dobek-Bell for this reference.

3. In a late interview, Borges acknowledged his specific debt to Kafka, saying, "If I had to choose a single piece by Kafka . . . I would choose 'The Great Wall of China,' which is a small masterpiece. That story was written in the second decade of this century, and yet it could have been written from time immemorial." Alifano, *Conversaciones,* p. 250.

4. Charbonnier, *El escritor,* p. 14.

5. Gamow, *One two three . . . infinity,* pp. 13–14.

6. da Cunha, *Rebellion in the Backlands,* trans. by Samuel Putnam, p. 149. The book and the incidents it narrates later served as the basis for Mario Vargas Llosa's novel, *The War of the End of the World.*

7. Charbonnier, *El escritor,* p. 75.

8. Ibid.

9. Barth, "The Literature of Exhaustion."

10. Christ, interview with Borges, p. 59.

11. Tamayo and Ruiz-Díaz, *Borges,* p. 25.

12. Charbonnier, *El escritor,* p. 14.

Chapter 7. *El Aleph* I: Doubles and Puzzles

1. Mentioned in Anderson-Imbert, "Un cuento de Borges," p. 138. In examining this story, I have depended in part on Professor Anderson-Imbert's essay.

2. Ibid., p. 140.

3. Santí, "Escritura y tradición," p. 311.

4. Hernández, *The Gaucho Martín Fierro,* trans. by Carrino, Carlos, and Mangouni. References to lines of verse in this translation will be indicated within the body of the text.

5. Santí, "Escritura y tradición," p. 311, discusses the idea of Fierro as a second "father" to Cruz.

6. This is the position taken by Santí in "Escritura y tradición," pp. 310–311.

7. Burgin, *Conversations*, p. 49.

8. Gibbon, *Decline and Fall*, vol. 2, ch. 45, p. 1501.

9. *Basic Writings of Saint Augustine*, vol. 2, p. 192.

10. *The Academics of Cicero*, pp. 53, 82.

11. Plutarch, *Moralia*, vol. 5, p. 435.

12. Pliny, *Natural History*, vol. 2, p. 121.

13. *The Koran*, p. 31.

14. Ibid, p. 338.

15. Ibid., p. 175.

16. Renan, *Averroës et l'averroïsme*, p. 47.

17. Ibid., p. 7, no. 1.

18. Ibid., p. 48.

19. Ibid.

Chapter 8. *El Aleph* II: Tales of Action and Violence

1. Alifano, *Últimas conversaciones*, p. 104.

2. Borges himself admitted to this verbal association, but he also noted that "Bandeira" was the name of the gardener of his friend, the writer Enrique Amorim. In Alifano, *Últimas conversaciones*, p. 104.

3. Interview with Enrique Estrázulas, in *Borges: Dos palabras antes de morir*, ed. Fernando Mateo, p. 44.

4. Alifano, *Últimas conversaciones*, p. 105.

5. Maier, *Borges and the European Avant-Garde*, p. 132.

6. Cited in Russell, *History*, p. 766.

7. Irby, "Encuentro," p. 8.

8. Ibid.

9. "Omnipotence," *New Catholic Encyclopedia*, vol. 10, p. 688.

10. Damiani, *De divina omnipotentia*, ch. 5, pp. 70–75. See also Russell, *History*, p. 413.

11. This latter according to Vázquez, in *Borges: Esplendor*, p. 187. Vázquez includes a photo, after p. 240.

12. Emerson, *Collected Poems*, p. 192.

Chapter 9. *El Aleph* III: The Visionary Experience

1. A literal translation of the title, alas, is unidiomatic and obscure. Other possibilities: "The Sensation of Death," "Feeling in Death."

2. Barnstone, *Borges at Eighty*, pp. 11, 73.

3. At the time Borges wrote this story, it should be noted, Mayan civilization was a mystery not only to educated people but to scholars and anthropologists,

and Mayan script remained a mute, undeciphered presence. In the intervening years our knowledge of Mayan culture has made strides that are nothing less than astonishing.

4. This account of mystical preparation and experience is based on Stace, *Teachings of the Mystics,* pp. 18–25. I am much indebted to Professor Glenn Yocum of Whittier College for having guided me in this area.

5. Ibid., p. 14.

6. Underhill, *Mysticism,* p. 79.

7. Ibid., p. 80.

8. Schimmel, *Mystical Dimensions of Islam,* p. 222.

9. Stace, *Teachings of the Mystics,* p. 91.

10. For a pioneering study of the presence of these works in Borges, see Alazraki, "Kabbalistic Traits."

11. Stace, *Teachings of the Mystics,* p. 91.

12. *Upanishads* (Mascaró edition), p. 49.

13. *Bhagavad-Gita,* pp. 89–93.

14. *Thirteen Principal Upanishads* (Robert Hume edition), p. 104.

15. Ibid, pp. 394–395.

16. Balderston, *Out of Context,* p.72.

17. Edmonson, introduction to *Popol Vuh,* p. 148.

18. *Popol Vuh,* translation and introduction by Edmonson. References to lines of verse in this translation will be made within the body of the text.

19. Cited in Stace, *Teachings of the Mystics,* p. 233.

20. Ibid.

21. Ibid., p. 235.

22. In an early version of the story that first appeared in *Sur* magazine, the woman's name was "Clementina." Borges later changed it to "Teodelina" when including the piece in *El Aleph,* presumably because of the religious overtones of the syllable "Teo" (from Greek *theos*). Dudley Fitts's translation in *Labyrinths,* originally published in *Partisan Review* in 1950, retains the "Clementina" of the original—certainly a more felicitous name in English.

23. Zaehner, *Mysticism,* pp. 85–86.

24. Gibbon, *Decline and Fall,* vol. 2, ch. 43, p. 1424.

25. Athenaeus, *Dneipnosophistae* (bk. 13), vol. 7, p. 81.

26. Melville, *Moby-Dick* (ch. 99, "The Doubloon"), pp. 540–546.

27. Carlyle, *French Revolution* (bk. 4, ch. 6), vol. 2, p. 206.

28. I am grateful to Professor Sarah Roche-Gerstein of Williams College for her help in this matter.

29. Canto, in *Borges a contraluz,* p. 191, considers this piece "one of Borges's less successful stories," and makes the interesting observation that it was written after "The Aleph."

30. In an interview, Borges notes that the "catalog of interminable things" was by far the hardest part of the story to write. "Such a chaotic list can only be simu-

lated, and each element that is random in our experience has to be connected to the following one either by some secret association or by way of contrast." Alifano, *Últimas conversaciones,* p. 152.

31. Borges, in his own commentary to this story (TA, 264), speaks with gentle irony of those critics who have sought Dantean parallels in "The Aleph." As we saw in chapter 2, however, Estela Canto (*Borges a contraluz,* p. 95) reports that, in the course of their own romance and at the very time he was writing this story, the author himself saw Ms. Canto as Beatrice to his Dante.

32. Franco, in "Utopia of a Tired Man," p. 72, speculates that Carlos's second surname "Daneri" might be an imperfect anagram for Pablo Neruda, who was famous, among other things, for his bardic tone, his lengthy enumerations, and eventually for his *Canto General,* a 500-page poem that takes on the entire history of the Americas. On the other hand, in 1923, in a letter written to the poet Jacobo Sureda, Borges ridicules the verse collection called *Hélices* ("propellers") recently published by his own brother-in-law Guillermo de Torre, and unfolds a mock-list of the "knick-knacks" ("cachivaches") catalogued in Torre's book: "Airplanes, railroad ties, trolleys, hydroplanes, rainbows, elevators, signs of the zodiac, stoplights." Barnatán, *Borges: Biografía,* p. 258.

33. Scholem, *Major Trends,* p. 76.

34. Suarès, introduction to *Sepher Yetsirah,* p. 25.

35. Scholem, *Major Trends,* pp. 15–16.

36. Rodman, interview with Borges, *Tongues of Fallen Angels,* p. 19.

37. Russell, *Introduction to Mathematical Philosophy,* p. 83.

38. Ibid., p. 97. Ellipses in original.

39. See Assawi, *Arab Philosophy of History.*

40. Ibn-Khaldun, *Muqaddimah,* vol. 2, p. 362.

41. Anderson, *Legend of the Wandering Jew,* p. 18.

42. Ibid., pp. 153–160.

43. Berg, "Non-Realistic Short Stories," p. 435.

44. Ibid.

45. Ibid.

46. Eliot, "Frontiers of Criticism," p. 121. Eliot drolly observes, "The notes to *The Waste Land!* I had at first intended only to put down all the references for my quotations, with a view to spiking the guns of critics of my earlier poems who had accused me of plagiarism. Then, when it came to print *The Waste Land* as a little book—for the poem on its first appearance in *The Dial* and in *The Criterion* had no notes whatever—it was discovered that the poem was inconveniently short, so I set to work to expand the notes, in order to provide a few more pages of printed matter, with the result that they became the remarkable exposition of bogus scholarship that is still on view to-day."

47. Christ, *Narrow Act,* p. 212.

48. Charbonnier, *El escritor,* p. 89.

49. Berg, "Non-Realistic Short Stories," p. 435.

Chapter 10. *Dreamtigers* and Later Works

1. The word "Maker" in English has strong religious overtones—hence the adoption of another title by its U.S. editors.

2. Burgin, *Conversations,* p. 141; Woodall, *Borges,* pp. 187–190.

3. Woodall, *Borges,* p. 188.

4. Burgin, *Conversations,* p. 143.

5. Ibid., p. 154.

6. Yates, "Behind 'Borges and I,'" p. 317.

7. Wood, "Borges's Surprise," p. 33.

8. Briggs, "Interview with Borges," p. 12.

9. The byline "Honorio Bustos Domecq" first emerged in the 1940s with some earlier parodies written in collaboration by Borges and his friend, the novelist Adolfo Bioy Casares. The name is "a cross between one of Borges's great-grandfathers (Bustos) and one of Bioy's (Domecq)." Woodall, *Borges,* p. 122.

10. Vázquez, in *Borges: Esplendor,* p. 52, relates an incident from the author's Swiss days. According to Vázquez, the young Borges, during his year in Lugano, once saw a tall, blonde woman standing and crying by a lamppost. The two of them talked, went off holding hands, and went to her small house on the outskirts of town, where they spent much of the night together. Next day, Borges was unable to find the house again. The woman's name was Ulrica. This incident is not reported in any other biographical work on Borges.

Chapter 11. Literature and Politics North and South

1. For an insightful political analysis combined with a fair and balanced biography, see Crassweller, *Perón and the Enigmas of Argentina.* The ideology and practice of Peronism are ably examined in depth in Ciria, *Partidos y poder* and *Perón y el justicialismo.* For a vivid dramatization of the grab-bag, opportunistic nature of the Peronist movement as well as the almost religious spell it could cast over its adherents, see Tomás Eloy Martínez, *La novela de Perón* (*The Perón Novel*).

2. Aizenberg, *Aleph Weaver,* p. 45.

3. Rodríguez Monegal, *Jorge Luis Borges,* pp. 397–398.

4. Vázquez, *Borges,* p. 55.

5. For a stance remarkably similar to that of Borges—though a great deal more peevish—see Nabokov's *The Real Life of Sebastian Knight* (originally published in 1941), where anti-Semitic Nazis and Popular Front activists are lumped together as "idle idiots." Vladimir Nabokov, *The Real Life of Sebastian Knight,* p. 166.

6. Barnatán, *Borges: Biografía,* p. 476.

7. Vázquez, *Borges: Sus días y su tiempo,* p. 231.

8. Frank MacShane, *The Life of Raymond Chandler.*

9. As further suggestion of a direct influence, one might mention that, in his work of advocacy entitled *On Moral Fiction,* p. 83, Gardner erroneously refers to Borges's story not as "The House of Asterion" but as "The Minotaur."

10. Pynchon, *Crying of Lot 49,* p. 88.

11. The enormous success of Isabel Allende's *The House of the Spirits*—a novel shamelessly derivative of *One Hundred Years of Solitude*—probably has a lot to do with the fact that its author avoids the touchy issue of direct U.S. involvement with the political repression in her native Chile.

Chapter 12. Borges as Argentine Author

1. Steiner, "The Archives of Eden," p. 85, and also "A P.S.," p. 251.

2. For an in-depth examination of this particular book by Borges, see Farías, *La metafísica del arrabal.*

3. Translations from this volume are largely my own, unless indicated otherwise. In this quotation I have availed myself partly of the fragment translated by Christ in *Narrow Act,* p. 49.

4. Christ, *Narrow Act,* p. 92.

5. Barnatán, *Borges: Biografía,* p. 206.

6. Scobie, *Argentina,* p. 305.

7. The best, and now-classic, account of the rise of right-wing nationalism in Argentina is Navarro Gerassi, *Los nacionalistas.* See also Falcoff and Dolkart, *Prologue to Perón.*

8. Romero, *History of Argentine Political Thought,* p. 238.

9. Ibid., p. 248.

10. The deputy was Leónidas Anastasi. Cited in Ciria, *Partidos y poder,* p. 70.

11. Sábato, *El otro rostro del peronismo,* p. 17.

12. Cited in Puiggrós, *Historia crítica de los partidos,* p. 333.

13. Fernández Retamar, *Calibán,* pp. 56–57.

14. Eliot, "American Literature and the American Language," pp. 55, 56.

15. Ronald Christ, ed., "Borges at N.Y.U.," in *Prose for Borges,* p. 456.

Selected Bibliography

Because the number of publications relating to Borges long ago surpassed the thousand mark, a bibliography presuming thoroughness would take up an entire volume. It is therefore not my aim to be exhaustive. In compiling the following list I have necessarily restricted myself to materials actually consulted in preparing the first and second editions of this book. These guidelines must of course result in unfortunate omissions of some fine works of scholarship, and for this oversight I offer my sincere apologies to all authors concerned.

Works by Borges

SPANISH LANGUAGE

El Aleph. Buenos Aires: Emecé, 1968.
Crónicas de Bustos Domecq. Adolfo Bioy Casares, coauthor. Buenos Aires: Losada, 1967.
Discusión. Buenos Aires: M. Gleizer, 1932.
Discusión. Buenos Aires: Emecé, 1966.
Ficciones. Buenos Aires: Emecé, 1966.
El hacedor. Buenos Aires: Emecé, 1971.
Historia de la eternidad. Buenos Aires: Emecé, 1966.
Historia universal de la infamia. Buenos Aires: Emecé, 1971.
El idioma de los argentinos. Buenos Aires: M. Gleizer, 1928.
El informe de Brodie. Buenos Aires: Emecé, 1971.
Inquisiciones. Buenos Aires: Editorial Proa, 1925.
"Los laberintos policiales y Chesterton," *Sur* 10 (July 1935):92–94.
El libro de arena. Buenos Aires: Emecé, 1975.
El libro de los seres imaginarios. Margarita Guerrero, coauthor. Mexico: Fondo de Cultura Económica, 1967.

"Nota sobre Joyce," *Sur* 77 (February 1941):60–62.

Obra poética, 1923–1967. Buenos Aires: Emecé, 1967.

Otras inquisiciones. Buenos Aires: Emecé, 1966.

Prólogo to *La invención de Morel*, by Adolfo Bioy Casares. Buenos Aires: Emecé, 1941.

El tamaño de mi esperanza. Buenos Aires: Editorial Proa, 1926.

Textos cautivos. Edited by Enrique Sacerio-Garí and Emir Rodríguez Monegal. With an introduction by Enrique Sacerio-Garí. Buenos Aires: Tusquets Editores, 1986.

ENGLISH TRANSLATIONS

The Aleph and Other Stories, 1933–1969. Translated by Norman Thomas di Giovanni in collaboration with the author. New York: E. P. Dutton, 1978.

The Book of Imaginary Beings. Margarita Guerrero, coauthor. Translated by Norman Thomas di Giovanni in collaboration with the author. New York: Avon Books, 1970.

The Book of Sand. Translated by Norman Thomas di Giovanni. New York: E. P. Dutton, 1976.

Chronicles of Bustos Domecq. Adolfo Bioy Casares, coauthor. Translated by Norman Thomas di Giovanni. New York: E. P. Dutton, 1976.

Doctor Brodie's Report. Translated by Norman Thomas di Giovanni in collaboration with the author. New York: E. P. Dutton, 1972.

Dreamtigers. Translated by Mildred Boyer and Harold Moreland. Austin: University of Texas Press, 1964.

Ficciones. Edited by Anthony Kerrigan, with various translators. New York: Grove Press, 1962.

Labyrinths. Edited by James Irby and Donald Yates. New York: New Directions, 1962.

Other Inquisitions. Translated by Ruth L. C. Simms. New York: Washington Square Press, 1966.

A Universal History of Infamy. Translated by Norman Thomas di Giovanni in collaboration with the author. New York: E. P. Dutton, 1972.

Works Dealing with Borges

Ion T. Agheana. *The Meaning of Experience in the Prose of Jorge Luis Borges*. New York: Peter Lang, 1988.

Aizenberg, Edna. *The Aleph Weaver: Biblical, Kabbalistic and Judaic Elements in Borges*. Potomac, Maryland: Scripta Humanistica, 1984.

Alazraki, Jaime. *Borges and the Kabbalah, and Other Essays on His Fiction and Poetry*. New York: Cambridge University Press, 1988.

————. *Jorge Luis Borges.* New York: Columbia University Press, 1969.

————. "Kabbalistic Traits in Borges's Narrations." *Studies in Short Fiction* 8, no. 1 (winter 1971):78–92.

————. *La prosa narrativa de Jorge Luis Borges.* Madrid: Gredos, 1971.

Alifano, Roberto. *Conversaciones con Borges.* Madrid: Editorial Debate, 1985.

————. *Últimas conversaciones con Borges.* Buenos Aires: Torres Agüero Editor, 1988.

Anderson-Imbert, Enrique. "Un cuento de Borges: 'La casa de Asterión.'" In *Jorge Luis Borges,* edited by Jaime Alazraki. Madrid: Taurus, 1976.

————. "Nueva contribución al estudio de las fuentes de Jorge Luis Borges." *Filología* (Buenos Aires) 8 (1962):7–13.

Balderston, Daniel. *Out of Context: Historical Reference and the Representation of Reality in Borges.* Durham: Duke University Press, 1993.

————. *El precursor velado: R. L. Stevenson en la obra de Borges.* Buenos Aires: Editorial Sudamericana, 1985.

Barnatán, Marcos. *Jorge Luis Borges.* Madrid: Ediciones Júcar, 1972.

Barnatán, Marcos-Ricardo. *Borges: Biografía total.* Madrid: Temas de Hoy, 1995.

Barnstone, Willis, ed. *Borges at Eighty: Conversations.* Bloomington: Indiana University Press, 1982.

————. *With Borges on an Ordinary Evening in Buenos Aires: A Memoir.* Urbana: University of Illinois Press, 1993.

Barrenechea, Ana María. *La expresión de la irrealidad en la obra de Jorge Luis Borges.* Mexico City: El Colegio de México, 1957.

————. *Borges: The Labyrinth Maker.* Translated by Robert Lima. New York: New York University Press, 1965.

Barth, John. "The Literature of Exhaustion." *Atlantic Monthly* 220, no. 2 (August 1967):29–34.

Becco, Horacio Jorge. *Jorge Luis Borges: Bibliografía total, 1923–1973.* Buenos Aires: Casa Pardo, 1973.

Berg, Mary Guyer. "The Non-Realistic Short Stories of Lugones, Quiroga, and Borges." Ph.D. dissertation, Harvard University, 1969.

Borges. [No editor listed]. Buenos Aires: Editorial El Mangrullo, 1976.

Bosco, María Angélica. *Borges y los otros.* Buenos Aires: Fabril Editores, 1967.

Botsford, Keith. "About Borges and Not about Borges." *Kenyon Review* 26 (Autumn 1964):723–737.

Briggs, John. "Interview with Borges." *University Review* (January 1970):12.

Burgin, Richard. *Conversations with Jorge Luis Borges.* New York: Avon Books, 1970.

Cañeque, Carlos. *Conversaciones sobre Borges.* Barcelona: Ediciones Destino, S.A., 1995.

Canto, Estela. *Borges a contraluz.* Madrid: Espasa-Calpe, 1989.

Chao, Ramon, and Ignacio Ramonet. "Entretien avec Jorge Luis Borges." *Le Monde,* 19 April 1978, p. 1.

Charbonnier, Georges. *El escritor y su obra.* Mexico: Siglo Veintiuno, 1967. Spanish translation of *Entretiens avec Borges.* Paris: Gallimard, 1967.

Christ, Ronald. "Jorge Luis Borges: An Interview." *Paris Review* 40 (winter–spring 1967): 6–64.(Included also in the second edition of Christ's *The Narrow Act,* pp. 147–289.)

———. *The Narrow Act: Borges' Art of Allusion.* New York: New York University Press, 1969.(Second ed., New York: Lumen Books, 1995.)

"Desagravio a Borges." *Sur* 94 (July 1942): 7–34.

di Giovanni, Norman Thomas. "Borges's Infamy: A Chronology and a Guide." *Review* (spring 1973):6–12.

———, ed. *In Memory of Borges.* London: Constable, 1988.

di Giovanni, Norman Thomas, Daniel Halpern, and Frank MacShane, eds. *Borges on Writing.* New York: E. P. Dutton, 1973.

Dunham, Lowell, and Ivar Ivask, eds. *The Cardinal Points of Borges.* Norman: University of Oklahoma Press, 1971.

Echavarría, Arturo. *Lengua y literatura de Borges.* Barcelona: Ariel, 1983.

———. "América y (en) Europa: Borges y la tradición literaria." In *Conjurados: Anuario Borgiano,* vol. 1, pp. 55–62. Edited by Antonio Fernández Ferrer. Alcalá: Universidad de Alcalá/Franco Maria Ricci, 1996.

Farías, Víctor. *La metafísica del arrabal: El tamaño de mi esperanza, un libro desconocido de Jorge Luis Borges.* Madrid: Anaya y Mario Muchnik, 1992.

Fernández Moreno, César. "Interview with Borges." *Encounter* 32 (April 1969): 6–12.

Fishburn, Evelyn, and Psiche Hughes. *A Dictionary of Borges.* London: Duckworth, 1990.

Franco, Jean. "The Utopia of a Tired Man: Jorge Luis Borges." *Social Text* no. 4 (fall 1981):52–71.

Friedman, Mary Lusky. *The Emperor's Kites: A Morphology of Borges' Tales.* Durham: Duke University Press, 1987.

Gallagher, D. P. "Jorge Luis Borges." In *Modern Latin American Literature,* pp. 94–121. New York: Oxford University Press, 1973.

Gass, W. H. "Imaginary Borges." *New York Review of Books,* 20 November 1969, pp. 5–8.

Génette, Gérard. "L'utopie littéraire." In *Figures I,* pp. 123–132. Paris: Éditions du Seuil, 1966.

Gilio, María Esther. Interview with Borges. In *Borges,* pp. 13–27. Buenos Aires: Editorial El Mangrullo, 1976.

Goloboff, Gerardo Mario. *Leer Borges.* Buenos Aires: Editorial Huemil, S.A., 1978.

Guibert, Rita. Interview with Borges. In *Seven Voices,* pp. 75–117. New York: Random House, 1973.

Gutiérrez Girardot, Rafael. *Jorge Luis Borges: Ensayo de interpretación.* Madrid: Editorial Ínsula, 1959.

Harss, Luis, and Barbara Dohman. "Jorge Luis Borges, or the Consolation by Philosophy." In *Into the Mainstream,* pp. 102–136. New York: Harper & Row, 1967.

L'Herne (biennial French magazine). *Jorge Luis Borges.* Paris, 1964.

Ibarra, Nestor. *Borges et Borges.* Paris: L'Herne, 1969.

Irby, James. "Encuentro con Borges." *Revista Universidad Nacional de México* 16, no. 10 (June 1962):4–10.

———. Introduction to *Labyrinths,* edited by James Irby and Donald Yates, pp. xv–xxiii. New York: New Directions, 1962.

———. "The Structure of the Stories of Jorge Luis Borges." Ph.D. dissertation, University of Michigan, 1962.

Jurado, Alicia. *Genio y figura de Borges.* Buenos Aires: Editorial Universitaria de Buenos Aires, 1964.

Kovacs, Katherine Singer. "Borges on the Right." *New Boston Review,* fall 1977, pp. 22–23.

Lida, Raimundo. "Notes a Borges." In *Letras hispánicas,* pp. 280–283. Mexico: El Colegio de México, 1958.

Lindstrom, Naomi. *Jorge Luis Borges: A Study of the Short Fiction.* Boston: Twayne Publishers, 1990.

López-Baralt, Luce. "Lo que había del otro lado del Zahir." *Conjurados: Anuario Borgiano,* vol. 1, pp. 90–108. Edited by Antonio Fernández Ferrer. Alcalá: Universidad de Alcalá/Franco Maria Ricci, 1996.

Maier, Linda S. *Borges and the European Avant-Garde.* New York: Peter Lang, 1996.

Marx, R., and Simon, J. "Interview with Jorge Luis Borges." *Commonweal* 89 (25 October 1968):107–110.

Matamoro, Blas. *Borges o el juego trascendente.* Buenos Aires: Editorial A. Peña Lillo, 1971.

Mateo, Fernando, ed. *Borges: Dos palabras antes de morir y otras entrevistas.* With an introduction by the editor. Buenos Aires: LC Editores, 1994.

McMurray, George R. *Jorge Luis Borges.* New York: Frederick Ungar, 1980.

Modern Fiction Studies 19, no. 3 (Autumn 1973). Special issue on Borges.

Murillo, Luis. *The Cyclical Night: Irony in James Joyce and Jorge Luis Borges.* Cambridge, Mass.: Harvard University Press, 1968.

La Nación (Buenos Aires). Interview with Borges (27 April 1976).

Olea Franco, Rafael. *El otro Borges, el primer Borges.* Mexico City: Fondo de Cultura Económica, 1993.

Naipaul, V. S. "Comprehending Borges." *New York Review of Books,* 19 October 1972, pp. 3–5.

La Opinión (Buenos Aires). Interview with Borges (15 September 1974).

———. Interview with Borges (9 May 1976).

Pérez, Alberto Julián. *Poética de la prosa de J. L. Borges.* Madrid: Editorial Gredos, 1986.

Prieto, Adolfo. *Borges y la nueva generación*. Buenos Aires: Letras Universitarias, 1954.

Prose for Borges. [No editor listed]. Evanston, Illinois: Northwestern University Press, 1972.

Read, Malcolm K. *Jorge Luis Borges and His Predecessors*. Chapel Hill: University of North Carolina Press, 1993 (North Carolina Studies in the Romance Languages and Literatures, Number 242).

Rest, Jaime. *El laberinto del universo: Borges y el pensamiento nominalista*. Buenos Aires: Ediciones Librería Fausto, 1976.

Review, spring 1973. Special issue dealing with *Universal History of Infamy*.

Rodman, Selden. Interview with Borges. In *Tongues of Fallen Angels*, pp. 5–37. New York: New Directions, 1974.

Rodríguez Monegal, Emir. *Borges: hacia una lectura poética*. Madrid: Guadarrama, 1976.

———. *Borges par lui-même*. Paris: Éditions du Seuil, 1970.

———. *Jorge Luis Borges: A Literary Biography*. New York: E. P. Dutton, 1978.

———. *El juicio de los parricidas: La nueva generación y sus maestros*. Buenos Aires: Deucalión, 1956.

———. "Borges, Lector Britannicae." *Review* (spring 1973): 33–38.

Rodríguez-Luis, Julio. *The Contemporary Praxis of the Fantastic*. New York: Garland Publishing, 1991.

Running, Thorpe. *Borges' Ultraist Movement and Its Poets*. Lathrop Village, Mich.: International Book Publishers, 1981.

Salas, Horacio. *Borges: Una biografía*. Buenos Aires: Planeta, 1994.

Santana, Lázaro. "La vida y la brújula" (interview with Borges). *Ínsula* 22, no. 258 (May 1968):1–5.

Santí, Enrico Mario. "Escritura y tradición: Martín Fierro en dos cuentos de Borges." *Revista Iberoamericana* 87/88 (1974):303–319.

Sarlo, Beatriz. *Jorge Luis Borges: A Writer on the Edge*. Edited by John King. New York: Verso, 1993.

Shaw, Donald L. *Borges' Narrative Strategy*. Leeds: Francis Cairns (Liverpool Monographs in Hispanic Studies, 11), 1992.

Sorrentino, Fernando. *Siete conversaciones con Jorge Luis Borges*. Buenos Aires: Editorial Casa Pardo, 1973.

Sosnowski, Saúl. *Borges y la cábala: La búsqueda del Verbo*. Buenos Aires: Pardes Ediciones, 1986.

Stabb, Martin S. *Borges Revisited*. Boston: Twayne Publishers, 1991.

———. *Jorge Luis Borges*. New York: Twayne Publishers, 1970.

Steiner, George. "Tigers in the Mirror." *The New Yorker*, 20 June 1970, pp. 109–119.

Sturrock, John. *Paper Tigers: The Ideal Fictions of Jorge Luis Borges*. New York: Oxford University Press, 1977.

Tamayo, Marcial, and Adolfo Ruiz-Díaz. *Borges: enigma y clave.* Buenos Aires: Editorial Nuestro Tiempo, 1955.

Todo Borges y. . . . Buenos Aires: Editorial Atlántida and *Gente* magazine, n. d.

Vaccaro, Alejandro. *Georgie, 1899–1930: Una vida de Jorge Luis Borges.* Buenos Aires: Editorial Proa/Alberto Casares, 1996.

Vázquez, María Esther. *Borges.* Caracas: Editorial Monte Avila, 1977.

———. *Borges: Esplendor y derrota.* Barcelona: Tusquets Editores, 1996.

———. *Borges: Sus días y su tiempo.* Madrid: Javier Vergara Editor, 1984.

———. "La pasión literaria." Conversation with Borges and Raimundo Lida. In *La Nación,* 13 February 1977.

Wheelock, Carter. *The Mythmaker: A Study of Motif and Symbol in the Short Stories of Jorge Luis Borges.* Austin: University of Texas Press, 1969.

Wood, Michael. "Borges's Surprise!" *New York Review of Books,* 1 June 1972, pp. 32–33.

Woodall, James. *Borges: A Life.* New York: Basic Books, 1996.

Yates, Donald. "Behind 'Borges and I.'" *Modern Fiction Studies* 19, no. 3 (Autumn 1973):317–324.

General Works

Anderson, George K. *The Legend of the Wandering Jew.* Providence, R.I.: Brown University Press, 1965.

Apollodorus. *Bibliothèque.* Translated to the French by E. Clavier. Paris, 1805.

Assawi, Charles. *An Arab Philosophy of History.* London: J. Murray, 1950.

Athenaeus. *Dneipnosophistae.* Translated by Charles Burton Gulick. Cambridge, Mass.: Harvard University Press, 1937.

Saint Augustine. *Basic Writings of Saint Augustine.* Edited by Whitney J. Oates. New York: Random House, 1948.

Bhagavad-Gita. Translated by Juan Mascaró. Baltimore: Penguin Books, 1962.

Carlyle, Thomas. *The French Revolution.* 6 vols. London: George Bell & Sons, 1902.

Chesterton, G. K. *The Man Who Was Thursday.* New York: Dodd, Mead, 1923.

Cicero. *The Academics.* Translated by James S. Reid. London: Macmillan, 1885.

Ciria, Alberto. *Partidos y poder en la Argentina moderna (1930–1946).* Buenos Aires: Jorge Álvarez Editores, 1964.

———. *Perón y el justicialismo.* Mexico: Siglo Veintiuno, 1971.

Cirlot, J. E. *A Dictionary of Symbols.* Translated by Jack Sage. Foreword by Herbert Read. New York: Philosophical Library, 1971.

Cortázar, Julio. *La vuelta al día en ochenta mundos.* Mexico City: Siglo Veintiuno, 1968.

Crassweller, Robert. *Perón and the Enigmas of Argentina.* New York: W. W. Norton, 1987.

Croce, Benedetto. *La poesia. Introduzione alla critica e storia della poesia e della letteratura.* Bari: G. Laterza e figli, 1937.

da Cunha, Euclides. *Rebellion in the Backlands.* Translated by Samuel Putnam. Chicago: University of Chicago Press, 1944.

Damiani, Pier. *De divina omnipotentia, e altri opuscoli.* Translated to the Italian by Bruno Nardi. Florence: Vallecchi, 1943.

Eliot, T. S. "American Literature and the American Language." In *To Criticize the Critic,* pp. 43–60. London: Faber and Faber, 1965.

———."The Frontiers of Criticism." In *On Poetry and Poets,* pp. 113–131. New York: Farrar, Straus and Cudahy, 1957.

Emerson, Ralph Waldo. *Collected Poems and Translations.* New York: Library of America, 1994.

Encyclopaedia Britannica. 11th ed. Cambridge, England: Cambridge University Press, 1910.

Esslin, Martin. *The Theatre of the Absurd.* New York: Doubleday, 1961.

Falcoff, Mark, and Ronald Dolkart. *Prologue to Perón: Argentina in Depression and War, 1930–1943.* Berkeley: University of California Press, 1975.

Fernández Retamar, Roberto. *Calibán: Apuntes sobre la cultura en nuestra América.* Mexico City: Editorial Diógenes, 1972.

Forster, E. M. *Aspects of the Novel.* New York: Harcourt Brace, 1954.

Fuentes, Carlos. *La nueva novela hispanoamericana.* Mexico City: Joaquín Mortiz, 1970.

Gamow, George. *One two three . . . infinity: Facts and Speculations of Science.* New York: Viking, 1947.

García Márquez, Gabriel, and Mario Vargas Llosa. *Diálogo.* New York: Ediciones Latinoamericanas, 1972.

Gardner, John. *Grendel.* New York: Alfred A. Knopf, 1972.

———. *On Moral Fiction.* New York: Basic Books, 1978.

Gerassi, Marysa Navarro. *Los nacionalistas.* Buenos Aires: Editorial Jorge Álvarez, 1968.

Gibbon, Edward. *The Decline and Fall of the Roman Empire.* 2 vols. New York: Heritage Press, 1946.

Guibert, Rita. Interview with Pablo Neruda. In *Seven Voices: Seven Latin American Writers Talk to Rita Guibert,* pp. 1–74. Translated by Frances Partridge. New York: Alfred A. Knopf, 1973.

Harding, D. W. Review of *The Mind of a Mnemonist,* by A. R. Luria. *New York Review of Books,* 9 May 1968, pp. 10–14.

Hernández, José. *The Gaucho Martín Fierro.* Translated by C. E. Ward, Frank G. Carrino, and Alberto J. Carlos. Albany: State University of New York Press, 1967.

———. *The Gaucho Martín Fierro.* Translated by Frank Carrino, Alberto J.

Carlos, and Norman Mangouni. Albany: State University of New York Press, 1974.

Ibn-Khaldun. *The Muqaddimah: An Introduction to History*. Translated by Franz Rosenthal. New York: Pantheon, 1958.

The Koran. Translation and commentary by George Sale. Philadelphia: J. B. Lippincott, 1923.

Lucian of Samosata. *The True History*. Translated by H. W. Fowler and F. G. Fowler. Oxford: Oxford University Press, 1905.

Luria, A. R. *The Mind of a Mnemonist*. Translated by Lynn Solotaroff. New York: Basic Books, 1968.

MacShane, Frank. *The Life of Raymond Chandler*. New York: E. P. Dutton, 1976.

Martínez, Tomás Eloy. *La novela de Perón*. Buenos Aires: Círculo de Lectores, 1985.

Melville, Herman. *Moby Dick*. New York: Penguin Books, 1972.

Nabokov, Vladimir. *The Real Life of Sebastian Knight*. London: Penguin Books, 1964.

"Omnipotence." *New Catholic Encyclopedia*. New York: McGraw Hill, 1969.

Paul the Deacon. *History of the Lombards*. Philadelphia: University of Pennsylvania Press, 1907.

Pliny. *The Natural History*. Translated by John Bostock. London: H. G. Bohn, 1855.

Plutarch. *Moralia*. Translated by Frank Cole Babbitt. Cambridge, Mass.: Harvard University Press, 1935.

The Popol Vuh. Translation and introduction by Munro S. Edmonson. New Orleans: Middle American Research Institute, Tulane University, 1971.

Puiggrós, Rodolfo. *Historia crítica de los partidos políticos argentinos*. Buenos Aires: Editorial Argumentos, 1956.

Pynchon, Thomas. *The Crying of Lot 49*. New York: Bantam Books, 1966.

Renan, Ernest. *Averroës et l'averroïsme*. Paris: Calmann Lévy, 1861.

Romero, José Luis. *A History of Argentine Political Thought*. Translated by Thomas McGann. Stanford: Stanford University Press, 1963.

Russell, Bertrand. *An Introduction to Mathematical Philosophy*. New York: Macmillan, 1919.

———. *A History of Western Philosophy*. New York: Simon and Schuster, 1945.

Sábato, Ernesto. *El otro rostro del peronismo*. Buenos Aires: n.p., 1956.

The Saga of the Volsungs. Translated by Margaret Schlauch. New York: W. W. Norton, 1930.

Schimmel, Anne Marie. *Mystical Dimensions of Islam*. Chapel Hill: University of North Carolina Press, 1975.

Schneider, Luis M. "Julio Cortázar" (interview). *Revista Universidad Nacional de México* 17, no. 9 (May 1963):24–25.

Scholem, Gershom. *Major Trends in Jewish Mysticism*. New York: Schocken Books, 1941.

Scobie, James. *Argentina: A City and a Nation.* New York: Oxford University Press, 1971.

Sepher Yetsirah. Edited by Carlo Suarès. Translated from the French by Micheline and Vincent Stuart. Boulder, Colo.: Shambhala Press, 1976.

Stace, W. T. *The Teachings of the Mystics.* New York: New American Library, 1960.

Steiner, George. "The Archives of Eden." *Salmagundi,* no. 50–51 (fall 1980–winter 1981):57–89.

———. "A P.S." *Salmagundi,* no. 50–51 (fall 1980–winter 1981):250–253.

Stevenson, Robert Louis. *The Strange Case of Dr. Jekyll and Mr. Hyde.* New York: Heritage Press, 1972.

Taylor, Philip Meadows. *The Story of My Life.* New York: Oxford University Press, 1920.

The Thirteen Principal Upanishads. Translated by Robert Ernest Hume. New York: Oxford University Press, 1921.

Todorov, Tzvetan. *Introduction a la littérature fantastique.* Paris: Éditions du Seuil, 1970.

Torre, Guillermo de. *Historia de las literaturas de vanguardia.* Madrid: Ediciones Guadarrama, 1965.

Underhill, Evelyn. *Mysticism.* New York: E. P. Dutton, 1961.

The Upanishads. Translated by Juan Mascaró. Baltimore: Penguin Books, 1965.

Wells, H. G. *Seven Famous Novels.* New York: Alfred A. Knopf, 1934.

Zaehner, R. C. *Mysticism: Sacred and Profane.* New York: Oxford University Press, 1961.

Index